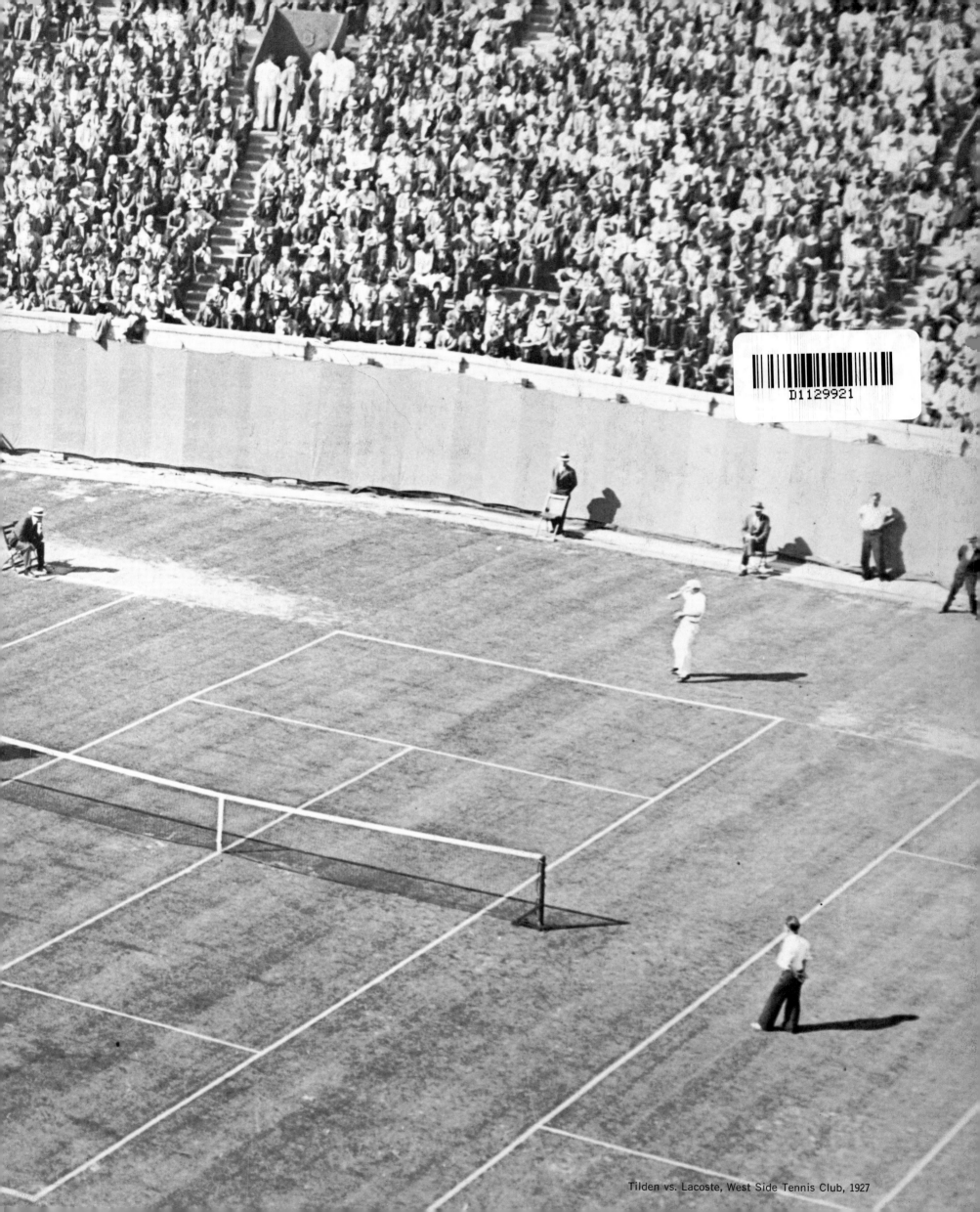

Tilden vs. Lacoste, West Side Tennis Club, 1927

tennis
OBSERVED

The USLTA Men's Singles Champions, 1881—1966

by BILL TALBERT
with PETE AXTHELM

BARRE PUBLISHERS, Barre, Massachusetts, 1967

THE
L. Nelson Bell
Library
MONTREAT—ANDERSON COLLEGE
Montreat, N. C.

"... if you can meet with triumph and disaster and treat these two imposters just the same ..."

Rudyard Kipling

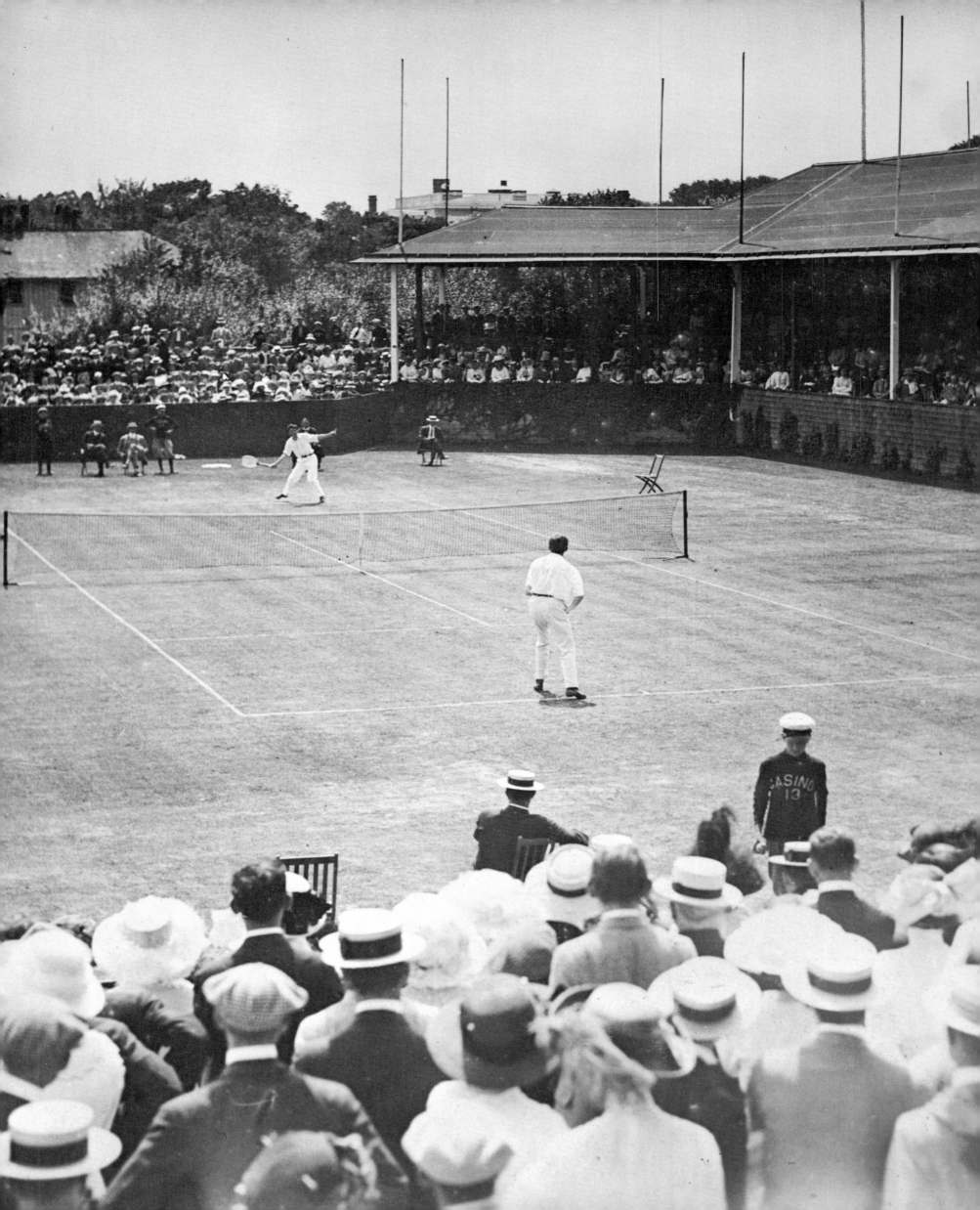

TENNIS OBSERVED

THE U.S. SINGLES CHAMPIONSHIP of 1881, a friendly competition among 26 young Eastern gentlemen, was in its third day when someone suggested that a few rows of folding chairs should be placed around the courts at the Newport Casino. The spectators who moved into the chairs were prominent and wealthy people, members of the remote and exclusive summer colony at Newport, R.I. The players were often scions of distinguished families, Ivy Leaguers and junior law partners who confessed certain qualms about neglecting their careers while they played a game that was just taking shape after only five years in America, a game that was called lawn tennis.

Eighty-five years later, the final round of the singles championship attracted 12,500 people—and the total was considered disappointing because the 14,000-seat stadium of the West Side Tennis Club in Forest Hills, N.Y., was not full. The finalists had emerged from a large field of players from all over the world. No one worried much about neglecting more lucrative pursuits, because modern professional tennis promises ample rewards to the best of the amateurs. The spectators—including those who watched on network television—were no longer a select group of the rich. Forest Hills, just 15 minutes from Manhattan by subway or train, is as accessible as the island of Newport was remote. Kids who know "lawn tennis" as a game played on chalk-marked asphalt streets with wornout rackets, to be interrupted in mid-point by passing cars, can join the most sophisticated club members in watching the very best amateur players compete under the best conditions.

The game was played at a leisurely pace in that first Newport tournament, with a round of singles in

Finals at Newport Casino, circa 1912

the morning and doubles after luncheon. The players' styles were equally casual; a few, still unaccustomed to the strokes being adapted from the English, served underhand. Almost all were satisfied to exchange cautious backcourt shots across a flimsy net that would have been ripped from its moorings by even the most modest of 1966 serves. The most advanced and aggressive player, Dick Sears, had little trouble winning that first title and holding it for six more years.

Now it takes eleven hectic days of play on numerous courts to narrow the field to the final two contenders. The game is dominated by an almost mechanical dedication to the serve and volley. In the absence of a Tilden or a Kramer who can add all-around precision to power and rise above all rivals, the sport is ruled by the man who can serve a little faster or volley a little more steadily than his opponent.

Tennis, like every other game that men invent and then seek to perfect, is always changing. Yet certain aspects of the sport remain surprisingly constant. The very first champion based his attack on the same serve-and-volley principles as the most successful modern players. The technical approach to tennis has certainly been refined, but the philosophy behind it has changed little. The game is still a harsh test of stamina and will, of the ability to play under pressure and react to a challenge—in short, of the quality that makes a sports champion worth talking about at all.

But while the essence of the game remained intact, the social setting of lawn tennis underwent drastic transformations. Court tennis, ancestor of the modern game, was called a "sport of kings" as early as medieval times; lawn tennis, in its first years in America, was still a sport of aristocrats. In the twentieth century, however, it gradually became a sport for all the people. California public parks produced as many good players as did the elite clubs

7

National Lawn Tennis Championships
Germantown Cricket Club, 1921

of the east. Bill Tilden, a colorful Philadelphia socialite, could dominate his era—but a Mexican-American school dropout named Pancho Gonzalez could also dominate his.

Newport, the setting for the first 34 U.S.L.T.A. national tournaments, exemplified the aristocratic atmosphere which surrounded lawn tennis at the time. Tennis was often of secondary interest there, as people compared notes on which socialites were seen with whom. The most distinguished members of the summer colony got the few choice seats around the court, and chatted happily as players tried to concentrate. Lesser social figures could see little of the action; even when a modest grandstand was built, it was quickly preempted by the local gentry. Mere tennis fans had to stand in the back and peer over the more favored observers—if they could

by some happy accident get to the courts at all.

As more people became interested in seeing tennis matches, and as the automobile gave more of them an opportunity to get to matches, the Newport Casino became an increasingly impractical place to run a national tournament. The island of Newport could be reached only by bridge or ferry; the Casino itself was accessible only by walking through a narrow tunnel. The legendary traffic jams that developed there compounded the frustrations of the spectators.

The arrival of brash, red-headed Maurice McLoughlin for the 1909 tournament seemed to signal the end of Newport's reign in tennis. McLoughlin was

the first of the California public parks players to suc-
ceed in the east, and the first proponent of the "Big
Game" based on the powerful serve and volley. (As
such, he was also one of the first to emphasize complete concentration, something that was almost im-
possible among Newport's courtside conversation-
alists.) McLoughlin became champion in 1912, the
year the "challenge round" system was abandoned
in favor of a more democratic system in which the
defending champion was required to play through
the entire tournament. Two years later he lost the
final round—and unknowingly participated in another historic moment. His match with Dick Williams
was the last national championship ever to be
played at Newport.

While Newport stood on its secluded site for years,
a symbol of an elite society impervious to the

changes in the outside world, the West Side Tennis
Club had always been right in the middle of that
hectic, commercial world. Begun in 1892 on Central
Park West at 88th and 89th Streets, the club was
forced from that spot by an apartment building ten
years later. It lasted six seasons at a location near
Columbia University at 117th Street, then retreated
further north to 238th Street and Broadway. At that
site, the club had its first grass courts; its previous
Manhattan courts had all been clay.

The adequate facilities and the location far north
of downtown Manhattan gave brief promise of a
solid future for the West Side Tennis Club at 238th
Street. But by 1912, real estate complications arose,
and the club was offered $12,000 for its lease. The
leaders, influenced by tournament chairman Calhoun Cragin, decided to accept the offer—mainly

because Cragin had already picked out a parcel of land in Forest Hills. By 1914, the club was in full operation on its new site; early the next year it was awarded the national championship tournament.

Bill Johnston won that first Forest Hills tournament; Bill Tilden won his initial title five years later. The characters had arrived for the most enduring attraction tennis has ever seen. But the West Side Tennis Club, ironically, lost the right to stage some of the very best Tilden-Johnston matches. In 1921 the U.S.L.T.A. assigned the nationals to Tilden's home club, the Germantown Cricket Club in Philadelphia.

The Germantown club was commodious and fashionable, but it was not in New York—and it became clear within a few years that the big crowds that now followed tennis could be most easily found in New York. Attendance for the three tournaments at Germantown was less than expected, and the West Side club made a bold move to regain the tournament; it proposed to build a concrete stadium that would seat 13,500. The national association agreed to return the tournament to Forest Hills in 1924, and the club went ahead with construction. The building, now even larger, is still the country's biggest permanent tennis stadium, and the tournament is still being played in it.

The West Side Tennis Club now lies as a striking patch of green amidst one of the world's most populous apartment areas. In the shadow of the railroad tracks and within walking distance of subways, it is in constant touch with the throbbing business of the city. As a social club it is still exclusive, and it certainly seems distant and even anachronistic to some apartment-dwellers around it. Yet compared to the

original seat of tennis at Newport, Forest Hills is a wild populist dream. It brings tennis into the middle of the most active city in the country, and makes it available to New York's divergent peoples. The Forest Hills setting gives stature to the national championship by its facilities and its large crowds, and by its undeniable role as a symbol of how much this sport has expanded.

Despite this feeling of expansion and improvement, however, there are doubts in many minds about the future of amateur tennis. The patterns of play that emerge in this study of the champions may give some idea about where the game is going; hopefully, that idea will be encouraging. Americans find little solace in the fact that Tony Trabert, in 1955, was the last American to win his own country's title; and all tennis enthusiasts may have been disturbed by the colorless exchange of strong serves that comprised the 1966 final match between Australians Fred Stolle and John Newcombe.

Yet there is certainly a future for American tennis, and for the exciting all-court styles that most great champions used. Jack Kramer and Pancho Gonzalez did not really bring on an era of simple power in tennis, but their followers have tended to over-emphasize the power. It is easier to emulate a serve than it is to practice the less spectacular and more difficult forehand of a Kramer, a backhand of a Budge or to train oneself into the incredible physical condition of a Gonzalez. A player can become good at the game by merely concentrating on the power; but he will never become good enough to win consistently. The all-around player, who can use ground strokes as well as aggressive volleys, has almost always overcome the man who has only power. Rod Laver and Ken Rosewall showed this recently for the Australians; the Americans will have to keep looking for promising young players with the understanding and patience and skill to do the same thing for the United States.

USLTA Men's Singles Championships, West Side Tennis Club, Forest Hills, N.Y. 1962

Richard D. Sears, 1881-87
The Volley

Eighty-five years ago, Dick Sears swept through all his opposition to win the first U.S. Lawn Tennis Association singles championship. Sears wore a striped jacket and cap, steel-rimmed glasses and a distinguished mustache; he played before a mildly interested gathering of socialites at Newport's exclusive Casino. It's not unusual for modern tennis people to take a condescending glance back at the 19th-century setting, and conclude that we have come a very long way since the first national tournament.

Actually, we haven't come so far, after all. Dick Sears won the first championship with the most familiar weapon of modern tennis—an effective volley at the net. He was the first American player to abandon the cautious backcourt game and charge the net. He experimented constantly to improve his all-court game, and he remained so far ahead of his contemporaries that he dominated the American game for seven years and retired undefeated.

Sears was a protegé of Dr. James Dwight, the patriarch of American tennis and one of the founders of the United States National Lawn Tennis Association. Dwight was a careful student of the game, and paid close attention to the styles of the more accomplished English players. He helped Sears adopt the overhead serve and volley of the English player O. E. Woodhouse; he took Sears to England in 1883 and assisted him in copying Herbert Lawford's strong forehand drive. Sears learned fast and improved much more quickly than his rivals in this country.

The 19-year-old Sears didn't lose a set in the first championship, and routed W. E. Glyn, 6-0, 6-3, 6-2 in the final match. Over the next six years, six different men rose to meet him in the finals; Sears easily maintained his place at the top. In 1884, his task was made simpler by the beginning of the "challenge round" system, in which the defending champion merely waited on the sidelines to meet

the winner of an "all-comers" tournament. In that year Howard Taylor became the first to win a set from Sears in title play, but the champion prevailed, 6-0, 1-6, 6-0, 6-2.

Sears' toughest match came in 1886 against Livingston Beeckman. The challenger was aggressive and fairly skillful, while Sears was suffering from cramps in his hands. With the help of a rest at a crucial time in the match, Sears overcame both obstacles to win, 4-6, 6-1, 6-3, 6-4. He concluded his reign the following year with an easy win over Henry Slocum. A neck injury forced him out of competition at that point. He retired, leaving an awesome record and a lasting influence on the style of tennis in this country.

Championship match at Newport, 1889

13

Henry W. Slocum, Jr. 1888-89
Physical Condition

Henry Slocum, an also-ran during the last four years of Dick Sears' domination of tennis, moved into the void left by Sears' retirement in 1888. Slocum could never match the powerful volleys or forehand drives of the first champion, but his consistent all-around play was good enough to defeat the undistinguished opposition of his time.

Slocum was a safe, sure player who remained in the backcourt most of the time, and carefully avoided any daring move which might make him vulnerable to a strong return. He looked unimpressive on the court, but he never seemed to get tired or discouraged. He took great pride in his physical condition, and credited it with his two national championships.

His onesided loss to Sears in the 1887 challenge round upset Slocum and made him determined to seek revenge. Sears' retirement deprived him of his opportunity, and he was somewhat annoyed by it. But he still worked extremely hard in 1888, and came into the tournament in his best shape. He routed Howard Taylor, 6-4, 6-1, 6-0, in the final match to become the second U.S. champion.

The 1889 tournament was more notable for the appearance of the first foreign entrant, E. G. Meers of Britain, than it was for quality of play. Oliver Campbell eliminated Meers in the semifinal round, and Quincy Shaw beat Campbell to enter the challenge match. Slocum defeated him in four sets with a typical exhibition of steady, consistent tennis.

Slocum was a lawyer, and he confessed pangs of conscience about practicing tennis more than law for several years. In 1889, he concentrated on his profession and did much less training. Without his superb conditioning, his moderate array of strokes couldn't sustain him, and he faded from the first line of American players.

Oliver S. Campbell, 1890-92
The Volley

Oliver Campbell, a student at Columbia University, was the most persistent and powerful volleyer of the nineteenth century. He rushed to the net at every opportunity and completely abandoned the cautious baseline play that many of his predecessors used. His volleys were as effective as those used by Dick Sears a few years before, and Campbell used them much more often.

Campbell geared his entire attack to the net game. He varied the direction of his serves, to keep his opponents off balance and give him more time to move forward. He was quick and agile, and learned to take the ball early on the rise, to keep the pressure on his rivals. His accurate volleys angled toward the lines and scored consistently against cautious players who remained too far back.

Henry Slocum put up a persistent battle in the challenge round of 1890 at Newport, but managed to win only one set from Campbell. In 1891, Clarence Hobart's backcourt drives gave Campbell considerable trouble. But Hobart had played many hard matches during the all-comers tournament while the champion awaited the challenge round, and he weakened badly in the last two sets. Campbell's volleys finally prevailed, 2-6, 7-5, 7-9, 6-1, 6-2.

By 1892, many American players were imitating the Campbell style; most were very unsuccessful. They seemed off balance as they tried to charge to the net, and were easily passed by Campbell's accurate shots. Campbell beat Fred Hovey in a match dominated by volleying to hold his title.

On his only foray in Europe, Campbell was badly beaten by the solid ground strokes and all-around play of the best foreign players. American players hardly seemed to notice; they fervently followed the Campbell pattern, and aggressive net play became a mark of American tennis.

Robert D. Wrenn, 1893-94, 1896-97
Defensive Strokes

Bob Wrenn may have been the best all-around athlete who ever won the U.S. tennis championship. He starred in football, hockey and baseball at Harvard, and brought good speed and power onto the tennis court. He had little finesse and his ground strokes were inadequate; but so were most of the ground strokes seen in America at the time. Wrenn's natural ability was enough to help him cope with the all-out volleyers against him, and he won the U.S. title four times in five years.

Like most of the successful early players, Wrenn experimented with many new styles and strokes. He developed a low offensive lob which was effective against close-in volleyers such as his main rival, Fred Hovey. He found that shots to the center of the court gave his opponents less chance to pass him when he moved forward to volley. Most important, he developed the ability to return his opponents' smashes with good defensive strokes.

Wrenn's 1893 victory over Hovey in the final match of the U.S. championships was one of the major tennis upsets of the time. Since Oliver Campbell didn't defend his title in the challenge match, Wrenn became champion. He kept the title by defeating a British challenger, Manlove Goodbody, in 1894. Hovey beat Wrenn in 1895, but in 1896 Wrenn's steady game and Hovey's occasional ineffectiveness —he had played little that year—enabled Wrenn to regain the title in five sets. He concluded his tenure as champion in 1897 by defeating another English player, W. V. Eaves.

Wrenn's strokes had little lasting impact on tennis, but his personality was impressive. His hard-fought matches with Hovey did a lot to popularize tennis, and his sense of humor delighted many of his fellow players and fans. Years later he was serving as a linesman when a pompous tournament official challenged him with one of a series of routine precautionary questions before a match: "Do you have a bet on this match?"

"No," replied Wrenn. "I'll bet you either way for any amount you want."

Fred H. Hovey, 1895
Ground Strokes

The many matches between Fred Hovey and Bob Wrenn in the 1890s are generally remembered as volleying duels; yet the only time Hovey was able to win a national championship from Wrenn, he did it with his ground strokes. Technically, Hovey's ground strokes were far from flawless; but strategically, they were perfect.

In 1893, Hovey lost to Wrenn when he concentrated on the volley and failed to cope with Wrenn's defensive lobs. When he got a chance for revenge in the 1895 finals, Hovey reversed his tactics. He stayed in the backcourt and let his opponent take the net. This deprived Wrenn of his best weapon—the lob over the head of the man at the net. With Wrenn volleying from the net, Hovey was able to pass him consistently with his ground strokes.

Hovey came into the 1895 challenge match after a series of impressive straight-set triumphs in the all-comers tournament. In most years, the opportunity for the champion to sit out the all-comers competition proved an advantage, but this time Hovey felt that his early matches had sharpened him up so well that he had the edge. In the all-comers final, he trounced Bill Larned, whom he called the "only man I ever really feared;" so Hovey felt confident coming into his match with Wrenn.

He justified his confidence with a series of beautiful passing shots, and took an early lead that he never relinquished. Hovey won convincingly, 6-3, 6-2, 6-4. He retired from active competition the next year, and played only in the challenge round of the championships. He gave Wrenn a surprisingly good battle before losing, 7-5, 3-6, 6-0, 1-6, 6-1.

Malcolm D. Whitman, 1898-1900
The Reverse Serve

The success of Malcolm Whitman in the last years of the nineteenth century was a sign of the growing improvement of all-around tennis play in this country. Whitman emphasized the importance of the net position, and tried to gain it whenever he could; but he also realized that volleying alone was not enough. He worked hard on his weaknesses, and developed a good forehand and a respectable backhand. He believed in relying "more on balance and control than speed and brilliance," and most of his shots were sound and well-controlled. He also mastered a very unusual serve.

Whitman struck his reverse serve from his right to his left, bringing the racket sharply across the ball and causing it to break away from the receiver to the right. It was a sharp departure from the spin service which most players had been using, but it worked well for Whitman. It was not a very hard serve, but Whitman varied its speed, making it even more difficult to judge and return.

Bob Wrenn and Bill Larned were fighting the war in Cuba when the 1898 championships were held, and Whitman had little trouble defeating the contenders who remained. He beat Dwight Davis in the finals by pressing his attack all the way, after losing the first set to some very good ground strokes by Davis. In 1899, he didn't press the attack, and defeated Parmly Paret with a steady backcourt game. Then he changed his tactics again, and charged the net frequently as he downed Larned in the 1900 challenge round.

Whitman felt that the reverse break on his serve helped him get position for the usually weak return shot. Actually, he didn't need too much help. The tall, blond and swift athlete was one of the best all-around shot-makers in the game.

William A. Larned, 1901-02, 1907-11
Ground Strokes

There are some striking similarities in the careers of Bill Larned and Bill Tilden. Both men developed slowly; Larned was 29 when he won his first U.S. championship, Tilden was 27. Once they had reached the top, both men dominated amateur tennis for years; each won seven titles. Both Larned and Tilden could put on a dramatic show on the court, and each man possessed a solid all-around game that was far too strong for his opponents.

Larned won with his ground strokes. He tried for nine years before he managed to take the U.S. championship, and during that period he worked hard to develop the soundest strokes in America. His backhand was the best anyone had seen in this country up to his time. It was accurate and varied, and Larned could hide its direction until the moment the ball left the racket. His forehand, hit with a lot of topspin, was almost as devastating. Larned's brilliant passing shots could make life miserable for anyone who depended on volleying at the net.

Larned's game was daring and aggressive. He tried to win on every shot, and never bothered with defensive lobs or cautious returns. He had tremendous confidence in his ability to drill the ball close to the lines and past his rival, and he was very effective on short angled shots. When he was off form, he could miss the lines all day and lose badly. But when he was hitting them, he was almost unbeatable.

His first long-awaited championship came in 1901, when Malcolm Whitman didn't defend his title, and Larned beat Beals Wright in the finals of the all-comers tournament. The next year, he defended successfully against the English challenger Reggie Doherty. In 1903, however, the younger Doherty brother, Laurie, defeated Larned. It was four years before Larned managed to regain the title.

Once he was back on top, Larned swept through four more challenge matches without defeat. The last one in 1911 was most memorable. The 39-year-old champion was challenged by Maurice McLough-lin, the 21-year-old Californian with the most powerful attack tennis had yet seen. McLoughlin served mightily and charged at Larned at all times—and Larned gave him a lesson in all-around shot-making, trouncing him, 6-4, 6-4, 6-2. The following year, the challenge round system was abandoned, and the defending champion was required to play through the whole tournament. Larned refused to do this, and retired with a record that marked him as America's finest player of the time.

H. L. Doherty, 1903
All-Around Game

The English Doherty brothers, Reggie and Laurie, were among the finest perfectionists in tennis. They didn't invent strokes and influence styles the way the earlier British brother team, Willie and Ernest Renshaw, had done. But they studied the strokes and brought many of them to a new degree of perfection. In 1903, the younger brother, Laurie Doherty, became the first foreign player ever to win the U.S. singles championship.

Laurie's best strokes were his serve, and overhead smash; he could kill a lob from almost any position on the court. His ground strokes and other shots were not as finely developed as Reggie's, and Reggie beat him in most of their matches. But Laurie had no real weakness, and his all-around ability and versatility made him very effective on his invasions of American courts.

The Dohertys—and the English—took particular pride in their 1903 success at Newport, because it came shortly after a controversial Davis Cup match. Laurie benefitted by a disputed call in his Cup victory over Bill Larned, and many Americans complained that England's first Davis Cup in the four years of international competition had been won by luck.

In the nationals, however, Doherty showed that he didn't need any luck to overcome Larned—and the other Americans he faced. He swept through all opposition until the fifth round, when he was matched against his brother. The year before, Reggie had tried and failed to beat Larned; this time, he didn't feel at his best, and defaulted to assure his brother of a chance. Laurie went on to beat Bill Clothier easily in the all-comers final, and then defeated Larned, 6-0, 6-3, 10-8, in a convincing display of British superiority.

Holcombe Ward, 1904
The Serve

Early in his career, Holcombe Ward found that he lacked the speed and the strokes to cope with good returns of a straight, hard serve. Defeats by solid all-around players like Malcolm Whitman and Bill Larned forced Ward to look for a more effective service that would give him more chance to get to a volleying position near the net.

Ward decided that he needed a twisting serve with a high bounce, which might give an opponent trouble and allow him time to get position. He hit the ball high in the air, bringing the racket sharply across and following through with a long swing. The ball curved effectively and the follow-through gave him impetus toward the net. He had developed the American twist service.

Dwight Davis worked closely with Ward to perfect the new serve, which broke the opposite way from the reverse serve that Whitman had used effectively in his earlier victories. When the first Davis Cup matches were played in 1900, the twist service was credited with the American victory over the English. In later years it was the principal weapon that kept the short, slight, and fairly slow-moving Ward among the leading players.

Ward won the title in 1904, a year in which Bill Larned played badly and Laurie Doherty, the defending champion, didn't play at all. While the Doherty brothers remained in England, Ward defeated the main American contenders, and won the match after a long duel with Bill Clothier, 6-4, 3-6, 2-6, 6-2, 6-3.

Beals C. Wright, 1905
The Chop Stroke

Beals Wright stood two feet inside the baseline as he awaited a serve. He tried to meet the ball on the rise and chop it low over the net. If his opponent rushed to net, Wright aimed the return at his feet. If the man stayed in the backcourt, Wright angled the shot short. This return kept the server off balance and allowed Wright to take the offensive, and it helped him to win the 1905 title.

Many of Wright's strokes were fairly weak, but he had a sound serve-and-volley attack. His lefthanded serve was not exceptionally fast, but he varied the spin and direction. He also had unusual control of his serve, and could play accurately and consistently to the spots he chose. Then he would charge the net and try to maintain the offensive at all times.

Wright was also gifted with very good tennis sense. Realizing that his natural ability would not win many titles by itself, he added sound strategy. When he got ahead in a match, he liked to switch his style of attack abruptly, to catch his rival off guard and win a few points by surprise. He studied his opponents and concentrated on their weaknesses with both his serves and his chop returns.

In his semifinal match in 1905, Wright played almost every shot to Clarence Hobart's backhand, the weakest part of a strong game. He gained complete control and won, 6-3, 6-2, 6-4. In the challenge round he handled Holcombe Ward's feared American twist service with his own effective returns, and beat Ward, 6-2, 6-1, 11-9, for the championship.

William J. Clothier, 1906
The Volley

Bill Clothier was a persistent volleyer who managed to stay among the leaders of American tennis for six years without making any particular impression with his strokes. His serve was weak and his ground strokes undistinguished, so he had little to follow to the net. But when he could gain a volleying position, he could win. In 1906, with the aid of a series of lucky breaks, Clothier took advantage of the ability he had, and won the U.S. singles championship.

Three men—Beals Wright, Holcombe Ward, and Bill Larned—had been ranked ahead of Clothier in the 1905 U.S. Lawn Tennis Association standings. In 1906, Clothier had slumped enough to be dropped from the Davis Cup team that lost to Britain. He was hardly recognized as a contender as the national tournament began. But he improved with every match, while his opposition faded from sight: Wright injured his hand, Ward retired from singles competition, and Larned played far below his best form.

Clothier's most difficult match came in the quarter-final round, against Fred Alexander. He needed a very good break to win it. Alexander, who lost the first two sets, staged a strong drive to win the third and fourth. He was leading 5-2 in the fifth set, and went to 40-0 in the eighth game. At match point, he served and Clothier's return sailed close to the baseline. It was very close—and it was called good. The call disturbed Alexander and his game fell apart. Clothier rallied to win the set and match, 8-6, 6-2, 4-6, 6-1, 7-5. He went on to defeat Karl Behr, who had eliminated Larned in an early round, and Wright, who played despite the hand injury that clearly bothered him.

Maurice McLoughlin, 1912-13
The Serve

If any one incident can be called the beginning of the "Big Game" of modern tennis, it is the 1912 rise of Maurice McLoughlin. The grinning redhead from California typified many of the changes that were taking place in the sport at the time. He was the first champion from the West, and the first public parks player to win the title that had previously been the province of Eastern socialites. Most important, McLoughlin was the first man to win with an attack based solely on the power of the serve and volley.

Early players had succeeded with volleying attacks, but had always succumbed when faced with the sound all-court game of a Bill Larned or a European champion. McLoughlin improved upon the first volleyers in several ways. First, he developed a true cannonball serve that could keep any opponent on the defensive while he began his own rush to net. In addition, he brought a new dash and speed to the game. Earlier players walked toward the attacking position at the net; McLoughlin raced there.

The McLoughlin style was the prototype of the California game that became a lasting influence in American tennis. He moved fast on the court and drilled his shots even faster. He played at top speed all the time and turned a sociable game into a vibrant, extremely strenuous activity. McLoughlin was always moving, always bearing down with his mighty serve or quick volley. He rarely gave an opponent a chance to think about defending against him.

McLoughlin beat Wallace Johnson in five sets in the 1912 final at Newport (below, McLoughlin serving) to win the first tournament in which the defender was no longer permitted to sit on the sidelines and await the challenge round. The next year he swept through the field again, and defended his title successfully in a four-set match with Dick Williams. Since McLoughlin's ground strokes were weak, he was dethroned as soon as shotmakers like Williams and Bill Johnston learned to handle his serve. His career was brief, but its impact is still felt in the powerful style of tennis that is played today.

R. Norris Williams, II, 1914-1916
Go-for-broke Shotmaking

Dick Williams never won a point with a soft, easy shot when a hard and dangerous smash would do instead. He did everything the hard and challenging way. Whether he was stroking a smooth backhand from a difficult position or a hard volley at the net, Williams would always aim for the lines. He left himself very little margin for error, but when he was on his game, he didn't need any margin at all. When he was off form, the result was disastrous—but he hardly seemed to think of that possibility. The daring Williams was one of the most spectacular shotmakers in the history of tennis.

There was nothing tentative in the Williams game. He charged forward at all times, and he liked to take the ball on the rise to gain a step on his opponent. Most players hit slightly over or under the ball to give it spin and help control it; Williams never bothered with such precautions. His hard, flat shots were extremely hard to handle.

Williams was born in Geneva and became something of a tennis prodigy, winning a Swiss tournament at the age of 12. He was 23 when he came into his own in this country by beating Maurice McLoughlin in the finals of the last national singles tournament played at Newport. He lost to Bill Johnston in the semifinals the next year at Forest Hills; then Williams and Johnston met in the 1916 finals.

The 1916 match was rated by some observers as the greatest ever seen up to that time. Typically, Williams won by playing boldly to Johnston's strength, his forehand. At that stage of his career, Johnston still had a tendency to play his forehand too often to the right court. Williams realized this and waited in position to smash it back. He won most of his points with sharply angled volleys, played as closely as possible to the lines—the only way Williams ever liked to play them.

William Johnston, 1915, 1919
The Forehand

Bill Johnston was one of the many good tennis players to come from the public parks of California; yet he stood out among California players, because his game included much more than the serve-and-volley attack that became the trademark of Western players. Johnston had a solid all-around game, with orthodox strokes and a variety of effective shots. The key to his success was the forehand.

He hit the forehand with the Western grip, which brought the racket back with the face closed, then swept it from far below the ball to finish above it. The shot was hit with a full sweep of the racket and a great curving follow-through, and the ball traveled with tremendous topspin. Johnston used it to win many points, and also to open the court, allowing him to get to net when he wanted to.

In each of his U.S. singles championship victories, Johnston met a stronger, more flamboyant opponent in the final round. In 1915, Maurice McLoughlin almost drove him from the court in a powerful first set; but Johnston recovered, concentrated on McLoughlin's weak backhand, and won, 1-6, 6-0, 7-5, 10-8. In 1919 Johnston faced Tilden, who was showing signs of his later greatness but who still had a weak backhand. Johnston aimed his forehand drives at Tilden's backhand at all times, and won easily, 6-4, 6-4, 6-3.

After that second triumph, Johnston was forced into a different role. Tilden corrected his flaws and began his reign—and Johnston remained as his main challenger. For years "Little Bill" battled "Big Bill," in dramatic matches that pitted the methodical small man against the spectacular big man. The galleries were invariably for Johnston, and Tilden usually disappointed them by winning. But even while losing to the best of all champions, Johnston established himself as a fine player—a player who might have been a dominant champion himself if he had played in another era.

R. Lindley Murray, 1917-18
The Serve

The official national championships were suspended in the war year of 1917, and replaced by a "patriotic tournament" for the benefit of the Red Cross. Bill Johnston, Dick Williams and other stars were overseas in the service; the players who were available to compete were no match for Lindley Murray and his strong left-handed serve.

Murray used a spinning serve that pulled his opponents far out of court and gave him ample time to get to the net. He was in outstanding physical condition for his steady rushes to net, partly because he had trained as a track man at Stanford. He defeated Bill Tilden in the second round of the patriotic tournament, and went on to meet Nat Niles in the finals. Niles was a good strategist, and he used an array of lobs and shots aimed at Murray's backhand to win the first two sets; then Murray wore him down and won, 5-7, 8-6, 6-3, 6-3.

The regular championships were resumed in 1918, and they provided the scene for Murray's most dramatic triumph. He hadn't played at all for three months before the tournament, and didn't want to enter. But the head of the wartime chemical plant where he worked prevailed upon him. He went into rigorous training only eight days before the matches began, and he kept improving throughout the tournament. When he reached the final against Tilden, in spite of a serious illness he was in his best condition. He also felt inspired by his boss, who managed to get to Forest Hills to see him.

Tilden probably didn't feel as inspired, and he definitely didn't feel as fit—a blister on his heel had become inflamed. Murray's serve overwhelmed him. Murray scored twelve aces and had Tilden reaching for almost every delivery as he scored an easy victory, 6-3, 6-1, 7-5.

William T. Tilden, II, 1920-25, 1929
The Maestro

Bill Tilden had everything. His shots and his attitude made him the most dominant champion in tennis history; his colorful style made him the most memorable champ. He could hit accurate shots from any position at any time, and he could come up with a dramatic winning shot whenever he needed one. Big Bill won seven U.S. championships against a generation of fine players, and still ranks as the premier player of all time.

Modern players and fans have speculated that Tilden, with the versatile and balanced game that won in the 1920's, would have failed against the all-out power of men like Budge, Kramer and Gonzalez. It's undoubtedly true that Tilden's style wouldn't have worked against such players. But it's also extremely likely that Tilden, a magnificent athlete and precise shotmaker, would have adjusted successfully to any style. He would have been a champion in any era.

William T. Tilden II was from an aristocratic Philadelphia family in which tennis was part of the good life. He won his first tournament at the age of eight, but didn't become national champion until he was 27. His slow rise gave him ample time to develop every phase of his game until it was very close to perfection.

When he finally did sweep to the U.S. singles title in 1920, Tilden did it with a characteristic flair. The first set of his final match against Bill Johnston has been called the most brilliant set ever played. Tilden won that match, 6-1, 1-6, 7-5, 5-7, 6-3, and went on to capture five straight titles—four of them over his perennial rival Johnston—before bowing to René Lacoste in 1926. In 1929, the 36-year-old Tilden rose up to win one final championship, bringing his still-unchallenged total to seven.

His greatest tournament probably came at the Germantown Cricket Club in Philadelphia in 1923. Playing at his awesome best, Tilden routed all opponents and trounced Johnston, 6-4, 6-1, 6-4, in the finals. But even Tilden's lesser victories were brilliant. He put drama into everything he did.

The tall, square-shouldered Tilden had a withering glare that struck fear into both opponents and linesmen. He also had a temper, but his controversial tirades never seemed to distract him from the concentration of winning an important match. As he established himself as the undisputed leader of tennis, he also developed the habit of falling behind early in his matches with sloppy play, then roaring back to win decisively.

Tilden never played carefully to a man's weakness. He preferred to challenge an opponent's strength, proving his own superiority until he broke the other man's game apart. He never relied on a particular shot. Whatever seemed most likely to bring the crowd to its feet was the shot Tilden would choose. In the "Golden Age" of sports, the age of Babe Ruth and Jack Dempsey and Red Grange, Big Bill Tilden stood among the best and most exciting of champions.

Rene Lacoste, 1926-27
Retrieving

René Lacoste was one of the greatest defensive players ever to win the U.S. championship. The quiet, unspectacular French star could return anything that came at him; no shot ever seemed to disturb him. Unlike his more colorful countrymen, Jean Borotra and Henri Cochet, Lacoste was a precise and patient player who always preferred to make his opponent miss rather than to smash a winning shot himself. He wore down his rivals with his remarkable retrieving ability.

Lacoste had an answer for everything that an opponent might try. If a man hit a hard shot at him, he would return it with a superbly controlled forehand, aimed either crosscourt or directly at the man's feet. Faced with a spinning shot, Lacoste would hit smoothly through the ball, robbing it of its spin and placing it just where he wanted it. He could handle a big serve quickly and accurately enough to force the server into a weak position; on a spinning serve, he could go wide and hit it down the line or crosscourt with precision.

He was a "made" player with very little natural ability, and he never even tried tennis until he was 16 years old. Yet Lacoste worked so hard at his game that he seemed to improve with every match. By the time he won the U.S. title, he had mastered solid ground strokes, and he had shown a rare ability to move his opponent around the court into precarious positions.

In the 1926 finals at Forest Hills, Lacoste kept the flamboyant, unpredictable Borotra constantly off balance. Borotra reacted by talking and needling throughout the match, trying to break down Lacoste's unswerving concentration. Lacoste never even showed that he heard Borotra, and won in straight sets. The following year he won again, with back-to-back victories over America's best, Johnston and Tilden. "It was one of the best matches I ever played," Tilden said later, "but it wasn't good enough to break down that French machine."

Henri Cochet, 1928
Ball Control

Henri Cochet was a short, graceful man with quick hands and unbelievably alert eyes. He never hit a tennis ball hard, but he always put it where he wanted it. He was a natural player, with amazing reflexes that made him exciting to watch. And his ability to control the ball made him one of the most frustrating opponents that Bill Tilden ever faced.

Ironically, Cochet's one victory in the U.S. singles championships came in 1928, the year that Tilden didn't play. The American champ was suspended by the U.S.L.T.A. for writing some newspaper stories that allegedly violated his amateur standing, so Cochet won a triumph that he had to consider hollow. His other wins over Tilden—at Wimbledon and in several Davis Cup matches—were more satisfying; and Cochet's overall performance marked him as one of the most brilliant players of his day.

Cochet, who came from Lyons, learned tennis on the clay courts of Paris, where speed afoot and defense were far more important than power. He developed a great ability to get to the ball and to hit it accurately. When he adapted this skill to the grass courts, he became a top player. His ground strokes were very sound and deceptive, because he hit them with a short flat swing that disguised their direction. His serve was not overwhelming, but it was low and deep.

The half-volley was one of Cochet's major weapons. This precise and demanding shot was hit just as the ball came off the ground, and it fit perfectly into Cochet's game. He never rushed to the net, but preferred to stroll casually forward, measuring his man for a winning shot. Since he didn't charge to the net, he was rarely in position for the regular volley. But he mastered the difficult half-volley so well that it became an advantage, and added to the style that made Cochet one of the most successful and dramatic players in the game.

John Doeg, 1930
The Serve

John H. Doeg was a strong left-handed player with a very hard serve. But in the crucial matches of the 1930 U.S. championship, a hard serve would not have helped Doeg. The 21-year-old player outlasted 37-year-old Bill Tilden in a grueling semifinal match; then he was faced with another long and testing match against Frank X. Shields. Doeg knew that he would have to conserve his energy as much as possible in these matches. But at the same time, he knew that he couldn't win unless he kept rushing to the net.

The solution to Doeg's problem was a spinning, twisting serve that gave his opponents trouble while allowing him time to get to the net for the volley. His serve often made the ball resemble an egg as it drifted toward his frustrated rivals. Because he was left-handed, the ball broke the "wrong" way, sometimes pulling a man out of court by five yards in an effort to return it.

Returning the Doeg serve was always difficult. Un-less you hit smoothly through the ball, it would spin off the racket to one side. He forced many opponents to stroke "foul balls" on their returns.

Even when they managed to return the serve, Doeg's rivals suffered. While they struggled with his elusive delivery, he had an opportunity to rush to the net. And that was the only way he could win. In his final match against Francis X. Shields, he pressed the attack at all times. Shields, on the other hand, stayed in the backcourt on many exchanges, allowing Doeg to take command of the play. Doeg was exhausted when it ended, but he won, 10-8, 1-6, 6-4, 16-14.

Without his serve, Doeg's game was unimpressive. His ground strokes were weak. His backhand was a kind of pushed chop, and his forehand was a top-spin. Everything else was average or below average. But the spinning, effective serve, and the ability to make the best use of it, won the 1930 title for Doeg.

H. Ellsworth Vines, Jr., 1931-32
Power Tennis

Nobody ever hit a tennis ball harder than H. Ellsworth Vines Jr., the tall, skinny kid who came out of the Los Angeles public parks to win his first U.S. singles championship at the age of 19. And nobody ever played tennis with less margin for error. Vines had a cannonball serve that had very little of the spin which other players needed for control. On all his shots, he tried to clear the net by inches or smash the ball as close as possible to the lines.

When he was hitting the small targets which he gave himself, Vines was as invincible as any player has ever been. When he was missing them, he could lose to almost anyone; after winning the U.S. title in 1931 and 1932, he was eliminated in 1933 by Bitsy Grant, who never approached Vines' ability on the grass courts. Vines' inconsistency kept him from being ranked alongside Tilden as a player; but he was certainly as dramatic to watch as any tennis champion.

Only Pancho Gonzalez has ever approached the power of Vines' hard, flat serve. Despite his lack of spin, Vines could usually control the serve well enough to win many points. And his forehand and backhand were almost as powerful as his serve. He lacked the all-around virtuosity of Tilden, and he didn't charge the net in the all-court offensive style that Jack Kramer later developed. Instead of charging forward, he won a great many points from the backcourt, simply drilling the ball past his opponents.

In his first title match, against George Lott in 1931, Vines made many mistakes. His daring shots missed often, and he had to struggle when he fell behind. But he recovered to win, 7-9, 6-3, 9-7, 7-5, in a remarkable exhibition of power tennis. The following year, he was just as strong—and more accurate. He routed the celebrated Frenchman Henri Cochet, 6-4, 6-4, 6-4. Vines had his faults; but the quiet, unemotional young star could generate an excitement that few tennis players have ever matched.

Frederick J. Perry, 1933-34, 1936
The Forehand

Every time Fred J. Perry walked onto a tennis court, he expected to win. Perry's ego occasionally made opponents wonder if the only word he knew was "I." He was completely convinced that he was superior to anyone that ventured across a net from him; and very often, the English champion was right. He dominated amateur tennis for several years, winning with a combination of self-confidence and a forehand that was one of the finest shots in tennis.

Perry hit his forehand with the continental grip, which kept the racket extremely "open" as it was taken back; the racket position can be compared to the angle of the face of a nine-iron in golf. This grip required tremendous wrist action as the racket met the ball. Perry used his strong wrist to turn the racket as he stroked the ball, sending a low, accurate shot toward his opponent. As this unusual shot became more and more effective, Perry made the best use of it. He always brought his forehand into play at every opportunity.

Perry was also unbelievably fast on the court. Most of his shots were just average, but he had the speed to stay in contention at all times. He took full advantage of what weapons he had, and distinguished himself as an exceptional match player.

In 1933, Perry lost two of the first three sets of the Forest Hills final match against Jack Crawford. But his steady play took its toll; Crawford began to make mistakes, and Perry routed him, 6-0, 6-1, in the last two sets. The following year he beat Wilmer Allison with the same kind of steady and persistent match play. In 1936, Perry won his third title in a grueling match against Don Budge, the rising challenger to his own tennis supremacy. Then Perry turned pro, leaving his position at the top to Budge and ending the four-year Davis Cup reign that he had brought to England.

Wilmer L. Allison, Jr., 1935
The Volley

Wilmer L. Allison was a good tennis player in a period when some very good players named Tilden and Vines and Perry were winning championships. Allison was never quite good enough to beat the best; until 1935, his best effort in a U.S. singles championship was a near-miss against Fred Perry in the 1934 finals. Then Allison got some very good luck to go with his ability. Perry, the odds-on favorite, fell and hurt himself in the first set of a 1935 semifinal match against Allison, and bowed, 6-4, 4-6, 8-6, 6-0. Allison went on to beat Sidney Wood Jr. in the finals to win his only national title.

Like Ted Schroeder, who labored in Jack Kramer's shadow in the 1940's, Allison was a tenacious battler who could make up for his physical faults with aggressive, hustling play. When his more gifted foes faltered, he could take advantage. There was no big weapon in his game, but he got the most out of what he possessed.

The volley was Allison's forte, and his game was geared to it. He followed a simple strategy: attack at all times. He was never tentative in his charges to the net. Since his serves and approaches were unimpressive, he should have been vulnerable as he charged. But he was such a spectacular volleyer that he could make his net play work. His fierce competitive spirit kept him on the offensive even when his opponents were scoring points; his relentless attack often reversed the trend of a match and helped him come from behind to win. Allison won enough hard matches to stay among the country's leaders for eight years.

J. Donald Budge, 1937-38

The Backhand

As a kid in Oakland, California, Don Budge was a lefthanded-hitting baseball player. When he switched his emphasis to tennis, he never forgot the smooth stroke of a good lefthanded batter. He developed a natural, fluid backhand motion, bringing the racket through the ball with his right arm the way Ted Williams would guide a bat through a baseball. And Budge's backhand left a mark on tennis that may last as long as Williams' hitting records.

In 1938, three years before Williams became the last major league .400 hitter, J. Donald Budge became the first winner of tennis' Grand Slam, as champion of England, France, Australia and the United States. He climaxed his feat with an easy win over his friend Gene Mako in the finals of the U.S. singles championships. A year earlier, the 21-year-old Budge had beaten Baron Gottfried von Cramm to win his first Forest Hills title. His records were impressive, but his best stroke was even more so. Budge gave tennis the greatest backhand ever developed.

He hit his backhand very hard or soft, with great control. He would move his shoulder and side as well as his arm into the shot, giving it a slight topspin. Only on the rare occasions when he was forced out of position would he play a defensive shot with underspin. He could place his backhand either crosscourt or down the line with the same accuracy.

Budge's game was built on power rather than speed. He used a heavy 16-ounce racket which did much of his work for him. He wasn't exceptionally fast, but he didn't have to be. His shots were so good that an opponent had to be lucky to get the ball past him when he came to the net. Budge's serve was deep and accurate, and he managed to control it with a minimum of spin, making it harder to return. His forehand suffered by comparison to his backhand, and most opponents would play to it; but it was effective enough to keep his game balanced.

Budge was a percentage player, with a good tennis sense and a magnificent attitude for match play. He decided early in his career that he would make up for his lack of speed by taking the ball early on the rise. He would save two yards each time he did this, keeping his opponent two yards further out of position. Budge was the only player I ever faced who could make me feel completely overwhelmed; he could force you into a hopeless position and keep you there with his relentless attack. He must be placed among the greatest players of all time.

Robert L. Riggs, 1939, 1941
Match Play Ability

Robert L. Riggs was probably the most underrated tennis player who ever lived. He followed Don Budge as leader of the game; he was succeeded a few years later by Jack Kramer. Between these recognized giants, Riggs seemed to get lost. He was small and unimposing. Most people never compared him to the stars of modern tennis' "Big Game."

But the players did. The one man that even Budge and Kramer always hated to face was Bobby Riggs. There was nothing overwhelmingly "big" about Riggs' game; but there was nothing small, either. He had a solid all-around game. He was clever, steady and deceptive. And in an important match, he would inevitably be at his very best.

Riggs was 21 when he won his first U.S. title, beating Welby Van Horn in the 1939 final. He lost to Don McNeill in the final match the next year, then came

back to defeat Frank Kovacs for the 1941 championship. His amateur career was marked by some surprising losses to less known players. But it included few defeats in the matches with the highest stakes.

Rarely has a player been able to out-think opponents the way Riggs could. Often he would give up points early in a match, in order to test his rival. He would lob frequently in the early sets, forcing his man to do a lot of running. Gradually, Riggs with the completeness of his game from his controlled lob to his excellent forehand and other strokes would wear down his opponent to get the victory.

Riggs complemented his clever tactics with steady and deceptive shotmaking. His opponents had difficulty anticipating his shots, so they were often caught off balance. In the most important matches, for the biggest stakes Riggs was at his best.

Donald McNeill, 1940
The Topspin Backhand

Don McNeill, a popular 22-year-old player from Oklahoma City, won the 1940 championship with a combination of luck, determination and one of the most unusual shots in tennis. The luck came when a long and crucial series of questionable linesmen's calls went against loser Bobby Riggs. The determination enabled McNeill to come back and beat Riggs after losing the first two sets of the final match. The shot that did the most for McNeill was a topspin backhand.

Even the best backhands in tennis are almost invariably hit with underspin or slight topspin. A Don Budge or a Ken Rosewall could keep a backhand so low, hard and well-placed that it was almost invulnerable. But a less precise underspin backhand is susceptible to attack.

A backhand with topspin is much more difficult to develop. But once developed, it is also much more difficult to attack. McNeill was able to use this rare shot to keep his opponents on the defensive, complementing his own aggressive style of play.

McNeill always attacked. He was not a great volleyer, but he designed his game so that he didn't have to depend on volleys. His ground strokes were so sound and deep that they could break an opponent before he had a chance to volley. McNeill's approaches hit close to the baseline, making it very hard for a man to get the ball past him.

McNeill's dogged competitive spirit added to the effectiveness of his attacking style. He had no real weakness himself, and he could force an opponent into many errors. These errors were enough to defeat Riggs at Forest Hills in 1940.

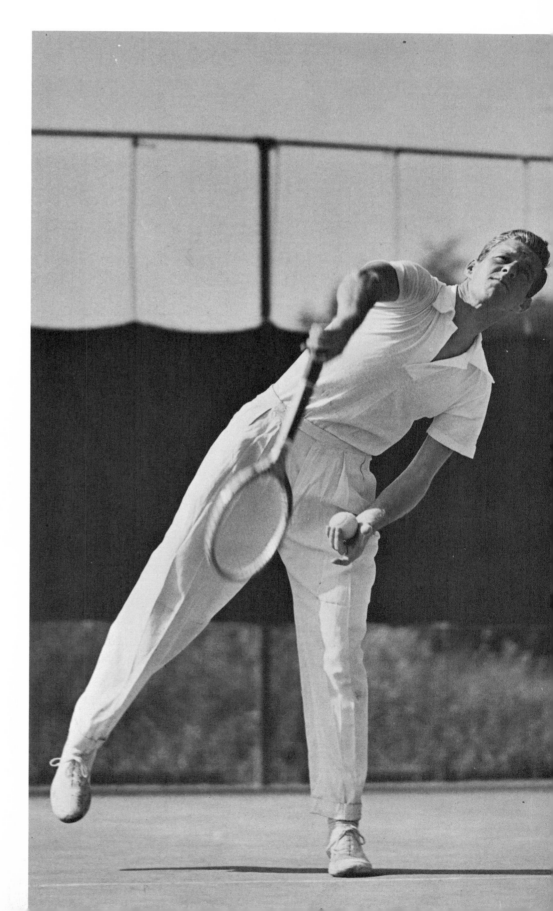

Frederick R. Schroeder, 1942
The Clutch Hitter

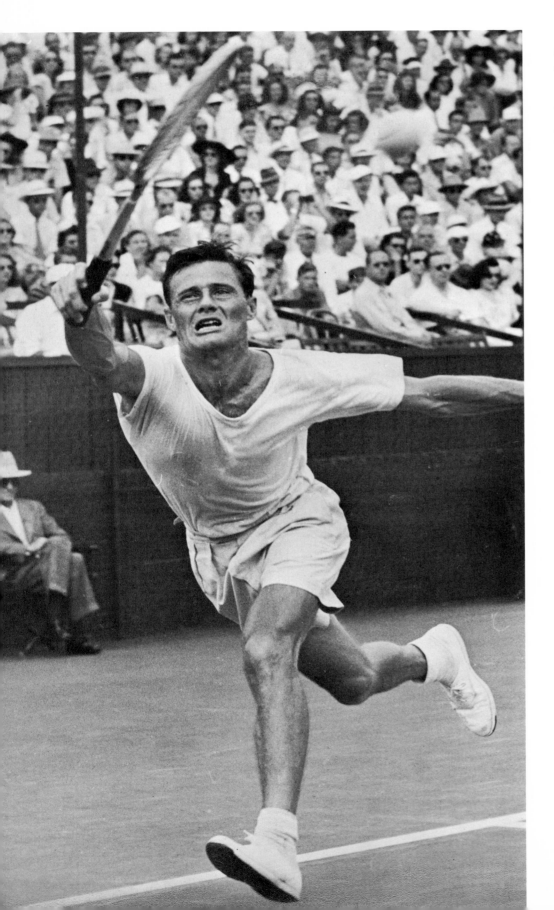

In the early 1940's, two young players came out of California, seeking to move toward Don Budge's vacated position as a tennis super-star. Frederick R. (Ted) Schroeder and Jack Kramer won the National doubles title together in 1940 and 1941, and also began advancing in singles competition. Kramer eventually proved to be the superior player; but it was Schroeder who developed most quickly. He won the U.S. singles championship when he was 21, defeating Frank Parker in the 1942 finals.

After his one wartime victory, Schroeder became overshadowed by Kramer and other stars. He lacked a big or frightening weapon to employ against the power of some opponents. Schroeder cannot be called a great champion. But he was a great match player. His ability to win important matches with determination and spirit kept him among amateur leaders for a decade after his championship year.

Schroeder had a good, steady serve and was quick as a cat. He won most of his points at the net. Since he was never overpowering, he found himself in many close matches. And the close matches brought out the best in Schroeder's game.

Like a clutch hitter with men on base in the late innings, Schroeder usually came up with the big shot when he needed it most. With a set tied at 4-all or 5-all, he was always most dangerous.

Schroeder was not unaware of his own abilities. He had a respectable repertory of shots, including an outstanding overhead which he could smash from almost anywhere on the court. But he never rushed to overwhelm his man with strength. He preferred to play carefully and accurately, keeping the match close. If Ted Schroeder could keep a match close, his ability to hit the big shot in the clutch would usually win it for him.

Joseph R. Hunt, 1943
The Serve and Volley

Joe Hunt was a typical product of the Southern California tennis circuit. He was tall, blond and good-looking, with a near-perfect physique. He was also extremely devoted to the game of tennis, and he worked hard to develop the shots which he first learned from his father, a successful Los Angeles player named Reuben Hunt.

Hunt made use of his power and speed in the serve-and-volley style that was becoming known as the "Big Game." His serve was strong, and his volleys were effective. He used a combination of accurate touch volleys and punch volleys to win most of his points. He possessed a very powerful overhead.

His ground strokes were lacking, but Hunt had the sound tennis sense to realize this and gear his game to his strong point. He also had a good attitude for match play. He won a series of Junior and Intercollegiate titles, and reached the final round of the U.S. men's singles against Jack Kramer in 1943.

When the 25-year-old Hunt beat Kramer, 6-3, 6-8, 10-8, 6-0, to win the championship, his game was still unpolished. He had the principal weapons of the "Big Game," and he might well have gone on to an outstanding career.

He never got the chance. Joseph R. Hunt, Navy lieutenant, was killed February 2, 1945, while flying a fighter plane on a training mission off Daytona Beach, Florida.

Frank Parker, 1944-45
Controlled Speed

In 1933, when he was seventeen, Frank A. Parker was placed eighth in the U.S.L.T.A. men's rankings. In 1949, when he turned pro, he was ranked fourth. And in every one of the 15 intervening years, Parker's name appeared in the top ten. He was never a great player, but he was an effective one for a long period. In the war years of 1944 and 1945, he was good enough to become national champion.

Parker had very little natural ability. But he was taught by an excellent coach, Mercer Beasley, and he was willing to work hard at the game. He had a good physique and kept rigid training, and he never ceased working on his shots. He finally won the U.S. title simply because he had hit so many practice shots that he could return almost anything that came toward him.

His game was based on controlled speed. He never tried to overpower the ball. Every shot was hit precisely and carefully—fast enough to be effective but slow enough to avoid errors. Parker never beat himself; he challenged his opponents to defeat him.

Parker never smiled on the court. He was grim and unemotional but he played his dogged, colorless game until he won. He beat me in the finals in both 1944 and 1945.

The backhand was the stroke Parker could really depend on. It was also the only one which remained constant throughout his career. He constantly experimented with different forehands and serves, seeking to improve his power and accuracy. He never quite found the strokes he wanted, but the ones he did possess gave him an all-around game that made him a perennial contender in major tournaments.

John A. Kramer, 1946-47
The Forehand

The post-war rise of Jack Kramer is sometimes hailed as the beginning of "modern" tennis. Kramer is occasionally credited with revising the whole sport by popularizing the "Big Game" based on the serve and volley.

Actually, Kramer's style wasn't a sharp break with the past. It was the result of a detailed study of the most effective ways to win at tennis. In fact, Kramer patterned his own game after that of Ellsworth Vines. But he became so successful that he was gradually pictured as the hero of a "new" power-happy era in tennis.

Kramer didn't really play his shots differently from his immediate predecessor. He just played them better. He set a schedule for himself in the 1930's, when he was still a junior player. He was 25 when he fulfilled some of his plans by defeating Tom Brown in the 1946 finals at Forest Hills. He won the U.S. title again in 1947, coming from behind to beat Frank Parker. Then he turned his athletic and promotional talents to the pro game.

The serve and volley of the powerful player from Southern California were justly praised. But fewer people realized that Kramer's most valuable weapon was his forehand. It was less dramatic than the serve, and more predictable than some of the volleys. It was also devastating.

Kramer always favored the forehand; sometimes he would drift far to the backhand side to play it. He usually played it to his opponent's backhand moving to net at the first opportunity. It was a hard shot, but it was hit with a little inside-out motion that gave it spin. The spin gave Kramer just the right amount of control over the ball.

The Kramer serve was deep and hard, but it wasn't quite as awesome as that of Pancho Gonzalez and a few others. Its greatest asset was placement. Kramer kept a high percentage of first serves in the court, forcing his opponents to play defensive shots back to him.

Kramer wasn't fast, but when in a difficult position he could compensate by making the big shot. He kept all the pressure on his opponent. Players like Parker and McNeill, who could at least return the ball against his relentless attack, were most successful against Kramer. But at its best, Kramer's game could overcome even the most persistent rival.

Richard A. Gonzales, 1948-49
The Serve

Pancho Gonzalez was preparing to serve. His eyes flashed across the net at his opponent. His dark face, cut by a thin scar, showed intense concentration. His taut and powerful 6′-3″ body leaned slightly forward. The gallery fell completely silent. It was like the moment when a brilliant racehorse is set to leap from the starting gate.

And it was a moment which was repeated many times. Richard A. Gonzalez was one of the most magnificent athletes ever to play tennis. He was also one of the sport's most dramatic and imposing champions. And the most exciting aspect of his game was his serve. It reached speeds up to 118 miles per hour, and it made Gonzalez a threat to break up a tense match at any time.

As a professional, Gonzalez went on to be rated by some people as the greatest player of all time. As an amateur, he was less polished and more vulnerable —but no less exciting and dangerous. When he was 20, he came to the 1948 Nationals as the seventeenth-ranked player on the U.S.L.T.A. lists. He beat Eric Sturgess in the finals to become the youngest U.S. champion since Ellsworth Vines won it at 19 in 1931.

The following year, after an inconsistent season, Gonzalez faced Ted Schroeder, who had skipped the Forest Hills tournament in 1948 and was anxious to assert his superiority over Gonzalez. In one of the most memorable matches ever played in the Nationals, Gonzalez came from behind to win, 16-18, 2-6, 6-1, 6-2, 6-4. Having proven himself the amateur champ again, he turned pro.

If American tennis could attract more athletes of Gonzalez' stature, the U.S. would never lose a Davis Cup. Pancho had physical traits rarely found in tennis. He was big and rangy, fast and extremely strong; and he had the quick eyes and hands that mark many sports champions.

He was also mean. He wanted to beat everybody. Because he refused to go to school, Gonzalez received little help from organized tennis as he was developing. He made it largely on his own incredible natural talent; and once he did make it, he remained proud and aloof from most of his opponents.

In addition to his serve, Gonzalez's forehand was hit with overspin and the backhand with underspin. His volleys were a strong complement to the serves. If he had a weakness, it was a vulnerability to an attack to his backhand. But it was difficult for a man to launch such an attack. Like Kramer, Gonzalez kept a high percentage of first serves in the court, keeping his opponents constantly on the defensive.

Arthur Larsen, 1950
Touch

The influence of Kramer and Gonzalez on amateur tennis was understandably widespread. It was not, however, uniformly good. By the end of Gonzalez' tenure as champion, the country was full of slightly less gifted players, ignoring fundamental strokes and trying to imitate the awesome power of the "Big Game."

The 1950 U.S. Singles tournament was marked by this dubious trend, as well as the fact that several very good players played badly that week. It was only natural that Art Larsen, who spent his whole career going against the trends and customs of tennis, should emerge as the new champ.

Larsen, a slim lefthander, had little power. What he did have was exceptional racket and ball control. He could vary the spin on his shots and place them just where he wanted them. He was adept at playing to his opponents' weaknesses, and he found many weaknesses to exploit in the 1950 field at Forest Hills. He beat Herbie Flam in the final match.

The quick 140-pound champ from San Francisco didn't exactly reverse the Kramer-Gonzalez power trend by his victory. But, he was an unusual character on and off the court.

He could be shocking to the staid gatherings at Newport or Forest Hills, abusive to meek ball boys, and delightful to everyone around him—all within a few hours. He was superstitious beyond belief, smiling benignly as "lucky birds" flew over him or insisting on serving a "lucky ball." His blithe after-dinner speeches were hysterical—and the players, to a man, were his friends.

His career ended the way he always moved—at full speed. He was seriously injured in a 1957 accident on an Italian motorscooter he had won in a tournament. Tennis lost its most colorful character.

Frank Sedgman, 1951-52
The All-Court Volley

The changes which Jack Kramer brought into tennis after the Second World War reached the Australian players a few years later. The new style was called the "Big Game" and it was based on a big serve and volley. Frank Sedgman had both attributes, and he developed the all-court volley to a degree which made him the first Australian ever to win the U.S. singles title.

Sedgman won his first championship in 1951, when he was 23. He repeated the following year, showing even more complete superiority over his rivals. In seven matches at Forest Hills in 1952, Sedgman didn't lose a set. He was at his best that year, and at his best, Sedgman was the finest player that has ever come out of Australia.

Sedgman charged every shot he possibly could. He always volleyed from just off the baseline, instead of waiting to play a ground stroke. His ground strokes were adequate, but he never used them when an aggressive volley would do. His volleys allowed him to rush toward the net. And at the net, he won most of his points.

In the 1951 U.S. finals, Sedgman's volleys ruined whatever chance Vic Seixas had. His returns blunted the effectiveness of Seixas' serve, and he kept his opponent in the backcourt most of the afternoon. He turned back Seixas' only serious threat late in the first set and won, 6-4, 6-1, 6-1. It was even easier the following year, as Sedgman routed Gardnar Mulloy, 6-1, 6-2, 6-3, in just 47 minutes.

The all-court game requires tremendous speed, and Sedgman had that quality. He was quick enough to take on the volley a shot that most players would play on the rise. He had a good, deep serve which kept his opponents on the defensive, but he was even more devastating with his volleys. And he was fit enough to sustain his speed. He could move as quickly in the fifth set of a hard match as he had in the first—if an opponent could manage to carry him that long.

Tony Trabert, 1953, 1955
The Backhand Volley

Tony Trabert was big, strong and fast—a natural tennis player. He was also a kid from Cincinnati—which is not a natural tennis proving ground. Trabert was faced with limited opportunities and fairly meager competition as he developed. Yet he was such a student of the game that he overcame all obstacles to become one of the very best U.S. champions.

Trabert was a pleasure to teach. He was a willing worker and a dogged competitor. He learned very fast and listened eagerly to suggestions. Yet the most powerful weapon in his game was probably the one thing that nobody ever taught him. He used a distinctive "punch" backhand volley, hit with his racket in front of his body. It was unorthodox, and a coach's first reaction would have been to change it. But it worked. So Trabert stayed with it, and made it into one of the outstanding shots in tennis.

When he was 23, Trabert won the 1953 Nationals, routing Vic Seixas in the record time of only 59 minutes. Two years later, he beat Ken Rosewall in the finals to climax an awesome tournament performance in which he didn't lose a set. When he turned pro after the 1955 victory, he was the world's best amateur.

When given a choice, Trabert would always knock you down rather than try to ease a shot past you for a point. His game was always forceful and aggressive. But he was also a smart player. He could adapt to any conditions or instructions, and he was always alert to an opponent's weaknesses.

Trabert is a sensitive individual, and in a few matches he became upset and this interfered with the task at hand. For the most part, however, he showed great powers of concentration. A fierce competitor, he could bear down for long periods and keep the pressure on until the match was won.

E. Victor Seixas, 1954
Competitive Spirit

E. Victor Seixas, of Philadelphia, never looked the part of a leading tennis player. His strokes were awkward, his strength moderate. He lunged and scrambled to hold his own in matches. He never presented a model of good tennis form for young players to copy. All Vic Seixas did was win.

You can call Seixas' weapon determination or will to win or spirit, but the words are overworked and sound too much like cliches. Seixas' quality isn't adequately described by glib phrases. To appreciate what he had, you have to talk in terms of what he lacked. This is a champion who has won many, many tournaments with very little of the classic strokes in his game.

In the 1954 final match at Forest Hills, Seixas lost the first set to Australian Rex Hartwig. Seixas was 31 at the time. His opponent was younger, stronger and faster, and he was off to an early lead. But Seixas wouldn't give up. Somehow, he won the title. It was an exhibition of consistency and drive—a typical Seixas triumph.

Seixas won all his matches at the net. He also left his stunned victims wondering how he had gotten to the net in the first place. He didn't advance to the net on a big backhand or a booming forehand. His serves weren't strong, and they often bounced far short. Seixas almost always appeared vulnerable, and rarely seemed to be launching an offensive. Yet somehow he would get to the net and win.

This persistent style made it very easy for Seixas' opponents to beat themselves. A shot that appeared to be a sure winner would suddenly come back across the net and catch a man off-balance. A few of his incredible recoveries could leave his rival surprised and demoralized.

His opponent's feelings were often understandable. Seixas' returns would be lunging and awkward. Some would career off the wood of his racket. Somehow his assortment of "junk" shots seemed to stay in play. When an opponent would try to over-power him, Seixas would be even more effective, and force his man into further mistakes.

Playing against Seixas was never easy. It became slightly less frustrating, however, when you finally adapted one attitude—You must expect everything you hit at him to come back at you. As soon as you start to think you've won a point with a fine shot, the ball comes squirting back, and the problems of playing Vic Seixas are just beginning.

Kenneth Rosewall, 1956
The Backhand

The small man's racket went back high in the air and swept down smoothly under the ball. As he followed through the backhand stroke, the ball sailed quickly, low and with underspin. And it always seemed to land at the most vulnerable spot in the other player's defenses. This was Ken Rosewall's backhand, and it is very close to the perfect way to hit this shot in tennis.

Rosewall stands 5'-7", but he has the chest and shoulders of a man 6'-4". His friends on the tennis circuit nicknamed him "Muscles" because of the unusual power he generated. Yet power wasn't the center of the game that won Rosewall the 1956 U.S. championship. It was a game based on precision, and Rosewall's backhand was as precise a shot as anyone has ever developed.

It was a hard powerful shot. Its underspin kept it low and made it difficult to handle. But the most effective thing about the backhand was its accuracy. He could hit it either down the line or crosscourt, making it hard to anticipate and even harder to return.

Rosewall beat another Australian, Lew Hoad, for the 1956 title. Both players were 21 at the time, and both had played one another many times. The match wasn't decided by surprises or tactics. It was a contest of shot-making, and Rosewall won it with his backhand.

Rosewall's forehand was not as strong or varied. He almost always played it crosscourt, so it could be anticipated and charged. In 1954, Vic Seixas helped the U.S. to the Davis Cup by playing to Rosewall's forehand.

However, few players ever managed to dominate a match against Rosewall. His all-around game was solid. His serves hit from a low toss were deep and accurate, and his volleys were aggressive. He developed an effective lob which forced his opponents back from the net. His overhead—another necessity for the small man—was equally solid. Nobody took advantage of Rosewall's stature, and many who tried finally succumbed to his remarkable backhand.

Malcolm Anderson, 1957
The All-Around Game

The 77th National championship, played in 1957, doesn't exactly stand as a milestone in tennis history. The biggest names in amateur tennis—Trabert, Rosewall, Lew Hoad—were all professionals by that year. The amateur ranks were left depleted, waiting for new leaders. The National tournament was an unpredictable event. With no dominant star, it figured to be won by the player who could make the fewest mistakes.

A 22-year-old Australian named Malcolm Anderson made fewer mistakes than any of his rivals. At the start of the week, Anderson was virtually unknown. He was unseeded in the tournament and overshadowed by his country man, topseeded Ashley Cooper. But he played steady and effective tennis, and managed to upset Cooper, 10-8, 7-5, 6-4, in the final match.

Anderson didn't possess any outstanding weapon. He had a solid all-around game and he made very few errors. With no real weakness for his rivals to exploit, Anderson stayed in contention in every match, and waited for the others to beat themselves.

He was very quick and fit, and used the court to his advantage with uncanny anticipation. Whenever Anderson saw his man out of position, he seemed to move directly to the best spot from which to make the point. When he forced a man wide with his backhand, or forehand for example, he could move quickly toward the net punching a winning volley past his man.

Anderson didn't have an overpowering serve, but he did have great control over it. It was always deep and heavy, forcing his opponent to play it with a firm wrist and a lot of effort. This kind of "heavy" serve can be compared to a ground ball which bounces at the feet of an infielder in baseball: the ball plays the man, and the man never gets a chance to play the ball.

The serve—undramatic but effective—was typical of Anderson's all-around game. He hit few spectacular shots, but many good ones. And his steady play was enough to win for him in 1957.

Ashley Cooper, 1958
Hard Work

In a rematch of the 1957 final, Ashley Cooper and Mal Anderson met in the last match of the 1958 Nationals. The two young Australians were clearly the best of the amateurs of the time, and they appeared evenly matched against one another. In 1958, Cooper reversed the previous year's result and took the title from Anderson.

Like Anderson, Cooper was a player without a dramatic weapon. In addition, he didn't have exceptional natural ability. Everything he did on the court appeared a little too stiff and labored. He had none of the fluency of motion that marked earlier Australian champs like Ken Rosewall or Frank Sedgman. But he made it to the top of amateur tennis, largely through hard work.

Cooper kept himself in almost unbelievable physical condition. He emphasized running, weight lifting and other exercise. He was never a really smooth player, but he made himself into a strong and durable one. He knew that he could wear down many opponents and eventually find a weakness to exploit. In fact, his physical fitness was the most important factor in Cooper's success.

He also practiced endlessly. He had a repertory of less-than-brilliant strokes, but he gradually and painstakingly molded them into a sound and consistent machine which was hard to beat. He could be beaten by superior shots, but he was rarely defeated by his own mistakes.

Cooper worked hard on his mental condition for an important match. He prepared himself carefully for the challenge ahead, and convinced himself that he could win. In an evenly-matched tournament such as the 1958 Nationals, this kind of confidence could have been a crucial factor.

Neale Fraser, 1959-60
The Serve

Neale Fraser won with his serve. It was left-handed, extremely powerful, and versatile. It stood far above the other aspects of an otherwise moderate tennis style. It was, in fact, one of the most dramatically effective weapons that any champion has ever used.

When he wasn't serving, Fraser was just another tournament player. He could be beaten in many ways, and he had a tendency to hurt himself with erratic play. But when he stepped back to deliver his serve, he became a fearsome and powerful figure. He could blast his serve at great speed, or put tremendous spin on slower deliveries. On his best spinning serves, the ball looked like an egg as it came toward the receiver.

Fraser's serve brought him two U.S. championships. When he was 25, he won the 1959 title, beating Alex Olmedo in the finals. He was aided by some luck that day—Olmedo played with a pulled shoulder muscle, and also played dangerously close to the net as he received Fraser's service. The following year, Fraser needed no luck as he overcame Rod Laver, another strong Australian left-hander, 6-4, 6-4, 10-8.

The rest of Fraser's game bore little resemblance to the serve. His whippy topspin forehand was erratic. His backhand was little more than a chip, an attempt to merely block the ball and keep it in play. If Fraser could be forced into an uncomfortable volleying position, he could be beaten.

This wasn't easy to do. Fraser's serve was as strong psychologically as it was physically. Some opponents would stay awake nights thinking about it, and enter the court prepared for the worst. This led to defeat. The only useful attitude against Fraser was a determination to get the serve back over the net. If you could do this, you had the edge. But against Fraser's serve, it wasn't an easy edge to get.

Roy Emerson, 1961, 1964
Speed

Roy Emerson won most of his points at the net, which doesn't make him unique among modern tennis champs. But the Australian leader got to the net with a speed that was unique. His brilliant and aggressive style of play was based on great natural speed and amazingly quick reactions.

In 1961, the 24-year-old Emerson won the U.S. title for the first time, trouncing Rod Laver in straight sets in the deciding match. Three years later, he beat another Australian, Fred Stolle, with the same methodical power. Neither of his wins was close or especially exciting. Emerson rarely lost his service, and rushed forward to execute a steady series of effective volleys at the net.

His serve was not overpowering, but it was very consistent. He sacrificed extreme speed for accuracy, and kept a large percentage of his first serves in play, setting up his swift charges to the net. He could also afford to stay at the net, because it was very hard to lob over his head. Emerson could jump as well as he ran, and possessed an excellent overhead.

His ground strokes didn't compare with those of men like Don Budge or Ken Rosewall. He couldn't beat a solid opponent from the backcourt. He also had the sound tennis sense to realize this fact; so he geared his whole attack to net play. He was never tentative or defensive in his ground strokes. If he could go for a shot, he always would with the clear purpose of following it quickly to net.

Emerson's speed was complemented by his exceptional physical fitness and an ideal temperament for tournament play. He was never upset by a linesman's call or an opponent's tactic, and he refused to be rattled by his own mistakes. Toward the end of his career, he was no longer "hungry" for every weekly event, but he could still prepare himself for any challenge–as he showed in the 1964 Nationals.

Rodney G. Laver, 1962
The Serve

Rodney George Laver has a lefthanded serve so powerful that he can take charge of a match from the start. His wrists are so strong that he can reach a ball that is almost behind him, and convert it into a winning shot. His speed made Pancho Gonzalez call him "the fastest tennis player I've ever seen."

Any one of these attributes might have taken Laver to the top ranks of tennis. In 1962, all of them worked together. Injuries that had bothered him earlier were absent. The 24-year-old Laver was at his very best. And Laver's best tennis was good enough to accomplish what only one player—Don Budge in 1938—had ever managed before him.

Laver won the Grand Slam—the Australian, French, Wimbledon and American titles—in 1962. As the slender redhead from Rockhampton, Queensland, Australia moved toward this rare goal, the odds against him increased. Yet during the climactic finish at Forest Hills, he seemed to get even better.

He won the U.S. title with an awesome display of power and consistency. He yielded only two sets in the course of the entire tournament. In the finals on September 10, he overpowered Roy Emerson, the defending champ, 6-2, 6-4, 5-7, 6-4. Emerson did not manage to reach 40 on Laver's service until the middle of the third set.

Laver's mighty serve was so striking that it almost overshadowed his other abilities. But a player doesn't win the testing Grand Slam on serves alone. Rod Laver was the complete player in 1962. His backhand returns of service were very effective, and his volleys were aggressive.

His power game was complemented by his incredible wrist action, which not only saved points but allowed him to change spin and placement a split second after his rival committed himself. Laver had almost everything going for him in 1962. He employed the modern big game as few have employed it, and he gave his generation the Grand Slam it had awaited for 24 years.

Rafael Osuna, 1963
Speed

Frank Froehling reached back and delivered his strongest serve. Rafael Osuna danced forward, caught the ball as it rose from the grass, and returned it to make the point. Froehling served again and moved toward the net. Osuna remained near the baseline, received the serve at the top of the bounce, and lobbed it back over Froehling for another point.

This was the pattern of the final match of the 1963 Nationals. Rafael Osuna had no overpowering weapon. His ground strokes were actually weak. But he played with incredible quickness and daring. Offensively and defensively, he never ceased moving. He varied his tactics and controlled the pace, winning in straight sets, 7-5, 6-4, 6-2.

As the match began on the afternoon of September 8, 1963, it appeared that Froehling, a large and powerful player from Florida, might drive his smaller opponent off the court. Froehling's serves quickly gave him a 40-0 lead in the first game, and Osuna drew laughs by dropping far behind the baseline to await the next serve.

But Osuna refused to weaken. He played percentage tennis, anticipating his slower rival's shots, getting to the ball and keeping it in play. Gradually his perseverance began to dominate the match. He gained control—physically and psychologically.

Osuna's speed made Froehling appear increasingly awkward. His changing tactics made Froehling increasingly confused. He won most of his points at the net, reaching for shots that seemed beyond even the fastest of players. And his carefully placed lobs forced Froehling's overhead to crumble, allowing Osuna to assume complete command of the action.

The lithe Mexican player won the U.S. championship a week before his 25th birthday. He lacked the power of most of his opponents, but he won it with speed and strategy—and a winning attitude. "I always have great confidence in myself," he said later. "I know I am good."

Manuel Santana, 1965
All-Around Game

On September 11, 1965, Manuel Santana fell behind Arthur Ashe in a semifinal match at Forest Hills. Ashe won the first set, 6-2, by overpowering his opponent with his serves. He appeared to have Santana on the defensive.

This happens to be just where Manuel Santana is at his best. The 23-year-old Spaniard, who had led his country to a Davis Cup win over the U.S. earlier in the season, never lost his intense enthusiasm for his task. He positioned himself perfectly. He made use of the entire court. And he left no area in which he could be exploited by his more powerful rival.

Soon he was breaking Ashe's service. He went on to win that match, and the following day he beat Cliff Drysdale of South Africa in the finals to become National champion.

The final match was close most of the way. Santana was ahead, 6-2, 7-9, 7-5, after three sets when it was delayed by rain. After the interruption, it took the winner just 26 minutes to route Drysdale, 6-1. "I cooled off during the break," said Drysdale. Santana, the model of concentration and exuberant Latin temperament, never cooled off at all.

Santana's own serves were only moderate. But his returns of his opponent's serves were consistently brilliant. "They fly by you," said Drysdale, "like a rocket."

Santana's entire repertory of strokes was unspectacular, but he executed every shot carefully and cleverly. He never overwhelmed anyone, but he managed to outmaneuver almost everyone. He made full use of the court, placing his shots so well that his opponents rarely had a chance to take the offensive. He was especially effective at drawing his man to the net, then hitting a topspin lob for a winner. When a rival did get an opportunity to overpower him, Santant rebounded immediately. He virtually ran and scrambled to the title.

Frederick Stolle, 1966
The Serve

The influence of the power tennis of Pancho Gonzalez and Jack Kramer may have reached its height in the final match of the 1966 nationals at Forest Hills. Two rangy Australians traded powerful serves for two hours and 15 minutes, and neither showed any real ability to make return shots. Modern players have managed to duplicate much of the strength of the Gonzalez-type game, but somehow they have failed to gain the accuracy and versatility that went with it.

Fred Stolle's serve had tremendous speed and twist, with little direction. In the past, a server had to think in terms of hitting the ball close to the line, or it would be returned effectively. Now the returns are less dangerous, and the serves no longer have to be carefully placed. So the Stolle attack was simple. He served as hard as he could, then charged to the net. John Newcombe, his opponent, was trying much the same thing; Stolle won because, on that particular day, his serve was sharper.

Actually, Stolle's game was not limited to the serve and volley. His ground strokes were adequate and his overhead was very strong. But he never felt comfortable in the backcourt; he always concentrated on his attack at the net. His service was erratic early in his match with Newcombe, but he got straightened out in time to win, 4-6, 12-10, 6-3, 6-4.

Stolle also benefitted from a psychological weapon provided by the American seeding committee, which left him unseeded while placing four Americans in the top eight before the tournament. He was determined to prove that he belonged among the top players in any world listing. His victory was popular with the other players on the amateur circuit, because, while he may not possess one of the most distinguished all-court games in tennis, the 27-year-old Stolle is well conditioned, persistent, and a well liked man.

THE DRAWS: 1881-1966

FIRST USLTA MEN'S SINGLES CHAMPIONSHIPS
The Casino, Newport, R.I., 1881

First Round	Second Round	Third Round	Semi-Finals	Final Round	Winner

```
First Round          Second Round       Third Round      Semi-Finals      Final Round       Winner

Sears ............... Sears
Powell .............. 6-0, 6-2
Anderson ............ Anderson           Sears
Randolph ............ 6-2, 6-0           6-1, 6-2
Nightingale ......... Nightingale                         Sears
Caldwell ............ 6-2, 6-0                             6-3, 6-5
Barnes .............. Barnes             Nightingale
Miller .............. 6-2, 1-6, 6-1      6-4, 6-3                          Sears
Gray ................ Gray                                                 6-3, 6-0
Hines ............... 6-5, 6-3           Gray
Coggswell ........... Coggswell          6-0, 6-0                          Gray
Conglon ............. 6-4, 6-5                             Gray            Bye
                                                          Bye                               R. D. Sears
Glyn ................ Glyn                                                                   6-0, 6-3, 6-2
Rives ............... 1-6, 6-1, 6-1      Glyn
Conover ............. Conover            6-5, 6-2
Morse ............... 6-1, 6-1                             Glyn
Gammell ............. Gammell                              6-4, 4-6, 6-4
Newbold ............. 1-6, 6-3, 6-1      Gammel
                                         Bye                               Glyn
Shaw ................ Shaw                                                 6-2, 6-2
 bye                                     Shaw
Rathbone ............ Rathbone           6-3, 6-5
Saunders ............ 6-5, 5-6, 6-5                        Shaw
Smith ............... Smith                                4-6, 6-3, 6-1
Eldridge ............ Default
Kessler ............. Kessler            Kessler
Pruyn ............... 6-1, 6-4           6-1, 6-2
```

SECOND USLTA MEN'S SINGLES CHAMPIONSHIPS
The Casino, Newport, R.I., 1882

```
First Round          Second Round      Third Round       Fourth Round     Semi-Final Round   Final Round   Winner

R. D. Sears ......... Sears
Johnson ............. 6-4, 6-1          Sears
W. E. Glyn .......... Glyn              6-1, 6-4
Hynes ............... 6-2, 6-0                            Sears
R. F. Conover ....... Conover           Conover          6-1, 6-4
Butler .............. 6-2, 6-3          2-6, 6-0, 6-2
                      Thorne ............                                  Sears
Rankine ............. Rankine                                             6-0, 6-4
Miller .............. 6-4, 8-6, 6-1     Rankine
Malcolmson .......... Malcolmson        6-0, 6-0                                             Sears
Brooks .............. 1-6, 6-4, 6-3                       Rankine                            bye
                      Powell ............                4-6, 5-6, 6-5
                                         Powell
                      Rathbone ..........6-0, 6-1
                                                                                                           R. D. Sears, 6-1, 6-4, 6-0
C. M. Clark ......... C. M. Clark       C. M. Clark
Boti ................ 6-3, 6-1          6-5, 6-1
                      Codman                              C. M. Clark
A. L. Rives ......... Rives             Rives             6-3, 2-6, 6-1
Thomas .............. 6-1, 6-0          4-6, 6-1, 6-5
Kneeland ............ Kneeland                                            Clark
LeRoy ............... 6-2, 6-2                                            Default
James Dwight ........ Dwight            Dwight
Boardman ............ 6-1, 6-0          Default
Allen ............... Allen                               Dwight                             Clark
Carryl .............. 6-4, 5-6, 6-2                       6-1, 6-0                            6-3, 6-2
J. S. Clark ......... Clark             J. S. Clark
Baillie ............. 6-3, 6-0          6-3, 6-0
Baillie ............. Baillie
W. F. Metcalfe ...... 6-1, 6-0
Nightingale ......... Nightingale       Nightingale
Draper .............. Default           6-4, 6-1
Eldridge ............ Eldridge                            Gray
Roby ................ Default                             6-4, 6-4          Gray
Gray ................ Gray                                                 bye
Agassiz ............. Default           Gray
G. A. Smith ......... Smith             6-1, 6-1
LeRoy ............... 6-2, 6-2
```

THIRD USLTA MEN'S SINGLES CHAMPIONSHIPS
The Casino, Newport, R.I., 1883

```
First Round          Second Round      Third Round       Semi-Finals       Finals            Winner

C. Farnum ........... Farnum
H. A. Taylor ........ 6-2, 4-6, 6-4     Sears
R. D. Sears ......... Sears             6-1, 6-4
 bye                                                      Sears
H. W. H. Powell ..... Powell            Powell            6-2, 6-0
Wharton ............. 6-2, 6-0          6-1, 6-5
W. H. Bucknall ...... Bucknall
W. Gammell, Jr. ..... 6-5, 6-5                                              Sears, 6-0, 6-0
Foxhall Keene ....... Keene             Keene
Johnson ............. 6-4, 6-1          6-2, 6-4
M. Post ............. Post                                Keene
J. H. Powell ........ 6-4, 6-4                            6-3, 6-4
G. M. Smith ......... Smith             Smith
Williams ............ Default           6-5, 6-1
F. Eldridge ......... Eldridge                                                                Richard D. Sears,
F. J. Hynes ......... 6-5, 3-6, 6-4                                                            6-2, 6-0, 9-7
M. S. Paton ......... Paton             Dwight
W. F. Metcalfe ...... 6-5, 6-4          6-3, 6-0
J. Dwight ........... Dwight                              Dwight
M. Thomas ........... 6-0, 6-2                            6-2, 6-3
G. M. Brinley ....... Brinley           Brinley
H. Hooper ........... 6-5, 6-1          6-4, 5-6, 6-3
A. Newbold .......... Newbold                                               Dwight, 6-4, 6-3
G. W. Beals ......... Default
R. F. Conover ....... Conover           Conover
J. Tooker ........... 5-6, 6-1, 6-1     6-2 6-2
W. B. Dixon ......... Dixon                               Conover
Leigh Bosnal ........ 4-6, 6-3, 6-1                       Bye
```

FOURTH USLTA MEN'S SINGLES CHAMPIONSHIPS
The Casino, Newport, R.I., 1884

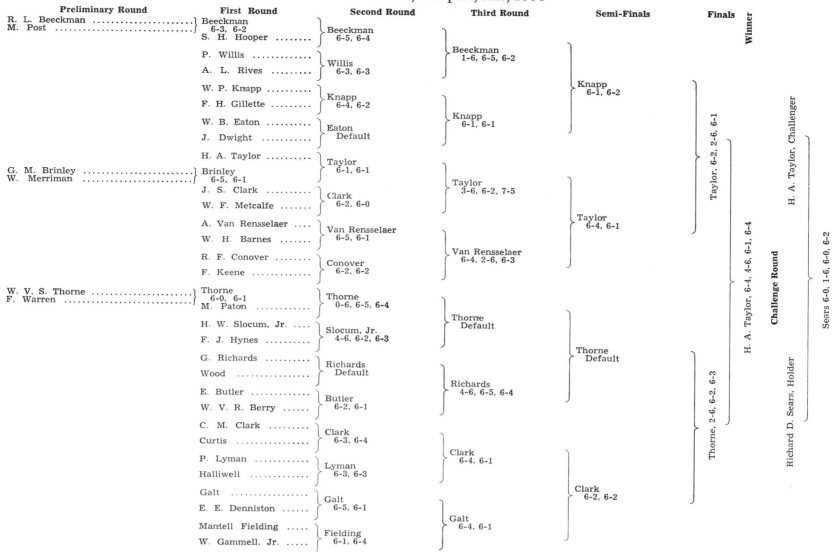

Preliminary Round	First Round	Second Round	Third Round	Semi-Finals	Finals	Winner
R. L. Beeckman / M. Post — Beeckman 6-3, 6-2	Beeckman vs S. H. Hooper — Beeckman 6-5, 6-4	Beeckman 1-6, 6-5, 6-2	Knapp 6-1, 6-2	Taylor 6-2, 2-6, 6-1	H. A. Taylor, 6-4, 4-6, 6-1, 6-4	H. A. Taylor, Challenger
	P. Willis vs A. L. Rives — Willis 6-3, 6-3					
	W. P. Knapp vs F. H. Gillette — Knapp 6-4, 6-2	Knapp 6-1, 6-1				
	W. B. Eaton vs J. Dwight — Eaton Default					
	H. A. Taylor vs Brinley — Taylor 6-1, 6-1	Taylor 3-6, 6-2, 7-5	Taylor 6-4, 6-1			
G. M. Brinley / W. Merriman — Brinley 6-5, 6-1	J. S. Clark vs W. F. Metcalfe — Clark 6-2, 6-0					
	A. Van Rensselaer vs W. H. Barnes — Van Rensselaer 6-5, 6-1	Van Rensselaer 6-4, 2-6, 6-3				
	R. F. Conover vs F. Keene — Conover 6-2, 6-2					
W. V. S. Thorne / F. Warren — Thorne 6-0, 6-1	Thorne vs M. Paton — Thorne 0-6, 6-5, 6-4	Thorne Default	Thorne Default	Thorne Default		
	H. W. Slocum, Jr. vs F. J. Hynes — Slocum, Jr. 4-6, 6-2, 6-3					
	G. Richards vs Wood — Richards Default	Richards 4-6, 6-5, 6-4				
	E. Butler vs W. V. R. Berry — Butler 6-2, 6-1					
	C. M. Clark vs Curtis — Clark 6-3, 6-4	Clark 6-4, 6-1	Clark 6-2, 6-2	Thorne, 2-6, 6-2, 6-3		
	P. Lyman vs Halliwell — Lyman 6-3, 6-3					
	Galt vs E. E. Denniston — Galt 6-5, 6-1	Galt 6-4, 6-1				
	Martell Fielding vs W. Gammell, Jr. — Fielding 6-1, 6-4					

Challenge Round — Richard D. Sears, Holder — Sears 6-0, 1-6, 6-0, 6-2

FIFTH USLTA MEN'S SINGLES CHAMPIONSHIPS
The Casino, Newport, R.I., 1885

Preliminary Round	First Round	Second Round	Semi-Finals	Finals	Winner
	J. S. Clark	Clark 6-2, 1-6, 8-6	Clark 7-6, 1-6, 6-3	Knapp, 6-4, 6-3	G. M. Brinley, 6-3, 6-3, 3-6, 6-4
R. L. Beeckman / G. A. Smith — Beeckman 6-1, 6-2	A. Moffat				
F. S. Mansfield / C. E. Garrett — Mansfield 6-3, 6-3	Moffat 6-0, 9-11, 6-3				
W. P. Knapp / W. Shippen — Knapp 6-1, 7-5	Knapp 6-0, 6-2	Knapp 4-6, 10-8, 6-2			
S. T. Hooper / F. J. Hynes — Hooper 9-7, 6-2					
	Taylor	Taylor 6-4, 6-2			
Nightingale / H. S. Morgan — Nightingale 6-3, 4-6, 7-5					
	Brinley	Brinley 6-1, 4-6, 6-2	Brinley 6-2, 6-1	Brinley, 3-6, 9-7, 6-1	G. M. Brinley, Challenger
	H. W. Slocum				
C. B. Davis / P. E. Presbrey — Davis 6-3, 7-5	Davis 6-1, 6-0				
H. Lilienthal / C. M. Clark — Lilienthal Default					
W. V. R. Berry / M. A. DeW. Howe — Berry 6-3, 6-1	Berry 6-3, 2-6, 6-3	Berry 6-2, 6-1			
F. Warren / W. Lewis — Warren 3-6, 6-3, 7-5					
F. Keene / F. H. Gillett — Keene 9-7, 6-2	Keene Default				
M. S. Paton					

Challenge Round — Richard O. Sears, Holder — Sears, 6-3, 4-6, 6-0, 6-3

SIXTH ANNUAL USLTA MEN'S SINGLES CHAMPIONSHIPS
The Casino, Newport, R.I., 1886

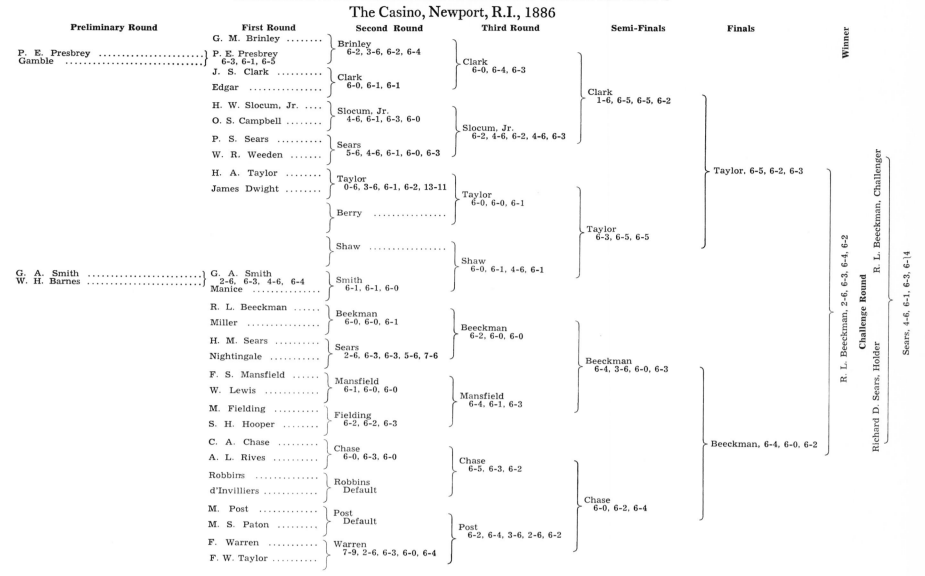

Preliminary Round	First Round	Second Round	Third Round	Semi-Finals	Finals	Winner

G. M. Brinley ....
Brinley
6-2, 3-6, 6-2, 6-4

P. E. Presbrey .... }
Gamble ....
P. E. Presbrey
6-3, 6-1, 6-5

J. S. Clark ....
Clark
6-0, 6-1, 6-1

Edgar ....

Clark
6-0, 6-4, 6-3

H. W. Slocum, Jr. ....
Slocum, Jr.
4-6, 6-1, 6-3, 6-0

O. S. Campbell ....

P. S. Sears ....
Sears
5-6, 4-6, 6-1, 6-0, 6-3

W. R. Weeden ....

Slocum, Jr.
6-2, 4-6, 6-2, 4-6, 6-3

Clark
1-6, 6-5, 6-5, 6-2

H. A. Taylor ....
Taylor
0-6, 3-6, 6-1, 6-2, 13-11

James Dwight ....

Berry ....

Taylor
6-0, 6-0, 6-1

Shaw ....

Shaw
6-0, 6-1, 4-6, 6-1

G. A. Smith .... }
W. H. Barnes ....
G. A. Smith
2-6, 6-3, 4-6, 6-4

Manice ....
Smith
6-1, 6-1, 6-0

Taylor
6-3, 6-5, 6-5

Taylor, 6-5, 6-2, 6-3

R. L. Beeckman ......
Beekman
6-0, 6-0, 6-1

Miller ....

H. M. Sears ....
Sears
2-6, 6-3, 6-3, 5-6, 7-6

Nightingale ....

Beekman
6-2, 6-0, 6-0

F. S. Mansfield ......
Mansfield
6-1, 6-0, 6-0

W. Lewis ....

M. Fielding ....
Fielding
6-2, 6-2, 6-3

S. H. Hooper ....

Mansfield
6-4, 6-1, 6-3

Beekman
6-4, 3-6, 6-0, 6-3

C. A. Chase ....
Chase
6-0, 6-3, 6-0

A. L. Rives ....

Robbins ....
Robbins
Default

d'Invilliers ....

Chase
6-5, 6-3, 6-2

M. Post ....
Post
Default

M. S. Paton ....

F. Warren ....
Warren
7-9, 2-6, 6-3, 6-0, 6-4

F. W. Taylor ....

Post
6-2, 6-4, 3-6, 2-6, 6-2

Chase
6-0, 6-2, 6-4

Beeckman, 6-4, 6-0, 6-2

R. L. Beeckman, 2-6, 6-3, 6-4, 6-2

Richard D. Sears, Holder

R. L. Beeckman, Challenger

Challenge Round

Sears, 4-6, 6-1, 6-3, 6-14

SEVENTH USLTA MEN'S SINGLES CHAMPIONSHIPS
The Casino, Newport, R.I., 1887

Preliminary Round	First Round	Second Round	Semi-Finals	Final Round	Winner

F. S. Mansfield ....
Mansfield
6-2, 8-6, 6-1

H. C. Bowers ....
W. R. Weeden ....
Bowers
Default

J. S. Clark ....
Clark
8-6, 6-3, 8-6

Q. A. Shaw, Jr. ....
A. E. Wright ....
Shaw, Jr.
Default

Clark
3-6, 6-2, 6-8, 6-1, 6-4

G. R. Fearing, Jr. ....
W. Lewis ....
Fearing, Jr.
6-4, 6-4, 6-0

C. E. Garrett ....
P. Manchester ....
Garrett
6-0, 6-2, 6-0

Fearing
8-6, 3-6, 6-4, 6-1

H. W. Slocum, Jr. ....
Slocum, Jr.
6-2, 4-6, 8-7, 6-3

Slocum, Jr.
6-1, 7-5, 6-2

R. L. Beeckman ....
M. Fielding ....
Beeckman
6-4, 6-4, 6-0

H. A. Taylor ....
O. S. Campbell ....
Taylor
6-3, 6-2, 7-5

Garrison Depew ....
Taylor
6-1, 6-4, 6-3

P. S. Sears ....
Sears
6-3, 6-2, 6-0

F. Warren ....

Taylor
6-1, 1-6, 6-3, 6-1

G. M. Brinley ....
Brinley
6-4, 6-1, 6-2

H. Emmons ....
W. H. Barnes ....
Emmons
6-1, 6-4, 6-1

W. L. Thacher ....
W. Cushman ....
Thacher
12-10, 5-7, 6-1, 6-3

F. W. Taylor ....
Thacher
6-3, 9-7, 6-3

Thacher
6-4, 8-6, 3-6, 6-4

Slocum, Jr., 6-8, 6-4, 6-3, 6-3

Taylor, 6-3, 6-1, 6-1

H. W. Slocum, Jr., 12-10, 7-5, 6-4

Richard D. Sears, Holder

H. W. Slocum, Jr., Challenger

Challenge Round

Sears, 6-1, 6-3, 6-2

EIGHTH USLTA MEN'S SINGLES CHAMPIONSHIPS
The Casino, Newport, R.I., 1888

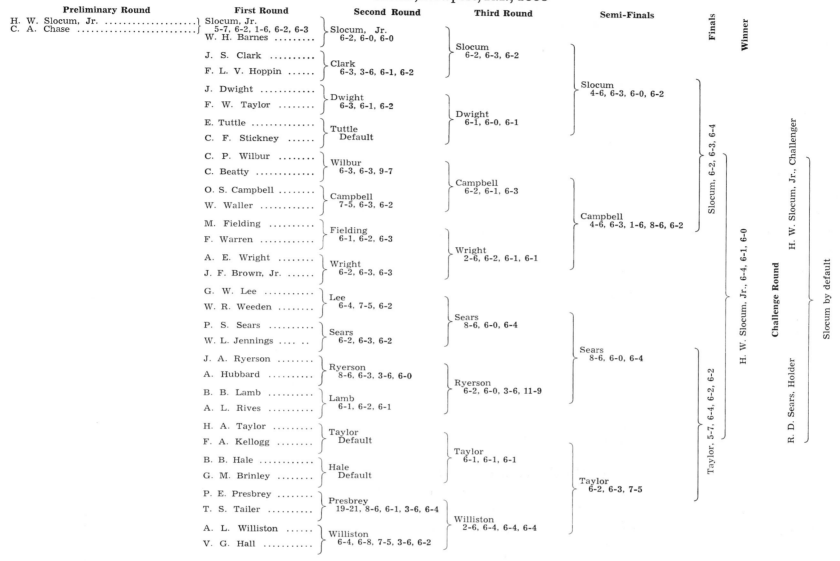

Preliminary Round	First Round	Second Round	Third Round	Semi-Finals	Finals	Winner

H. W. Slocum, Jr. .... Slocum, Jr.
C. A. Chase 5-7, 6-2, 1-6, 6-2, 6-3
Slocum, Jr. 6-2, 6-0, 6-0
W. H. Barnes ....
Slocum 6-2, 6-3, 6-2
J. S. Clark .... Clark 6-3, 3-6, 6-1, 6-2
F. L. V. Hoppin ......
Slocum 4-6, 6-3, 6-0, 6-2
J. Dwight .... Dwight 6-3, 6-1, 6-2
F. W. Taylor ....
Dwight 6-1, 6-0, 6-1
E. Tuttle .... Tuttle Default
C. F. Stickney ......
Slocum, 6-2, 6-3, 6-4
C. P. Wilbur .... Wilbur 6-3, 6-3, 9-7
C. Beatty ....
Campbell 6-2, 6-1, 6-3
O. S. Campbell .... Campbell 7-5, 6-3, 6-2
W. Waller ....
Campbell 4-6, 6-3, 1-6, 8-6, 6-2
M. Fielding .... Fielding 6-1, 6-2, 6-3
F. Warren ....
Wright 2-6, 6-2, 6-1, 6-1
A. E. Wright .... Wright 6-2, 6-3, 6-3
J. F. Brown, Jr. ......
H. W. Slocum, Jr., 6-4, 6-1, 6-0
G. W. Lee .... Lee 6-4, 7-5, 6-2
W. R. Weeden ....
Sears 8-6, 6-0, 6-4
P. S. Sears .... Sears 6-2, 6-3, 6-2
W. L. Jennings .... ..
Sears 8-6, 6-0, 6-4
J. A. Ryerson .... Ryerson 8-6, 6-3, 3-6, 6-0
A. Hubbard ....
Ryerson 6-2, 6-0, 3-6, 11-9
B. B. Lamb .... Lamb 6-1, 6-2, 6-1
A. L. Rives ....
Taylor, 5-7, 6-4, 6-2, 6-2
H. A. Taylor .... Taylor Default
F. A. Kellogg ....
Taylor 6-1, 6-1, 6-1
B. B. Hale .... Hale Default
G. M. Brinley ....
Taylor 6-2, 6-3, 7-5
P. E. Presbrey .... Presbrey 19-21, 8-6, 6-1, 3-6, 6-4
T. S. Tailer ....
Williston 2-6, 6-4, 6-4, 6-4
A. L. Williston ...... Williston 6-4, 6-8, 7-5, 3-6, 6-2
V. G. Hall ....

Challenge Round

H. W. Slocum, Jr., Challenger

R. D. Sears, Holder

Slocum by default

NINTH USLTA MEN'S SINGLES CHAMPIONSHIPS
The Casino, Newport, R.I., 1889

First Round	Second Round	Third Round	Semi-Finals	Finals	Challenge Round

C. A. Chase .... Chase 6-0, 6-3, 6-1
F. O. Reade ....
R. B. Hale .... Hale 6-2, 6-2, 6-1
A. L. Rives ....
Chase 6-4, 6-0, 6-3
R. V. Beach .... Beach 6-2, 6-2, 8-6
F. W. Taylor ....
Q. A. Shaw .... Shaw 7-9, 7-5, 6-3, 6-4
A. E. Wright ....
Shaw 7-9, 6-7, 6-0, 6-2
J. A. Ryerson .... Ryerson 6-0, 5-7, 6-0, 7-5
A. L. Williston ....
W. P. Knapp .... Knapp 6-2, 8-6, 4-6, 6-2
M. Fielding ....
Knapp 7-5, 8-6, 6-2
Deane Miller .... Miller 6-4, 8-6, 6-1
R. C. Sands ....
G. R. Fearing, Jr. .... Fearing, Jr. 6-3, 6-2, 6-4
W. W. Reece ....
Miller 6-2, 6-2, 6-3
F. L. V Hoppin .... Hoppin 6-3, 6-0, 6-1
S. C. Fox ....
F. S. Mansfield .... Mansfield 9-7, 6-0, 6-1
T. S. Tailer ....
Mansfield 7-5, 6-0, 6-1
M. R. Wright .... Wright 6-3, 6-0, 6-2
E. W. Gould, Jr. ....
E. G. Meers .... Meers 6-4, 6-3, 6-4
C E. Sands ....
Meers 7-5, 6-3, 6-4
S. T. Chase .... Chase 8-6, 6-4, 2-6, 6-4
G. A. Hurd ....
J. S. Clark .... Clark 6-3, 7-5, 6-4
W. R. Weeden ....
Clark 2-6, 6-1, 0-6, 6-4, 7-5
H. A. Taylor .... Taylor 6-3, 6-3, 6-0
R. P. Huntington, Jr. ....
O. S. Campbell .... Campbell 6-4, 6-1, 6-2
E. A. Thompson ....
Campbell 6-4, 6-2, 7-5

Shaw 6-4, 6-4, 4-6, 6-3

Knapp 6-4, 6-3, 6-2

Meers 6-1, 6-2, 6-2

Campbell 10-12, 7-5, 6-3, 6-3

Shaw, 4-6, 6-1, 6-4, 6-4

Campbell 5-7, 6-1, 5-7, 6-4, 6-2

Q. A. Shaw, Jr., 1-6, 6-4, 6-3, 6-4

H. W. Slocum, Jr., Holder

Q. A. Shaw Challenger

Slocum. Jr., 6-3, 6-1, 4-6, 6-2

TENTH USLTA MEN'S SINGLES CHAMPIONSHIPS
The Casino, Newport, R.I., 1890

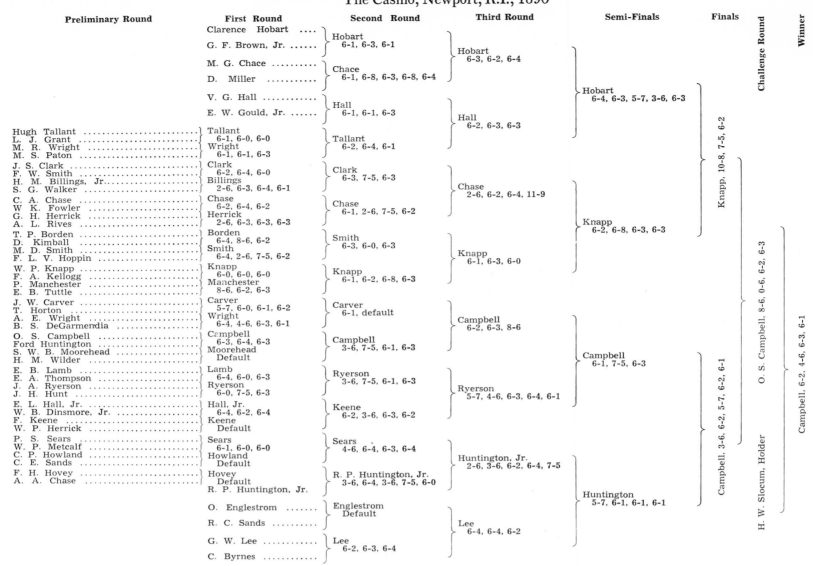

Preliminary Round	First Round	Second Round	Third Round	Semi-Finals	Finals	Challenge Round	Winner

Clarence Hobart ....
G. F. Brown, Jr. ......
— Hobart 6-1, 6-3, 6-1

M. G. Chace ....
D. Miller ....
— Chace 6-1, 6-8, 6-3, 6-8, 6-4

Hobart 6-3, 6-2, 6-4

V. G. Hall ....
E. W. Gould, Jr. ......
— Hall 6-1, 6-1, 6-3

Hall 6-2, 6-3, 6-3

Hobart 6-4, 6-3, 5-7, 3-6, 6-3

Hugh Tallant .... Tallant 6-1, 6-0, 6-0
L. J. Grant .... Wright 6-1, 6-1, 6-3
M. R. Wright ....
M. S. Paton ....
— Tallant 6-2, 6-4, 6-1

J. S. Clark .... Clark 6-2, 6-4, 6-0
F. W. Smith .... Billings 2-6, 6-3, 6-4, 6-1
H. M. Billings, Jr. ....
S. G. Walker ....
— Clark 6-3, 7-5, 6-3

C. A. Chase .... Chase 6-2, 6-4, 6-2
W. K. Fowler .... Herrick 2-6, 6-3, 6-3, 6-3
G. H. Herrick ....
A. L. Rives ....
— Chase 6-1, 2-6, 7-5, 6-2

Chase 2-6, 6-2, 6-4, 11-9

T. P. Borden .... Borden 6-4, 8-6, 6-2
D. Kimball .... Smith 6-4, 2-6, 7-5, 6-2
M. D. Smith ....
F. L. V. Hoppin ....
— Smith 6-3, 6-0, 6-3

W. P. Knapp .... Knapp 6-0, 6-0, 6-0
F. A. Kellogg .... Manchester 8-6, 6-2, 6-3
P. Manchester ....
E. B. Tuttle ....
— Knapp 6-1, 6-2, 6-8, 6-3

Knapp 6-1, 6-3, 6-0

Knapp 6-2, 6-8, 6-3, 6-3

Hobart, Knapp, 10-8, 7-5, 6-2

J. W. Carver .... Carver 5-7, 6-0, 6-1, 6-2
T. Horton .... Wright 6-4, 4-6, 6-3, 6-1
A. E. Wright ....
B. S. DeGarmendia ....
— Carver 6-1, default

O. S. Campbell .... Campbell 6-3, 6-4, 6-3
Ford Huntington .... Moorehead Default
S. W. B. Moorehead ....
H. M. Wilder ....
— Campbell 3-6, 7-5, 6-1, 6-3

Campbell 6-2, 6-3, 8-6

E. B. Lamb .... Lamb 6-4, 6-0, 6-3
E. A. Thompson .... Ryerson 6-0, 7-5, 6-3
J. A. Ryerson ....
J. H. Hunt ....
— Ryerson 3-6, 7-5, 6-1, 6-3

E. L. Hall, Jr. .... Hall, Jr. 6-4, 6-2, 6-4
W. B. Dinsmore, Jr. .... Keene Default
F. Keene ....
W. P. Herrick ....
— Keene 6-2, 3-6, 6-3, 6-2

Ryerson 5-7, 4-6, 6-3, 6-4, 6-1

Campbell 6-1, 7-5, 6-3

Campbell, 3-6, 6-2, 5-7, 6-2, 6-1

P. S. Sears .... Sears 6-1, 6-0, 6-0
W. P. Metcalf .... Howland Default
C. P. Howland ....
C. E. Sands ....
— Sears 4-6, 6-4, 6-3, 6-4

F. H. Hovey .... Hovey Default
A. A. Chase .... R. P. Huntington, Jr. 3-6, 6-4, 3-6, 7-5, 6-0
R. P. Huntington, Jr.
— R. P. Huntington, Jr. 2-6, 3-6, 6-2, 6-4, 7-5

O. Englestrom .... Englestrom Default
R. C. Sands ....
— Lee 6-4, 6-4, 6-2

Huntington 5-7, 6-1, 6-1, 6-1

G. W. Lee .... Lee 6-2, 6-3, 6-4
C. Byrnes ....

O. S. Campbell, 8-6, 0-6, 6-2, 6-3

H. W. Slocum, Holder

Campbell, 6-2, 4-6, 6-3, 6-1

ELEVENTH USLTA MEN'S SINGLES CHAMPIONSHIPS
The Casino, Newport, R.I., 1891

First Round	Second Round	Third Round	Fourth Round	Fifth Round	Finals	Challenge Round	Winner

H. A. Colby .... Colby 6-1, 4-6, 6-1, 6-1
E. K. Rowland ....
F. L. V. Hoppin .... Hoppin Default
F. J. Bentley ....
— Colby 1-6, 11-9, 6-4, 3-6, 6-3

E. L. Hall .... Hall 6-2, 6-3, 2-6, 6-4
M. Fielding ....
S. McCormick .... McCormick 5-7, 7-5, 6-1, 6-2
W. Hoopes ....
— Hall 5-7, 7-5, 6-1, 6-2

Hall 6-0, 3-6, 6-0, 6-4

W. V. Johnson .... Johnson 6-2, 6-2, 6-2
S. Woodward ....
C. Hobart .... Hobart 8-6, 6-3, 6-3
T. P. Borden ....
— Hobart 6-1, 6-4, 6-3

C. M. Bunting .... Bunting 6-4, 6-8, 4-6, 7-5, 6-4
J. A. Hovey ....
J. A. Ryerson .... Ryerson 6-2, 6-3, 6-3
M. L. Pratt ....
— Ryerson 6-1, 6-2, 6-4

Hobart Default

Hobart 3-6, 6-4, 11-9, 6-4

C. T. Lee .... Lee 6-0, 6-1, 6-1
H. Satterlee ....
W. P. Jenks .... Jenks 6-0, 6-0, 9-7
J. F. Turrill ....
— Lee 6-1, 6-1, 6-2

E. Colby .... Colby 11-9, 4-6, 6-3, 7-5
B. J. Carroll ....
W. A. Larned .... Larned 8-6, 6-4, 8-6
H. F. McCormick ....
— Larned 6-1, 6-1, 6-1

Lee 6-2, 6-2, 6-4

V. G. Hall .... Hall 6-1, 6-1, 6-1
F. M. Pile ....
Richard Stevens .... Stevens 2-6, 6-3, 4-6, 6-2, 6-1
B. B. Lamb ....
— V. G. Hall 2-6, 6-2, 6-4, 6-1

S. T. Chase .... Chase 6-2, 6-2, 6-1
G. P. Herrick ....
R. P. Huntington, Jr. .... Huntington, Jr. Default
R. Johnson ....
— Chase 3-6, 6-4, 6-3, 6-3

Hall 6-4, 2-6, 6-2, 6-3

Hall 6-4, 6-4, 0-6, 6-0

Hobart, 6-2, 6-4, 6-2

F. H. Hovey .... Hovey 6-1, 6-3, 6-1
L. R. Parker ....
H. G. Bixby .... Bixby 6-4, 6-4, 6-1
J. W. Nichols, Jr. ....
— Hovey 6-3, 6-4, 2-6, 6-4

P. S. Sears .... Sears 5-7, 6-3, 6-2, 10-8
Deane Miller ....
W. D. Orcutt .... Orcutt 6-3, 10-8, 6-1
E. W. Gould, Jr. ....
— Sears 6-4, 6-3, 2-6, 7-5

Hovey 5-7, 3-6, 6-2, 13-11, 6-2

H. I. Wilcox .... Wilcox 6-4, 2-6, 6-3, 6-4
W. K. Fowler ....
C. R. Budlong .... Budlong 3-6, 6-4, 6-3, 6-2
E. S. Rushmore ....
— Wilcox 6-4, 6-2, 6-2

A. W. Post .... Post 6-3, 6-3, 6-2
G. I. Scott ....
G. R. Fearing, Jr. .... Fearing, Jr. 6-0, 6-1, 6-1
C. A. Brown ....
— Post 6-3, 6-3, 4-6, 6-4

Post 0-6, 6-2, 6-3, 6-1

Hovey 4-6, 6-4, 6-3, 6-0, 2-6

Hovey, 6-4, 6-2, 3-6, 1-6, 6-4

M. D. Smith .... Smith 7-5, 6-2, 6-1
D. W. Candler ....
G. F. Brown, Jr. .... Brown, Jr. 6-1, 6-0, 8-6
B. S. DeGarmendia ....
— Smith 6-0, 6-4, 6-2

Burdette O'Connor .... O'Connor 6-0, 7-5, 8-6
G. N. Norton ....
P. S. Oscanyan .... Oscanyan 6-2, 4-6, 6-4, 6-3
E. Stille ....
— O'Connor 6-3, 6-2, 6-1

Smith 6-2, 6-2, 6-3

T. Horton .... Horton 6-2, 6-2, 6-2
E. A. Thompson ....
J. S. Clark .... Clark 6-1, 4-6, 6-1, 6-3
E. I. White ....
— Clark 6-0, 6-1, 6-3

J. H. Hunt .... Hunt 6-3, 6-4, 6-1
W. S. Post ....
A. E. Wright .... Wright Default
W. H. Trotter, Sr. ....
— Hunt Default

Clark 6-4, 6-2, 6-4

Smith 6-1, 6-0, 6-4

C. Hobart, 6-4, 3-6, 6-4, 6-8, 6-0

O. S. Campbell, Champion

Campbell, 2-6, 7-5, 7-9, 6-1, 6-2

TWELFTH USLTA MEN'S SINGLES CHAMPIONSHIPS
The Casino, Newport, R.I., 1892

Preliminary Round	First Round	Second Round	Third Round	Fourth Round	Semi-Finals	Finals	Challenge Round	Winner

A. E. Wright ....
R. D. Wrenn ....
Wrenn
6-1, 10-8, 6-1

M. G. Chace ....
W. P. Knapp ....
Knapp
6-4, 4-6, 6-1, 2-6, 6-4

Wrenn
12-14, 6-2, 4-6, 9-7, 6-1

C. R. Budlong ....
J. S. Clark ....
Budlong
3-6, 6-2, 2-6, 8-6, 6-3

H. D. Betts ....
G. H. Pratt ....
Betts
6-4, 6-2, 6-3

Budlong
6-1, 6-4, 6-2

Wrenn
8-6, 6-4, 6-1

R. M. Thomas ....
G. S. Scott ....
R. M. Thomas
6-4, 6-2, 5-7, 6-4

M. Fielding ....
E. D. Hewins ....
Fielding
6-0, 6-1, 6-1

Fielding
Default

N. H. Emmons ....
C. R. Wyckoff ....
N. H. Emmons
4-6, 7-5, 7-5, 2-6, 6-4

W. V. Johnson ....
G. P. Herrick ....
Herrick
Default

Herrick
7-5, 6-3, 6-1

Fielding
2-6, 3-6, 6-2, 7-5, 6-2

Wrenn
6-1, 4-6, 9-7, 6-0

T. P. Borden ....
R. Stevens ....
Stevens
6-2, 6-4, 6-0

E. K. Rowland ....
H. F. McCormick ....
McCormick
6-2, 6-1, 6-3

Stevens
6-0, 4-6, 7-5, 6-1

Wm. Ames, Jr. ....
A. N. Winslow ....
Ames
7-5, 8-6, 6-4

B. S. de Garmendia ..
J. W. Nichols, Jr. .....
Nichols
Default

Ames
4-6, 8-6, 6-4, 6-1

Stevens
6-1, 6-1, 6-2

R. S. Howland ....
A. Codman ....
Codman
4-6, 2-6, 6-1, 8-6, 6-4

G. S. Bryan ....
F. H. Hovey ....
Hovey
6-1, 6-1, 6-2

Hovey
6-3, 6-1, 6-3

H. M. Billings ....
Billings
6-3, 6-2, 6-8, 6-4

Hovey
6-2, 6-4, 5-7, 6-0

Hovey
6-1, 6-4, 6-0

Hovey, 6-4, 7-5, 6-3

W. McKittrick ....
F. B. Stevens ....
McKittrick
7-5, 6-1, 6-0

H. W. Cozzens, Jr. ....
K. S. Green ....
Green
9-7, 6-4, 6-1

A. W. Post ....
H. G. Bixby ....
Post
6-4, 6-8, 8-6, 3-6, 6-2

Post
6-1, 6-0, 6-1

Post
6-0, 6-4, 7-5

H. H. Pigott ....
B. B. Manchester ....
Manchester
6-4, 6-4, 6-3

E. Stelle ....
T. Horton ....
Horton
6-4, 6-1, 6-1

Horton
7-5, 6-3, 6-1

C. E. Lord ....
E. L. Hall ....
E. L. Hall
By default

J. C. Davidson ....
E. L. Hall
6-2, 6-4, 6-4

E. L. Hall
6-4, 6-2, 6-2

E. L. Hall
8-6, 4-6, 4-6, 6-2, 6-3

C. Hobart ....
G. C. Thomas ....
Hobart
6-1, 6-1, 6-3

M. Bruce ....
C. P. Hubbard ....
Hubbard
6-2, 6-3, 6-4

Hobart
6-1, 6-1, 6-2

Q. A. Shaw ....
G. T. Rice ....
Shaw
6-0, 6-4, 6-4

S. T. Chase ....
D. W. Candler ....
Chase
7-5, 11-13, 4-6, 6-2, 6-2

Chase
6-4, 6-0, 6-3

Chase
7-5, 5-7, 6-3, 2-6, 6-1

E. L. Hall
1-6, 6-3, 4-6, 6-2, 6-3

M. D. Smith ....
R. P. Huntington, Jr.
Smith
7-5, 6-3, 6-1

W. Floyd ....
E. A. Thomson ....
Floyd
Default

Smith
6-2, 6-1, 7-5

H. W. Slocum, Jr. ....
W. N. Ryerson ....
Slocum
6-0, 6-0, 6-0

W A. Larned ....
G. R. Fearing, Jr. .....
Larned
7-5, 6-3, 6-1

Larned
6-1, 6-3, 3-6, 6-4

Larned
6-0, 6-3, 6-3

Larned, 2-6, 6-0, 6-4, 1-6, 8-6

W. H. Barnes ....
J. Geer ....
Barnes
Default

W. R. Roberts ....
W. D. Goforth ......
Goforth
6-4, 6-2, 6-4

Goforth
6-3, 6-4, 6-1

V. G. Hall ....
P. S. Sears ....
V. G. Hall
6-3, 3-6, 8-6, 6-4

C. Tete, Jr. ....
R. N. Dana ....
Dana
6-4, 6-4, 6-1

V. G. Hall
6-3, 6-2, 6-2

Larned
6-4, 6-3, 7-5

H. E. Woodworth .....
A. B. Emmons ....
Emmons
6-4, 7-5, 10-8

W. P. Metcalf ....
F. B. Winslow ....
Winslow
5-7, 6-1, 8-6, 6-0

Winslow
6-1, 6-3, 6-2

V. G. Hall
6-4, 6-4, 6-3

Hovey, 6-0, 6-2, 7-5

Campbell, 7-5, 3-6, 6-3, 7-5

O. S. Campbell, Champion

THIRTEENTH USLTA MEN'S SINGLES CHAMPIONSHIPS
The Casino, Newport, R.I., 1893

Preliminary Round	First Round	Second Round	Third Round	Fourth Round	Semi-Finals	Finals	Challenge Round	Winner

S. R. McCormick .....
Gordon I. Willis ......
  Willis — By default

F. M. Pile ....
M. R. Wright ....
  Wright — 6-0, 6-0, 6-0

    Wright — 4-6, 6-4, 6-3, 6-1

R. D. Wrenn ....
H. H. Dickey ....
  Wrenn — 6-1, 6-0, 6-0

G. T. Warren ....
S. D. Reed ....
  S. D. Reed — By default

    Wrenn — 6-1, 6-0, 6-1

      Wrenn — 6-2, 11-9, 4-6, 3-6, 6-4

S. V. R. Thayer ......
R. C. Thomas ....
  Thomas — 6-2, 6-3, 6-4

Charles Tete, Jr .....
H. Clews, Jr. ....
  Tete, Jr. — 6-3, 6-4, 6-2

    Tete, Jr. — 0-6, 6-4, 6-4, 6-3

Richard Stevens ......
H. F. McCormick ....
  Stevens — 6-1, 3-6, 6-4, 7-5

H. M. Billings ......
J. S. Morris ....
  Morris — By default

    Seevens — 6-1, 6-3, 6-0

      Stevens — 6-2, 6-0, 6-1

        Wrenn — 6-1, 6-2, 2-6, 6-2

S. T. Chase ....
Geo. C. Hinckley ....
  S. T. Chase — By default

M. A. Agelasto ......
H. D. Cleveland ......
  Cleveland — By default

    S. T. Chase — 6-2, 6-0, 6-2

Deane Miller ....
S. G. Thompson ......
  Miller — 6-0, 6-4, 6-2

J. Bertram ....
H. H. Pigott ....
  Pigott — By default

    Miller — 6-1, 6-2, 7-5

      S. T. Chase — 6-3, 6-4, 6-3

        S. T. Chase — 6-3, 6-4, 6-2

W. H. A. Willing ....
Roberston Honey ....
A. W. Cobb ....
E. Colby ....
  Willing — By default
  E. Colby — 6-1, 6-4, 6-1

O. M. Bostwick ....
E. A. Wilkie ....
J. B. Read ....
P. Frazer, Jr. ....
  Bostwick — 6-1, 6-0, 6-0
  J. B. Read — 6-1, 6-4, 6-3

    E. Colby — 6-2, 6-2, 7-5

C. H. Farnam, Jr. ....
H. A. Colby ....
A. W. Post ....
P T. Wright ....
  H. A. Colby — By default
  Post — 6-3, 6-3, 12-10

H. Bruen ....
J. F. Talmadge, Jr. ....
E. C. Rushmore ....
Duncan W. Candler ....
  Talmadge — 6-2, 6-1, 6-0
  Candler — 6-3, 3-6, 6-2, 6-1

    J. B. Read — 7-5, 6-1, 6-2

    H. A. Colby — 6-4, 6-8, 8-6 (d.)

    Candler — 4-6, 6-4, 6-0, 6-3

      E. Colby — 12-10, 6-2, 4-6, 7-5

      Candler — 4-6, 6-4, 6-2, 2-6, 6-4

F. K. Ward ....
Alfred Codman ....
G. L. Herrick ....
A. B. Emmons, 2d ....
  Ward — 6-0, 6-1, 6-0
  Herrick — 6-2, 4-6, 7-5, 6-4

G. C. Hetz ....
M. Bruce ....
E. A. Thompson ....
F. E. Donohue ....
  Bruce — 1-6, 4-6, 6-3, 6-4, 6-3
  Donohue — By default

    Ward — 2-6, 6-1, 6-3, 6-3

G. P. Dodge ....
Wm. Ames, Jr. ....
K. S. Greene ....
C. M. Bunting ....
  Ames, Jr. — By default
  Bunting — 4-6, 5-7, 6-1, 6-1, 6-3

W. A. Larned ....
J. C. Davidson ....
  Larned — 6-3, 6-4, 6-4
  Malcolm G. Chace ....

    Bruce — By default

    Ames, Jr. — 6-3, 6-4, 6-1

    Larned — 2-6, 6-2, 6-3, 6-4

      Ward — 6-0, 6-4, 7-5

      Larned — 12-10, 6-1, 6-4

        Candler — 6-1, 6-4, 6-4

        Larned — 6-2, 6-3, 6-3

N. H. Lord ....
Clarence Hobart ......
  Hobart — 6-0, 6-0, 6-2

W. G. Parker ....
J. A. Fowler ....
  Parker — 6-1, 6-2, 6-4

    Hobart — 6-4, 8-6, 6-1

G. S. Bryan ....
C. R. Budlong ....
  Budlong — 7-5, 6-2, 6-0

A. P. Simmonds ....
S. L. Smith ....
  Simmonds — 11-9, 7-5, 6-4

    Budlong — 6-2, 6-0, 6-2

      Hobart — 6-3, 6-1, 6-2

        Hobart — 6-3, 6-4, 3-6, 5-7, 6-2

O. A. Shaw, Jr. ......
F. H. Hovey ....
  Hovey — 6-0, 7-5, 7-5

A E. Foote ....
H. S. Russell ....
  Foote — 6-0, 6-1, 6-1

    Hovey — 4-6, 6-3, 6-2, 6-2

C. E. Sands ....
J. S. Clark ....
  Sands — 6-4, 6-2, 4-6, 6-3

John Howland ....
E. L. Hall ....
  E. L. Hall — 6-4, 6-1, 6-4

    E. L. Hall — 10-8, 3-6, 6-0, 4-6, 6-3

      Hovey — 6-3, 6-2, 6-1

V. G. Hall ....
H. B. Bartow ....
  V. G. Hall — 6-0, 6-2, 6-2

W. P. Knapp ....
E. Hewitt ....
  Hewitt — By default

    V. G. Hall — 6-2, 7-5, 6-2

F. Whitall ....
G. T. Rice ....
  Whitall — 6-4, 7-5, 6-2

E. D. Hewins.........
W. W. Reese ....
  Reese — 6-3, 6-2, 6-1

    Whitall — 5-7, 5-7, 6-4, 6-0, 6-4

      V. G. Hall — 6-2, 6-3, 6-2

        Hovey — 6-2, 5-7, 8-6, 6-2

Semi-Finals:
Wrenn — 8-6, 6-1, 6-2
Hovey — 7-5, 6-0, 6-3

Finals:
Wrenn — 6-4, 3-6, 6-4, 6-4

Challenge Round:
Wrenn, by default

Winner:
O. S. Campbell, Champion 1890, 91, 92

FOURTEENTH USLTA MEN'S SINGLES CHAMPIONSHIPS
The Casino, Newport, R.I., 1894

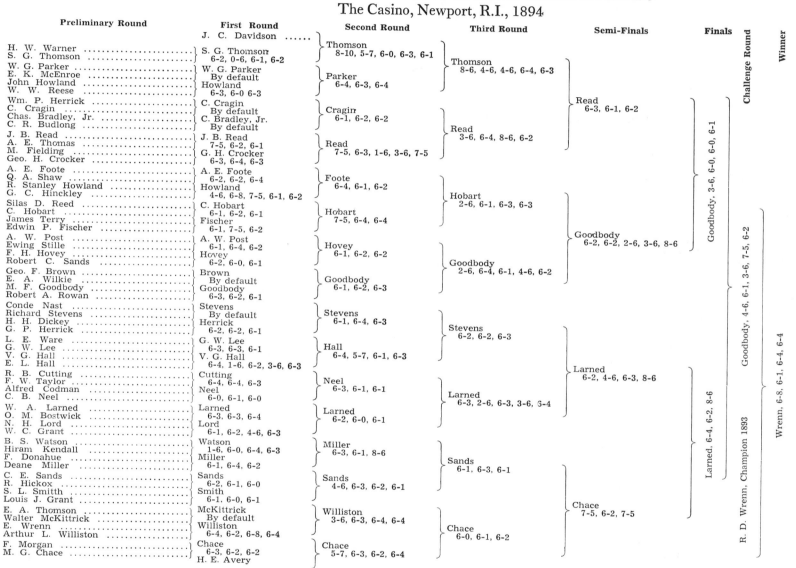

Preliminary Round	First Round	Second Round	Third Round	Semi-Finals	Finals	Challenge Round	Winner

Preliminary Round

H. W. Warner
S. G. Thomson
W. G. Parker
E. K. McEnroe
John Howland
W. W. Reese
Wm. P. Herrick
C. Cragin
Chas. Bradley, Jr.
C. R. Budlong
J. B. Read
A. E. Thomas
M. Fielding
Geo. H. Crocker
A. E. Foote
Q. A. Shaw
R. Stanley Howland
G. C. Hinckley
Silas D. Reed
C. Hobart
James Terry
Edwin P. Fischer
A. W. Post
Ewing Stille
F. H. Hovey
Robert C. Sands
Geo. F. Brown
E. A. Wilkie
M. F. Goodbody
Robert A. Rowan
Conde Nast
Richard Stevens
H. H. Dickey
G. P. Herrick
L. E. Ware
G. W. Lee
V. G. Hall
E. L. Hall
R. B. Cutting
F. W. Taylor
Alfred Codman
C. B. Neel
W. A. Larned
O. M. Bostwick
N. H. Lord
W. C. Grant
B. S. Watson
Hiram Kendall
F. Donahue
Deane Miller
C. E. Sands
R. Hickox
S. L. Smith
Louis J. Grant
E. A. Thomson
Walter McKittrick
E. Wrenn
Arthur L. Williston
F. Morgan
M. G. Chace

First Round

J. C. Davidson ......
S. G. Thomson
6-2, 0-6, 6-1, 6-2
W. G. Parker
By default
Howland
6-3, 6-0 6-3
C. Cragin
By default
C. Bradley, Jr.
By default
J. B. Read
7-5, 6-2, 6-1
G. H. Crocker
6-3, 6-4, 6-3
A. E. Foote
6-2, 6-2, 6-4
Howland
4-6, 6-8, 7-5, 6-1, 6-2
C. Hobart
6-1, 6-2, 6-1
Fischer
6-1, 7-5, 6-2
A. W. Post
6-1, 6-4, 6-2
Hovey
6-2, 6-0, 6-1
Brown
By default
Goodbody
6-3, 6-2, 6-1
Stevens
By default
Herrick
6-2, 6-2, 6-1
G. W. Lee
6-3, 6-3, 6-1
V. G. Hall
6-4, 1-6, 6-2, 3-6, 6-3
Cutting
6-4, 6-4, 6-3
Neel
6-0, 6-1, 6-0
Larned
6-3, 6-3, 6-4
Lord
6-1, 6-2, 4-6, 6-3
Watson
1-6, 6-0, 6-4, 6-3
Miller
6-1, 6-4, 6-2
Sands
6-2, 6-1, 6-0
Smith
6-1, 6-0, 6-1
McKittrick
By default
Williston
6-4, 6-2, 6-8, 6-4
Chace
6-3, 6-2, 6-2
H. E. Avery

Second Round

Thomson
8-10, 5-7, 6-0, 6-3, 6-1
Parker
6-4, 6-3, 6-4
Cragin
6-1, 6-2, 6-2
Read
7-5, 6-3, 1-6, 3-6, 7-5
Foote
6-4, 6-1, 6-2
Hobart
7-5, 6-4, 6-4
Hovey
6-1, 6-2, 6-2
Goodbody
6-1, 6-2, 6-3
Stevens
6-1, 6-4, 6-3
Hall
6-4, 5-7, 6-1, 6-3
Neel
6-3, 6-1, 6-1
Larned
6-2, 6-0, 6-1
Miller
6-3, 6-1, 8-6
Sands
4-6, 6-3, 6-2, 6-1
Williston
3-6, 6-3, 6-4, 6-4
Chace
5-7, 6-3, 6-2, 6-4

Third Round

Thomson
8-6, 4-6, 4-6, 6-4, 6-3
Read
3-6, 6-4, 8-6, 6-2
Hobart
2-6, 6-1, 6-3, 6-3
Goodbody
2-6, 6-4, 6-1, 4-6, 6-2
Stevens
6-2, 6-2, 6-3
Larned
6-3, 2-6, 6-3, 3-6, 6-4
Sands
6-1, 6-3, 6-1
Chace
6-0, 6-1, 6-2

Semi-Finals

Read
6-3, 6-1, 6-2
Goodbody
6-2, 6-2, 2-6, 3-6, 8-6
Larned
6-2, 4-6, 6-3, 8-6
Chace
7-5, 6-2, 7-5

Finals

Goodbody, 3-6, 6-0, 6-0, 6-1

Larned, 6-4, 6-2, 8-6

Challenge Round

Goodbody, 4-6, 6-1, 3-6, 7-5, 6-2

Winner

Wrenn, 6-8, 6-1, 6-4, 6-4

R. D. Wrenn, Champion 1893

69

FIFTEENTH USLTA MEN'S SINGLES CHAMPIONSHIPS
The Casino, Newport, R.I., 1895

Column headings: Preliminary Round — First Round — Second Round — Third Round — Fourth Round — Semi-Finals — Finals — Challenge Round — Winner

---

First Round

Chas. Bradley, Jr. / G. C. Hinckley — Hinckley 6-2, 6-3, 6-0

J. W. Wear / C. H. Hatch — Wear 8-6, 6-3, 6-4

R. Stevens / S. L. Smith — Smith By default

Arthur Taylor / M. Baker — Baker 2-6, 6-4, 6-2, 3-6, 6-3

Scott Griffin / B. S. de Garmendia — Griffin 6-3, 4-6, 6-2, 7-5

F. H. Hovey / W. L. Jennings — Hovey 6-2, 6-2, 3-6, 6-4

H. B. Bartow / R. C. Sands — Bartow 9-7, 6-4, 7-5

E. A. Crowninshield / J. F. Hobart — Crowninshield 6-2, 5-7, 6-2, 7-5

C. F. Walz / Ewing Stille — Walz 6-3, 6-3, 3-6, 6-0

C. Tete, Jr. / J. D. E. Jones — Jones 6-2, 6-2, 6-0

C. B. Neel / H. E. Avery — Neel 3-6, 7-5, 6-1, 6-1

H. Clews, Jr. — Clews 2-6, 6-3, 6-3, 6-1

Preliminary Round / First Round (lower half)

B. Needham / Deane Miller — Needham By default

F. M. Scudder / J. F. Talmadge, Jr. — Talmage 6-3, 6-3, 4-6, 6-4

E. P. Fischer / K. Brice — Fischer By default

J. C. Davidson / F. Davis — Davidson 9-7, 4-6, 6-3, 6-1

P. Herrick / F. Wise — Wise 7-5, 6-4, 7-5

A. S. Lewis / G. W. Lee — Lee 6-2, 6-3, 6-2

Fred S. Taylor / J. A. Hovey — Hovey 4-6, 6-4, 2-6, 6-4, 7-5

C. E. Sands / M. G. Chace — Chace 6-2, 6-3, 6-4

V. P. Matthews / A. Jones — Matthews 6-3, 6-4, 7-5

Alfred Codman / Hale — Codman 6-2, 6-1, 6-3

P. Hawes / M. Pile — Hawes 2-6, 7-5, 6-3, 7-9, 6-2

H. Barnes / S. Ward — Ward 6-2, 6-2, 6-3

K. Willing / James Terry — Terry 4-6, 7-5, 4-6, 6-4, 6-3

Evarts Wrenn / H. Lord — Wrenn 6-2, 6-3, 6-0

C. Millett / R. P. Davis — Millett 6-3, 5-7, 6-2, 7-5

J. P. Paret / G. Beaman — Paret 6-1, 6-4, 7-5

C. W. Brooks / R. Stanley Howland — Howland 6-3, 6-1, 6-2

R. H. Palmer / W. Herrick — Palmer 6-4, 6-3, 3-6, 1-6, 6-3

First Round (continued, lower section)

F. S. Butler — Palmer By default

J. S. Cushman / J. A. Ryerson — Ryerson 6-0, 6-3, 6-3

C. C. Stillman / S. D. Reed — Reed 7-5, 6-2, 6-2

C. R. Budlong / J. C. Neely — Budlong By default

H. F. Robinson / E. A. Thomson — Thomson By default

A. W. Post / W. A. Larned — Larned 6-3, 4-6, 2-6, 6-1, 6-3

S. Henshaw / H. D. Cleveland — Henshaw 4-6, 6-2, 2-6, 6-2, 6-3

W. H. Brown / E. K. McEnroe — Brown By default

W. P. Herrick / Leo E. Ware — Ware 6-2, 6-1, 6-2

Wm. Boag / A. L. Willston — Williston 6-3, 6-2, 6-4

A. F. Foote / G. L. Wrenn, Jr. — Foote 6-2, 6-8, 6-2, 6-0

C. A. Gould / J. H. Masson, Jr. — Gould 6-2, 6-3, 6-3

Second Round

- Hinckley 6-4, 6-1, 6-1
- Smith 6-3, 6-0, 4-6, 7-5
- Hovey 6-2, 6-0, 6-1
- Crowninshield 6-2, 7-5, 3-6, 6-4
- Jones 6-2, 7-5, 6-2
- Neel 6-1, 6-2, 6-2
- Fischer 6-4, 6-4, 6-4
- Davidson 6-4, 6-2, 3-6, 4-6, 6-2
- Lee 6-4, 6-1, 6-1
- Chace 6-0, 6-2, 6-1
- Codman 6-0, 6-3, 6-4
- Terry 6-2, 5-7, 7-5, 8-6
- Millett 7-5, 6-1, 6-3
- Howland 6-2, 6-4, 7-5
- Palmer By default
- Ryerson 6-0, 6-3, 6-3
- Reed 7-5, 6-2, 6-2
- Budlong By default
- Thomson By default
- Larned 6-2, 6-2, 6-3
- Henshaw 6-3, 6-0, 6-3
- Brown By default
- Ware 6-2, 6-2, 6-2
- Williston 6-3, 6-2, 6-4
- Foote 6-2, 6-1, 6-2

Third Round

- Hinckley 6-3, 5-7, 1-6, 6-2, 6-3
- Hovey 6-2, 6-0, 6-1
- Crowninshield 6-2, 7-5, 3-6, 6-4
- Neel 8-6, 8-6, 6-4
- Fischer 6-2, 6-0, 6-2
- Chace 6-3, 6-7, 6-4
- Terry 4-6, 5-7, 6-3, 6-4, 6-0
- Howland 9-7, 6-2, 6-3
- Ryerson 3-6, 6-2, 6-4, 6-3
- Budlong 4-6, 6-2, 6-2, 6-1
- Larned 6-2, 6-2, 6-3
- Larned 6-0, 6-0, 6-1
- Ware 6-2, 6-2, 6-2
- Foote 4-6, 6-4, 6-0, 8-10, 8-6

Fourth Round

- Hovey 6-1, 6-2, 7-5
- Hovey 2-1, by default
- Neel 6-4, 6-1, 6-4
- Chace 6-4, 7-5, 9-7
- Howland 6-3, 6-4, 1-6, 6-1
- Budlong 6-2, 6-2, 6-2
- Larned 6-3, 6-4, 3-6, 6-1
- Foote

Semi-Finals

- Hovey
- Neel
- Howland 6-3, 2-6, 6-4, 6-3
- Larned

Finals

- Hovey 6-4, 6-4, 6-4
- Larned 7-5, 8-6, 6-1
- Hovey 6-1, 9-7, 6-4

Challenge Round

- Hovey, 6-3, 6-2, 6-4
- R. D. Wrenn, Champion 1893 and 1894

Winner

Hovey, 6-3, 6-2, 6-4

SIXTEENTH USLTA MEN'S SINGLES CHAMPIONSHIPS
The Casino, Newport, R.I., 1896

Preliminary Round	First Round	Second Round	Third Round	Semi-Finals	Finals	Challenge Round	Winner

C. B. Neel ....
J. R. Carpenter ....

Neel
6-1, 6-2, 6-2

E. Lyman ....
C. Cragin ....

Cragin
3-6, 7-5, 6-3, 5-7, 6-3

Neel
6-4, 6-2, 6-4

F. B. Stevens, Jr. ....

Neel
6-4, 6-0, 7-9, 9-7

A. W. Post ....
C. R. Budlong .... Budlong
7-5, 6-4, 6-2

Budlong
6-2, 6-1, 6-1

W. C. Grant ....
R. Stevens .... Stevens
6-2, 6-3, 6-3

Stevens
6-4, 6-1, 6-4

Stevens
6-4, 0-6, 6-4, 6-4

R. H. Palmer ....
G. H. Miles .... Miles
8-6, 6-1, 6-1

C. M. Pope ....
H. D. Cleveland .... Pope
9-7, 7-5, 6-2

Pope

Paret
6-3, 6-2, 6-3

J. P. Paret ......
C. X. Cordier, Jr .... Paret
By default

G. L. Wrenn
6-1, 6-0, 6-3

A. Hawes ....
J. McL. Walton .... Hawes
6-1, 4-6, 6-3, 6-2

Wrenn
6-4, 7-9, 6-4, 6-1

L. H. Turner ....
G. L. Wrenn .... G. L. Wrenn
6-1, 6-1, 6-2

R. D. Wrenn
2-6, 9-7, 7-5, 9-7

C A. Gould ....
H. E. Avery .... Gould
2-6, 6-2, 7-5, 6-3

E. Wrenn
6-0, 6-1, 6-0

E. Wrenn ....
W. J. Clothier .... E. Wrenn
6-1, 6-2, 6-0

R. D. Wrenn
6-4, 6-4, 12-10

R. D. Wrenn ....
N. P. Hallowell .... R. Wrenn
7-9, 3-6, 6-1, 6-1, 6-3

R. D. Wrenn
6-1, 6-8, 9-7, 6-2

J. C. Davidson ......
D. Davis .... Davis
6-4, 6-3, 6-2

Wrenn, 2-6, 14-12, 4-6, 6-4, 6-1

S. Ward ....
E. Stille .... Stille
9-7, 6-2, 4-6, 6-2

Larned
6-3, 6-4, 6-0

W. A. Larned ....
Deane Miller .... Larned
6-4, 6-3, 6-3

Larned
6-4, 6-2, 6-4

G. W. Lee ....
W. A. Bethel .... Lee
3-6, 6-4, 6-4, 6-8, 6-3

Lee
6-3, 8-6, 6-2

J. K. Willing ....
E. A. Thomson .... Willing
By default

Larned
6-4, 6-1, 6-2

M. D. Whitman ....
J. F. Talmadge, Jr. .... Whitman
6-1, 6-4, 6-3

Whitman
6-0, 6-2, 6-0

C. Cleveland, Jr. ....
A. Von W. Leslie .... Cleveland
6-4, 8-6, 6-0

Whitman
6-3, 6-2, 6-0

H. Ward ....
L. J. Grant .... Ward
6-1, 6-3, 6-2

Ward
2-6, 8-6, 4-6, 6-4, 6-2

W. W. Reese ....
R. P. Davis .... Davis
6-3, 6-1, 6-3

K. Horton ....
G. P. Sheldon, Jr. .... Sheldon
7-5, 6-3, 8-6

Sheldon
4-6, 6-2, 6-4, 6-2

R. T. Parke ....
J. C. Neely .... Neely
4-6, 6-1, 6-2, 9-7

Sheldon
6-1, 6-8, 6-4, 3-6, 8-6

R. Fincke ....
L. E. Ware .... Ware
6-1, 8-6, 6-2

Ware
6-2, 6-0, 6-3

Y. M. Edwards ......

Fischer
6-4, 7-5, 2-6, 8-6

W. D. Brownell ......
R. H. Carleton .... Carleton
By default

Fischer
6-3, 8-6, 6-1, 6-0

W. Jordan ....
E. P. Fischer .... Fischer
6-1, 6-3, 6-2

Larned, 6-1, 6-2, 6-1

Wrenn, 4-6, 3-6, 6-4, 6-4, 6-3

Wrenn, 7-5, 3-6, 6-0, 1-6, 6-1, Champion of 1896

F. F. Hovey, Champion 1895

SEVENTEENTH USLTA MEN'S SINGLES CHAMPIONSHIPS
The Casino, Newport, R.I., 1897

Preliminary Round	First Round	Second Round	Third Round	Semi-Finals	Finals	Challenge Round	Winner

F. F. Brooks

M. D. Whitman ....
W. J. Clothier .... Whitman
6-3, 6-0, 6-0

Whitman
By default

H. S. Mahony ....
Erving Stille .... Mahony
6-3, 6-3, 6-3

Whitman
9-7, 6-3, 3-6

T. R. Pell ....
J. C. Goodfellow .... Goodfellow
6-3, 6-8, 6-2, 6-2

Mahony
6-4, 6-0, 6-1

J. K. Willing ....
J. F. Talmadge, Jr. .... Willing
By default

Nisbet
6-3, 6-2, 6-4

H. H. Hackett ....
H. A. Nisbet .... Nisbet
2-6, 6-4, 6-3, 6-4

Nisbet
8-6, 4-6, 6-4, 3-6, 7-5

John A. Ryerson ....
R. D. Little .... Ryerson
6-3, 11-9, 3-6, 6-3

Nisbet
6-3, 6-4, 6-3

B. C. Wright ....
Percival Marshall .... Wright
6-0, 6-1, 6-1

Wright
6-2, 6-4, 3-6, 5-7, 6-3

Arthur P. Hawes ....
W. A. Larned .... Larned
6-2, 6-3, 6-0

Larned
8-6, 3-6, 6-2, 8-6

Clarence P. Dodge ....
George Wrenn .... Wrenn
6-3, 3-6, 6-3, 5-7, 6-3

Larned
6-3, 6-1, 6-4

E. S. White ....
J. D. Forbes .... Forbes
6-3, 6-4, 6-2

Forbes
6-1, 6-3, 1-6, 6-0

Deane Miller ....
Paul Macmahon .... Macmahon
By default

Larned
6-4, 6-1, 6-3

Richard Stevens ....
M. G. Chace .... Stevens
By Default

Smith
By default

M. D. Smith ....
Ralph McKettrick .... Smith
6-2, 7-5, 6-4

Fischer
7-5, 8-6, 6-2

E. P. Fischer ....
C. A. Gould .... Fischer
6-1, 6-4, 6-3

Fischer
4-6, 6-3, 2-6, 6-2, 6-4

A. W. Post ....
W. S. Bond .... Bond
6-1, 6-3, 6-1

Nisbet, 3-6, 2-6, 9-7, 6-4, 6-4

D. F. Davis ....
Richard Hooker .... Davis
1-6, 6-1, 6-4, 6-4

Wrenn
7-5, 6-2, 6-0

Evarts Wrenn ....
R. D. Thurber .... Wrenn
6-4, 6-3, 6-0

Paret
6-3, 5-7, 6-4, 6-1

H. McKittrick ....
Marcus Goodbody .... Goodbody
By default

Paret
6-4, 6-4, 6-0

G. P. Sheldon, Jr. ....
J. P. Paret .... Paret
6-0, 6-0, 6-3

Eaves
6-4, 6-1, 3-6, 6-3

W. V. Eaves ....
F. B. Stevens, Jr. .... Eaves
6-2, 6-2, 6-3

Eaves
6-4, 4-6, 6-0, 6-3

W. K. Auchincloss ....
C. R. Budlong .... Budlong
6-3, 6-3, 6-1

Eaves
7-5, 6-2, 6-2

E. T. Gross ....
J. C. Neely .... Neely
4-6, 6-2, 6-2, 2-6, 6-3

Neely
6-2, 6-4, 6-2

H. E. Avery ....
John C. Davidson .... Davidson
6-3, 6-4, 6-2

Eaves
6-2, 6-1, 6-4

O. M. Bostwick ....
B. Goodbody .... Bostwick
9-7, 9-7, 6-3

Ward
6-1, 6-2, 6-3

Holcomb Ward ....
Alfred Codman .... Ward
6-3, 6-3, 6-4

Ward
6-4, 4-6, 6-4, 6-4

H. A. Plummer ....
W. W. Reese .... Reese
2-6, 6-4, 5-7, 6-4, 10-8

Lee
6-4, 6-1, retired

G. W. Lee ....
W. D. Brownell .... Lee
6-1, 6-2, 6-4

Ware
6-3, 6-4, 6-4

Rodney Proctor ....
J. S. Cushman .... Cushman
6-1, 6-2, 6-1

Ware
6-2, 6-2, 6-1

E. Freshman ....
L. E. Ware .... Ware
6-1, 6-2, 6-1

Ware
6-3, 6-2, 6-1

B. Marshall ....
E. K. McEnroe .... Marshall
By default

Holt
By default

H. J. Holt

Eaves, 6-0, 6-2, 6-4

W. V. Eaves, 7-5, 6-3, 6-2

Champion, Wrenn, 4-6, 8-6, 6-3, 2-6, 6-2

R. D. Wrenn, Champion of 1896

EIGHTEEENTH USLTA MEN'S SINGLES CHAMPIONSHIPS
The Casino, Newport, R.I., 1898

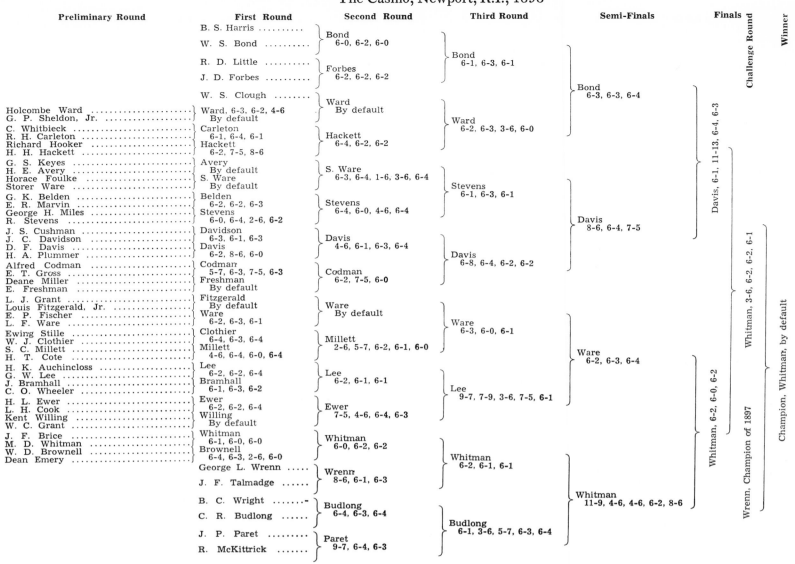

Preliminary Round	First Round	Second Round	Third Round	Semi-Finals	Finals	Challenge Round	Winner

B. S. Harris ....
W. S. Bond .... } Bond 6-0, 6-2, 6-0

R. D. Little ....
J. D. Forbes .... } Forbes 6-2, 6-2, 6-2

} Bond 6-1, 6-3, 6-1

W. S. Clough ....
Holcombe Ward .... Ward, 6-3, 6-2, 4-6
G. P. Sheldon, Jr. .... By default } Ward By default

C. Whitbieck .... Carleton 6-1, 6-4, 6-1
R. H. Carleton ....
Richard Hooker .... Hackett 6-2, 7-5, 8-6
H. H. Hackett .... } Hackett 6-4, 6-2, 6-2

} Ward 6-2, 6-3, 3-6, 6-0

} Bond 6-3, 6-3, 6-4

G. S. Keyes .... Avery By default
H. E. Avery ....
Horace Foulke .... S. Ware By default
Storer Ware .... } S. Ware 6-3, 6-4, 1-6, 3-6, 6-4

G. K. Belden .... Belden 6-2, 6-2, 6-3
E. R. Marvin ....
George H. Miles .... Stevens 6-0, 6-4, 2-6, 6-2
R. Stevens .... } Stevens 6-4, 6-0, 4-6, 6-4

} Stevens 6-1, 6-3, 6-1

} Davis 8-6, 6-4, 7-5

J. S. Cushman .... Davidson 6-3, 6-1, 6-3
J. C. Davidson ....
D. F. Davis .... Davis 6-2, 8-6, 6-0
H. A. Plummer .... } Davis 4-6, 6-1, 6-3, 6-4

Alfred Codman .... Codman 5-7, 6-3, 7-5, 6-3
E. T. Gross ....
Deane Miller .... Freshman By default
E. Freshman .... } Codman 6-2, 7-5, 6-0

} Davis 6-8, 6-4, 6-2, 6-2

} Davis, 6-1, 11-13, 6-4, 6-3

L. J. Grant .... Fitzgerald By default
Louis Fitzgerald, Jr. ....
E. P. Fischer .... Ware 6-2, 6-3, 6-1
L. F. Ware .... } Ware By default

Ewing Stille .... Clothier 6-4, 6-3, 6-4
W. J. Clothier ....
S. C. Millett .... Millett 4-6, 6-4, 6-0, 6-4
H. T. Cote .... } Millett 2-6, 5-7, 6-2, 6-1, 6-0

} Ware 6-3, 6-0, 6-1

} Ware 6-2, 6-3, 6-4

H. K. Auchincloss .... Lee 6-2, 6-2, 6-4
G. W. Lee ....
J. Bramhall .... Bramhall 6-1, 6-3, 6-2
C. O. Wheeler .... } Lee 6-2, 6-1, 6-1

H. L. Ewer .... Ewer 6-2, 6-2, 6-4
L. H. Cook ....
Kent Willing .... Willing By default
W. C. Grant .... } Ewer 7-5, 4-6, 6-4, 6-3

} Lee 9-7, 7-9, 3-6, 7-5, 6-1

} Whitman 6-2, 0-0, 6-2

J. F. Brice .... Whitman 6-1, 6-0, 6-0
M. D. Whitman ....
W. D. Brownell .... Brownell 6-4, 6-3, 2-6, 6-0
Dean Emery .... } Whitman 6-0, 6-2, 6-2

George L. Wrenn .... Wrenn 8-6, 6-1, 6-3
J. F. Talmadge ...... } Wrenn 8-6, 6-1, 6-3

} Whitman 6-2, 6-1, 6-1

B. C. Wright .... Budlong 6-4, 6-3, 6-4
C. R. Budlong ...... } Budlong 6-4, 6-3, 6-4

J. P. Paret .... Paret 9-7, 6-4, 6-3
R. McKittrick .... } Paret 9-7, 6-4, 6-3

} Budlong 6-1, 3-6, 5-7, 6-3, 6-4

} Whitman 11-9, 4-6, 4-6, 6-2, 8-6

Whitman, 3-6, 6-2, 6-2, 6-1

Whitman, 6-2, 6-0, 6-2

Wrenn, Champion of 1897

Whitman, Champion of 1897

Champion, Whitman, by default

NINETEENTH USLTA MEN'S SINGLES CHAMPIONSHIPS
The Casino, Newport, R.I., 1899

Preliminary Round	First Round	Second Round	Third Round	Semi-Finals	Finals	Challenge Round	Winner

J. A. Allen ....
N. H. Mundy .... } Mundy By default

Holcombe Ward ......
C. R. Budlong .... } Ward 6-4, 6-4, 4-6, 6-2

} Ward 4-6, 10-8, 6-2, 6-0

E. A. Freshman ......
Alfred Codman ...... } Codman 6-2, 6-4, 6-3

Norman McLeod ......
L. E. Ware .... } Ware By default

} Ware 9-7, 6-3, 6-3

} Ware 3-6, 6-4, 9-11, 6-2, 6-4

M. G. Chace ....
J. P. Paret .... } Paret 3-6, 10-8, 6-0, 6-3

W. A. Larned ....
H. E. Avery .... } Avery By default

} Paret 6-2, 6-3, 6-3

H. W. Stines ....
Deane Miller .... Stevens, By default
R Stevens .... } Stevens By default

Ford Huntington .... Little By default
R. D. Little ....
R. P. Huntington .... Huntington 6-2, 8-6, 6-4
R. McKittrick .... } Huntington 6-4, 8-6, 6-4

} Huntington 2-6, 3-6, 6-3, 6-3, 6-1

} Paret 3-6, 6-3, 4-6, 6-4, 6-0

} Paret 7-5, 6-2, 6-4

W. S. Bond .... Bond 6-3, 4-6, 6-4, 6-4
W. J. Clothier ....
Payne Whitney .... Bridges By default
J. S. Bridges .... } Bond 6-1, 6-2, 6-0

G. P. Sheldon, Jr. .... Wright By default
R. C. Wright .... } Wright 6-2, 6-2, 6-1
L. J. Grant .... }

} Bond 4-6, 6-4, 7-5, 4-6, 6-3

C. N. Beard ....
D. S. Ricker .... } Beard 6-2, 6-2, 8-6

D. F. Davis ....
H. G. Whitehead ...... } Davis 6-2, 6-4, 6-0

} Davis 6-2, 6-0, 6-1

} Davis 6-4, 6-4, 1-6, 6-4

Geo. L. Wrenn, Jr. ...
E. P. Fisher .... } Wrenn, Jr. 5-7, 8-6, 7-5, 6-2

J. S. Taylor ....
J. K. Willing .... } Taylor 5-7, 8-6, 6-3, 3-6, 6-2

} Wrenn 6-2, 6-3, 6-3

Thos. Sturgis, Jr. ......
Kriegh Collins .... } Collins 6-3, 6-1, 6-1

W. C. Grant ....
Ewing Stille .... } Grant By default

} Collins 6-1, 6-1, 6-2

} Collins 8-6, 4-6, 4-6, 6-4, 6-3

} Davis 6-4, 6-1, 8-6

Paret, 7-5, 8-10, 6-3, 2-6, 6-4

M. D. Whitman, Champion 1898

Champion, M. D. Whitman, 6-1, 6-2, 3-6, 7-5

TWENTIETH USLTA MEN'S SINGLES CHAMPIONSHIPS
The Casino, Newport, R.I., 1900

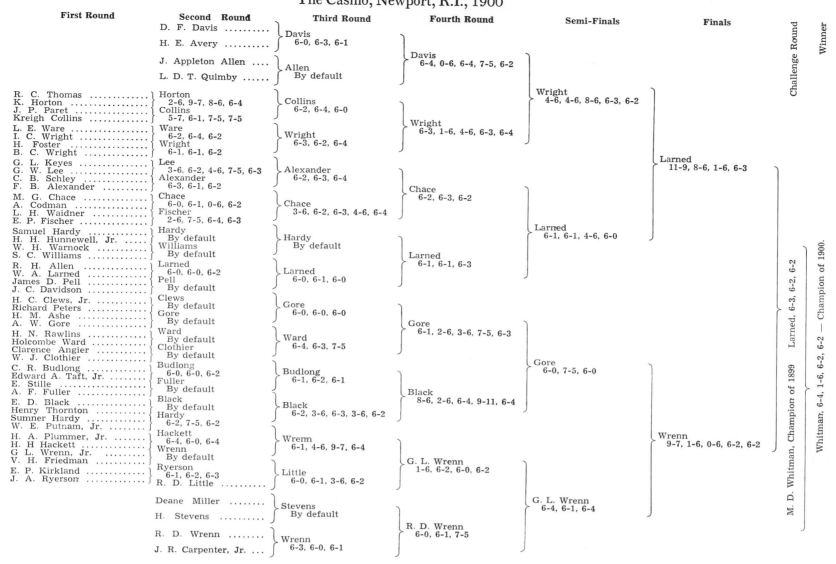

First Round	Second Round	Third Round	Fourth Round	Semi-Finals	Finals		Winner

D. F. Davis ....
H. E. Avery ....
Davis 6-0, 6-3, 6-1

J. Appleton Allen ....
L. D. T. Quimby ......
Allen By default

Davis 6-4, 0-6, 6-4, 7-5, 6-2

R. C. Thomas .... Horton
K. Horton 2-6, 9-7, 8-6, 6-4
J. P. Paret .... Collins
Kreigh Collins 5-7, 6-1, 7-5, 7-5
Collins 6-2, 6-4, 6-0

L. E. Ware .... Ware
I. C. Wright 6-2, 6-4, 6-2
H. Foster .... Wright
B. C. Wright 6-1, 6-1, 6-2
Wright 6-3, 6-2, 6-4

Wright 6-3, 1-6, 4-6, 6-3, 6-4

Wright 4-6, 4-6, 8-6, 6-3, 6-2

G. L. Keyes .... Lee
G. W. Lee 3-6, 6-2, 4-6, 7-5, 6-3
C. B. Schley .... Alexander
F. B. Alexander 6-3, 6-1, 6-2
Alexander 6-2, 6-3, 6-4

M. G. Chace .... Chace
A. Codman 6-0, 6-1, 0-6, 6-2
L. H. Waidner .... Fischer
E. P. Fischer 2-6, 7-5, 6-4, 6-3
Chace 3-6, 6-2, 6-3, 4-6, 6-4

Chace 6-2, 6-3, 6-2

Larned 11-9, 8-6, 1-6, 6-3

Samuel Hardy .... Hardy
H. H. Hunnewell, Jr. ... By default
W. H. Warnock .... Williams
S. C. Williams .... By default
Hardy By default

R. H. Allen .... Larned
W. A. Larned 6-0, 6-0, 6-2
James D. Pell .... Pell
J. C. Davidson .... By default
Larned 6-0, 6-1, 6-0

Larned 6-1, 6-1, 6-3

Larned 6-1, 6-1, 4-6, 6-0

H. C. Clews, Jr. .... Clews
Richard Peters .... By default
H. M. Ashe .... Gore
A. W. Gore .... By default
Gore 6-0, 6-0, 6-0

H. N. Rawlins .... Ward
Holcombe Ward .... By default
Clarence Angier .... Clothier
W. J. Clothier .... By default
Ward 6-4, 6-3, 7-5

Gore 6-1, 2-6, 3-6, 7-5, 6-3

Gore 6-0, 7-5, 6-0

C. R. Budlong .... Budlong
Edward A. Taft, Jr. 6-0, 6-0, 6-2
E. Stille .... Fuller
A. F. Fuller .... By default
Budlong 6-1, 6-2, 6-1

E. D. Black .... Black
Henry Thornton .... By default
Sumner Hardy .... Hardy
W. E. Putnam, Jr. 6-2, 7-5, 6-2
Black By default

Black 6-2, 3-6, 6-3, 3-6, 6-2

Black 8-6, 2-6, 6-4, 9-11, 6-4

H. A. Plummer, Jr. ..... Hackett
H. H Hackett 6-4, 6-0, 6-4
G. L. Wrenn, Jr. .... Wrenn
V. H. Friedman .... By default
Wrenn 6-1, 4-6, 9-7, 6-4

E. P. Kirkland .... Ryerson
J. A. Ryerson 6-1, 6-2, 6-3
Little 6-0, 6-1, 3-6, 6-2

Little 6-0, 6-1, 3-6, 6-2

R. D. Little ....

G. L. Wrenn 1-6, 6-2, 6-0, 6-2

Wrenn 9-7, 1-6, 0-6, 6-2, 6-2

Deane Miller ....
H. Stevens ....
Stevens By default

R. D. Wrenn ....
J. R. Carpenter, Jr. ...
Wrenn 6-3, 6-0, 6-1

R. D. Wrenn 6-0, 6-1, 7-5

G. L. Wrenn 6-4, 6-1, 6-4

Larned, 6-3, 6-2, 6-2

M. D. Whitman, Champion of 1899 Larned, 6-3, 6-2, 6-2 — Champion of 1900.

Whitman, 6-4, 1-6, 6-2, 6-2

Challenge Round

TWENTY-FIRST USLTA MEN'S SINGLES CHAMPIONSHIPS
The Casino, Newport, R.I., 1901

First Round	Second Round	Third Round	Quarter-Finals	Semi-Finals	Finals		Winner

L. E. Ware ....
D. B. Eldridge ....
Ware 6-0, 6-1, 6-1

Harry Oelrichs ....
Joseph Seabury ......
Seabury 6-4, 6-2, 6-1

Ware 6-1, 6-4, 6-2

R. C. Sever .... Mahoney
F. C. Mahoney .... By default
LeBaron Adams .... Avery
H. E. Avery 6-0, 6-2, 6-4
Avery 6-0, 6-2, 6-1

E. W. Leonard .... Leonard
Ewing Stille .... By default
R. G. Vaughan .... Vaughan
Crawford Allison 4-6, 6-2, 6-1, 3-6, 6-1
Leonard 6-4, 3-6, 6-3, 6-1

Leonard 6-3, 6-8, 6-3, 6-2

Ware 6-2, 6-2, 6-1

I. C. Wright .... Wright
J. R. Pell 7-5, 2-6, 6-2, 2-6, 6-3
Robert LeRoy .... Stevens
Richard Stevens 6-4, 6-2, 6-3
Stevens 8-6, 6-4, 6-0

F. B. Alexander .... Alexander
C. Pell 6-1, 6-1, 6-2
W. A. Larned .... Larned
T A. McGinley 6-0, 6-2, 6-2
W. A. Larned 6-2, 6-3, 6-2

W. A. Larned 6-1, 7-5, 8-6

W. A. Larned By default

George Griswold, 2d ..... Eldridge
D. G. Eldridge 6-1, 6-2, 4-6, 6-0
W. L. Foulke .... Foulke
J. J. Astor 6-2, 6-2, 6-4
Foulke 6-1, 6-3, 6-0

H. H Hackett .... McEnroe
E. K. McEnroe .... By default
E. P. Larned .... Larned
Norman G. Johnson 6-1, 6-2, 6-0
E. P. Larned By default

E. P. Larned 6-0, 6-1, 6-1

Larned, 6-3, 6-2, 6-2

E. C. Potter, Jr. ...... Appleton, 2d
D. F. Appleton, 2d 6-0, 6-1, 6-0
L. Wilmerding .... Little
R. D. Little 6-3, 8-6, 8-6
Little 6-1, 6-2, 6-1

I. T. Burden, Jr. ...... Maundy
N. H. Mundy .... By default
W. B. Kurtz .... Kurtz
Robertson Honey 6-1, 6-2, 6-0
Kurtz 6-0, 6-2, 6-0

Little 6-1, 6-3, 6-4

Little 6-3, 10-8, 1-6, 6-1

C. S. Lee .... Clothier
W. J. Clothier 6-0, 6-1, 6-1
E. P. Fischer .... Stillman
Alfred Stillman .... By default
Clothier 6-2, 6-0, 6-1

J. P. Paret .... Paret
C. E. Sands 6-3, 6-3, 6-2
K. Collins .... Read
J. B. Read .... By default
Paret 5-7, 6-3, 9-7, 6-1

Clothier 6-1, 0-6, 6-3, 4-6, 6-4

D. F. Davis .... Davis
S. C. Whipple 6-2, 6-1, 6-2
Holcombe Ward .... Ward
G. S. Keyes .... By default
Davis 1-6, 6-2, 6-3, 6-4

C. L. Childs .... Wright
B. C. Wright 6-2, 6-3, 6-1
Pennington Pierson ..... Pierson
H. A. Plummer .... By default
Wright 6-1, 6-0, 6-2

Wright 6-2, 8-6, 6-3

Wright 6-3, 8-6, 6-4

C. L. Grimestead ....
Louis DeForest ......
DeForest By default

Clarence Hobart ....
A. F. Fuller ....
Hobart 6-2, 6-0, 6-3

Hobart 6-0, 6-3, 6-0

Wright, 7-5, 2-6, 6-1, 6-2

Larned, 6-2, 6-8, 6-4, 6-4

M. D. Whitman, Champion of 1900 Larned, by default, champion of 1901

Challenge Round

73

TWENTY-SECOND USLTA MEN'S SINGLES CHAMPIONSHIPS
The Casino, Newport, R.I., 1902

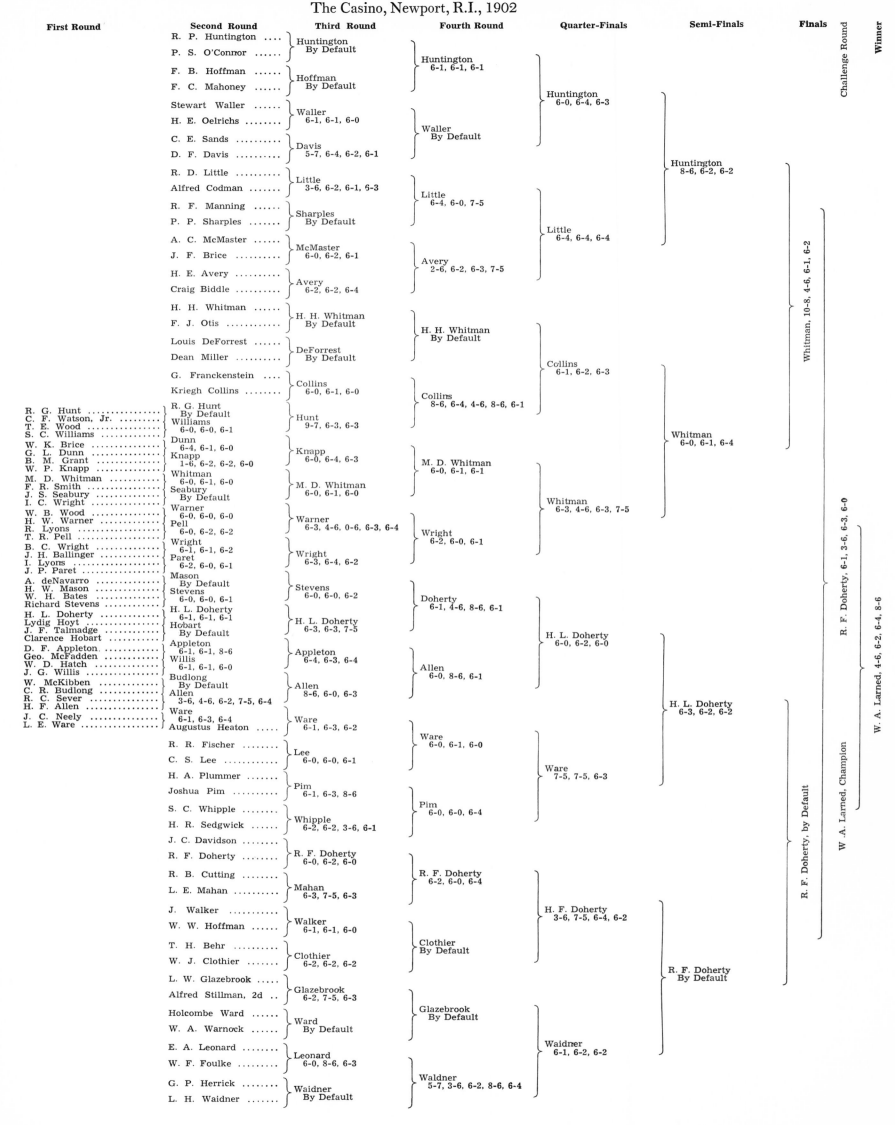

First Round — Second Round — Third Round — Fourth Round — Quarter-Finals — Semi-Finals — Finals — Challenge Round — Winner

R. P. Huntington ....
P. S. O'Connor ......
Huntington By Default

F. B. Hoffman ......
F. C. Mahoney ......
Hoffman By Default

Huntington 6-1, 6-1, 6-1

Stewart Waller ......
H. E. Oelrichs ....
Waller 6-1, 6-1, 6-0

C. E. Sands ....
D. F. Davis ....
Davis 5-7, 6-4, 6-2, 6-1

Waller By Default

Huntington 6-0, 6-4, 6-3

R. D. Little ....
Alfred Codman ....
Little 3-6, 6-2, 6-1, 6-3

R. F. Manning ......
P. P. Sharples ....
Sharples By Default

Little 6-4, 6-0, 7-5

A. C. McMaster ......
J. F. Brice ....
McMaster 6-0, 6-2, 6-1

H. E. Avery ....
Craig Biddle ....
Avery 6-2, 6-2, 6-4

Avery 2-6, 6-2, 6-3, 7-5

Little 6-4, 6-4, 6-4

Huntington 8-6, 6-2, 6-2

H. H. Whitman ......
F. J. Otis ....
H. H. Whitman By Default

Louis DeForrest ......
Dean Miller ....
DeForrest By Default

H. H. Whitman By Default

G. Franckenstein ....
Kriegh Collins ....
Collins 6-0, 6-1, 6-0

R. G. Hunt ....
R. G. Hunt By Default
Hunt 9-7, 6-3, 6-3

Collins 8-6, 6-4, 4-6, 8-6, 6-1

Collins 6-1, 6-2, 6-3

C. F. Watson, Jr. ....
T. E. Wood ....
S. C. Williams ....
Williams 6-0, 6-0, 6-1

W. K. Brice ....
G. L. Dunn ....
B. M. Grant ....
W. P. Knapp ....
Dunn 6-4, 6-1, 6-0
Knapp 1-6, 6-2, 6-2, 6-0

Knapp 6-0, 6-4, 6-3

Whitman 6-0, 6-1, 6-4

M. D. Whitman ....
F. R. Smith ....
J. S. Seabury ....
I. C. Wright ....
Whitman 6-0, 6-1, 6-0
Seabury By Default

M. D. Whitman 6-0, 6-1, 6-0

M. D. Whitman 6-0, 6-1, 6-1

W. B. Wood ....
H. W. Warner ....
R. Lyons ....
T. R. Pell ....
Warner 6-0, 6-0, 6-0
Pell 6-0, 6-2, 6-2

Warner 6-3, 4-6, 0-6, 6-3, 6-4

B. C. Wright ....
J. H. Ballinger ....
I. Lyons ....
J. P. Paret ....
Wright 6-1, 6-1, 6-2
Paret 6-2, 6-0, 6-1

Wright 6-3, 6-4, 6-2

Wright 6-2, 6-0, 6-1

Whitman 6-3, 4-6, 6-3, 7-5

A. deNavarro ....
H. W. Mason ....
W. H. Bates ....
Richard Stevens ....
Mason By Default
Stevens 6-0, 6-0, 6-1

Stevens 6-0, 6-0, 6-2

H. L. Doherty ....
Lydig Hoyt ....
J. F. Talmadge ....
Clarence Hobart ....
H. L. Doherty 6-1, 6-1, 6-1
Hobart By Default

H. L. Doherty 6-3, 6-3, 7-5

Doherty 6-1, 4-6, 8-6, 6-1

D. F. Appleton ....
Geo. McFadden ....
W. D. Hatch ....
J. G. Willis ....
Appleton 6-1, 6-1, 8-6
Willis 6-1, 6-1, 6-0

Appleton 6-4, 6-3, 6-4

W. McKibben ....
C. R. Budlong ....
R. C. Sever ....
H. F. Allen ....
Budlong By Default
Allen 3-6, 4-6, 6-2, 7-5, 6-4

Allen 8-6, 6-0, 6-3

Allen 6-0, 8-6, 6-1

H. L. Doherty 6-0, 6-2, 6-0

J. C. Neely ....
L. E. Ware ....
Ware 6-1, 6-3, 6-4

Augustus Heaton .....
Ware 6-1, 6-3, 6-2

Ware 6-0, 6-1, 6-0

R. R. Fischer ....
C. S. Lee ....
Lee 6-0, 6-0, 6-1

H. A. Plummer ....
Joshua Pim ....
Pim 6-1, 6-3, 8-6

Ware 7-5, 7-5, 6-3

S. C. Whipple ....
H. R. Sedgwick ......
Whipple 6-2, 6-2, 3-6, 6-1

Pim 6-0, 6-0, 6-4

H. L. Doherty 6-3, 6-2, 6-2

J. C. Davidson ....
R. F. Doherty ....
R. F. Doherty 6-0, 6-2, 6-0

R. B. Cutting ....
L. E. Mahan ....
Mahan 6-3, 7-5, 6-3

R. F. Doherty 6-2, 6-0, 6-4

J. Walker ....
W. W. Hoffman ......
Walker 6-1, 6-1, 6-0

T. H. Behr ....
W. J. Clothier ....
Clothier 6-2, 6-2, 6-2

Clothier By Default

H. F. Doherty 3-6, 7-5, 6-4, 6-2

L. W. Glazebrook .....
Alfred Stillman, 2d ..
Glazebrook 6-2, 7-5, 6-3

Holcombe Ward ......
W. A. Warnock ......
Ward By Default

Glazebrook By Default

R. F. Doherty By Default

E. A. Leonard ....
W. F. Foulke ....
Leonard 6-0, 8-6, 6-3

G. P. Herrick ....
L. H. Waidner ....
Waidner By Default

Waidner 6-1, 6-2, 6-2

Waidner 5-7, 3-6, 6-2, 8-6, 6-4

R. F. Doherty, by Default

Whitman, 10-8, 4-6, 6-1, 6-2

R. F. Doherty, 6-1, 3-6, 6-3, 6-0

W. A. Larned, 4-6, 6-2, 6-4, 8-6

W. A. Larned, Champion

74

TWENTY-THIRD USLTA MEN'S SINGLES CHAMPIONSHIPS
The Casino, Newport, R.I., 1903

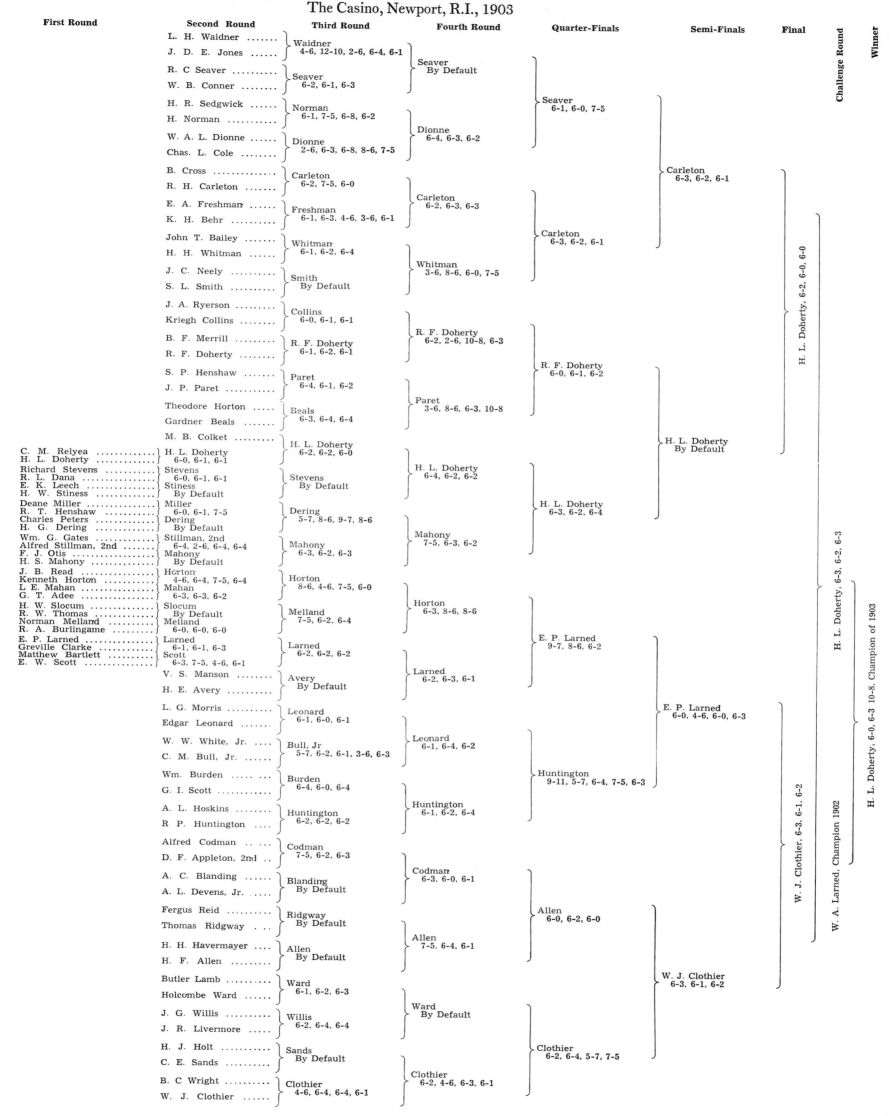

First Round	Second Round	Third Round	Fourth Round	Quarter-Finals	Semi-Finals	Final	Challenge Round	Winner

L. H. Waidner ....
J. D. E. Jones ......
Waidner 4-6, 12-10, 2-6, 6-4, 6-1

R. C Seaver ....
W. B. Conner ....
Seaver 6-2, 6-1, 6-3

Seaver By Default

H. R. Sedgwick ......
H. Norman ....
Norman 6-1, 7-5, 6-8, 6-2

W. A. L. Dionne ......
Chas. L. Cole ....
Dionne 2-6, 6-3, 6-8, 8-6, 7-5

Dionne 6-4, 6-3, 6-2

Seaver 6-1, 6-0, 7-5

B. Cross ....
R. H. Carleton ....
Carleton 6-2, 7-5, 6-0

E. A. Freshman ......
K. H. Behr ....
Freshman 6-1, 6-3, 4-6, 3-6, 6-1

Carleton 6-2, 6-3, 6-3

Carleton 6-3, 6-2, 6-1

John T. Bailey ....
H. H. Whitman ......
Whitman 6-1, 6-2, 6-4

J. C. Neely ....
S. L. Smith ....
Smith By Default

Whitman 3-6, 8-6, 6-0, 7-5

Carleton 6-3, 6-2, 6-1

J. A. Ryerson ....
Kriegh Collins ....
Collins 6-0, 6-1, 6-1

B. F. Merrill ....
R. F. Doherty ....
R. F. Doherty 6-1, 6-2, 6-1

R. F. Doherty 6-2, 2-6, 10-8, 6-3

S. P. Henshaw ....
J. P. Paret ....
Paret 6-4, 6-1, 6-2

Theodore Horton .....
Gardner Beals ....
Beals 6-3, 6-4, 6-4

Paret 3-6, 8-6, 6-3, 10-8

R. F. Doherty 6-0, 6-1, 6-2

M. B. Colket ....
H. L. Doherty 6-2, 6-2, 6-0

C. M. Relyea .... } H. L. Doherty 6-0, 6-1, 6-1
H. L. Doherty ....
Richard Stevens .... } Stevens 6-0, 6-1, 6-1
R. L. Dana ....
E. K. Leech .... } Stiness By Default
H. W. Stiness ....

Stevens By Default

H. L. Doherty 6-4, 6-2, 6-2

Deane Miller .... } Miller 6-0, 6-1, 7-5
R. T. Henshaw ....
Charles Peters .... } Dering By Default
H. G. Dering ....

Dering 5-7, 8-6, 9-7, 8-6

Wm. G. Gates .... } Stillman, 2nd 6-4, 2-6, 6-4, 6-4
Alfred Stillman, 2nd ....
F. J. Otis .... } Mahony By Default
H. S. Mahony ....

Mahony 6-3, 6-2, 6-3

Mahony 7-5, 6-3, 6-2

H. L. Doherty 6-3, 6-2, 6-4

J. B. Read .... } Horton 4-6, 6-4, 7-5, 6-4
Kenneth Horton ....
L E. Mahan .... } Mahan 6-3, 6-3, 6-2
G. T. Adee ....

Horton 8-6, 4-6, 7-5, 6-0

H. W. Slocum .... } Slocum By Default
R. W. Thomas ....
Norman Melland .... } Melland 6-0, 6-0, 6-0
R. A. Burlingame ....

Melland 7-5, 6-2, 6-4

Horton 6-3, 8-6, 8-6

E. P. Larned .... } Larned 6-1, 6-1, 6-3
Greville Clarke ....
Matthew Bartlett .... } Scott 6-3, 7-5, 4-6, 6-1
E. W. Scott ....

Larned 6-2, 6-2, 6-2

E. P. Larned 9-7, 8-6, 6-2

V. S. Manson ....
H. E. Avery ....
Avery By Default

Larned 6-2, 6-3, 6-1

L. G. Morris ....
Edgar Leonard ....
Leonard 6-1, 6-0, 6-1

W. W. White, Jr. ....
C. M. Bull, Jr. ......
Bull, Jr 5-7, 6-2, 6-1, 3-6, 6-3

Leonard 6-1, 6-4, 6-2

E. P. Larned 6-0, 4-6, 6-0, 6-3

Wm. Burden ....
G. I. Scott ....
Burden 6-4, 6-0, 6-4

A. L. Hoskins ....
R P. Huntington ....
Huntington 6-2, 6-2, 6-2

Huntington 6-1, 6-2, 6-4

Huntington 9-11, 5-7, 6-4, 7-5, 6-3

Alfred Codman ......
D. F. Appleton, 2nd ..
Codman 7-5, 6-2, 6-3

A. C. Blanding ......
A. L. Devens, Jr. .....
Blanding By Default

Codman 6-3, 6-0, 6-1

Fergus Reid ....
Thomas Ridgway ...
Ridgway By Default

H. H. Havermayer ....
H. F. Allen ....
Allen By Default

Allen 7-5, 6-4, 6-1

Allen 6-0, 6-2, 6-0

W. J. Clothier 6-3, 6-1, 6-2

Butler Lamb ....
Holcombe Ward ......
Ward 6-1, 6-2, 6-3

J. G. Willis ....
J. R. Livermore .....
Willis 6-2, 6-4, 6-4

Ward By Default

H. J. Holt ....
C. E. Sands ....
Sands By Default

Clothier 6-2, 6-4, 5-7, 7-5

B. C Wright ....
W. J. Clothier ......
Clothier 4-6, 6-4, 6-4, 6-1

Clothier 6-2, 4-6, 6-3, 6-1

W. J. Clothier 6-3, 6-1, 6-2

H. L. Doherty, 6-2, 6-0, 6-0

H. L. Doherty. 6-3, 6-2, 6-3

H. L. Doherty, 6-3, 6-1, 6-2

W. J. Clothier, 6-3, 6-1, 6-2

W. A. Larned, Champion 1902

H. L. Doherty, 6-0, 6-3 10-8, Champion of 1903

TWENTY-FOURTH USLTA MEN'S SINGLES CHAMPIONSHIPS
The Casino, Newport, R.I., 1904

First Round	Second Round	Third Round	Fourth Round	Quarter-Finals	Semi-Finals	Finals	Challenge Round	Winner

Alexander Phelps — B. C. Wright — 6-1, 6-1, 6-3
B. C. Wright

Paulding Fosdick — Dana — By Default
R. N. Dana

B. C. Wright — 1-6, 6-2, 6-3, 6-3

Marion Wright — M. Wright — 6-1, 6-3, 6-4
Philip A. Carroll

E. J. Sulloway — Sulloway — By Default
Ernest Lambert

Sulloway — 2-6, 6-1, 6-3, 6-2

Wright — 6-2, 6-2, 4-6, 6-1

Richard Stevens — Stevens — 6-4, 6-0, 6-2
B. B. V. Lyon

Ralph Hickox — Lee — 6-0, 6-1, 6-1
G. W. Lee

Stevens — 6-1, 6-1, 6-2

W. J. Hull — Watson, Jr. — 6-0, 6-2, 6-1
C. F. Watson, Jr

J. D. E. Jones — Larned — 6-2, 6-0, 3-6, 6-1
W. A. Larned

Larned — 6-1, 7-5, Default

Larned — 6-3, 6-1, 6-2

Larned — 6-1, 6-0, 6-3

W. F. Keene — Read — By Default
J. B. Read

M. G. Chace — Brice — By Default
J. F. Brice

Read — 6-1, 6-1, 6-2

George Baker — Burden — 6-3, 6-0, 6-0
W. P. Burden

F. C. Colston — Bell — 6-2, 5-7, 6-4, 8-6
A. E. Bell
G. H. Nettleton — Nettleton — 7-5, 6-1, 6-4
George A. Lyon, Jr.

Bell — 6-3, 6-2, 6-3

Bell — 6-3, 6-1, 6-4

Bell — 7-5, 6-1, 6-3

Gardner Beals — Allen — 3-6, 6-3, 6-0, 6-3
H. F. Allen
William J. Clothier — Clothier — 6-4, 6-2, 6-0
C. E. Sands

Clothier — 6-4, 6-1, 6-4

E. B. Dewhurst — Dewhurst — 6-1, 6-1, 6-2
H. R. Sedgwick
G. C. Hickley — Hickley — 2-6, 6-1, 6-4, 6-1
H. A. Sands

Dewhurst — 6-2, 6-8, 6-1, 6-1

Clothier — 6-1, 7-5, 6-4

Clothier — 6-3, 7-5, 6-3

Clothier — 5-7, 6-2, 6-2, 6-3

S. C. Whipple — Whipple — 6-1, 8-6, 6-4
E. Catlin, Jr.
Frank R. Tucker — Phetteplace — By Default
T. M. Phetteplace

Whipple — 6-2, 6-3, 4-6, 6-1

F. J. Otis — Mills — By Default
Ogden Mills, Jr.
Karl H. Behr — Behr — 6-2, 7-5, 9-7
A. L. Hoskins

Behr — By Default

Behr — 6-8, 6-1, 6-0, 6-2

H. Whitman — Huntington — By Default
Ford Huntington
J. S. A. Johnson — Cross — 6-0, 6-3, 6-0
Eliot Cross

Huntington — 6-0, 6-2, 6-3

H. W. Warner — Warner — By Default
Horace Brown
J. D. Forbes — Anderson — 6-1, 6-1, 6-4
Fred Anderson

Anderson — 6-4, 6-2, 6-0

Huntington — 6-4, 4-6, 6-4, 6-3

Alexander — 7-5, 6-1, 8-6

J. W. Burden — Ledyard — 6-2, 6-4, 7-5
Lewis Cass Ledyard
F. R. Budlong — Millett — 6-0, 6-1, 6-1
S. C. Millett

Millett — 6-0, 6-3, 6-1

Kenneth Horton — Thomas — By Default
Ralph A. Thomas
D. F. Appleton — Alexander — 6-1, 6-0, 6-9
F. B. Alexander

Alexander — 6-0, 6-1, 6-1

Alexander — 6-1, 6-3, 6-3

Ward — 6-4, 9-7, 7-5

Holcombe Ward — Ward — 6-4, 6-1, 6-1
C. S. Brigham
H. J. Holt — Ward — 6-3, 6-3, 6-1

Ward — 6-4, 6-3, 6-4

W. F. Johnson — Johnson — By Default
H. E. Avery

R. D. Little — Little — 6-1, 6-4, 5-7, 8-6
B. S. Prentice

Collins — 13-11, 3-6, 2-6, 6-4, 6-3

J. O. Ames — Collins — 6-3, 6-3, 7-5
Kriegh Collins

H. Ward — 6-2, 8-6, 6-2

Herbert G. Dering — Adee — 7-5, 6-4, 6-3
G. T. Adee

Charles Bull — Bull — By Default
Sydney J. Smith

Bull — 1-6, 7-5, 4-6, 6-4, 6-2

E. W. Leonard — Leonard — By Default
Alfred Codman

Leonard — 6-2, 6-2, 6-4

George T. Scott — LeRoy — By Default
Robert LeRoy

Leonard — 6-2, 7-5, 10-8

Leonard — 6-0, 6-1, 6-1

Ward — 6-3, 6-4, 6-4

F. H. Potter — Flourney — By Default
B. C. Flournery

Frank Foster — Howland — By Default
Merideth Howland

Howland — 6-3, 6-3, 6-0

H. W. Niles — Niles — By Default
R. C. Seaver

Niles — 6-0, 6-2, 6-1

Charles L. Oelrichs — Oelrichs — By Default
Deane Miller

Niles — 6-1, 6-0, 6-3

Clothier, 6-4, 3-6, 2-6, 6-2, 6-3

Ward, 10-8, 6-4, 9-7

Ward, By Default, Champion of 1904

H. L. Doherty, Champion 1903

TWENTY-FIFTH USLTA MEN'S SINGLES CHAMPIONSHIPS
The Casino, Newport, R.I., 1905

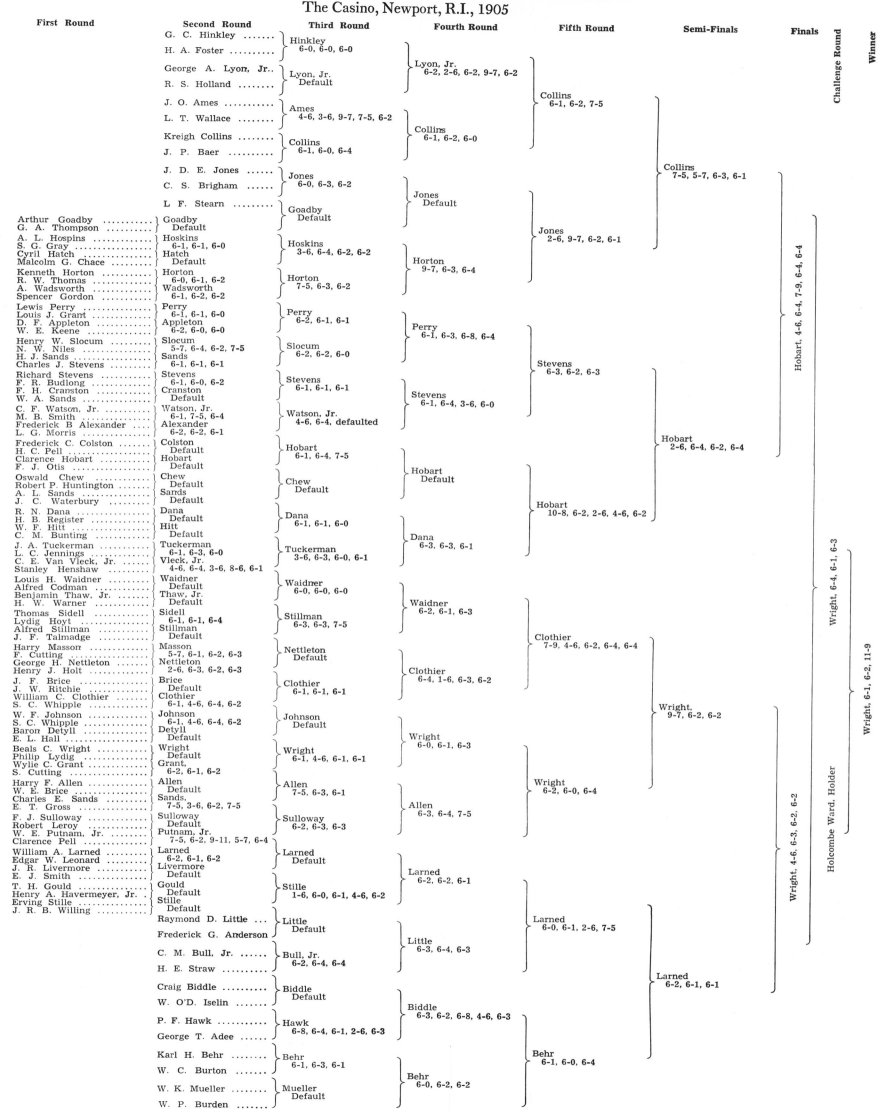

First Round | Second Round | Third Round | Fourth Round | Fifth Round | Semi-Finals | Finals | Challenge Round | Winner

G. C. Hinkley — Hinkley 6-0, 6-0, 6-0
H. A. Foster

George A. Lyon, Jr. — Lyon, Jr. Default — Lyon, Jr. 6-2, 2-6, 6-2, 9-7, 6-2
R. S. Holland

J. O. Ames — Ames 4-6, 3-6, 9-7, 7-5, 6-2
L. T. Wallace

Kreigh Collins — Collins 6-1, 6-0, 6-4 — Collins 6-1, 6-2, 6-0 — Collins 6-1, 6-2, 7-5
J. P. Baer

J. D. E. Jones — Jones 6-0, 6-3, 6-2
C. S. Brigham

L. F. Stearn — Goadby Default — Jones Default

Arthur Goadby — Goadby Default
G. A. Thompson

A. L. Hoskins — Hoskins 6-1, 6-1, 6-0 — Hoskins 3-6, 6-4, 6-2, 6-2
S. G. Gray

Cyril Hatch — Hatch Default
Malcolm G. Chace

Kenneth Horton — Horton 6-0, 6-1, 6-2 — Horton 7-5, 6-3, 6-2 — Horton 9-7, 6-3, 6-4 — Jones 2-6, 9-7, 6-2, 6-1
R. W. Thomas

A. Wadsworth — Wadsworth 6-1, 6-2, 6-2
Spencer Gordon

Lewis Perry — Perry 6-1, 6-1, 6-0 — Perry 6-2, 6-1, 6-1
Louis J. Grant

D. F. Appleton — Appleton 6-2, 6-0, 6-0
W. E. Keene

Henry W. Slocum — Slocum 5-7, 6-4, 6-2, 7-5 — Slocum 6-2, 6-2, 6-0 — Perry 6-1, 6-3, 6-8, 6-4
N. W. Niles

H. J. Sands — Sands 6-1, 6-1, 6-1
Charles J. Stevens

Richard Stevens — Stevens 6-1, 6-0, 6-2 — Stevens 6-1, 6-1, 6-1
F. R. Budlong

F. H. Cranston — Cranston Default
W. A. Sands

C. F. Watson, Jr. — Watson, Jr. 6-1, 7-5, 6-4 — Watson, Jr. 4-6, 6-4, defaulted — Stevens 6-1, 6-4, 3-6, 6-0 — Stevens 6-3, 6-2, 6-3
M. B. Smith

Frederick B Alexander — Alexander 6-2, 6-2, 6-1
L. G. Morris

Frederick C. Colston — Colston Default — Hobart 6-1, 6-4, 7-5
H. C. Pell

Clarence Hobart — Hobart Default
F. J. Otis

Oswald Chew — Chew Default — Chew Default — Hobart Default
Robert P. Huntington

A. L. Sands — Sands Default
J. C. Waterbury

R. N. Dana — Dana Default — Dana 6-1, 6-1, 6-0
H. B. Register

W. F. Hitt — Hitt Default
C. M. Bunting

J. A. Tuckerman — Tuckerman 6-1, 6-3, 6-0 — Tuckerman 3-6, 6-3, 6-0, 6-1 — Dana 6-3, 6-3, 6-1 — Hobart 10-8, 6-2, 2-6, 4-6, 6-2
L. C. Jennings

C. E. Van Vleck, Jr. — Vleck, Jr. 4-6, 6-4, 3-6, 8-6, 6-1
Stanley Henshaw

Louis H. Waidner — Waidner Default — Waidner 6-0, 6-0, 6-0
Alfred Codman

Benjamin Thaw, Jr. — Thaw, Jr. Default
H. W. Warner

Thomas Sidell — Sidell 6-1, 6-1, 6-4 — Stillman 6-3, 6-3, 7-5 — Waidner 6-2, 6-1, 6-3
Lydig Hoyt

Alfred Stillman — Stillman Default
J. F. Talmadge

Harry Masson — Masson 5-7, 6-1, 6-2, 6-3 — Nettleton Default
F. Cutting

George H. Nettleton — Nettleton 2-6, 6-3, 6-2, 6-3
Henry J. Holt

J. F. Brice — Brice Default — Clothier 6-1, 6-1, 6-1 — Clothier 6-4, 1-6, 6-3, 6-2 — Clothier 7-9, 4-6, 6-2, 6-4, 6-4
J. W. Ritchie

William C. Clothier — Clothier 6-1, 4-6, 6-4, 6-2
S. C. Whipple

W. F. Johnson — Johnson 6-1, 4-6, 6-4, 6-2 — Johnson Default
S. C. Whipple

Baron Detyll — Detyll Default
E. L. Hall

Beals C. Wright — Wright Default — Wright 6-1, 4-6, 6-1, 6-1 — Wright 6-0, 6-1, 6-3
Philip Lydig

Wylie C. Grant — Grant, 6-2, 6-1, 6-2
S. Cutting

Harry F. Allen — Allen Default — Allen 7-5, 6-3, 6-1 — Wright 9-7, 6-2, 6-2
W. E. Brice

Charles E. Sands — Sands, 7-5, 3-6, 6-2, 7-5
E. T. Gross

F. J. Sulloway — Sulloway Default — Sulloway 6-2, 6-3, 6-3 — Allen 6-3, 6-4, 7-5
Robert Leroy

W. E. Putnam, Jr. — Putnam, Jr. 7-5, 6-2, 9-11, 5-7, 6-4
Clarence Pell

William A. Larned — Larned 6-2, 6-1, 6-2 — Larned Default
Edgar W. Leonard

J. R. Livermore — Livermore Default
E. J. Smith

T. H. Gould — Gould Default — Stille 1-6, 6-0, 6-1, 4-6, 6-2 — Larned 6-2, 6-2, 6-1 — Wright 6-2, 6-0, 6-4
Henry A. Havermeyer, Jr. — Stille Default

Erving Stille — Stille Default
J. R. B. Willing

Raymond D. Little — Little Default — Little 6-3, 6-4, 6-3
Frederick G. Anderson

C. M. Bull, Jr. — Bull, Jr. 6-2, 6-4, 6-4
H. E. Straw

Craig Biddle — Biddle Default — Biddle 6-3, 6-2, 6-8, 4-6, 6-3 — Larned 6-0, 6-1, 2-6, 7-5
W. O'D. Iselin

P. F. Hawk — Hawk 6-8, 6-4, 6-1, 2-6, 6-3
George T. Adee

Karl H. Behr — Behr 6-1, 6-3, 6-1 — Behr 6-0, 6-2, 6-2 — Behr 6-1, 6-0, 6-4 — Larned 6-2, 6-1, 6-1
W. C. Burton

W. K. Mueller — Mueller Default
W. P. Burden

Semi-Finals: Wright, 9-7, 6-2, 6-2
Finals: Wright, 6-4, 6-1, 6-3 — Wright, 4-6, 6-3, 6-2, 6-2
Wright, 6-1, 6-2, 11-9
Challenge Round: Wright, 4-6, 6-3, 6-2, 6-2 — Holcombe Ward, Holder
Challenge Round: Hobart, 4-6, 6-4, 7-9, 6-4, 6-4

77

TWENTY-SIXTH USLTA MEN'S SINGLES CHAMPIONSHIPS
The Casino, Newport, R.I., 1906

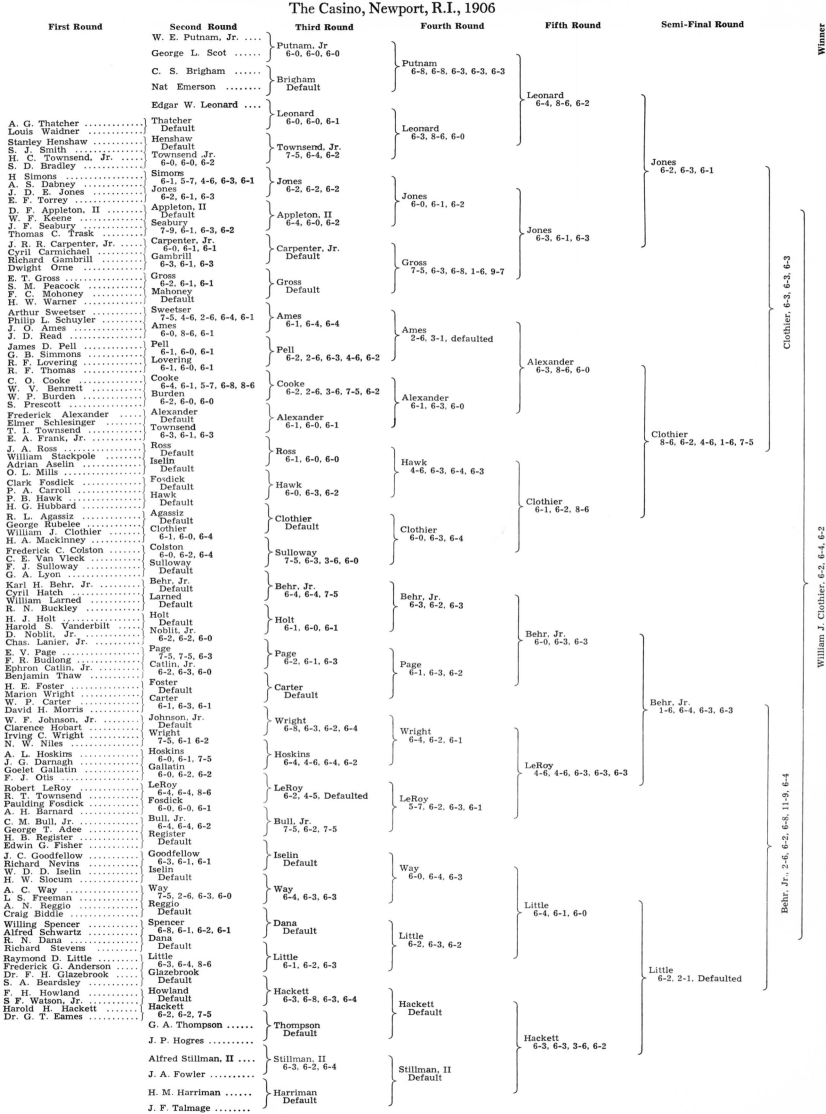

TWENTY-SEVENTH USLTA MEN'S SINGLES CHAMPIONSHIPS
The Casino, Newport, R.I., 1907

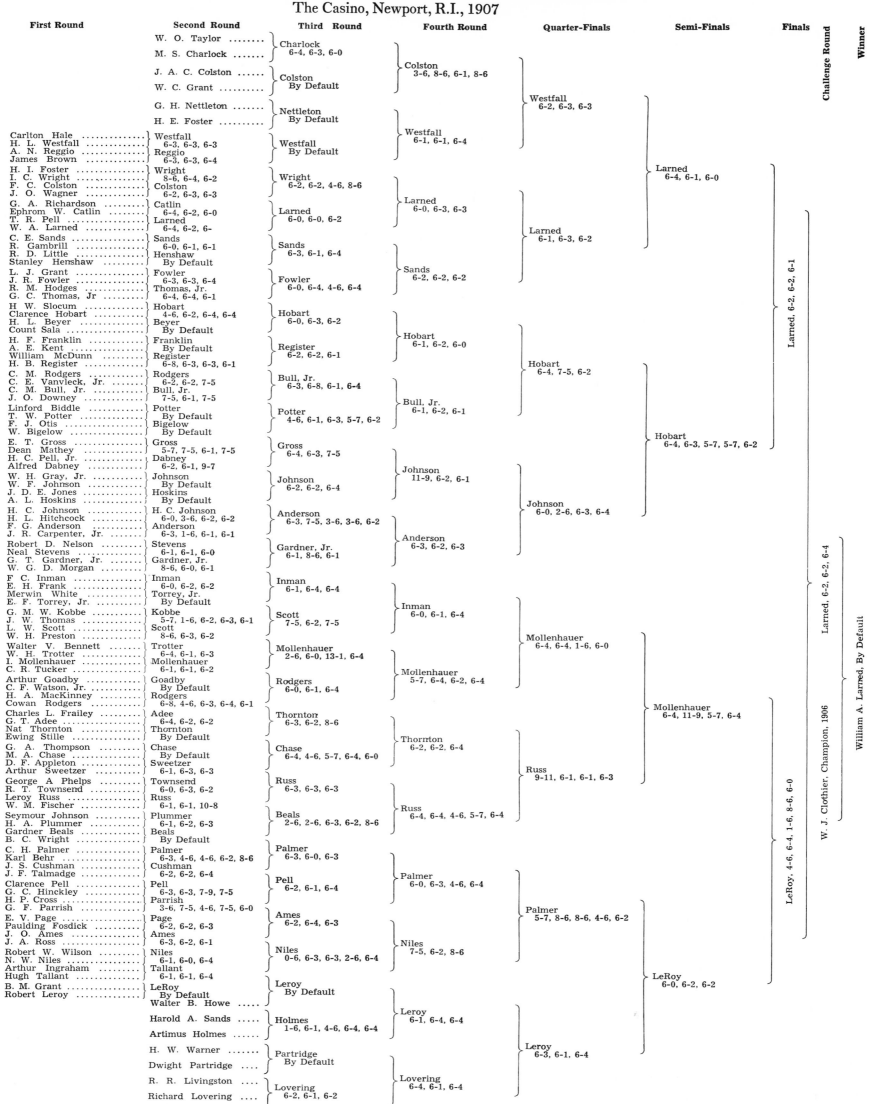

First Round | Second Round | Third Round | Fourth Round | Quarter-Finals | Semi-Finals | Finals | Challenge Round | Winner

W. O. Taylor — / Charlock 6-4, 6-3, 6-0
M. S. Charlock —
J. A. C. Colston — / Colston By Default
W. C. Grant —
G. H. Nettleton — / Nettleton By Default
H. E. Foster —
Colston 3-6, 8-6, 6-1, 8-6
Westfall 6-2, 6-3, 6-3

Carlton Hale — / Westfall 6-3, 6-3, 6-3
H. L. Westfall —
A. N. Reggio — / Reggio 6-3, 6-3, 6-4
James Brown —
Westfall By Default
Westfall 6-1, 6-1, 6-4

H. I. Foster — / Wright 8-6, 6-4, 6-2
I. C. Wright —
F. C. Colston — / Colston 6-2, 6-3, 6-3
J. O. Wagner —
Wright 6-2, 6-2, 4-6, 8-6

G. A. Richardson — / Catlin 6-4, 6-2, 6-0
Ephrom W. Catlin —
T. R. Pell — / Larned 6-4, 6-2, 6-
W. A. Larned —
Larned 6-0, 6-0, 6-2
Larned 6-0, 6-3, 6-3
Larned 6-4, 6-1, 6-0

C. E. Sands — / Sands 6-0, 6-1, 6-1
R. Gambrill —
R. D. Little — / Henshaw By Default
Stanley Henshaw —
Sands 6-3, 6-1, 6-4

L. J. Grant — / Fowler 6-3, 6-3, 6-4
J. R. Fowler —
R. M. Hodges — / Thomas, Jr. 6-4, 6-4, 6-1
G. C. Thomas, Jr —
Fowler 6-0, 6-4, 4-6, 6-4
Sands 6-2, 6-2, 6-2
Larned 6-1, 6-3, 6-2

H. W. Slocum — / Hobart 4-6, 6-2, 6-4, 6-4
Clarence Hobart —
H. L. Beyer — / Beyer By Default
Count Sala —
Hobart 6-0, 6-3, 6-2

H. F. Franklin — / Franklin By Default
A. E. Kent —
William McDunn — / Register 6-8, 6-3, 6-3, 6-1
H. B. Register —
Register 6-2, 6-2, 6-1
Hobart 6-1, 6-2, 6-0

C. M. Rodgers — / Rodgers 6-2, 6-2, 7-5
C. E. Vanvleck, Jr. —
C. M. Bull, Jr. — / Bull, Jr. 7-5, 6-1, 7-5
J. O. Downey —
Bull, Jr. 6-3, 6-8, 6-1, 6-4

Linford Biddle — / Potter By Default
T. W. Potter —
F. J. Otis — / Bigelow By Default
W. Bigelow —
Potter 4-6, 6-1, 6-3, 5-7, 6-2
Bull, Jr. 6-1, 6-2, 6-1
Hobart 6-4, 7-5, 6-2

E. T. Gross — / Gross 5-7, 7-5, 6-1, 7-5
Dean Mathey —
H. C. Pell, Jr. — / Dabney 6-2, 6-1, 9-7
Alfred Dabney —
Gross 6-4, 6-3, 7-5

W. H. Gray, Jr. — / Johnson By Default
W. F. Johnson —
J. D. E. Jones — / Hoskins By Default
A. L. Hoskins —
Johnson 6-2, 6-2, 6-4
Johnson 11-9, 6-2, 6-1

H. C. Johnson — / H. C. Johnson 6-0, 3-6, 6-2, 6-2
H. L. Hitchcock —
F. G. Anderson — / Anderson 6-3, 1-6, 6-1, 6-1
J. R. Carpenter, Jr. —
Anderson 6-3, 7-5, 3-6, 3-6, 6-2

Robert D. Nelson — / Stevens 6-1, 6-1, 6-0
Neal Stevens —
G. T. Gardner, Jr. — / Gardner, Jr. 8-6, 6-0, 6-1
W. G. D. Morgan —
Gardner, Jr. 6-1, 8-6, 6-1
Anderson 6-3, 6-2, 6-3
Johnson 6-0, 2-6, 6-3, 6-4

F. C. Inman — / Inman 6-0, 6-2, 6-2
E. H. Frank —
Merwin White — / Torrey, Jr. By Default
E. F. Torrey, Jr. —
Inman 6-1, 6-4, 6-4

G. M. W. Kobbe — / Kobbe 5-7, 1-6, 6-2, 6-3, 6-1
J. W. Thomas —
L. W. Scott — / Scott 8-6, 6-3, 6-2
W. H. Preston —
Scott 7-5, 6-2, 7-5
Inman 6-0, 6-1, 6-4

Walter V. Bennett — / Trotter 6-4, 6-1, 6-3
W. H. Trotter —
I. Mollenhauer — / Mollenhauer 6-1, 6-1, 6-2
C. R. Tucker —
Mollenhauer 2-6, 6-0, 13-1, 6-4

Arthur Goadby — / Goadby By Default
C. F. Watson, Jr. —
H. A. MacKinney — / Rodgers 6-8, 4-6, 6-3, 6-4, 6-1
Cowan Rodgers —
Rodgers 6-0, 6-1, 6-4
Mollenhauer 5-7, 6-4, 6-2, 6-4
Mollenhauer 6-4, 6-4, 1-6, 6-0

Charles L. Frailey — / Adee 6-4, 6-2, 6-2
G. T. Adee —
Nat Thornton — / Thornton By Default
Ewing Stille —
Thornton 6-3, 6-2, 8-6

G. A. Thompson — / Chase By Default
M. A. Chase —
D. F. Appleton — / Sweetzer 6-1, 6-3, 6-3
Arthur Sweetzer —
Chase 6-4, 4-6, 5-7, 6-4, 6-0
Thornton 6-2, 6-2, 6-4

George A Phelps — / Townsend 6-0, 6-3, 6-2
R. T. Townsend —
Leroy Russ — / Russ 6-1, 6-1, 10-8
W. M. Fischer —
Russ 6-3, 6-3, 6-3

Seymour Johnson — / Plummer 6-1, 6-2, 6-3
H. A. Plummer —
Gardner Beals — / Beals By Default
B. C. Wright —
Beals 2-6, 2-6, 6-3, 6-2, 8-6
Russ 6-4, 6-4, 4-6, 5-7, 6-4
Russ 9-11, 6-1, 6-1, 6-3

C. H. Palmer — / Palmer 6-3, 4-6, 4-6, 6-2, 8-6
Karl Behr —
J. S. Cushman — / Cushman 6-2, 6-2, 6-4
J. F. Talmadge —
Palmer 6-3, 6-0, 6-3

Clarence Pell — / Pell 6-3, 6-3, 7-9, 7-5
G. C. Hinckley —
H. P. Cross — / Parrish 3-6, 7-5, 4-6, 7-5, 6-0
G. F. Parrish —
Pell 6-2, 6-1, 6-4
Palmer 6-0, 6-3, 4-6, 6-4
Mollenhauer 6-4, 11-9, 5-7, 6-4

E. V. Page — / Page 6-2, 6-2, 6-3
Paulding Fosdick —
J. O. Ames — / Ames 6-3, 6-2, 6-1
J. A. Ross —
Ames 6-2, 6-4, 6-3

Robert W. Wilson — / Niles 6-1, 6-0, 6-4
N. W. Niles —
Arthur Ingraham — / Tallant 6-1, 6-1, 6-4
Hugh Tallant —
Niles 0-6, 6-3, 6-3, 2-6, 6-4
Niles 7-5, 6-2, 8-6
Palmer 5-7, 8-6, 8-6, 4-6, 6-2

B. M. Grant — / LeRoy By Default
Robert Leroy —
Walter B. Howe — / Leroy By Default
Harold A. Sands — / Holmes 1-6, 6-1, 4-6, 6-4, 6-4
Artimus Holmes —
Leroy 6-1, 6-4, 6-4

H. W. Warner — / Partridge By Default
Dwight Partridge —
R. R. Livingston — / Lovering 6-2, 6-1, 6-2
Richard Lovering —
Lovering 6-4, 6-1, 6-4
Leroy 6-3, 6-1, 6-4
LeRoy 6-0, 6-2, 6-2

Mollenhauer 6-4, 11-9, 5-7, 6-4
LeRoy, 4-6, 6-4, 1-6, 8-6, 6-0
Larned, 6-2, 6-2, 6-4
W. J. Clothier, Champion, 1906
Larned, 6-2, 6-2, 6-1
William A. Larned, By Default

TWENTY-EIGHTH USLTA MEN'S SINGLES CHAMPIONSHIPS
The Casino, Newport, R.I., 1908

Winner

W. A. Larned, 6-1, 6-2, 8-6

Challenge Round

Wright, 6-3 6-3, 6-3

W. A. Larned - Holder

Finals

Alexander, 7-5, 7-5, 6-3

Semi-Finals

Alexander, 6-1, 6-3, 6-1

Clothier, 6-1, 8-6, 6-0

Sixth Round

Alexander 7-5, 6-3, 6-4

Sulloway 1-6, 7-5, 6-0, 6-4

Touchard 6-8, 2-6, 7-2, 6-2, 7-5

Clothier 6-2, 6-2, 6-1

Fifth Round

Mathey 5-7, 6-4, 6-4, 6-3

Alexander 6-1, 8-6, 6-0

Martin 6-4, 5-7, 4-6, 6-1, 6-3

Sulloway 5-7, 4-6, 6-4, 7-5, 9-7

Touchard 6-4, 5-7, 8-6, 12-10

Westfall 6-1, 3-6, 6-1, 6-3

Church 6-2, 1-6, 6-4, 6-3

Clothier 6-2, 6-2, 6-1

Fourth Round

Hinckley 6-0, 6-0, 6-1

Mathey By default

Alexander 6-0, 6-3, 6-4

Beals By default

Martin By default

Hoskins 6-3, 6-4, 0-6, 6-4, 6-0

Sulloway 6-4, 6-2, 6-3

Leroy 6-2, 8-6, 6-4

Thornton 8-6, 6-3, 4-6, 7-5

Touchard By default

Westfall 7-5, 6-2, 6-2

Russ 6-2, 6-2, 6-3

Rosenbaum 6-3, 6-3, 3-6, 6-3

Church 6-4, 6-4, 6-3

Clothier 7-5, 6-2, 7-5

Ames 2-6, 6-4, 6-3, 6-3

Third Round

Wigham By default

Hinckley 6-0, 6-1, 6-0

Mathey 6-2, 6-0, 6-2

Pearson By default

Alexander 6-0, 6-2, 6-2

White By default

Beals By default

Martin 6-3, 6-2, 6-4

Grant By default

Pell, Jr. 8-6, 6-0, 6-2

Hoskins By default

Sulloway By default

Hawk 6-3, 6-3, 6-1

Leroy By default

Watrous 6-4, 6-0, 6-0

Wagner 7-5, 6-3, 2-6, 2-6, 6-1

Thornton 5-7, 8-6, 6-2, 7-5

Agassiz By default

Touchard 6-2, 6-3, 6-2

Westfall 7-5, 6-2, 7-5

Dabney 6-1, 6-3, 6-1

Jordan 6-0, 6-1, 6-0

Russ By default

Wilson By default

Rosenbaum By default

Ingraham 6-1, 6-8, 6-3, 6-3

Church 6-1, 6-0, 6-1

Clothier 6-2, 6-0, 6-3

Wright 6-8, 6-3, 6-2, 7-5

Ames 6-1, 7-5, 6-0

Biddle 6-3, 6-2, 6-2

Second Round

R. E. Wigham
Roderick Terry, Jr. ..... By default
S. E. Hinckley
W. D. Isglin
Goelet Gallatin
T. K. Miller, Jr.
Dean Mathey
W. L. Pate
R. H. Pearson
F. S. Seabury
F. B. Alexander
E. F. Torrey, Jr.
S. C. Williams
Merwin White
H. W. Stiness
Gardner Beals
Thos. Ridgway
H. C. Martin
Berrall Hoffman
B. M. Grant
Russell Sard
H. C. Pell, Jr.
A. L. Hoskins
H. J. Holt
F. G. Anderson
Frank Sulloway
Harold Rowe
P. B. Hawk
Cyril Hatch
Robert Leroy
J. J. Darragh
F. W. Watrous
H. W. Slocum
G. O. Wagner
L. H. Burt
N. Thornton
R. L. Agassiz
C. E. Sands
G. F. Touchard
D. W. Dillworth
A. L. Westfall
R. S. Hardy
A. G. Dabney
A. G. Gammell
E. W. Pittman
Wm. Jordan
Semp Russ
A. T. Baker
Robert W. Wilson
R. C. Seaver
G. T. Adee
Wm. Rosenbaum
Arthur Ingraham
Stanley Henshaw
G. M. Church

Day 10-8, 6-2, 6-1

Cushman By default

Clothier 6-2, 6-2, 6-3

Wright 6-1, 6-1, 6-1

Niles 6-0, 6-2, 6-0

Parrish By default

Ames 6-0, 6-3, 6-0

Biddle By default

Davidson, Jr.

First Round

G. H. Frank
F. L. Day
J. S. Cushman
Eugene Hale, Jr
R. D. Little
W. J. Clothier
H. E. Thomas
I. C. Wright
S. R. Fahnstock
N. W. Niles
L. F. Parrish
T. W. Potter
J. O. Ames
P. S. P. Randolph, Jr.
D. B. Miller
Craig Biddle
H. T. Peters

Emerson
6-2, 4-6, 6-2, 6-1

Jones
6-1, 6-1, 6-2

Wright
6-1, 6-1, 6-1

Torrance
6-4, 6-2, 6-3

Emerson
6-2, 4-6, 6-2, 6-1

Nettleton
6-1, 6-3, 6-3

Stevens
9-7, 6-1, 6-0

Jones
5-7, 2-6, 6-4, 6-2, 6-2

Wright
6-4, 7-5, 6-2

Hale
6-2, 7-5, 6-2

Torrance
6-3, 6-0, 6-1

James
3-6, 6-4, 6-2, 8-6

Emerson
6-2, 6-8, 6-3

Bull
6-2, 6-2, 8-6

Fielding
6-0, 6-1, 6-2

Nettleton
6-2, 6-0, 6-1

Stevens
6-4, 6-0, 6-1

Johnson
6-1, 6-0, 6-1

Jones
6-2, 6-3, 12-10

Tallant
6-3, 6-8, 6-3, 6-2

Johnson
6-1, 6-3, 6-1

Wright
6-1, 6-1, 6-2

Hale
0-6, 6-0, 6-8, 9-7, 7-5

Gambrill
By default

Butler
2-6, 4-6, 6-1, 6-3, 6-0

Torrance
6-2, 7-5, 6-3

Stillman
6-0, 6-1, 6-8, 6-1

James
6-1, 6-4, 6-3

Colston — By default — 6-0, 6-3, 6-3
Blair — Emerson — 8-6, 7-9, 5-7, 7-5
Emerson — By default
Emerson — By default — 5-7, 7-5, 6-4, 6-1
Inman — By default
Inman — Livingston — 6-1, 6-2, 6-1
By default
Bull, Jr. — By default
Bull, Jr. — Whitney — 6-2, 2-6, 3-6, 6-3, 6-0
By default — 6-4, 6-0, 6-3
V. Sorchan — Clarke
C. Clarke — Fielding — By default
M. Fielding — By default
L. H. Waldner — Jennings — By default
L. C. Jennings — Nettleton
H. C. Davis — By default
G. H. Nettleton — 6-2, 6-1, 6-2
E. V. Page — Thayer — By default
A. T. Baker — Stevens — By default
A. D. Thayer
R. Stevens — By default
T. S. Tailer — Penniman — By default
B. Penniman — Johnson — By default
R. Brooks — By default
S. Johnson — Johnson — By default
F. W. Burnham — By default
H. C. Johnson — Jones — By default
G. A. Thompson — By default
T. R. Pell — Jones — By default
J. D. E. Jones — By default
G. W. C. Thomas — Tallant — 6-3, 6-3, 6-4
H. Tallant — Charlock — By default
M. S. Charlock — By default
J. S. Phipps — Johnson — 3-6, 6-4, 6-4, 6-1
R. H. Palmer — Cooke — 6-3, 6-3, 6-4
W. F. Johnson
C. C. Cooke — Wright — 6-3, 6-1, 6-4
E. Stille — Connell — By default
B. C. Wright
M. G. Chace — Palmer
W. H. Connell — Johnson — 6-3, 6-8, 6-4, 2-6, 6-1
R. Palmer — Hale
N. Johnson — 6-1, 6-1, 6-0
S. W. Merrihew — Allison — 6-3, 6-4, 6-1
S. B. French, Jr. — Gambrill — By default
G. C. Allison
C. R. Frailey — Butler — By default
E. K. MacEnroe — Babcock — By default
W. Gambrill
H. M. Harriman — Torrance — 6-3, 6-3, 6-3
A. C. Butler — Trotter — 8-6, 6-1, 6-4
M. Babcock
T. V. P. Knapp — Stillman — 6-0, 6-1, 6-1
H. Torrance, Jr. — Mackinney — 8-6, 6-1, 6-0
B. Buckwalter
A. Thurber — Thomas — 6-2, 6-2, 3-6, 6-1
W. H. Trotter — James — By default
A. Stillman, 2nd
W. D. Bourne
H. A. Mackinney
D. F. Appleton
E. W. Donn, Jr.
R. W. Thomas
R. L. James
H. R. Fortescue

T. C. Trask
J. A. C. Colston
E. S. Blair
Geo. A. Phelps
Lydig Hoyt
N. Emerson
F. N. Inman
W. S. Temis
C. G. Plimpton
R. R. Livingston
C. M. Bull, Jr.
P. M. Lydig
Doneldson Nickols
E. H. Whitney

TWENTY-NINTH USLTA MEN'S SINGLES CHAMPIONSHIPS
The Casino, Newport, R.I., 1909

First Round
H. G. Simmons
W. L. Jones
R. T. Gaunt
W. O. Manice
G. T. Adee
C. Woodward
Richard Stevens
Geo. Brooke, Jr.
J. F. Darragh
H. W. H. Powell, Jr.
W. H. Connell
H. C. Martin
W. B. Cragin, Jr.
W. W. Finley, Jr.
I. M. Thomas
R. A. McCloud
A. S. Cassils
Suydam Cutting
Goodwin Hobbs
C. Amory
Carl Gardner
G. C. Hinckley
Ewing Taylor
C. T. Porter
N. W. Niles, Jr.
Sydney Beals
A. N. Reggio
Clarence Hobart
J. D. E. Jones
A. G. Neargaard
A. G. Thatcher
J. P. Snow
G. O. Wagner
S. P. Pell

Second Round
W. D. Bourne
Karl H. Behr
N. Wadsworth
Frank Soule
N. M. Vose
H. Alexander
Chas. E. Sands
Thomas Blumer
H. W. Slocum
G. A. Thompson
Carman Runyan
N. C. Peebles
G. F. Parrish
F. R. Hughes
A. S. Dabney, Jr.
W. J. Clothier
Chas. O. Cooke
Wm. Grosvenor
J. N. DuBarry, 2nd
E. M. Sheppard
H. D. Kirkover
Paulding Fosdick
F. T. Thomas
Henry R. Scott
E. H. Whitney
S. M. Sinsabaugh
R. L. Oakley
W. Rosenbaum
H. A. MacKinney
Frank W. Paul, Jr.
G. S. Groesbeck
H. W. Stiness
Stanley Henshaw
E. H. Frank, Jr.
Edgar F. Leo
G. W. Knowlton
Thomas C. Bundy
W. V. Bennett
Ezra Gould
G. M. Church
Seymour Johnson
G. Brock Smith
Gordon Douglas
Norman Johnson
E. T. Cross
H. W. Ballou

Simmons — By default
Gaunt 6-1, 6-3, 6-0
Adee — By default
Stevens — By default
Powell 6-3, 4-6, 6-4, 6-3
Martin 6-0, 6-3, 8-6
Cragin 6-0, 6-0, 6-1
Thomas 3-6, 6-4, 6-1, 6-4
Cutting 6-2, 6-2, 6-4
Hobbs — By default
Hinckley — By default
Taylor 4-6, 6-2, 6-4, 6-3
Niles — By default
Reggio — By default
Neargaard — By default
Snow — By default
Millett — By default
Pell — By default

Third Round
Behr 6-2, 6-0, 6-1
Wadsworth 6-0, 6-2, 9-2
Vose — By default
Sands — By default
Slocum — By default
Peebles — By default
Hughes — By default
Clothier — By default
Cooke 6-1, 6-0, 6-2
Sheppard 6-2, 6-1, 6-0
Fosdick — By default
Scott 6-2, 6-2, 6-0
Whitney 7-5, 6-2, 6-1
Rosenbaum — By default
MacKinney 8-6, 7-5, 6-3
Groesbeck — By default
Henshaw 6-0, 6-1, 6-2
Leo 6-2, 7-5, 6-3
Bundy 6-1, 6-3, 6-1
Church 7-5, 6-1, 6-3
Smith 4-6, 6-3, 3-6, 6-3, 6-2
Johnson — By default
Ballou — By default
Gaunt 4-8, 8-6, 6-0, 2-6, 6-3
Stevens 3-6, 6-2, 9-7, 6-1
Martin 6-3, 6-2, 6-4
Cragin 6-0, 6-0, 6-0
Cutting 6-1, 6-0, 6-0
Hinckley 7-5, 6-2, 3-6, 4-6, 6-2
Niles 6-3, 6-1
Neargaard — By default
Pell 6-3, 6-4, 6-1

Fourth Round
Behr 6-4, 1-6, 6-2, 6-1
Sands 6-1, 6-2, 6-4
Slocum 6-3, 3-6, 7-5, 6-3
Clothier — By default
Cooke 6-0, 6-0, 7-5
Scott 7-5, 7-5
Whitney — By default
MacKinney 6-2, 8-6, 6-2
Henshaw 7-5, 3-6, 6-4, 6-3
Bundy 4-6, 6-1, 7-5, 6-3
Johnson 6-4, 6-8, 6-3, 6-2
Gaunt 6-2, 6-4, 6-1
Stevens — By default
Cragin 9-7, 6-4, 6-4
Niles — By default
Pell 6-2, 6-2, 6-1

Fifth Round
Behr — By default
Clothier 8-6, 6-3, 6-4
Scott
Whitney 5-7, 6-2, 6-0, 8-6
Bundy 6-2, 6-3, 6-1
Johnson 5-7, 6-4, 6-3, 6-1
Cragin 3-6, 6-0, 6-2, 6-3
Pell 3-6, 6-4, 3-6, 6-4, 8-6

Sixth Round
Clothier 2-6, 6-2, 6-3, 6-4
Whitney 5-7, 6-0, 6-2, 6-3
Bundy 6-0, 6-0, 6-1
Cragin 2-6, 6-2, 6-4, 6-3

Semi-Finals
Clothier 6-1, 7-5, 6-4
Bundy 6-1, 7-5, 6-2

Finals
Clothier 6-3, 6-3, 6-8, 7-5

Challenge Round
Clothier 7-5, 6-4, 9-11, 6-3
W. A. Larned, Champion, 1909

Winner
W. A. Larned 6-1, 6-2, 5-7, 1-6, 6-1

Championship Draw

Winner: McLoughlin, 6-3, 4-6, 7-5, 6-2

Entrants
- J. A. Williams
- G. P. Gardner, Jr.
- Wm. F. Keene
- C. C. Pell
- P. B. Hawk
- J. O. Ames
- F. C. Colston
- E. W. Donn, Jr.
- S. W. Merrihew
- Andrew Winsor
- W. F. Johnson
- O. H. Hinck
- W. L. Pate
- S. F. Bain
- E. F. Torrey, Jr
- Louis J. Grant
- Walter Roberts
- W. C. Grant
- R. Terry, Jr.
- G. Rushmore
- E. P. Larned
- Carleton Hale
- D. W. Dilworth
- Thomas Slidell
- W. L. Stewart
- Robert Leroy
- C. L. Johnston, Jr.
- R. H. Palmer
- C. F. Watson
- Hugh Tallant
- H. C. Pell, Jr.
- Bayard Rives
- P. S. P. Randolph
- Rowland Hazard
- A. E. Peterson
- M. E. McLoughlin
- Joseph G. Willis
- Melville H. Long
- F. M. Harris
- C. S. Mills
- T. C. Trask
- G. A. L. Dionne
- C. M. Bull, Jr.
- G. W. Pike
- J. S. Seabury
- R. W. Thomas
- George Hollister
- Alfred Stillman
- L. T. Wallis
- J. C. Neely, Jr.
- R. C. Seaver
- F. P. Williams
- F. C. Inman
- C. G. Plimpton
- W. S. Patten
- Richard Bishop
- A. A. Gammell
- T. W. Potter
- C. King
- Ewing Stille
- G. A. Phelps
- Dr. J. C. Kopf
- Chas. S. Rogers
- D. Woodward
- F. N. Burnham
- F. J. Sulloway
- Gardner Beals
- A. T. Baker
- G. McFadden, Jr.
- G. C. Keeler
- R. Gambrill
- G. F. Touchard
- D. Meyer
- Peter D. Martin
- Charles Runyan
- S. B. French, 2nd
- S. H. Pendergast
- S. H. Boshell
- Basil Wagner
- Bunyan Colie
- George Leamy

First Round
- Williams — 6-1, 6-0, 6-2
- Gardner — by default
- Hawk — 8-6, 1-6, 1-6, 7-5, 8-6
- Colston — 6-3, 6-4, 6-4
- Johnson — 6-0, 6-1, 6-1
- Hinck — 6-2, 6-1, 6-3
- Bain — 8-6, 3-6, 6-4, 1-6, 6-2
- Roberts — 6-3, 6-0, 6-1
- Grant — by default
- Larned — by default
- Dilworth — by default
- Slidell — by default
- Johnston — 6-3, 12-10, 4-6, 3-6, 6-4
- Palmer — by default
- Pell — by default
- Rives — by default
- Hazard — by default
- McLoughlin — 6-1, 6-2, 6-2
- Long — 6-4, 6-4
- Trask — 6-0, 6-2, 6-0
- Bull — 6-2, 6-1, 3-6, 6-0
- Seabury — 4-6, 7-5, 6-4, 6-0
- Thomas — by default
- Stillman — 8-10, 6-1, 10-8, 6-4
- Seaver — 6-0, 6-4, 6-4
- Inman — by default
- Plimpton — by default
- Gammell — by default
- King — 2-6, 6-4, 6-4, 6-4
- Stille — by default
- Rogers — 6-1, 6-4, 6-3
- Burnham — 6-3, 6-3, 6-0
- Sulloway — 6-3, 6-4, 6-1
- Baker — by default
- Gambrill — 6-0, 6-0, 6-0
- Touchard — by default
- Runyan — by default
- Pendergast — 6-1, 6-0, 6-0
- Wagner — 6-3, 6-1, 6-2
- Colie — by default

Second Round
- Colston — 6-2, 3-6, 6-1, 7-5
- Johnson — 6-1, 6-4, 6-1
- Larned — 6-2, 6-0, 6-4
- Palmer — 6-4, 6-2, 6-3
- McLoughlin — 6-3, 6-1, 6-1
- Long — 6-3, 6-4, 6-0
- Bull — 2-6, 6-2, 6-2, 6-4
- Stillman — by default
- Inman — 6-0, 6-4, 6-4
- Plimpton — by default
- Stille — 6-1, 6-3, 3-3, default
- Rogers — by default
- Sulloway — 6-2, 6-1, 6-2
- Touchard — 6-0, 6-0, 6-4
- Pendergast — 6-0, 6-0, 6-3
- Wagner — 6-0, 6-1 6-1

Third Round
- Colston — 3-6, 6-4, 6-3, 1-6, 6-3
- Palmer — 5-7, 6-4, 6-2, 6-1
- McLoughlin — 7-5, 6-2, 5-7, 2-6, 10-8
- Bull — 8-10, 5-7, 6-0, 6-1, 6-4
- Inman — 6-4, 6-4, 6-3
- Rogers — 6-0, 7-5, 6-0
- Touchard — 6-3, 4-6, 6-4, 6-4
- Wagner — 6-4, 4-6, 6-2, 9-7

Fourth Round
- Palmer — 0-6, 6-4, 6-1, 5-7, 6-4
- McLoughlin — 6-4, 6-4, 6-2
- Inman — 6-4, 6-2, 6-2
- Touchard — 6-3, 6-2, 10-8

Semi-Finals
- McLoughlin — 7-5, 6-4, 6-2
- Touchard — 6-4, 4-6, 8-6, 6-2

Final
- McLoughlin — 6-3, 4-6, 7-5, 6-2

THIRTIETH USLTA MEN'S SINGLES CHAMPIONSHIPS
The Casino, Newport, R.I., 1910

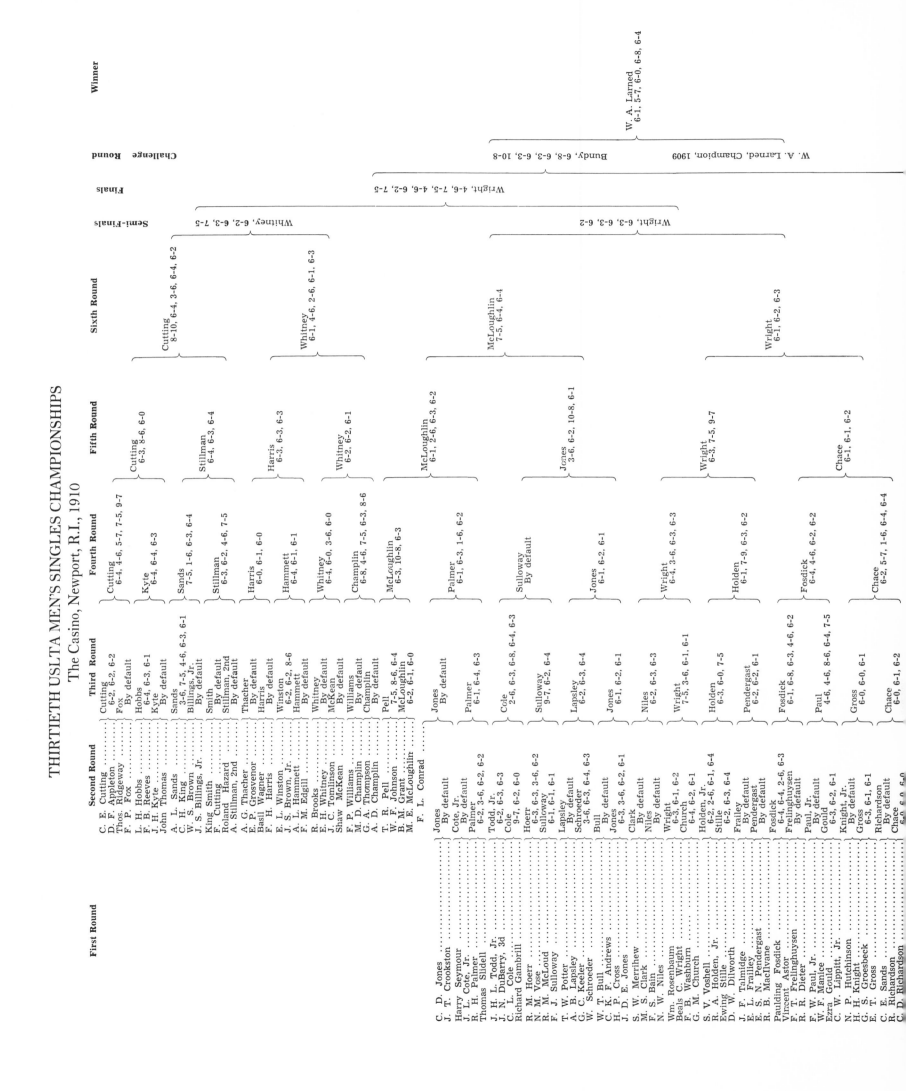

Tennis tournament draw (bracket). Reading from the left: entrants, then successive rounds with scores.

Entrants:

Norman Johnson
E. M. Sheppard
G. F. Parrish
Walter L. Pate
F. C. Inman
A. S. Dabney, Jr.
S. J. Wagstaff
C. L. Cooke
E. F. Torrey, Jr.
W. M. Washburn
Goodwin Hobbs
C. L. Sherman
T. W. Hendrick
G. S. Hinckley
R. R. Livingston
Russell Perkins
Alex. Yarnel
Dean Mathey
P. A. Degener
A. T. S. Baker
F. H. Burr
G. P. Touchard
P. B. Hawk
C. M. Bull, Jr.
H. A. MacKinney
W. E. Heyl, Jr
Wm. D. Bourne
A. N. Reggio
G. T. Adee
J. C. Cushman
F. F. Derham
J. P. Jackson
W. F. Symington
W. T. Cooke, Jr.
S. I. Beals
Wm. McCreath
Chas. Garland
F. M. Watrous
H. E. Colton
Alfred Codman
W. D. Siverd
F. T. Thomas
Thomas Jay
Gardner Beals
Walter Roberts
Douglas Campbell
L. N. Thomas
Edgar F. Leo

First round:

Sheppard 6-4, 6-8, 6-4, 6-4
Inman 6-4, 2-6, 3-6, 6-3, 7-5
Inman 6-4, 10-8, 6-4
Dabney, Jr. 6-2, 6-3, 6-1
Cooke 6-1, 6-1, 6-3
Washburn 6-2, 6-0, 6-2
Hendrick 6-1, 6-0, 6-1
Hinckley By default
Perkins By default
Mathey By default
Blumer 6-1, 6-3, 6-1
Burr By default
Bull Jr. By default
MacKinney By default
Reggio 6-1, 6-2, 6-1
Reggio 6-4, 6-2, 5-7, 6*4
Adee By default
Cushman By default
Gardner By default
Cooke, Jr. 6-2, 6-3, 6-2
Beals By default
Watrous 6-4, 2-6, 6-3, 6-2
Codman 6-2, 8-6, 10-8
Siverd 6-4, 6-1, 6-4
Beals 6-0, 6-2, 6-1
Roberts By default
Leo 12-10, 6-3, 3-6, 6-3

Second round:

Inman 8-6, 6-2, 6-1
Inman 6-4, 6-4, 9-7
Washburn 6-3, 6-3, 6-4
Hendrick 6-3, 6-2, 6-3
Mathey 6-0, 6-1, 6-0
Burr 6-2, 2-6, 6-2, 6-1
Bull 8-6, 11-9, 6-2
Reggio 6-3, 4-6, 8-6, 6-3
Gardner 6-2, 6-2, 6-3
Beals 6-0, 6-3, 6-2
Watrous 6-0, 6-2, 1-6, 6-3
Siverd 7-9, 9-7, 6-4, 6-4
Leo By default

Third round:

Inman 6-3, 6-4, 4-6, 6-3
Hendrick 5-7, 6-3, 6-0, 4-6, 6-4
Mathey 6-4, 9-7, 4-6, 6-4
Bull 6-8, 3-6, 6-2, 4-6, 7-5
Gardner 6-4, 6-2, 4-6, 6-4
Siverd 6-4, 6-4, 6-1
Colston 6-3, 6-1, 6-1
Charlock 6-2, 6-3, 3-6, 6-2
Thomas 6-3, 7-5, 6-2
Hoffman By default
Nickerson 7-9, 7-9, 6-2, 6-4, 6-3
Bundy 6-2, 6-4, 6-1
Cragin 6-0, 6-2, 6-0
Ames 3-6, 6-2, 6-2, 6-3
Biddle 6-3, 6-2, 6-1
Slocum 6-4, 6-3, 6-1

Fourth round:

Inman 6-3, 6-4, 4-6, 6-3
Mathey 6-4, 9-7, 4-6, 6-4
Gardner 6-4, 6-2, 4-6, 6-4
Colston 2-6, 6-1, 6-3, 6-4
Thomas 6-0, 6-2, 6-2
Bundy 6-4, 6-2, 6-4
Cragin 7-5, 6-3, 8-6

Fifth round:

Mathey 6-3, 6-2, 6-2
Colston 2-6, 6-2, 6-3, 6-4
Bundy 6-3, 6-4
Cragin 1-6, 6-4, 6-2, 6-4

Semifinals / Final:

Colston, 6-4, 8-6, 6-4
Bundy, 4-6, 6-3, 6-2
Bundy, 6-8, 6-1, 6-3, 6-3

Lower half entrants (right side):

F. T. Mauslan
F. C. Colston
L. H. Roper
R. C. Black
Acton Griscom
M. S. Charlock
R. Wilson
R. Griswold
G. T. Thomas, Jr.
H. L. Williamson
T. J. Mullin
F. B. Hoffman, Jr.
Robert Taylor
C. Amory
J. M. Holcombe, Jr.
J. H. Taylor
H. Nickerson
R. W. Grant
P. S. P. Randolph
T. C. Bundy
G. A. Lyons, Jr.
Stanley Henshaw
W. B. Gragin, Jr.
H. W. MacVickar
C. A. Gammell
M. A. Colton
Colket Caner
J. O. Ames
Louis N. Noel
Ewing Taylor
C. D. Winslow
F. W. Prichett
Dorr Newton
Craig Biddle
H. G. Simmons
H. W. Slocum
H. M. R. Kermochan

Lower half first round:

Colston 6-2, 6-2, 6-1
Roper 6-4, 6-2, 6-8, 2-6, 6-3
Charlock 6-1, 8-6, 6-3
Wilson 6-3, 6-2, 6-3
Thomas, Jr. By default
Hoffman, Jr. By default
Amory By default
Holcombe, Jr. 6-1, 6-1, 6-3
Nickerson By default
Bundy 6-0, 6-0, 6-0
Henshaw By default
Cragin, Jr. 6-0, 6-0, 6-0
Colton 3-6, 7-5, 8-6, 3-6, 6-4
Ames 6-2, 13-11, 6-0
Taylor By default
Prichett By default
Biddle By default
Slocum 6-2, 7-5, 6-1
Stiness By default
Kermochan By default

THIRTY-FIRST USLTA MEN'S SINGLES CHAMPIONSHIPS
The Casino, Newport, R.I., 1911

Winner

Larned
6-4, 6-2

Challenge Round

W. A. Larned - Holder

McLoughlin, 6-4, 4-6, 7-5, 6-3

Finals

McLoughlin, 6-2, 6-4, 6-3

Semi-Finals

Touchard 6-3, 6-4, 7-5

McLoughlin 6-1, 6-2, 6-4

Sixth Round

Gardner 3-6, 6-3, 6-4, 6-3

Touchard 6-1, 6-3, 6-4

Washburn 9-7, 5-7, 3-6, 6-2, 6-4

McLoughlin 6-4, 6-4, 8-6

Fifth Round

Gross 6-3, 3-6, 6-4, 6-3

Gardner 6-1, 6-2, 6-2

Touchard 6-4, 8-6, 6-2

Palmer 6-4, 4-6, 2-6, 8-6, 6-2

Little 6-0, 10-8, 6-8, 1-6, 6-4

Washburn 6-8, 6-3, 6-3

McLoughlin 6-3, 6-2, 7-5

Gardner, Jr. 6-3, 6-2, 6-2

Fourth Round

Slocum 6-3, 6-0, 6-2

Gross 6-3, 6-4, 6-2

Armstrong 6-3, 6-3, 6-2

Gardner 7-5, 6-3, 6-4

Pate 6-3, 6-4, 6-2

Touchard 6-3, 4-6, 5-7, 6-3, 6-1

Palmer 6-1, 6-2, 6-2

Ames 10-8, 6-1, 6-1

Little 6-4, 6-1, 6-3

Behr 6-3, 4-6, 6-2, 6-0

Slidwell 6-2, 6-0, 6-0

Washburn 6-3, 6-3, 6-4

Dabney 6-4, 6-0, 6-1

McLoughlin 6-2, 6-1, 6-1

Cutting 6-3, 6-2, 6-1

Gardner, Jr. 6-1, 6-0, 6-4

Third Round

Slocum 6-3, 6-1, 6-0
Curtis, 2nd 6-1, 2-6, 7-5, 1-6, 6-2
Roberts 7-5, 2-6, 13-11, 2-6, 6-2
Gross 6-1, 7-5, 6-3
Armstrong 6-1, 6-0, 6-1
Brown, Jr. 6-1, 6-1, 6-4
Burton 6-3, 3-6, 6-3, 6-1
Gardner 6-3, 6-3, 6-4
Pate Default
Peaslee
Touchard Default
Gates 6-1, 6-4, 6-1
Grier 3-6, 8-6, 6-0, 6-0
Palmer 6-2, 6-4, 1-6, 6-3
Dana 6-0, 6-1, 6-0
Ames 6-1, 6-2, 5-7, 5-7, 6-4
Little 6-1, 6-2, 6-2
Harris 6-0, 6-0, 6-0
Behr 6-0, 6-1, 6-3
Hall 6-0, 6-1, 6-1
Vose 6-3, 7-5, 6-0
Slidwell 6-2, 6-3, 6-0
Washburn 6-4, 6-4, 6-2
Middleton Default
Groesbeck 7-5, 6-0, 6-0
Dabney 6-2, 2-6, 6-2, 9-11, 6-1
Cole 6-2, 2-6, 6-2, 4-6, 6-3
McLoughlin Default
Cutting 6-1, 6-2, 6-1
Cushman 6-1, 7-5, 6-1
Ridgeway 6-1, 2-6, 7-5, 6-4
Gardner, Jr.

Second Round

H. W. Slocum
S. C. Adams
L. Curtis, 2nd
A. S. Cassils
Walter Roberts
F. B. Washburn
E. T. Gross
A. L. Sands
J. J. Armstrong
C. S. Beck
J. S. Brown, Jr.
W. V. Astor
W. C. Burton
R. C. Bray
C. R. Gardner
F. M. Watrous
Walter Pate
F. W. Paul
F. W. Peaslee
H. C. Simmons
G. F. Touchard
J. H. MacVeagh
H. C. Gates
R. S. Lyman
G. W. Grier
R. Stevenson
R. F. Palmer

Rosenbaum Default
Dana
Pepper Default
Nelson 6-1, 6-3, 6-3
Ames 6-0, 6-2, 6-2
Little Default
Fall
Bell Default
Harris Default
Schwengers Default
Behr 6-4, 4-6, 6-4, 6-4
Hall Default
Robinson 4-6, 6-4, 5-7, 6-3, 8-6
Emmons Default
Vose Default
Slidwell Default
Thomas Default
Cragin 6-3, 6-1, 6-3
Washburn Default
Woods Default
Middleton Default
Webber 6-3, 1-6, 6-1, 7-5
Groesbeck 6-3, 6-0
Larned 6-0, 6-0, 6-1
Dabney 6-1, 6-1, 6-4
Billings, Jr.
Cole 6-1, 6-3, 6-1
McLoughlin 6-2, 6-4, 6-3
Pell Default
Roche 7-5, 6-2, 6-3
Cutting 6-2, 6-2, 6-1
Fosdick 6-1, 6-2, 6-1
Cushman 6-1, 6-0, 6-1
Law Default
Ridgeway 6-3, 10-8, 6-3
Gardner, Jr. Default

First Round

W. Rosenbaum
G. F. Parrish
R. D. Dana
Norman Johnson
O. H. P. Pepper
A. G. Kennedy, Jr.
J. G. Nelson
T. O. Sailor
R. B. McClave
R. D. Little
F. O. French
D. Noblit, Jr.
Alfred Bell
E. W. Palmer
F. H. Harris
W. R. Harper
R. P. Schwengers
L. R. Brown
Karl Behr
Richard Stevens
W. M. Hall
F. W. Bates
F. W. Robinson
L. H. Hobbs
N. H. Emmons
M. T. Wendall
N. M. Vose
R. C. Crouse
Thomas Slidwell
G. T. Hill, Jr.
H. E. Thomas
Haven Clark
A. S. Cragin
Ewing Stille
W. M. Washburn
E. S. Carrol
E. H. Woods
P. H. Harrower
Elliott Middleton
G. T. Adee
H. W. Webber
G. L. Fralley
G. S. Groesbeck
B. M. Phillips
E. P. Larned
A. D. Champlin
A. D. Dabney
A. W. Merriam
J. S. Billings, Jr.
E. S. Cole
C. L. Peck
E. H. Frank, Jr.
M. E. McLoughlin
G. H. Nettleton
T. R. Pell
M. G. Chace
Frank Roche
W. O'D Iselin
C. S. Cutting
W. E. Heyl, Jr.
Paulding Fosdick
J. S. Cushman
J. W. Lippincott
B. C. Law
G. B. Post, 3rd
Thomas Ridgeway
S. W. Merrihew
G. P. Gardner, Jr.
P. Cummings, Jr.

Quarterfinals

- Andrews 6-1, 6-4, 4-6, 6-2
- Niles 6-1, 6-1, 6-2
- Bundy 8-6, 3-6, 6-8, 6-1, 7-5
- Jones 6-0, 8-10, 6-4, 6-1

Round of 16

- Andrews 6-1, 6-1, 6-4
- Wright 6-3, 6-4, 6-4
- Niles 6-4, 6-2, 3-6, 6-3
- Caner 6-3, 6-3, 6-3
- Bundy 6-3, 6-4, 6-4
- Church 6-3, 6-1, 8-6
- Bull, Jr. 4-6, 6-3, 6-4, 6-3
- Jones 6-4, 6-0, 6-0

Round of 32

- Andrews 6-3, 6-2, 6-4
- Carpenter 6-1, 6-1, 6-4
- Lyon, Jr. 6-3, 6-1, 6-3
- Wright 6-0, 6-1, 6-2
- Niles 6-3, 6-0, 6-3
- Long 6-3, 3-6, 7-5, 6-1
- Devereaux Default
- Caner 6-4, 6-2, 6-2
- Bundy 6-1, 6-2, 0-6, 6-3
- Burden 6-0, 6-0, 6-2
- MacKinney 6-4, 4-6, 6-2, 10-8
- Church 6-2, 6-0, 6-2
- Hammett 6-2, 4-6, 6-4, 6-3
- Bull, Jr. 6-4, 6-8, 6-8, 7-5, 6-4
- Leonard 6-2, 6-4, 6-3
- Jones 6-3, 6-2, 6-1

Round of 64

- Andrews Default
- Bartholomew Default
- Carpenter, Jr. 6-2, 6-2, 6-3
- Pearson 7-5, 2-6, 8-6, 6-3
- Lyon, Jr. 0-6, 6-0, 6-1, 6-0
- Brown, Jr. 3-6, 6-4, 6-2, 6-2
- Wright 6-0, 6-1, 6-1
- Anderson 6-0, 6-1, 6-0
- Niles 6-0, 6-0, 6-0
- Wightman 6-0, 6-0, 6-0
- Waidner 6-1, 6-0, 6-2
- Long 6-3, 6-2, 6-4
- Devereaux Default
- Nicholl 4-6, 0-6, 10-8, 6-1, 6-0
- Whiting 6-4, 6-1, 6-0
- Caner 6-4, 6-2, 6-3
- Mathey 2-6, 8-6, 7-5, 7-5
- Bundy 6-3, 6-0, 7-5
- Burden 6-1, 6-0, 6-0
- Schroeder
- MacKinney 11-9, 6-3, 6-2
- Adams Default
- Church 6-1, 6-1, 6-1
- Wagner 6-1, 7-5, 5-7, 6-2
- Hammett 6-2, 4-6, 6-4, 6-3
- Grant Default
- Johnson 6-0, 6-3, 6-4
- Bull, Jr. 6-2, 6-2, 6-2
- Leonard 7-9, 6-0, 6-2, 2-6, 6-2
- Izard 8-6, 6-4, 6-3
- Biddle 6-3, 6-0, 6-1
- Jones 6-4, 6-0, 6-0

First round

- Default
- Andrews 6-0, 6-3, 6-2
- Carroll Default
- Bartholomew Default
- Carpenter, Jr. 6-0, 6-0, 6-3
- Beals Default
- Connell 6-1, 6-3, 6-1
- Pearson 6-3, 5-7, 6-2, 4-6, 6-2
- Lipscom Default
- Lyon, Jr. 6-4, 6-3, 6-2
- Josephs 6-3, 6-3, 6-3
- Brown, Jr. Default
- Hunt Default
- Wright 6-0, 6-1, 6-0
- Lloyd Default
- Anderson 6-1, 7-5, 6-2
- Niles Default
- Chormley Default
- Williams 6-1, 6-3, 6-0
- Wightman 6-0, 6-1, 6-2
- Gates Default
- Waidner 6-1, 6-0, 6-2
- Minot Default
- Long Default
- Devereaux 6-3, 6-0, 6-0
- Leonard Default
- Nicholl Default
- Charlock Default
- Peck Default
- Whiting Default
- Gallatin Default
- Caner Default
- Mathey Default
- Whitney 6-1, 6-4, 6-2
- Bundy 4-6, 6-4, 6-0, 6-2
- Seaver 6-1, 5-7, 6-3, 6-4
- Weeden Default
- Burden Default

Entrants

- A. P. Lapsley
- C. D. Richardson
- C. K. F. Andrews
- C. L. Neibel
- E. S. Carroll
- H. C. Johnson
- G. H. Bartholomew
- C. E. Sands
- J. R. Carpenter, Jr.
- William D. Bourne
- Gardner Beals
- Spencer Heaton
- W. H. Connell
- C. W. Smith
- S. W. Pearson
- F. J. Hall
- C. E. Lipscom
- Richard Bishop
- G. A. Lyon, Jr.
- F. Freylinghuysen
- D. C. Josephs
- J. M. Thomas
- J. N. Brown, Jr.
- W. P. Hunt
- J. C. Tomlinson
- Beals C. Wright
- J. B. Alexander
- Edward Lloyd, Jr.
- A. E. Thurber
- W. S. Anderson
- H. E. Colton
- N. W. Niles
- C. M. Bull
- H. L. Ghormley
- G. A. Thompson
- William Williams
- L. J. Grant
- G. W. Wightman
- W. F. Low
- R. C. Gates
- G. I. Drew
- L. H. Waidner
- Goodwin Hobbs
- Sedgwick Minot
- O. B. Marshall
- M. H. Long
- L. Wilmerding, Jr.
- J. C. Devereaux
- Godwin Ordway
- Cyril Hatch
- J. S. Nicholl
- W. J. Clothier
- M. S. Charlock
- T. P. Williams
- H. D. Peck
- P. Ingraham
- M. T. Whiting
- L. N. Walthall
- G. Gallatin
- F. J. Bassett
- G. C. Caner
- Philip Winsor
- Dean Mathey
- E. H. Whitney
- D. F. Appleton
- T. C. Bundy
- F. C. Inman
- R. C. Seaver
- C. R. Fisher
- R. B. Weeden
- C. F. Cutting

- W. Schroeder
- E. F. Woods
- H. A. MacKinney
- R. C. Black
- Carlton Adams
- E. F. Torrey, Jr.
- G. M. Church
- J. P. Jackson
- Basil Wagner
- Q. A. S. Mackean
- A. D. Hammett
- S. Henshaw
- B. M. Grant
- P. B. Hawk
- W. F. Johnson
- F. W. Pelzer
- C. M. Bull, Jr.
- E. Pendergast
- C. R. Leonard
- W. L. O'Brion
- W. B. Izard
- L. S. Freeman
- Craig Biddle
- G. R. Nichols, Jr.
- R. C. McCloud

87

THIRTY-SECOND USLTA MEN'S SINGLES CHAMPIONSHIPS
The Casino, Newport, R.I., 1912

Winner

M. E. McLoughlin
3-6, 2-6, 6-2, 6-4, 6-2

Finals

McLoughlin, 8-6, 6-2, 3-6, 6-4

Semi-Finals

McLoughlin 6-4, 5-7, 6-4, 3-6, 6-3

Clothier 7-5, 6-0, 6-1

Preliminary Round	First Round	Second Round	Third Round	Fourth Round	Fifth Round
	Craig Biddle	Biddle 6-1, 6-1, 6-1	Biddle 6-0, 6-2, 6-1	Williams 7-9, 6-3, 6-0, 6-0	Williams 6-1, 6-1, 6-1
	W. D. Brownell	Maynard 6-1, 6-1, 6-4			
	R. S. Maynard		Williams, Jr. 6-3, 6-2, 6-1		
	Ezra Gould	Williams, Jr. 6-0, 6-3, 6-2			
	R. N. Williams, Jr.	Porter 6-0, 6-1, 6-2			
	N. M. Vose				
	Seaton Parker	Hall	Hall 6-3, 6-3, 6-2	Herd 6-4, 7-5, 7-5	
	J. N. DuBarry, 3rd				
	W. M. Hall				
	H. W. Stiness	Gatewood 4-6, 2-6, 6-4 7-5, 6-3	Herd 6-4, 6-3, 2-6, 6-3		
	R. D. Gatewood				
	H. G. Smith	Herd			
	Clifton B. Herd				
	Jerry H. Weber	Kuhn Default	Charlock 6-0, 6-0, 6-2	Slocum 6-2, 6-0, 6-2	McLoughlin 6-1, 6-4, 6-2
	W. S. Kuhn				
	H. E. Thomas	Charlock 6-1, 6-1, 6-2			
	Miles S. Charlock	Hubbard, Jr.			
	Abbott Phillips				
	J. F. Hubbard, Jr.	Slocum 6-0, 6-1, 6-1	Slocum 6-4, 6-0, 3-6, 6-2		
	W. G. Parsons				
	H. W. Slocum	Seabury 15-13, 5-7, 6-2, 6-3			
	Ewing Stille				
	R. W. Seabury	Washburn Default	McLoughlin 6-4, 6-2, 6-1	McLoughlin 6-1, 6-2, 6-3	
	H. G. Simmons	McLoughlin Default			
	F. B. Washburn				
	Whitney Preston	Montgomery 6-0, 6-2, 6-1	Montgomery Default		
	M. E. McLoughlin				
	F. B. McNair	Kennedy, Jr. Default			
	J. R. Montgomery				
	A. E. Kennedy, Jr.	Williams 6-2, 6-1, 6-1	Whiting, 2-6, 4-6, 6-2, 12-10, 13-11	Preston 9-7, 6-4, 6-3	Clothier 6-1, 6-1, 6-1
	R. Auspitzer				
	J. A. Williams	Whiting Default			
	Geoffrey Taylor				
	M. J. Whiting	Preston Default	Preston 6-0, 3-6, 6-4, 6-4		
	Edgar Leonard	Harvey 6-1, 6-2, 6-4			
	Whiting Preston				
	H. H. Braley				
	H. D. Harvey	Fralley Default	Beals 6-3, 6-1, 6-3	Clothier 6-1, 8-6, 6-0	
	R. Griswold	Beals Default			
	C. L. Fralley				
	C. M. Amory	Williams 6-2, 9-7, 6-3	Clothier 7-5, 6-4, 12-10		
	Gardner Beals	Clothier 6-1, 6-2, 6-1			
	Allen Tobey				
	E. P. Larned				
	Preston Gibson	Man. Jr.			
	William J. Clothier				
Edward M. Pickman	John Reece	Clothier 6-0, 6-1, 6-0			
W. P. Burden	Pickman 7-5, 4-6, 4-6, 6-1, 7-5				
A. H. Man, Jr.	Man, Jr.		Gardner, Jr. 6-4, 6-1, 4-6, 6-3	Gardner 6-3, 4-6, 4-6, 6-1, 6-3	Little 6-4, 7-5, 6-2
D. H. Codington	Default				
G. P. Gardner, Jr.	Gardner, Jr. 3-6, 6-2, 6-4, 6-3	Gardner, Jr. 6-2, 6-1, 6-2			
F. J. Sulloway					
G. C. Caner	Caner 4-6, 9-7, 6-2, 6-2				
H. Kleinschroth					
E. S. H. Pendergast	Pendergast 6-1, 6-3, 6-1	Niles	Niles 6-1, 6-4, 6-4		
A. D. Champlin	Niles 6-2, 6-0, 6-0				
N. W. Niles					
H. A. Mackinney					
Walter Roberts	Roberts 6-4, 6-2, 6-3	Evans		Little 6-0, 6-1, 6-0	
Rowland Evans, Jr.	Evans, Jr. 6-0, 6-1, 6-1				
F. M. Letson					
William D. Bourne	Bourne 6-4, 6-3, 3-6, 3-6, 6-3	Rosenbaum	Stevens 6-4, 6-4, 6-4		
C. S. Beck	Rosenbaum 6-3, 6-3, 6-2				
William Rosenbaum					
Hammatt Norton					
C. D. Jones	Jones 6-3, 6-1, 6-3	Stevens		Little 7-5, 6-2, 6-1	
F. W. Easton, Jr.	Stevens 6-0, 6-0, 6-2				
J. R. Quinn					
J. S. Brown, Jr.	Brown, Jr. 6-1, 6-3, 6-1	Little	Little 7-5, 6-2, 6-1		
C. L. Neibel	Little 6-3, 6-2, 6-1				
G. F. Touchard					
S. Miller, Jr.	Miller, Jr. Default	Dana			
W. H. Connell	Dana				
R. N. Dean					

Tournament Draw (reading bottom-to-top / left-to-right)

Final: Johnson, 4-6, 6-0, 6-3, 6-2

Semifinals: Behr 6-2, 6-2, 6-0 — Johnson 8-6, 6-2, 3-6, 6-3

First round (players)	Second round	Third round	Fourth round	Fifth round
E. W. Peaslee ... Default	Peaslee	McKim 4-6, 6-2, 11-13, 6-2	Bundy 6-0, 6-2, 6-4	Church Default
E. H. Rodgers, Jr. ... Devens, Jr. 1-6, 6-2, 6-2, 6-4	McKim			
A. L. Devens, Jr.				
R. A. McCloud ... McKim 3-6, 6-3, 6-4				
Witham L. McKim				
L. Curtis, 2nd ... Lipscomb Default				
C. E. Lipscomb				
W. L. Gilven				
W. L. Pate ... Pate 6-2, 6-3, 6-3	Pate 6-0, 6-0, 6-1	Bundy 6-0, 6-0, 6-2		
H. G. W. Wightman				
H. R. Boyer ... Boyer Default				
E. H. Miller				
R. L. Harte ... Baggs Default	Bundy 6-3, 6-1, 6-1			
Thomas C. Bundy ... Bundy Default				
G. T. Adee				
J. G. Nelson ... Nelson 6-2, 6-2, 2-6, 11-9	Church	Church 6-0, 6-3, 6-0	Church 6-4, 4-6, 6-1, 4-6, 6-1	
F. C. Colston ... Church Default				
G. M. Church				
R. H. Palmer				
S. Mckean ... Mckean Default	Mckean 6-2, 6-2, 6-3			
H. D. Carpenter				
Rex Crouse ... Crouse Default				
G. B. McKinney				
C. S. Cutting ... Cutting Default	Cutting 7-5, 6-3, 9-7	Cutting 6-2, 6-3, 6-4		
E. H. Frank, Jr.				
A. S. Cragin ... Cragin 6-4, 3-6, 6-4, 6-2				
Rowland Hazard				
H. B. Register ... Register 6-2, 6-1, 6-1	Register 6-4, 6-2, 6-0	Behr 6-2, 8-6, 6-4	Behr 6-3, 6-2, 6-2	Behr 7-5, 6-4, 6-4
E. B. Boyer ... E. F. Torrey				
Karl H. Behr ... Behr 6-1, 6-2, 6-3	Behr 6-1, 6-2, 6-3			
S. R. Smith				
A. D. Hammett ... Hammett	Hammett			
C. R. Leonard				
A. E. Kennedy ... Kennedy Default	Kennedy	Ward 6-4, 6-2, 7-5		
Dean Mathey				
V. D. Ward ... Ward Default	Ward Default			
S. T. Frelinghausen				
C. S. Rogers ... Rogers 6-0, 6-1, 6-4	Rogers 6-0, 6-1, 6-4	Rogers 6-1, 6-1, 6-1	Rogers 6-3, 6-0, 6-1	
William Dear				
Edward Law ... Law 6-2, 6-4, 6-2	Law 6-2, 6-4, 6-2			
P. W. Foster, Jr.				
R. Cowan ... Cowan 6-3, 6-2, 6-1	Cowan 6-3, 6-2, 6-1	Porter 2-6, 6-4, 6-2, 7-5		
R. C. Thayer				
C. T. Porter ... Parker 6-2, 2-6, 8-6, 6-3	Parker 6-2, 2-6, 8-6, 6-3			
Phillip Roberts				
H. W. Webber ... Webber 6-4, 2-6, 6-4, 6-3	Webber 6-4, 2-6, 6-4, 6-3	Johnson 6-1, 6-2, 6-2	Johnson 6-3, 6-0, 6-1	Johnson 6-4, 6-2, 6-1
S. W. Merrihew				
W. F. Johnson ... Johnson 6-2, 6-3, 6-4	Johnson 6-2, 6-3, 6-4			
W. M. Tilden				
F. W. Paul, Jr. ... Paul, Jr. 6-1, 6-3, 6-4	Paul, Jr. 6-1, 6-3, 6-4	Carpenter, Jr. 6-0, 6-8, 6-0, 6-1		
Murray Taylor				
J. R. Carpenter, Jr. ... Carpenter, Jr. Default	Carpenter, Jr. Default			
G. C. Adams				
J. S. Cushman ... Cushman Default	Cushman Default	Dabney 4-6, 6-1, 6-8, 6-3, 6-2	Dabney 6-1, 6-4, 4-6, 2-6	
J. O. Downey				
A. S. Dabney ... Dabney Default	Dabney Default			
F. H. Harris				
S. H. Voshell ... Voshell 6-1, 6-2, 6-0	Voshell 6-1, 6-2, 6-0	Inman 6-3, 9-7, 6-3		
G. W. Knowlton, Jr.				
F. C. Inman ... Inman 6-3, 6-2, 6-2	Inman 6-3, 6-2, 6-2			
A. L. Sands				
H. C. Johnson ... Johnson 6-1, 6-4, 6-1	Johnson 6-8, 6-3, 6-4, 6-2	Johnson 6-8, 6-3, 6-4, 6-2	Washburn 4-6, 6-2, 6-3, 9-7	Washburn 10-12, 6-4, 6-1, 6-3
G. W. Phillips				
H. Nickerson ... Nickerson 6-4, 6-0, 6-0	Nickerson			
M. R. Volek				
W. M. Washburn ... Washburn Default	Washburn Default	Washburn 2-6, 6-1, 7-5, 6-4		
H. Taylor				
W. B. Izard ... Izard 8-6, 6-1, 6-2	Izard 8-6, 6-1, 6-2			
F. R. Feitshans				
S. Henshaw ... Henshaw Default	Henshaw Default	Henshaw 4-6, 9-7, 6-4, 7-5	Seaver 6-1, 6-2, 6-3	
Beals C. Wright				
J. C. Devereaux ... Devereaux Default	Devereaux Default			
H. E. Colton				
H. L. Ewer ... Ewer 6-4, 6-3, 6-3	Ewer 6-4, 6-3, 6-3	Seaver 6-1, 6-2, 6-8, 6-1		
W. E. Heyl, Jr.				
R. C. Seaver ... Seaver 6-1, 6-1, 6-2	Seaver 6-1, 6-1, 6-2			
M. Hamilton				

THIRTY-THIRD USLTA MEN'S SINGLES CHAMPIONSHIPS

The Casino, Newport, R.I., 1913

First Round

Roberton Griswold
Charles Beck
J. W. Calvert
George Burgess
Wm. M. Johnston
George T. Adee
I. B. Shelley
William Blair
C. E. Lipscom
C. R. Leonard
G. C. Caner
Joseph Dwight
Baron K Von Lersner
E. C. Wilson
S. H. Voshell
Harold Hartshorn
G. F. Touchard
Walter Roberts
R. C. Seaver

Second Round

W. A. Thomson
F. W. Cole
C. L. Fralley
Harold Swain
H. H. Hackett
W. E. Huyl, Jr.
George Wightman
E. H. Diepholz
Leonard Beekman
Allan Tobey
Paulding Fosdick
D. D. Morgan
W. P. Burden
Leonard Thomas
L. Goldman
A. D. Champlin
G. P. Gardner, Jr.
Ewing Taylor
Ewing Stille
H C. Owen
R. U. N. Gambrill
Paul Sheldon
C. L. Childs
H. A. MacKinney
N. W. Niles
J R. Carpenter
N. M. Vose
W. L. McKim
Gardner Beals
A. H. Dutton
C. M. Buchanan
A. D. Hammett
Francis Roche
J. H. Weber
Alfred Dabney
P. A. Valle
Rowland Evans, Jr.
Richard Stevens
G. W. Phillips
E. P. Pearson
A. W. Merriam
Alfred Codman
H. C. Johnson
George M. Rushmore
Stewart A. Cushman
W. D. Kenyon
D. C. Josephs
W. M. Washburn
H. D. Harvey
C. S. Cutting
B. C. Law
F. E. Dixon
J. S. Cameron, Jr.
F. M. Harris
Griswold, 9-7, 9-7, 6-3
Geo. Burgess, 6-0, 6-2, 6-1
W. M. Johnston, By Default
Wm. Blair, 6-4, 6-4, 8-6
Lipscom, By Default
G. C. Caner, 6-1, 6-2, 6-3
E. C. Wilson, 6-2, 3-6, 6-1, 2-6, 4-5, default
Voshell, By Default
G. F. Touchard, 6-2, 6-0, 6-3
Williams

Third Round

Cole, By Default
Swain, 6-2, 6-4, 6-1
Huyl, By Default
Wightman, 6-3, 6-1, 6-1
Beekman, By Default
Beekman, 6-4, 6-3, 6-3
Fosdick, 6-4, 6-1, 6-0
W. F. Burden, 6-0, 6-2, 6-1
Champlin, By Default
Gardner, By Default
Owen, 3-6, 6-3, 6-8, 6-2, 10-8
Sheldon, By Default
MacKinney, 6-3, 6-0, 6-3
N. W. Niles, 6-2, 6-3, 6-1
McKim, 6-2, 6-3, 7-5
Beals, 6-0, 6-2, 6-3
Hammett, 6-3, 6-0, 6-2
Weber, 6-8, 8-6, 6-1, 6-2
Dabney, 6-0, 6-2, 6-0
Evans, 6-3, 6-4, 6-2
Phillips, 7-5, 2-6, 6-3, 7-5
Codman, By Default
H. C. Johnson, 6-3, 6-1, 6-0
Kenyon, 6-1, 6-3, 6-1
Washburn, 6-2, 6-1, 6-3
Cutting, 6-3, 6-3, 6-3
Law, 6-1, 6-3, 6-4
Cameron, By Default
Burgess, 6-4, 6-1, 6-0
Wm. Johnston, 6-3, 6-2, 6-2
Caner, By Default
Voshell, 6-2, 7-5, 6-1
Williams, 3-6, 6-4, 6-4, 1-6, 6-4, 7-5

Fourth Round

Cole, 6-1, 6-3, 6-1
Wightman, 6-3, 6-1, 6-1
Beekman, 6-0, 6-1, 6-0
Burden, 6-0, 6-1, 6-4
Gardner, 6-1, 6-2, 6-1
MacKinney, 6-3, 6-0, 6-2
Niles, 6-3, 6-1, 6-2
Beals, 8-6, 6-3, 6-1
Dabney, 12-10, 6-1, 6-4
Evans, 6-4, 6-4, 7-5
H. C. Johnson, 6-3, 6-4, 6-2
Washburn, 6-0, 6-0, 6-0
Law, 7-5, 6-4, 3-6, 6-3
Burgess, By Default
W. Johnston, 8-6, 6-1, 6-2
Williams, 6-2, 6-3, 3-6, 6-4

Fifth Round

Cole, 8-6, 6-1, 6-3
Beekman, 6-4, 7-5, 6-1
Gardner, 6-2, 6-3, 6-4
Niles, 6-2, 6-3, 6-4
Evans, 6-3, 6-1, 9-7
Washburn, 6-4, 6-3, 6-3
Law, 4-6, 6-0, 6-0, 6-3
Williams, 6-3, 6-4, 3-6, 8-6

Quarter Finals

Beekman, 3-6, 4-6, 7-5, 6-2, 6-3
Niles, 6-3, 6-4, 4-6, 6-1
Washburn, 6-2, 6-2, 2-6, 6-2
Williams, 6-4, 8-6, 6-1

Semi-Finals

Niles, 6-0, 9-7, 6-2
Williams, 6-1, 7-5, 6-3

Finals

Williams, 6-4, 7-5, 3-6, 6-1

Winner

McLoughlin, 6-4, 5-7, 6-3, 6-1

Tennis tournament draw — final: **McLoughlin, 6-0, 7-5, 6-1**

Semi-finals:
- Johnson, 2-6, 6-2 6-2, 6-4
- McLoughlin, 6-3, 7-5, 6-4

Quarter-finals / later rounds:
- Strachan 6-4, 8-6, 6-1
- Johnson 6-3, 6-1, 6-3
- McLoughlin 6-2, 6-4, 6-4
- Clothier 6-0, 6-2, 6-1

Entrant	Round 1	Round 2	Round 3	Round 4	Round 5
C. M. Bull, Jr.	6-2, 6-0, 6-1	Bull 8-6, 7-5, 6-3	Bull 10-8, 5-7, 5-7, 6-2, 6-4	Strachan 6-1, 6-3, 6-2	
F. S. Marden, Jr.	Marden, 6-2, 6-2, 10-8				
S. W. Merrihew					
J. G. Thomas	Inman	Inman 2-6, 6-4, 6-2, 6-1			
F. C. Inman	6-4, 10-8, 11-9				
Stanley Rogers	Colston 7-9, 6-2, 6-3, 5-7, 7-5				
A. E. Kennedy, Jr.	Kennedy 7-5, 6-1, 2-6, 6-3	Strachan 6-1, 6-4, 6-1	Strachan 6-2, 6-3, 6-4		
R. L. Baggs					
F. T. Frelinghuysen	Strachan 6-1, 6-2, 6-3				
J. R. Strachan					
A. E. Kennedy	T. C. Bundy 6-1, 6-1, 6-0	Bundy 6-0, 6-1, 6-2			
T. C. Bundy					
Louis H. Hobbs	Baron H. vonLernser 6-2, 6-2, 6-1				
Baron H. Von Lersner					
Dean Mathey	Mathey 6-1, 6-1, 6-1	Mathey By Default	Mathey 6-2, 6-0, 7-5		
R. A. Johnson					
Clarence J. Griffin	Griffin By Default				
E. H. Woods					
G. S. Groesbeck	Groesbeck 6-3, 6-2, 3-6, 6-2		Whitney 1-6, 6-3, 6-3, 6-3	Whitney 8-6, 9-7, 7-5	
G. L. Lewis					
M. R. Kernochan	Whitney 6-1, 6-0, 6-0				
E. H. Whitney					
Wm. Dean	Seabury 6-0, 6-3, 6-0				
R. W. Seabury					
Edgar Leonard	Behr By Default		Hazard By Default		
K. H. Behr					
Rowland Hazard	Hazard 8-6, 8-6, 6-3				
A. L. Sands					
E. H. Peaslee	Brown By Default		Brown 6-2, 6-2, 2-6, 6-1	Brown 6-3, 3-6, 6-3, 6-1	
J. G. Brown Jr.					
Stanley Henshaw	Henshaw 6-2, 6-0, 6-2				
J. H. H. Taylor					
E. C. Conlin	Conlin 2-6, 7-5, 3-6, 6-4, 7-5		Moore 6-2, 6-4, 6-1		
E. D. Donn, Jr					
L. J. Dreyfus	Moore By Default				
J. B. Moore					
Wallace F Johnson	W. F. Johnson By Default		W. F. Johnson 6-1, 6-3, 6-3	W. F. Johnson 6-2, 6-0, 6-2	
Shaw McKean					
H. W. Slocum	Slocum 6-3, 6-2, 6-3				
Lawrence Curtis, 2nd					
S. S. Palme	Drew 6-1, 6-4, 6-0		Brownell 2-6, 6-2, 7-9, 6-2, 6-1		
F. A. Drew					
W. D. Brownell	Brownell By Default				
F. C. Fearing					
Amos Pinchot	McLoughlin 6-2, 6-0, 6-2		McLoughlin 6-3, 6-1, 6-3	McLoughlin 6-0, 6-1, 6-2	
M. E. McLoughlin					
Hoffman Nickerson	Nickerson 6-2, 6-2, 6-3				
W. D. Bourne					
R. H. Palmer	Palmer 6-1, 6-1, 6-2		Palmer 6-4, 6-3, 6-3		
J. D. Gratz					
Thomas Dunlap	Felton 6-0, 6-0, 6-1				
C. C. Felton					
J. J. Armstrong	Armstrong 7-5, 6-3, 6-4		Leroy 6-4, 4-6, 6-1, 7-5	Leroy 6-0, 6-2, 6-1	
J. C. Bell, Jr.					
A. E. Peterson	Leroy 6-1, 6-1, 6-1				
Robert Leroy					
E. S. H. Pendergast	Pendergast 6-4, 6-3, 6-4		Watrous 7-5, 4-6, 6-1, 6-3		
E. F. Torrey					
F. M Watrous	Watrous 6-4, 6-1, 6-1				
R. J. Sommer					
G. M. Church	Church 6-4, 6-2, 6-1		Clothier 6-0, 3-6, 6-3, 6-3	Clothier 6-1, 6-2, 6-0	
W. S. Kuhn					
Basil Wagner	Clothier 6-2, 6-0, 6-3				
W. J. Clothier					
H. L. Beyer	Pate 6-0, 6-1, 6-2		Pate 6-2, 6-3, 2-6, 6-3	Pate 6-3, 6-3, 6-2	
W. L. Pate					
G. V. Peak, Jr.	Paul By Default				
E. B. Krumbhaar	Rosenbaum 6-3, 7-5, 7-5		Rosenbaum 6-2, 6-1, 6-2		
Wm. Rosenbaum					
F. S. Woodward	Woodward By Default				
Wm. A. Larned					

THIRTY-FOURTH USLTA MEN'S SINGLES CHAMPIONSHIPS
The Casino, Newport, R.I., 1914

First Round	Second Round	Third Round	Fourth Round	Fifth Round	Quarter-Finals	Semi-Finals	Finals

First Round

B. C. Hoppin — Hoppin
F. R. Budlong — By Default
H. C. Johnson — H. C. Johnson 6-3, 6-3, 6-1
J R. Carpenter, Jr.
Louis H Hobbs — Inman
F. C. Inman — 6-3, 6-1, 6-4
N. G. Johnson — Cunningham
D. Cunningham — 6-1, 7-5, 6-1
R. B. Weeden — Whitney
E. H. Whitney — 6-1, 6-1, 6-3
J. P. Jackson — Heyl
W. E. Heyl — 6-1, 6-3, 6-2
G. F. Touchard — Touchard
E. F. Torrey — 6-1, 6-1, 6-2
W. L. Pate — Pate
R. Rowell — By Default
G. Roberts — G. Roberts 6-8, 6-3, 6-2, 6-0
L. C. Jennings
A. Phillips — Fottrell
E. F. Fottrell — By Default
H. G. Simmonds — Simmonds
S. Hoffman — By Default
C. L. Childs — Childs
Kenneth Stern — 6-2, 6-4, 7-5
Vincent Astor — Mathey
Dean Mathey — By Default
A. Watters — J. S. Brown, Jr.
J. S. Brown, Jr. — 6-0, 6-1, 6-0
N. W. Niles — Niles
D. S. Watters — 6-3, 7-5, 6-2
G. Humphreys — Humphreys
R. L. Swain — By Default
J. F. Hubbard — Hubbard
N. E. Brooks — By Default
Wm. Rosenbaum — Thayer
S. Thayer, Jr. — 4-6, 6-2, 4-6, 6-3, 6-4
A. L. Sands — Sands
J. S. Cushman — By Default
C. A. Major — Major 6-1, 4-6, 6-1,
Francis Roche — By Default
R. N. Williams, 2d — R. N. Williams, 2nd
H. J. Schmidt — By Default
C. M. Bull, Jr — Johnston
Wm. M. Johnston — 6-3, 6-3, 6-4
Alfred Dabney — Dabney
D. C. Josephs — 6-2, 6-2, 10-8
A. D. Champlin — Voshell
S. H. Voshell — 6-1, 6-2, 6-1
G. A. Lyon — Leroy
Robt Leroy — 6-1, 6-0, 6-1
A. Chouteau — Phillips
W. A. Phillips — 8-6, 6-0, 6-4
O. J. Sweet — Sweet
J. E. Gignoux — By Default
Karl Behr — Behr
N. M. Vose — 6-2, 6-0, 6-1
R. L. Murray — Murray
F. W. Paul, Jr — By Default
R. W. Stevenson, Jr. — Wagner 6-1, 6-4, 6-3

G. L. Wrenn — Wagner, 7-5, 7-5, 6-1
Basil Wagner
G. Achelis — Achelis 6-1, 6-0, 6-4
Ewing Stille
L. S. Tailer — Tailer 3-6, 6-3, 6-3, 6-2
J. C. Waterbury
J. W. Geary, Jr — Geary 6-0, 6-8, 7-9, 6-1, 9-7
F. P. Magoun, Jr
H. A. MacKinney — MacKinney By Default
R. D. Gatewood
Leonard Beekman — Beekman,, 13-11, 8-6, 4-4, by Default
A. M. Kidder
Chas. Beck — Devereux 6-3, 6-0, 6-1
J. C. Devereux
R. H. Palmer — Marden By defaulit
F. S. Marder
F T. Frelinghuysen — Frelinghuysen 4-6, 6-3, 6-0, 6-4
H. W. Webber
R. D. Little — Little, 6-2, 6-2, 6-3
Wm. Blair

Second Round (continued)

R. C. Sailer — Little 6-1, 6-0, 6-2
C. F. Watson, Jr — Clothier
W. J. Clothier — By Default
H. Throckmorton — Throckmorton 6-2, 11-9, 6-3
J H. Randolph
L. D. Causey — Seaver 6-0, 6-2, 6-1
R. C. Seaver
W. M. Washburn — Washburn 6-2, 6-4, 4-6, 6-4
B. C. Law
R. Harte — Harte 6-1, 6-2, 6-3
W. J. Wright
H. C. Owen — Owen 4-6, 6-3, 3-6, 6-1
W. D. Bourne
K. Robottom — Robottom 10-8, 2-6, 6-2, 6-4
C. L. Sherman
G. M. Church — Pell By Default
T. R. Pell
F W. Hopkins — Groesbeck 6-4, 5-7, 6-4, 6-3
G. S. Groesbeck
R. C. Thomas — R. C. Thomas By Default
A. F. Wilding
H. D. Harvey — Harvey By Default
Gordon Boyd
Wallace F Johnson — W. F. Johnson 6-1, 6-2, 6-2
J. H. Bruns
Lawrence Curtis, 2d — Curtis 6-4, 6-4, By Default
C. Craigin
W. D. Brownell — Griffin 6-1, 6-3, 6-3
Clarence J. Griffin
Boris Yonine — J. G. Thomas 6-1, 6-2, 6-0
J. G. Thomas
A. D. Hammett — Hammett 6-0, 6-1, 6-1
C. C. Wistar
Gardner Beals — Fox 6-3, 2-6, 2-6, 6-2, 6-1
Alan Fox
Wm A. Larned — Morgan By Default
E. F. A. Morgan
Richard Stevens — Stevens 6-2, 6-0, 6-1
C. S. Landers
E. R. McCormick — McCormick 7-5, 6-0, 6-1
S. H. Merrihew
E. K. Swift — Gardner 6-2, 6-1, 6-3
G. P. Gardner, Jr.
C. W. Smith — Smith By Default
Hoffman Nickerson
H. K. Sturdy, Jr. — McLoughlin 6-1, 6-2, 6-2
M. E. McLoughlin
L. B. Cooper — Cooper By Default
R. S. Maynard
I. C. Wright — I. C. Wright 6-3, 6-4, 6-8, 6-4
W. M. Hall
V. B. Miner — Hazard 6-3, 4-6, 6-3, 6-2
R. Hazard
E. P. Pearson — Pearson 6-1, 6-0, 6-1
E. J. Carey
R. I. Brown — P. T. Wright By Default
P. T. Wright
Walter Roberts — Gould By Default
Ezra Gould

Third Round

H. C. Johnson 6-0, 6-3, 6-0
Inman 6-0, 6-1, 6-4
Whitney 6-0, 6-1, 6-1
Touchard 6-2, 6-2, 6-3
Fottrell 6-4, 6-2, 4-6, 6-1
Childs 6-0, 6-4, 6-1
Mathey 6-3, 7-5, 6-0
Niles 6-0, 6-0, 6-1
Thayer 6-0, 6-1, 6-3
Major 7-5, 7-9, 6-4, 7-9, 6-4
Williams 9-7, 3-6, 6-3, 6-3
Dabney 6-3, 16-14, 6-8, 3-6, 8-6
Leroy 6-4, 6-4, 6-2
Behr 6-0, 6-3, 6-1
Murray 6-1, 6-1, 6-3
MacKinney 6-3, 6-1, 6-3
Beekman 6-2, 6-3, 6-2
Clothier 6-0, 6-0, 6-0
Throckmorton 2-6, 6-2, 6-3, 4-6, 6-3
Washburn 1-6, 6-3, 7-5, 7-5
Owen 6-2, 6-2, 6-4
Pell 6-0, 6-1, 6-1
Harvey 6-2, 6-2, 6-2
W. F. Johnson 6-0, 6-3, 6-1
Griffin 6-1, 6-4, 8-6
Hammett 6-3, 6-3, 6-4
Stevens 6-0, 6-0, 6-1
Gardner 6-4, 4-6, 6-0, 6-2
McLoughlin 6-1, 6-2, 6-0
I. C. Wright 2-6, 6-2 ,6-2, 6-3
Pearson 6-0, 6-0, 6-2
P. T. Wright 6-0, 7-5, 3-6, 6-0

Fourth Round

Inman 6-2, 6-8, 6-4, 6-8, 9-7
Touchard 6-4, 5-7, 6-3, 4-6, 12-10
Fottrell 6-1, 6-2, 6-4
Niles 6-3, 6-3, 6-3
Major 2-6, 6-4, 6-3, 4-6, 10-8
Williams 6-3, 6-4, 6-1
Behr 6-2, 6-4, 2-6, 6-3
Murray 7-5, 6-1, 6-1
Clothier 6-4, 8-6, 6-2
Washburn 6-1, 6-1, 6-1
Pell 6-0, 6-0, 6-1
W. F. Johnson 6-3, 6-1, 6-3
Griffin 6-3, 6-3, 6-3
Gardner 6-1, 6-2, 6-2
McLoughlin 6-0, 6-2, 6-1
Pearson 8-6, 6-1, 6-1

Fifth Round

Touchard 4-6, 1-6, 6-3, 6-3, 6-0
Fottrell 2-6, 9-7, 8-6, 6-2
Williams 7-5, 7-5, 6-1
Murray
Clothier 6-2, 6-4, 4-6, 6-1
W. F. Johnson 3-6, 6-1, 6-0, 6-4
Griffin By Default
McLoughlin 6-1, 6-2, 6-3

Quarter-Finals

Fottrell, 6-1, 6-1, 6-2
Williams, 6-1, 6-2, 7-5
Clothier, 6-2, 9-7, 6-1
McLoughlin, 6-1, 6-4, 3-6, 8-6

Semi-Finals

Williams, 6-4, 6-3, 6-2
McLoughlin, 6-4, 6-4, 6-3

Finals

R. N. Williams, 2nd, 6-3, 8-6, 10-8

92

THIRTY-FIFTH USLTA MEN'S SINGLES CHAMPIONSHIPS
West Side Tennis Club, Forest Hills, N.Y., 1915

First Round

Louis Graves
Norman Johnson
J. G. McKay
Ward Dawson
W. D. Cunningham
C. S. Garland
C. J. Griffin
Sid. Thayer, Jr.
G. W. Wightman
C. W. MacMullen
Fenimore Cady
E. D. Toland
J. S. O'Neale, Jr.
W. M. Blair
C. A. Major
B. C. Law
A. H. Man, Jr.
D. S. Watters
J. W. Anderson
Hugh Tallant
H. H. Hackett
W. M. Johnston
C. C. Pell
L. F. Turnbull
H. C. Martin
K. H. Behr
H. L. Bowman
G. W. Phillips
H. S. Parker
Chas Chambers
Wm. Rosenbaum
Robert LeRoy
S. E. Palmer
R. C. Thomas
J. S. Eaton
A. E. Copeland
J B. Adoue, Jr.
P. S. Brinsmade
Richard Stevens
A. M. Kidder
F. C. Inman
C. L. Childs
Adrian Riker
R. N. Williams, 2d
W. F. Johnson
E. H. Hooker
W M. Hall
Chand. Burrows
H. W. Forster
Craig Biddle
Robert Rand
E. W. Peaslee
L. W. Knox
J. W. Geary, Jr.
L. I. Grinnell
T. A. Robinson
J. H. Blackstone
F. A. Fall
W. L. Pate
B. F. Drake
J. G. Thomas
William Rand, 3d
W. I. Plitt
B. Da Silva
S. P. Henshaw
W. S. Anderson
F. T. Hunter
M. Sargeant
G. A. L. Dionne
Middl'n De Camp
P. A. Vaile
S. R. McAllister
F. W. Cole
C J. Post, Jr.
Russell Brown
J S. Pfaffman
W. A. Campbell
Felix Doubleday
J. T. Allen
P. W. Gibbons
R. S. Stoddart
W. H. Wood
A. H. Allen
Leonard Beekman
Dudley Roberts
Dean Mathey
E. F. Kuhn
M. E. McLoughlin
A. S. Cragin
C. L. Johnston, Jr.
S. H. Voshell
R. B. McClave
Walter Roberts
Phillip Roberts
N. W. Niles
F. B. Alexander
B. S. Prentice
W D. Bourne
A. H. Coffey
Harold Swain
Cornelius Boocock
R. L. Baggs
T. H. S. Andrews
B. M Phillips
R J. Sommer
I. C. Wright
J. S. Cushman
G. C. Caner
F. T. Frelinghuysen
E. F. Thomas, Jr.
Irving Riker
H. D. Harvey
E. H. Whitney
Harold Throckmorton
T. R. Pell
Alan Fox
E. J. Newhouse
W. M. Washburn
G. S. McKearin
G. M. Church
G. H. Nettleton
A. Bassford, Jr
C. M. Bull, Jr
L E. Mahan
Lud. Van Deventer
H. A. Plummer
F. H. Harris
C L. Russell

Second Round

Graves 6-3, 6-4, 6-4
Dawson 6-3, 2-6, 4-6, 6-2, 6-1
Garland 6-3, 3-6, 7-5, 6-3
Griffin 6-2, 6-2, 6-1
Wightman 6-3, 6-1, 5-7, 6-4
Toland 6-3, 6-4, 2-6, 8-6
O'Neale 9-7, 6-2, 6-2
Law 4-6, 6-2, 6-4, 7-5
Watters 4-6, 1-6, 8-6, 8-6, 6-2
Tallant 6-4, 6-0, 8-6
W M. Johnston 6-1, 6-2, 10-8
C. C. Pell 6-1, 9-7, 9-7
Behr 6-1, 6-3, 8-6
G. W. Phillips 6-2, 6-4, 6-0
Parker 6-3, 4-6, 6-2, 6-3
Le Roy 7-5, 6-3, 6-0
Thomas 6-2, 6-3, 6-1
Copeland 6-4, 5-7, 6-0, 6-4
Adoue 3-6, 6-2, 6-3, 6-1
Stevens 6-4, 3-6, 6-2, 6-3
Inman 7-5, 6-2, 6-3
Williams By Default
W. F. Johnson 6-0, 6-1, 6-1
Hall 6-2, 0-6, 6-1, 6-2
Biddle 6-2, 6-3, 6-2
Peaslee 6-3, 6-2, 6-2
Knox 6-4, 4-6, 6-4, 6-2
Grinnell 6-2, 6-2, 6-2
Blackstone 7-5, 4-6, 7-5, 6-1
Pate 3-6, 6-3, 7-5, 6-2
Rand 6-0, 7-9, 6-1, 5-7, 6-4
Plitt 6-1, 6-0, 6-2
Anderson 6-4, 6-1, 6-1
Hunter 6-3, 6-2, 6-2
Dionne 7-5, 6-2, 11-9
Vaile 2-6, 6-4, 7-5, 6-4
Post By Default
Pfaffman 6-3, 3-6, 6-0, 6-2
Campbell 6-3, 6-2, 7-5
Allen 7-9, 6-1, 5-7, 6-0, 7-5
Wood 6-3, 3-6, 7-5, 6-1
Beekman By Default
Mathey 6-1, 7-5, 6-0
McLoughlin 6-1, 6-1, 6-0
C. L. Johnston, Jr. 8-6, 10-8, 8-6
Voshell 6-3, 6-4, 6-2
P. Roberts 6-3, 0-6, 6-4, 4-6, 6-4
Alexander 6-3, 5-7, 7-5, 8-10, 6-2
Prentice 6-0, 6-3, 6-0
Coffey 6-4, 6-4, 6-1
Baggs 6-0, 6-1, 6-2
B. M. Phillips 6-3, 6-2, 6-3
Wright 6-0, 6-0, 6-0
Caner 6-2, 6-2, 6-1
Frelinghuysen 6-2, 6-1, 8-6
Harvey 7-5, 6-1, 4-6, 7-5
Whitney 6-3, 4-6, 6-4, 6-1
T. R. Pell 6-2, 6-0, 6-2
Washburn 6-0, 6-2, 6-4
Church 6-1, 6-0, 6-2
Bassford 6-4, 7-9, 6-2, 7-5
Bull 4-6, 12-10, 6-2, 6-4
Plummer 6-4, 6-3, 6-2
Harris 6-1, 6-1, 6-1

Third Round

Dawson 6-2, 8-6, 10-8
Griffin 6-3, 2-6, 6-2, 6-3
Wightman 6-3, 6-1, 6-1
Law 4-6, 6-2, 6-4, 6-4
Watters 6-1, 6-2, 6-4
W. M. Johnston 8-6, 6-4, 6-4
Behr 6-0, 6-3, 6-4
Le Roy 6-2, 6-4, 10-8
Thomas 3-6, 6-2, 6-4, 6-3
Adoue 6-3, 1-6, 6-4, 2-6, 7-5
Williams 7-5, 6-1, 9-7
Hall 18-16, 4-6, 6-2, 4-6, 6-2
Biddle 6-2, 6-1, 6-0
Grinnell 7-5, 6-2, 6-1
Pate 6-1, 6-1, 6-4
Rand 6-0, 6-0, 6-2
Hunter 7-5, 4-6, 4-6, 6-1, 6-1
Dionne 6-3, 6-0, 6-2
Pfaffman 6-3, 6-0, 6-0
Campbell 7-5, 6-3, 3-6, 6-2
Beekman 6-1, 6-1, 6-2
McLoughlin 6-1, 6-2, 8-6
Voshell 6-2, 8-6, 6-2
Alexander 6-4, 6-1, 6-1
Prentice 6-8, 7-5, 7-5, 6-1
B. M. Phillips 7-9, 6-2, 4-6, 6-4, 6-0
Wright 6-2, 0-6, 6-1, 6-3
Frelinghuysen 3-6, 6-1, 9-7, 4-6, 6-4
T. R. Pell 6-3, 6-4, 0-6, 6-3
Washburn 7-5, 9-11, 6-4, 6-2
Bull 4-6, 6-4, 6-4, 6-2
Harris 6-4, 6-2, 3-6, 6-3

Fourth Round

Griffin 6-3, 7-5, 6-2
Law 5-7, 2-6, 6-4, 7-5, 6-4
W. M. Johnston 6-2, 6-1, 6-2
Behr 4-6, 6-4, 6-4, 6-4
Adoue 6-2, 7-5, 6-4
Williams 6-3, 9-7, 2-6, 6-1
Biddle 6-1, 6-2, 6-2
Rand 6-1, 6-4, 6-1
Hunter 10-8, 6-3, 2-6, 2-6, 6-3
Pfaffman 7-5, 6-4, 6-1
McLoughlin 6-2, 3-6, 6-2, 6-2
Alexander 6-4, 6-4, 6-2
Prentice 6-0, 6-3, 5-7, 6-0
Wright 6-3, 6-2, 6-0
Pell 6-4, 6-4, 6-3
Bull 8-6, 7-5, 5-7, 6-2

Quarter-Finals

Griffin 6-2, 6-4, 6-2
Johnston 3-6, 6-3, 6-2, 7-5
Williams 6-3, 6-1, 6-0
Rand 3-6, 6-3, 6-3, 2-6, 6-3
Hunter 3-6, 6-3, 6-3, 2-6, 6-3
McLoughlin 6-3, 6-2, 1-6, 6-3
Wright 7-5, 6-4, 6-1
Pell 6-1, 6-2, 6-3

Semi-Finals

Johnston 6-2, 6-1, 6-8, 5-7, 6-1
Williams 8-6, 7-5, 6-1
McLoughlin 6-2, 6-4, 6-0
Pell 6-3, 6-1, 6-1

Finals

Johnston, 5-7, 6-4, 5-7, 6-2, 6-2

McLoughlin, 6-2, 6-0, 7-5

William M. Johnston, 1-6, 6-0, 7-5, 10-8

THIRTY-SIXTH USLTA MEN'S SINGLES CHAMPIONSHIPS
West Side Tennis Club, Forest Hills, N.Y., 1916

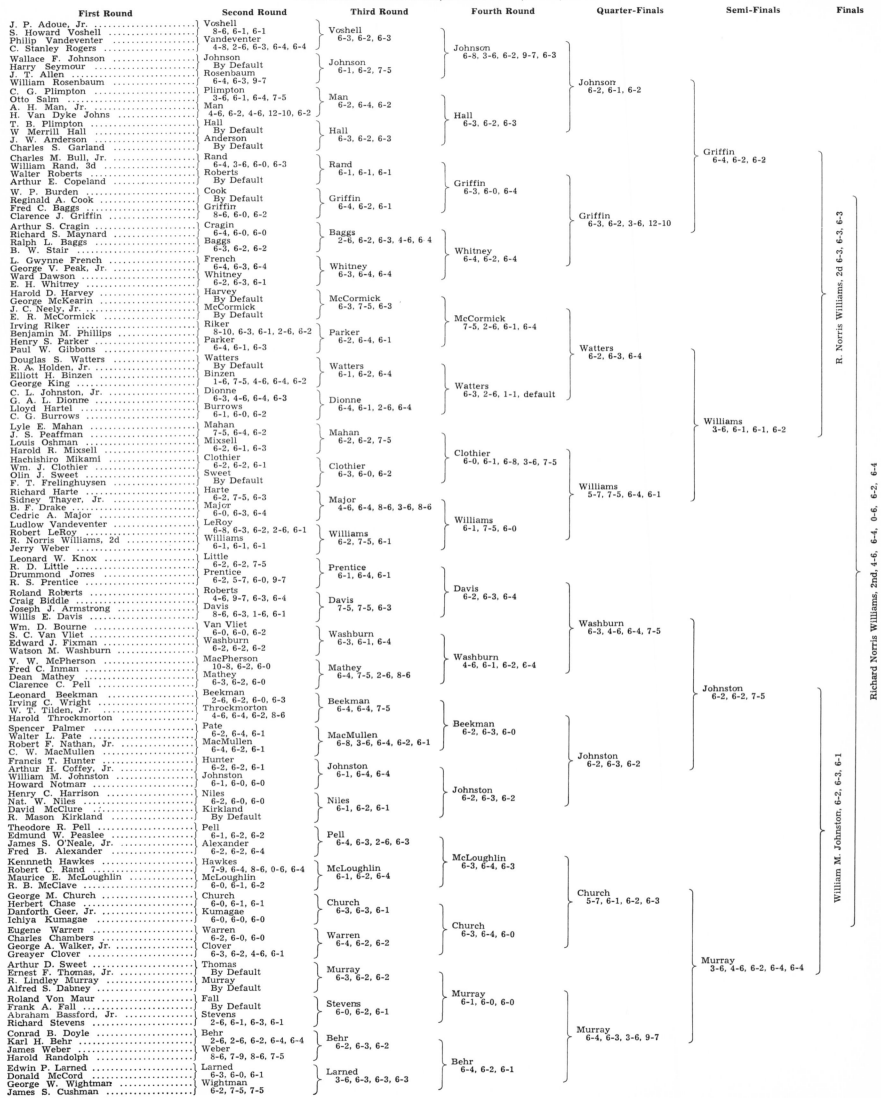

NATIONAL PATRIOTIC TOURNAMENT
West Side Tennis Club, Forest Hills, N.Y., 1917

First Round

- E. J. Fixman
- R. L. Murray
- Gerald B. Emerson
- H. L. Westfall
- T. R. Pell
- W. Rosenbaum
- Otto Salm
- W. T. Tilden, Jr.
- Dean Mathey
- G. G. Burrows
- George A. Walker, Jr.
- Harry Seymour
- F. B. Alexander
- A. Bassford, Jr.
- Craig Biddle
- C. A. Major
- John R. Strachan
- Benjamin H. Letson
- H. L. Bowman
- E. H. Binzen
- A. W. MacPherson
- F. H. Harris
- George O. Wagner
- Moses Berk
- Douglas Watters
- John T. Allen
- Sehchiro Kashio
- F. Brown Ransom
- Charles S. Garland
- Lyle E. Mahan
- G. A. L. Dionne
- Karl H. Behr
- S. H. Voshell
- Holcombe Ward
- F. C. Inman
- H. S. Parker
- N. W. Niles
- Marshall Allen
- Charles Chambers
- J. B. Adoue, Jr.
- J. J. Armstrong
- R. M. Beck
- Herbert Vail
- Kenneth F. Vilsack
- C. J. Griffin
- C. W. MacMullen
- Ludlow VanDeventer
- Christian Mack
- Har'd A. Throckmorton
- Harry C. Johnson
- Fred C. Baggs
- J. S. O'Neale, Jr.
- W. M. Washburn
- Hunt T. Dickinson
- George Tilden
- R. B. McClave
- M. D. Whitman
- Irving C. Wright
- Philip VanDeventer
- Leonard Beekman
- R. N. Williams, 2nd
- W. L. Pate
- L. G. French
- R. L. James

Second Round

- Murray — By default
- Westfall — 6-2, 6-1
- Pell — 6-3, 6-3
- Tilden — 6-0, 6-1
- Mathey — By default
- Walker — 6-2, 6-0
- Alexander — 6-1, 6-0
- Biddle — By default
- Strachan — By default
- Binzen — By default
- MacPherson — By default
- Wagner — 6-3, 6-0
- Watters — 7-5, 6-4
- Kashio — 7-9, 7-5, 10-8
- Garland — 6-1, 7-5
- Behr — 6-4, 2-6, 6-0
- Ward — 6-4, 1-6, 6-3
- Parker — 6-1, 6-3
- Niles — 6-4, 6-2
- Chambers — By default
- Beck — By default
- Vail — 6-3, 9-7
- Griffin — 6-2, 6-3
- VanDeventer — By default
- Throckmorton — 6-4, 6-4
- Baggs — By default
- Washburn — 6-3, 6-3
- McClave — By default
- Wright — By default
- Beekman — 6-2, 6-4
- Williams — 6-2, 6-2
- French — 3-6, 6-3, 6-1

Third Round

- Murray — 6-2, 6-2
- Tilden — 6-3, 6-3
- Mathey — 6-3, 6-1
- Biddle — 6-1, 6-4, 6-0
- Strachan — 6-1, 6-1
- MacPherson — 6-1, 6-4
- Watters — 6-3, 6-4
- Garland — 6-2, 6-4
- Ward — 6-2, 6-2
- Niles — 6-4, 6-1
- Beck — 6-1, 6-3
- Griffin — 6-2, 6-2
- Throckmorton — 7-5, 6-3
- Washburn — 6-0, 6-2
- Beekman — 5-7, 12-10, 6-2
- Williams — 6-3, 6-2

Fourth Round

- Murray — 3-6, 6-4, 6-3, 6-3
- Biddle — 6-4, 12-14, 6-3, 6-3
- Strachan — 6-1, 2-6, 6-0, 6-3
- Garland — 6-4, 6-1, 6-3
- Niles — 3-6, 6-3, 6-1, 6-2
- Griffin — 6-2, 8-6, 6-2
- Throckmorton — 4-6, 6-2, 6-4, 6-4
- Williams — 6-8, 6-4, 9-7, 6-3

Semi-Finals

- Murray — 4-6, 6-1, 6-4, 4-6, 6-2
- Strachan — 6-1, 2-6, 6-2, 6-3
- Niles — 6-1, 6-3, 6-0
- Williams — 4-6, 6-3, 7-5

Finals

- Murray — 4-6, 6-3, 6-3, 6-1
- Niles — 6-2, 4-6, 6-4, 6-3

Winner: Murray — 5-7, 8-6, 6-3, 6-3

THIRTY-SEVENTH USLTA MEN'S SINGLES CHAMPIONSHIPS
West Side Tennis Club, Forest Hills, N.Y., 1918

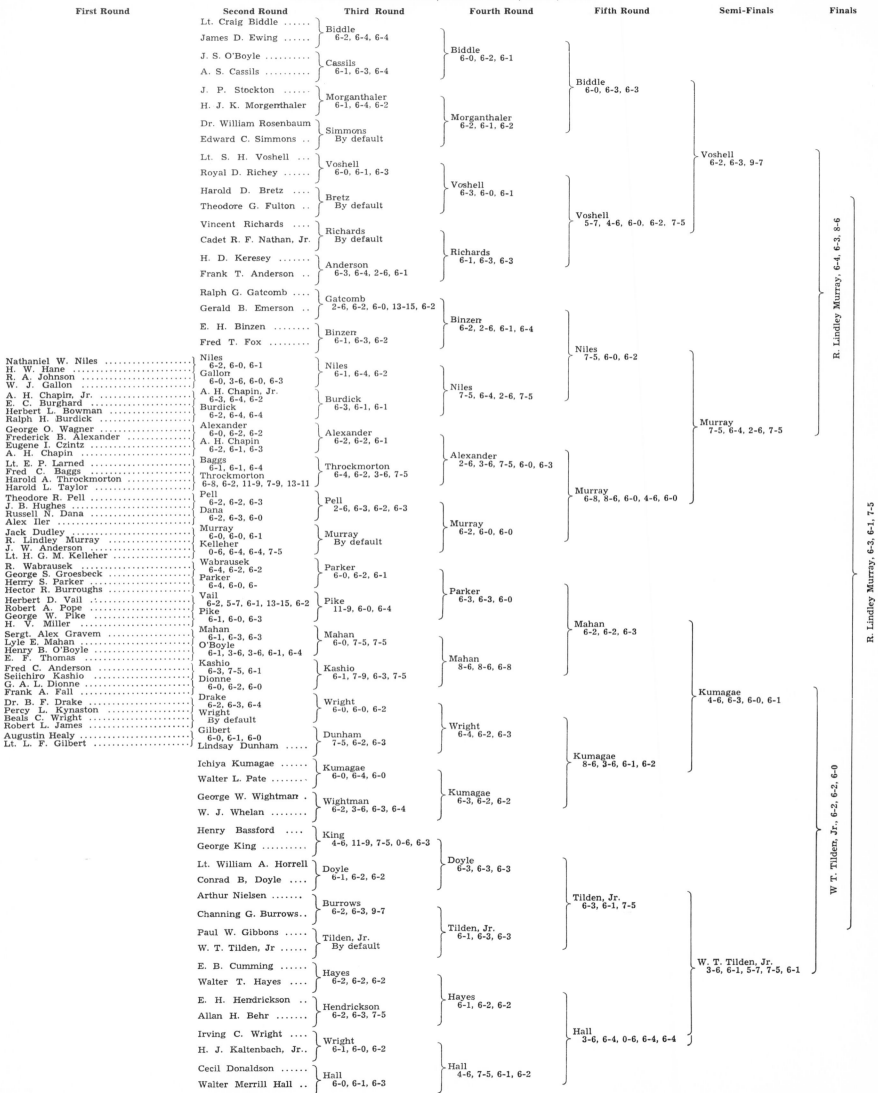

First Round — Second Round — Third Round — Fourth Round — Fifth Round — Semi-Finals — Finals

Lt. Craig Biddle ......
James D. Ewing ...... — Biddle 6-2, 6-4, 6-4

J. S. O'Boyle ....
A. S. Cassils .... — Cassils 6-1, 6-3, 6-4

Third Round: Biddle 6-0, 6-2, 6-1

J. P. Stockton ......
H. J. K. Morganthaler — Morganthaler 6-1, 6-4, 6-2

Dr. William Rosenbaum
Edward C. Simmons .. — Simmons By default

Third Round: Morganthaler 6-2, 6-1, 6-2

Fourth Round: Biddle 6-0, 6-3, 6-3

Lt. S. H. Voshell ...
Royal D. Richey ...... — Voshell 6-0, 6-1, 6-3

Harold D. Bretz ....
Theodore G. Fulton .. — Bretz By default

Third Round: Voshell 6-3, 6-0, 6-1

Vincent Richards ....
Cadet R. F. Nathan, Jr. — Richards By default

H. D. Keresey ....
Frank T. Anderson .. — Anderson 6-3, 6-4, 2-6, 6-1

Third Round: Richards 6-1, 6-3, 6-3

Fourth Round: Voshell 5-7, 4-6, 6-0, 6-2, 7-5

Fifth Round: Voshell 6-2, 6-3, 9-7

Ralph G. Gatcomb ....
Gerald B. Emerson ... — Gatcomb 2-6, 6-2, 6-0, 13-15, 6-2

E. H. Binzen ....
Fred T. Fox .... — Binzen 6-1, 6-3, 6-2

Third Round: Binzen 6-2, 2-6, 6-1, 6-4

Nathaniel W. Niles ...
H. W. Hane .... — Niles 6-2, 6-0, 6-1

R. A. Johnson ......
W. J. Gallon .... — Gallon 6-0, 3-6, 6-0, 6-3

Third Round: Niles 6-1, 6-4, 6-2

Fourth Round: Niles 7-5, 6-4, 2-6, 7-5

Fifth Round: Niles 7-5, 6-0, 6-2

A. H. Chapin, Jr. .....
E. C. Burghard ..... — A. H. Chapin, Jr. 6-3, 6-4, 6-2

Herbert L. Bowman ..
Ralph H. Burdick ... — Burdick 6-2, 6-4, 6-4

Third Round: Burdick 6-3, 6-1, 6-1

George O. Wagner ...
Frederick B. Alexander — Alexander 6-0, 6-2, 6-2

Eugene I. Czintz ......
A. H. Chapin .... — A. H. Chapin 6-2, 6-1, 6-3

Third Round: Alexander 6-2, 6-2, 6-1

Fourth Round: Alexander 2-6, 3-6, 7-5, 6-0, 6-3

Fifth Round: Murray 6-8, 8-6, 6-0, 4-6, 6-0

Lt. E. P. Larned ......
Fred C. Baggs ...... — Baggs 6-1, 6-1, 6-4

Harold A. Throckmorton
Harold L. Taylor ... — Throckmorton 6-8, 6-2, 11-9, 7-9, 13-11

Third Round: Throckmorton 6-4, 6-2, 3-6, 7-5

Theodore R. Pell ......
J. B. Hughes .... — Pell 6-2, 6-2, 6-3

Russell N. Dana ....
Alex Iler .... — Dana 6-2, 6-3, 6-0

Third Round: Pell 2-6, 6-3, 6-2, 6-3

Fourth Round: Murray 6-2, 6-0, 6-0

Jack Dudley ....
R. Lindley Murray .. — Murray 6-0, 6-0, 6-1

J. W. Anderson .....
Lt. H. G. M. Kelleher — Kelleher 0-6, 6-4, 6-4, 7-5

Third Round: Murray By default

Semi-Finals: Murray 7-5, 6-4, 2-6, 7-5

R. Wabrausek ......
George S. Groesbeck — Wabrausek 6-4, 6-2, 6-2

Henry S. Parker ....
Hector R. Burroughs — Parker 6-4, 6-0, 6-

Third Round: Parker 6-0, 6-2, 6-1

Herbert D. Vail .:..
Robert A. Pope .... — Vail 6-2, 5-7, 6-1, 13-15, 6-2

George W. Pike ....
H. V. Miller ...... — Pike 6-1, 6-0, 6-3

Third Round: Pike 11-9, 6-0, 6-4

Fourth Round: Parker 6-3, 6-3, 6-0

Sergt. Alex Gravem ...
Lyle E. Mahan ..... — Mahan 6-1, 6-3, 6-3

Henry B. O'Boyle ..
E. F. Thomas ...... — O'Boyle 6-1, 3-6, 6-1, 6-4

Third Round: Mahan 6-0, 7-5, 7-5

Fred C. Anderson ..
Seiichiro Kashio .. — Kashio 6-3, 7-5, 6-1

G. A. L. Dionne ...
Frank A. Fall ..... — Dionne 6-0, 6-2, 6-0

Third Round: Kashio 6-1, 7-9, 6-3, 7-5

Fourth Round: Mahan 8-6, 8-6, 6-8

Fifth Round: Mahan 6-2, 6-2, 6-3

Dr. B. F. Drake ......
Percy L. Kynaston . — Drake 6-2, 6-3, 6-4

Beals C. Wright ...
Robert L. James ... — Wright By default

Third Round: Wright 6-0, 6-0, 6-2

Augustin Healy ....
Lt. L. F. Gilbert ... — Gilbert 6-0, 6-1, 6-0

Lindsay Dunham ..... — Dunham 7-5, 6-2, 6-3

Third Round: Wright 6-4, 6-2, 6-3

Fourth Round: Kumagae 8-6, 3-6, 6-1, 6-2

Semi-Finals: Kumagae 4-6, 6-3, 6-0, 6-1

Ichiya Kumagae ......
Walter L. Pate .... — Kumagae 6-0, 6-4, 6-0

George W. Wightman .
W. J. Whelan .... — Wightman 6-2, 3-6, 6-3, 6-4

Third Round: Kumagae 6-3, 6-2, 6-2

Fourth Round: Kumagae 6-3, 6-2, 6-2

Henry Bassford ....
George King .... — King 4-6, 11-9, 7-5, 0-6, 6-3

Lt. William A. Horrell
Conrad B. Doyle .... — Doyle 6-1, 6-2, 6-2

Third Round: Doyle 6-3, 6-3, 6-3

Arthur Nielsen ....
Channing G. Burrows.. — Burrows 6-2, 6-3, 9-7

Paul W. Gibbons .....
W. T. Tilden, Jr ...... — Tilden, Jr. By default

Third Round: Tilden, Jr. 6-1, 6-3, 6-3

Fourth Round: Tilden, Jr. 6-3, 6-1, 7-5

Fifth Round: Tilden, Jr. 3-6, 6-1, 5-7, 7-5, 6-1

E. B. Cumming ......
Walter T. Hayes .... — Hayes 6-2, 6-2, 6-2

E. H. Hendrickson ..
Allan H. Behr .... — Hendrickson 6-2, 6-3, 7-5

Third Round: Hayes 6-1, 6-2, 6-2

Irving C. Wright ....
H. J. Kaltenbach, Jr.. — Wright 6-1, 6-0, 6-2

Cecil Donaldson ......
Walter Merrill Hall .. — Hall 6-0, 6-1, 6-3

Third Round: Hall 4-6, 7-5, 6-1, 6-2

Fourth Round: Hall 3-6, 6-4, 0-6, 6-4, 6-4

Semi-Finals: R. Lindley Murray, 6-4, 6-3, 8-6 — W. T. Tilden, Jr., 6-2, 6-2, 6-0

Finals: R. Lindley Murray, 6-3, 6-1, 7-5

THIRTY-EIGHTH USLTA MEN'S SINGLES CHAMPIONSHIPS
West Side Tennis Club, Forest Hills, N.Y., 1919

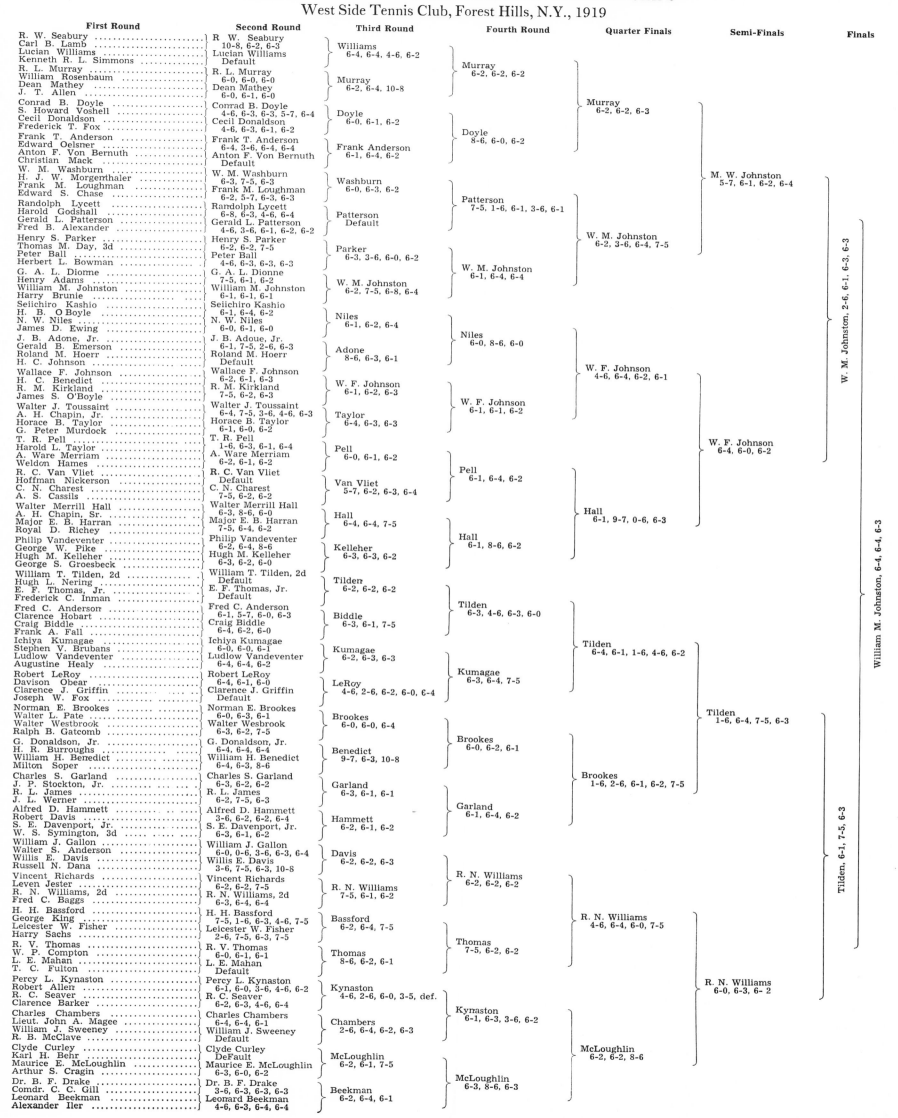

First Round	Second Round	Third Round	Fourth Round	Quarter Finals	Semi-Finals	Finals

R. W. Seabury
Carl B. Lamb
R W. Seabury
10-8, 6-2, 6-3
Williams
6-4, 6-4, 4-6, 6-2

Lucian Williams
Kenneth R. L. Simmons
Lucian Williams
Default

R. L. Murray
William Rosenbaum
R. L. Murray
6-0, 6-0, 6-0
Murray
6-2, 6-4, 10-8
Murray
6-2, 6-2, 6-2

Dean Mathey
J. T. Allen
Dean Mathey
6-0, 6-1, 6-0

Conrad B. Doyle
S. Howard Voshell
Conrad B. Doyle
4-6, 6-3, 6-3, 5-7, 6-4
Doyle
6-0, 6-1, 6-2
Murray
6-2, 6-2, 6-3

Cecil Donaldson
Frederick T. Fox
Cecil Donaldson
4-6, 6-3, 6-1, 6-2

Frank T. Anderson
Edward Oelsner
Frank T. Anderson
6-4, 3-6, 6-4, 6-4
Frank Anderson
6-1, 6-4, 6-2
Doyle
8-6, 6-0, 6-2

Anton F. Von Bernuth
Christian Mack
Anton F. Von Bernuth
Default

W. M. Washburn
H. J. W. Morgenthaler
W. M. Washburn
6-3, 7-5, 6-3
Washburn
6-0, 6-3, 6-2

Frank M. Loughman
Edward S. Chase
Frank M. Loughman
6-2, 5-7, 6-3, 6-3
Patterson
7-5, 1-6, 6-1, 3-6, 6-1

Randolph Lycett
Harold Godshall
Randolph Lycett
6-8, 6-3, 4-6, 6-4
Patterson
Default

Gerald L. Patterson
Fred B. Alexander
Gerald L. Patterson
4-6, 3-6, 6-1, 6-2, 6-2
W. M. Johnston
6-2, 3-6, 6-4, 7-5

Henry S. Parker
Thomas M. Day, 3d
Henry S. Parker
6-2, 6-2, 7-5
Parker
6-3, 3-6, 6-0, 6-2

Peter Ball
Herbert L. Bowman
Peter Ball
4-6, 6-3, 6-3, 6-3
W. M. Johnston
6-1, 6-4, 6-4

G. A. L. Dionne
Henry Adams
G. A. L. Dionne
7-5, 6-1, 6-2
W. M. Johnston
6-2, 7-5, 6-8, 6-4

William M. Johnston
Harry Brunie
William M. Johnston
6-1, 6-1, 6-1

M. W. Johnston
5-7, 6-1, 6-2, 6-4

Selichiro Kashio
H. B. O Boyle
Selichiro Kashio
6-1, 6-4, 6-2
Niles
6-1, 6-2, 6-4

N. W. Niles
James D. Ewing
N. W. Niles
6-0, 6-1, 6-0
Niles
6-0, 8-6, 6-0

J. B. Adoue, Jr.
Gerald B. Emerson
J. B. Adoue, Jr.
6-1, 7-5, 2-6, 6-3
Adone
8-6, 6-3, 6-1

Roland M. Hoerr
H. C. Johnson
Roland M. Hoerr
Default

Wallace F. Johnson
H. C. Benedict
Wallace F. Johnson
6-2, 6-1, 6-3
W. F. Johnson
6-1, 6-2, 6-3
W. F. Johnson
4-6, 6-4, 6-2, 6-1

R. M. Kirkland
James S. O'Boyle
R. M. Kirkland
7-5, 6-2, 6-3

Walter J. Toussaint
A. H. Chapin, Jr.
Walter J. Toussaint
6-4, 7-5, 3-6, 4-6, 6-3
Taylor
6-4, 6-3, 6-3
W. F. Johnson
6-1, 6-1, 6-2

Horace B. Taylor
G. Peter Murdock
Horace B. Taylor
6-1, 6-0, 6-2

T. R. Pell
Harold L. Taylor
T. R. Pell
1-6, 6-3, 6-1, 6-4
Pell
6-0, 6-1, 6-2

A. Ware Merriam
Weldon Hames
A. Ware Merriam
6-2, 6-1, 6-2
Pell
6-1, 6-4, 6-2

W. F. Johnson
6-4, 6-0, 6-2

R. C. Van Vliet
Hoffman Nickerson
R. C. Van Vliet
Default
Van Vliet
5-7, 6-2, 6-3, 6-4

C. N. Charest
A. S. Cassils
C. N. Charest
7-5, 6-2, 6-2

Walter Merrill Hall
A. H. Chapin, Sr.
Walter Merrill Hall
6-3, 3-8-6, 6-0
Hall
6-4, 6-4, 7-5
Hall
6-1, 9-7, 0-6, 6-3

Major E. B. Harran
Royal D. Richey
Major E. B. Harran
7-5, 6-4, 6-2

Philip Vandeventer
George W. Pike
Philip Vandeventer
6-2, 6-4, 8-6
Kelleher
6-3, 6-3, 6-2
Hall
6-1, 8-6, 6-2

Hugh M. Kelleher
George S. Groesbeck
Hugh M. Kelleher
6-3, 6-2, 6-0

William T. Tilden, 2d
Hugh L. Nering
William T. Tilden, 2d
Default
Tilden
6-2, 6-2, 6-2

E. F. Thomas, Jr.
Frederick C. Inman
E. F. Thomas, Jr.
Default
Tilden
6-3, 4-6, 6-3, 6-0

Fred C. Anderson
Clarence Hobart
Fred C. Anderson
6-1, 5-7, 6-0, 6-3
Biddle
6-3, 6-1, 7-5

Craig Biddle
Frank A. Fall
Craig Biddle
6-4, 6-2, 6-0
Tilden
6-4, 6-1, 1-6, 4-6, 6-2

Ichiya Kumagae
Stephen V. Brubans
Ichiya Kumagae
6-0, 6-0, 6-1
Kumagae
6-2, 6-3, 6-3

Ludlow Vandeventer
Augustine Healy
Ludlow Vandeventer
6-4, 6-4, 6-2
Kumagae
6-3, 6-4, 7-5

Robert LeRoy
Davison Obear
Robert LeRoy
6-4, 6-1, 6-0
LeRoy
4-6, 2-6, 6-2, 6-0, 6-4

Clarence J. Griffin
Joseph W. Fox
Clarence J. Griffin
Default

Tilden
1-6, 6-4, 7-5, 6-3

Norman E. Brookes
Walter L. Pate
Norman E. Brookes
6-0, 6-3, 6-1
Brookes
6-0, 6-0, 6-4

Walter Westbrook
Ralph B. Gatcomb
Walter Wesbrook
6-3, 6-2, 7-5
Brookes
6-0, 6-2, 6-1

G. Donaldson, Jr.
H. R. Burroughs
G. Donaldson, Jr.
6-4, 6-4, 6-4
Benedict
9-7, 6-3, 10-8

William H. Benedict
Milton Soper
William H. Benedict
6-4, 6-3, 8-6
Brookes
1-6, 2-6, 6-1, 6-2, 7-5

Charles S. Garland
J. P. Stockton, Jr.
Charles S. Garland
6-3, 6-2, 6-2
Garland
6-3, 6-1, 6-1

R. L. James
J. L. Werner
R. L. James
6-2, 7-5, 6-3
Garland
6-1, 6-4, 6-2

Alfred D. Hammett
Robert Davis
Alfred D. Hammett
3-6, 6-2, 6-2, 6-4
Hammett
6-2, 6-1, 6-2

S. E. Davenport, Jr.
W. S. Symington, 3d
S. E. Davenport, Jr.
6-3, 6-1, 6-2

William J. Gallon
Walter S. Anderson
William J. Gallon
6-0, 0-6, 3-6, 6-3, 6-4
Davis
6-2, 6-2, 6-3

Willis E. Davis
Russell N. Dana
Willis E. Davis
3-6, 7-5, 6-3, 10-8

Tilden
6-1, 7-5, 6-3

Vincent Richards
Leven Jester
Vincent Richards
6-2, 6-2, 7-5
R. N. Williams
7-5, 6-1, 6-2

R. N. Williams, 2d
Fred C. Baggs
R. N. Williams, 2d
6-3, 6-4, 6-4
R. N. Williams
6-2, 6-2, 6-2

H. H. Bassford
George King
H. H. Bassford
7-5, 1-6, 6-3, 4-6, 7-5
Bassford
6-2, 6-4, 7-5

Leicester W. Fisher
Harry Sachs
Leicester W. Fisher
2-6, 7-5, 6-3, 7-5
R. N. Williams
4-6, 6-4, 6-0, 7-5

R. V. Thomas
W. P. Compton
R. V. Thomas
6-0, 6-1, 6-1
Thomas
8-6, 6-2, 6-1

L. E. Mahan
T. C. Fulton
L. E. Mahan
Default
Thomas
7-5, 6-2, 6-2

Percy L. Kynaston
Robert Allen
Percy L. Kynaston
6-1, 6-0, 3-6, 4-6, 6-2
Kynaston
4-6, 2-6, 6-0, 3-5, def.

R. C. Seaver
Clarence Barker
R. C. Seaver
6-2, 6-3, 4-6, 6-4
Kynaston
6-1, 6-3, 3-6, 6-2

Charles Chambers
Lieut. John A. Magee
Charles Chambers
6-4, 6-4, 6-1
Chambers
2-6, 6-4, 6-2, 6-3

William J. Sweeney
R. B. McClave
William J. Sweeney
Default
McLoughlin
6-2, 6-2, 8-6

Clyde Curley
Karl H. Behr
Clyde Curley
DeFault
McLoughlin
6-2, 6-1, 7-5

Maurice E. McLoughlin
Arthur S. Cragin
Maurice E. McLoughlin
6-3, 6-0, 6-2
McLoughlin
6-3, 8-6, 6-3

Dr. B. F. Drake
Comdr. C. C. Gill
Dr. B. F. Drake
3-6, 6-3, 6-3, 6-3
Beekman
6-2, 6-4, 6-1

Leonard Beekman
Alexander Iler
Leonard Beekman
4-6, 6-3, 6-4, 6-4

R. N. Williams
6-0, 6-3, 6-2

W. M. Johnston, 2-6, 6-1, 6-3, 6-3

William M. Johnston, 6-4, 6-4, 6-3

THIRTY-NINTH USLTA MEN'S SINGLES CHAMPIONSHIPS
West Side Tennis Club, Forest Hills, N.Y., 1920

First Round	Second Round	Third Round	Fourth Round	Quarter Finals	Semi-Finals	Finals
R. L. Baggs	Baggs 6-0, 6-3, 8-6	Baggs 6-4, 4-6, 6-4, 6-4				
K. D. Fisher						
John G. McKay	John G. McKay 6-2, 6-3, 6-2		Mahan 6-3, 2-6, 6-1, 6-1			
H. R. Hathaway						
L. E. Mahan	L. E. Mahan 6-1, 6-1, 1-0, default	Mahan 6-3, 2-6, 6-1, 6-1				
Paul A. Vanneman, Jr.				Caner 6-1, 6-3, 6-2		
Philip Van Deventer	Philip Van Deventer 6-4, 4-6, 5-7, 3-6, 6-4					
Wm. V. Burrill						
Willard H. Botsford	Willard H. Botsford 6-1, 6-1, 6-4	Botsford 1-6, 6-2, 6-3, 5-7, 6-4				
Henry Parsons						
Herbert L. Bowman	Herbert L. Bowman 6-3, 6-2, 7-9, 6-3		Caner 6-4, 6-0, 7-9, 6-4			
A. Ware Merriam						
James D. Ewing, Jr.	James D. Ewing, Jr. 1-6, 7-5, 9-7, 3-6, 6-3	Caner 6-3, 6-1, 6-1				
Frederick C. Inman						
C. C. Caner	G. C. Caner 4-6, 6-2, 6-2, 6-4				Caner 6-3, 6-4, 6-2	
Walter T. Hayes						
G. A. L. Dionne	G. A. L. Dionne 6-0, 6-0, 6-1	Emerson 3-6, 6-4, 6-4, 9-7				
Leicester W. Fisher						
Gerald B. Emerson	Gerald B. Emerson 6-2, 6-4, 6-8, 9-7		Wright 6-1, 6-0, 6-2			
H. J. Morgenthaler						
William M. Fischer	William M. Fischer 3-6, 6-3, 6-3, 6-2	Wright 6-2, 2-6, 6-2, 6-2				
S. V. Brubans				Wright 6-4, 6-2, 9-7		
Irving C. Wright	Irving C. Wright 6-4, 8-6, 4-6, 1-6, 6-2					
Marshall Allen						
Ralph H. Burdick	Ralph H. Burdick 4-6, 6-1, 8-6, 6-2	Burdick 6-3, 6-4, 6-2				
R. Mason Kirkland						
J. C. Donaldson	J. C. Donaldson 6-4, 6-1, 1-6, 6-2		Burdick 6-3, 6-1, 3-6, 6-4			
Hammett Norton						
Murray Vernon	Murray Vernon 3-6, 6-3, 6-2, 6-1	Kynaston 6-3, 6-3, 6-2				
Frank A. Fall						
Percy L. Kynaston	Percy L. Kynaston 6-2, 6-1, 6-2					
H. B. O'Boyle						
Leonard W. Knox	Leonard W. Knox 6-2, 6-4, 4-6, 6-2	Knox 3-6, 6-0, 6-2, 6-3				
Davison Obear						
Valentine B. Havens	Valentine B. Havens 6-0, 6-2, 1-6, 1-6, 6-3		Washburn 6-3, 6-1, 7-5			
Edgar T. Appleby						
Watson Washburn	Watson Washburn 6-3, 6-4, 6-3	Washburn 7-5, 0-6, 6-4, 6-0				
John A. Magee				Washburn 7-5, 7-5, 7-5		
Harold A. Throckmorton	H. A. Throckmorton 7-5, 6-2, 4-6, 6-3					
Robert LeRoy						
Frank T. Anderson	Frank T. Anderson 9-7, 6-2, 3-6, 6-4	Anderson 6-1, 4-6, 6-2, 6-3				
R. C. Seaver						
A. J. Ostendorf	A. J. Ostendorf 2-6, 6-3, 9-7, 6-1		Garland 6-2, 6-0, 6-4			
Walter S. Anderson						
Charles S. Garland	Charles S. Garland 6-0, 6-1, 6-1	Garland 6-2, 6-0, 6-0				
J. P. Stockton					W. M. Johnston 6-4, 6-4, 7-5	
Edward B. Benedict	Edward B. Benedict 6-0, 6-1, 6-1					
R. A. Johnson						
S. Howard Voshell	S. Howard Voshell 6-1, 6-0, 6-2	Williams 3-6, 6-2, 7-5, 6-3				
Hugh L. Nehring						
R. N. Williams, 2d	R. N. Williams, 2d 8-6, 3-6, 6-2, 10-8		Williams 4-6, 6-4, 6-4, 6-2			
Francis T. Hunter						
Willis E. Davis	Willis E. Davis 4-6, 6-0, 4-6, 6-1, 6-1	Davis 6-2, 6-4, 6-2				
Theodore R. Pell				W. M. Johnston 6-3, 6-4, 7-5		
Andrew Morgan	Andrew Morgan 6-3, 10-12, 9-7, 7-5					
Harry Sachs						
William M. Johnston	William M. Johnston 6-2, 6-3, 10-8	W. M. Johnston 6-2, 6-4, 6-4				
Carl Fischer						
Alfred D. Hammett	Alfred D. Hammett 6-2, 6-3, 6-1		W. M. Johnston 6-4, 8-10, 7-5, 6-2			
Edward S. Chase						
A. S. Dabney	A. S. Dabney 6-3, 6-3, 6-2	Niles 6-1, 6-4, Default				
Harry F. Vories, Jr.						
N. W. Niles	N. W. Niles Default					M. W. Johnston, 6-3, 4-6, 8-6, 6-4
J. B. Adoue, Jr.						
Fred B. Alexander	Fred B. Alexander 9-11, 6-2, 6-2, 6-3	Alexander 6-3, 6-2, 6-2				
William Rosenbaum						
R. L. James	R. L. James 2-6, 2-6, 7-5, Default		Griffin Default			
Russell N. Dana						
Clarence J. Griffin	Clarence J. Griffin 7-5, 6-3, 6-2	Griffin 6-2, 7-5, 7-5				
A. J. Cawse				Griffin 6-2, 6-3, 6-1		
Richard Harte	Richard Harte 6-1, 6-1, 6-1					
Robert B. McClave						
H. H. Bassford	H. H. Bassford 6-4, 2-6, 6-4, 6-2	Bassford 6-1, 7-5, 6-2				
C. M. Charest						
Allen Behr	Allen Behr 6-2, 6-1, 7-5		Lowrey 4-6, 3-6, 6-4, 6-2, 6-3			
Edward D. Toland						
Joseph W. Fox, Jr.	Joseph W. Fox, Jr. 8-6, 7-5, 6-8, 6-3	Lowrey 6-4, 3-6, 6-3, 4-6, 6-0				
Fred Anderson					W. F. Johnson 6-1, 6-3, 2-6, 6-4	
A. J. Lowrey	A. J. Lowrey 6-2, 6-3, 6-3					
Walter L. Pate						
Dwight P. Robinson	Dwight P. Robinson 6-0, 6-4, 6-1	Mathey 6-1, 6-3, 6-3				
John W. Dudley						
Dean Mathey	Dean Mathey 6-4, 6-3, 6-3		W. F. Johnson Default			
Morris Duane						
Wallace F. Johnson	Wallace F. Johnson 6-1, 6-1, 6-4	W. F. Johnson 6-4, 6-0, 6-1				
Alex. Iler				W. F. Johnson 6-2, 3-6, 6-3, 4-6, 6-4		
W. W. Ingraham	W. W. Ingraham 6-1, 6-2, 6-3					
Milton Soper						
John Hennessey	John Hennessey 6-2, 7-5, 6-3	Hennessey 6-4, 6-3, 6-3				
Victor F. Hockmeyer						
James Weber	James Weber 6-4, 6-4, 7-5		Roberts 6-1, 7-5, 3-6, 6-3			
Paul Martin						
Roland Roberts	Roland Roberts 12-10, 6-2, 6-1	Roberts 6-2, 6-0, 6-0				
Cedric A. Major						W. F. Johnson
Hoffman Nickerson	Hoffman Nickerson 6-1, 6-1, 6-1					
William Felstiner						
Clyde J. Curley	Clyde J. Curley 6-2, 7-5, 11-9	Hardy 6-3, 6-2, 6-3				
John A. Collom						
Samuel Hardy	Samuel Hardy 6-2, 6-3, 6-4		Tilden 3-6, 6-2, 6-4, 6-2			
William J. Gallon						
William T. Tilden, 2d	Wm. T. Tilden, 2d 6-4, 6-3, 6-2	Tilden 6-3, 6-4, 9-7				
Lawrence B. Rice				Tilden 6-3, 3-6, 6-3, 6-0		
M. Thos. Ackerland	M. Thos. Ackerland 6-0, 6-0, 3-6, 6-2					
Richard W. Seabury						
Vincent Richards	Vincent Richards 6-2, 6-2, 2-6, 6-0	Richards 6-3, 6-2, 6-4				
Henry S. Parker						
Leonard Beekman	Leonard Beekman 6-2, 6-2, 6-1		Richards 6-4, 6-1, 6-1			
Augustin Healey						
Edward Oelsner	Edward Oelsner Default	Josties 6-3, 5-7, 6-4, 6-4			Tilden 6-3, 8-6, 6-1	
Hugh Kelleher						
Fred O. Josties	Fred O. Josties 6-1, 6-2, 6-3					
Raymond E. Snow						
H. Broockman	H. Broockman 1-6, 6-2, 2-6, 6-2, 6-0	Broockman 6-2, 6-3, 6-3				
James W. Anderson						
Thomas M. Day, 3d	Thomas M. Day, 3d Default		Broockman 8-6, 8-6, 6-4			
Fritz Bastian						
Charles M. Bull, Jr.	C. M. Bull, Jr. 6-4, 8-6, 6-4	Baggs 6-8, 6-2, 2-6, 8-6, 11-9				Tilden, 14-12, 6-4, 6-4
Edmund W. Peaslee						
Frederick C. Baggs	Frederick C. Baggs Default		Wesbrook 6-1, 6-4, 6-2			
W. M. Hall						
Armand L. Bruneau	Armand L. Bruneau 6-2, 6-0, 6-2	Wesbrook 6-2, 6-3, 6-0				
Geo. Drexel Biddle						
Walter Westbrook	Walter Wesbrook 6-4, 6-2, 6-0		Wesbrook 6-4, 6-1, 6-3			
Royal D. Richey						
John S. Nicholl	John S. Nicholl 7-5, 6-3, 2-6, 5-7, 6-2	L. Van Deventer 6-4, 6-1, 6-3				
W. J. Toussaint						
Ludlow Van Deventer	L. Van Deventer 6-2, 6-0, 6-2					
Dr. B. F. Drake						

William T. Tilden, 2d, 6-1, 1-6, 7-5, 5-7, 6-3

FORTIETH USLTA MEN'S SINGLES CHAMPIONSHIPS
Germantown Cricket Club, Philadelphia, Pa., 1921

First Round	Second Round	Third Round	Fourth Round	Quarter Finals	Semi-Finals	Finals

Henry S. Parker .....
D. P. Robinson, Jr. ...
Parker 6-4, 6-4, 6-2

Craig Biddle ....
R. W. Gilmore ......
Biddle 6-2, 6-1, 6-1

Biddle 4-6, 6-4, 6-1, 6-3

W. C. Crawford ....
S. S. Pannock ......
Crawford 10-8, 6-3, 6-4

Alfred D. Hammett ..
B. D. Golden ....
Hammett 6-4, 6-2, 6-2

Hammett 6-3, 3-6, 6-2, 6-4

Biddle 6-1, 3-6, 6-3, 6-1

Hatson T. Knight ....
H. R. Hathaway ......
Knight 6-4, 6-2, 6-1

Howard Kinsey ....
L. C. Putnam ....
Kinsey 6-1, 6-3, 6-4

Kinsey 6-2, 6-4, 6-4

Kinsey 6-2, 6-3, 10-8

E. C. Oelsner ....
J. P. Stockton ....
Oelsner 4-6, 6-4, 9-7, 6-0

E. M. Edwards ....
I. M. Vanneman, Jr. ....
Edwards 6-3, 7-9, 5-7, 6-3, 6-1

Edwards 4-6, 6-4, 6-4, 4-6, 6-4

A. W. Meyers ....
Paul W. Gibbons ....
Meyers 2-6, 6-0, 6-1, 3-6, 7-9

Watson Washburn ....
A. D. Thayer ....
Washburn 6-0, 6-2, 6-2

Johnson 6-3, 5-7, 2-6, 6-3, 6-3

Johnson 6-0, 6-1, 6-2

Johnson 4-6, 8-6, 6-2, 6-1

Wallace J. Johnson ....
Fred M. Mercur ....
Johnson 6-1, 6-3, 6-4

G. A. L. Dionne ....
Rowland Evans ....
Dionne 7-5, 7-5, 10-8

Fischer 6-3, 6-1, 6-3

Carl Fischer ....
S. Kashio ....
Fischer Default

F. T. Hunter ....
F. C. Anderson ....
Hunter 6-3, 5-7, 6-3, 3-6, 6-3

Hunter 6-2, 6-3, 6-3

Hunter 4-6, 1-6, 6-4, 6-3, 6-0

Morton Bernstein ....
W. A. Larned ....
Bernstein Default

R. L. Baggs ....
Charles S. Garland ....
Baggs Default

King 6-3, 6-1, 6-4

George King ....
James D. Ewing ....
King 6-1, 6-2, 6-0

Hunter 6-3, 6-3, 6-1

A. W. Jones ....
Olin J. Sweet ....
Jones 6-0, 6-1, 6-1

Anderson 6-4, 6-1, 7-5

Frank T. Anderson ....
F. C. Baggs ....
Anderson 6-2, 6-2, 6-1

Anderson 6-2, 6-3, 12-10

J. B. Adoue, Jr. ....
Eric T. Wood ....
Adoue, Jr. 6-1, 6-3, 8-6

Adoue, Jr. 6-2, 2-6, 6-4, 6-4

S. H. Voshell ....
I. Kumagae ....
Voshell Default

W. W. Ingraham ....
Norman Peach ....
Ingraham 6-3, 6-1, 6-4

Williams 6-1, 7-5, 6-2

Williams 7-5, 6-3, 6-2

R. N. Williams ....
Sidney Thayer ....
Williams 6-0, 6-2, 6-1

Anderson 6-3, 6-3, 2-6, 4-6, 6-4

R. Le Roy ....
I. de La Borbolla ....
LeRoy 6-4, 6-2, 6-3

Hawkes 6-1, 6-2, 6-3

J. B. Hawkes ....
William Rosenbaum ....
Hawkes 6-2, 6-3, 6-3

Anderson 10-8, 6-0, 6-3

W. S. Symington ....
G. Colket Caner ....
Symington Default

Anderson 6-1, 6-0, 7-5

James O. Anderson ....
L. B. Rice ....
Anderson 1-6, 6-2, 6-3, 6-3

Anderson 6-1, 6-3, 6-4

Hugh Talland ....
R. L. Murray ....
Talland Default

Mathey Default

A. H. Chapin, Jr. ....
Dean Mathey ....
Mathey Default

Lowe Default

A. S. Morgan ....
L. O. Kamber ....
Morgan 6-4, 6-2, 4-6, 6-2

Lowe 6-2, 6-2, 6-2

F. G. Lowe ....
L. J. Werner ....
Lowe Default

Lowe 6-2, 6-3, 6-3

T. M. Banks, Jr. ....
P. R. Edralin ....
Banks, Jr. Default

Banks, Jr. 6-3, 6-3, 9-11, 6-2

J. W. Dudley ....
N. Garcia ....
Dudley Default

Pearson 6-3, 6-3, 6-4

S. W. Pearson ....
James M. Davis ....
Pearson 6-3, 6-2, 6-4

Pearson 5-7, 3-6, 6-3, 6-4, 6-3

N. W. Niles ....
M. G. Miller, Jr. ....
Niles 6-1, 6-0, 6-2

Tilden, II 6-4, 6-3, 6-4

Wm. M. Johnston ....
H. G. M. Kelleher ....
Johnston 6-4, 6-4, 6-4

Johnston 6-4, 6-1, 6-4

Johnston 2-6, 3-6, 6-3, 9-7, 6-2

E. C. Hall ....
M. T. Ackerland ....
Hall 2-6, 3-6, 7-5, 8-6, 7-5

Walter T. Hayes ....
L. H. Richards, Jr. ....
Hayes 6-1, 6-1, 6-0

Richards 6-3, 6-4, 6-4

Vincent Richards ....
E. T. Herndon ....
Richards 6-1, 6-1, 3-6, 6-4

Tilden, II 4-6, 7-5, 6-4, 6-3

Marshall Allen ....
John Hennessey ....
Allen 6-2, 7-5, 6-1

Shimidzu 6-3, 6-0, 12-10

Tilden, II 6-4, 6-4, 6-1

Z. Shimidzu ....
Arthur C. Nielsen ....
Shimidzu 6-1, 6-1, 6-1

William T. Tilden, II ....
Irving G. Wright ....
Tilden, II 6-0, 6-0, 6-1

Tilden, II 6-2, 6-1, 6-4

P. L. Goldsborough, Jr. ....
Manfred Goldman ....
Goldsborough, Jr. 6-2, 7-5, 6-2

Tilden, II 4-6, 3-6, 8-6, 6-3

J. A. Magee ....
Albert I. Gore ....
Magee 4-6, 6-0, 2-6, 7-5, 8-6

Neer 6-2, 10-8, 6-2

Phil Neer ....
Lyman Tremaine ....
Neer 6-2, 6-1, 9-7

Davis 6-3, 6-4, 2-6, 6-4

Clarence V. Todd ....
G. S. Groesbeck ....
Todd 6-1, 6-1, 6-0

Davis 4-6, 3-6, 6-4, 6-3, 6-3

W. E. Davis ....
Harold Ingersoll ....
Davis Default

Davis 9-7, 5-7, 14-12, 6-3

Gerald B. Emerson ....
P. S. Osborne ....
Emerson 6-3, 6-4, 5-7, 6-1

Emerson 6-3, 6-8, 6-4, 6-4

Leon de Turenne ....
Armand Bruneau ....
de Turenne 6-0, 6-4, 10-8

Clothier 6-1, 6-4, 6-1

W. J. Clothier ....
Clothier 6-1, 6-0, 6-2

Davis 6-3, 4-6, 6-4, 1-6, 6-4

William Taylor ......

C. S. Rogers ....
Paul Martin ....
Rogers 6-1, 6-4, 6-2

Gallon 6-4, 2-6, 6-2, 10-12, 6-2

W. J. Gallon ....
J. C. Neeley ....
Gallon 6-3, 6-1, 6-2

Kinsey 6-0, 6-1, 6-4

R. G. Kinsey ....
Charles Watson ......
Kinsey 6-3, 6-2, 6-2

Kinsey 6-0, 6-0, 6-3

Frank A. Full ....
Edward Wilson ....
Fall 7-5, 6-1, 6-2

Johnson, 6-4, 3-6, 8-6, 6-3

Tilden, II 6-1, 6-3, 6-1

Tilden, II, 10-8, 6-2, 6-1

FORTY-FIRST USLTA MEN'S SINGLES CHAMPIONSHIPS
Germantown Cricket Club, Philadelphia, Pa., 1922

First Round	Second Round	Third Round	Fourth Round	Fifth Round	Semi-Finals	Final

William Johnston .....
Craig Biddle ....
— Johnston 6-3, 6-1, 6-4

Leonard Beekman
Charles S. Rogers — Beekman 6-0, 6-0, 6-1
Stanley W. Pearson — Pearson 6-2, 6-1, 6-1
I. S. Cravis
— Pearson 7-5, 6-4, 6-1

Johnston 9-7, 6-1, 6-2

Howard Kinsey — Kinsey 6-2, 6-4, 6-1
Arthur L. Reed
Phil Bagby — Bagby 6-1, 0-6, 4-6, 6-4, 6-0
Alex Iler
— Kinsey 6-1, 6-2, 10-8

Williiam J. Clothier — Clothier 6-0, 6-0, 6-0
Harold E. Lane
Jose M. Alonso — Alonso 3-6, 3-6, 6-1, 7-5, 7-5
Fred C. Anderson
— Clothier 6-1, 6-0, 4-6, 3-6, 6-4

Kinsey 2-6, 7-10, 6-4, 6-4, 6-1

Johnston 4-6, 6-2, 6-2, default

Watson Washburn — Washburn 6-1, 6-1, 6-2
Ralph L. Baggs
A. H. Chapin, Jr. — Chapin, Jr. 6-3, 6-1, 6-4
Earl C. Bache
— Washburn 6-1, 6-4, 6-2

C M. Charest — Charest 6-3, 6-2, 6-2
Harold Colburn
William T. Campbell — Campbell 6-3, 6-4, 6-3
Joseph M. Lewin
— Charest 8-6, 6-2, 6-1

Washburn 4-6, 9-7, 6-0, 6-4

S. Howard Voschell — Voschell 6-1, 6-3, 6-4
Paul A. Casey
Watson T. Knight — Knight 6-1, 6-1, 6-2
Louis S. de Lone
— Voschell 6-0, 6-3, 6-1

Robert Le Roy — LeRoy 6-1, 6-2, 6-1
Armand Marion
Manuel Alonso — Alonso 6-1, 6-1, 6-1
Robert W. Gilmore
— Alonso 6-3, 6-3, 6-0

Alonso 6-2, 6-1, 6-3

Alonso 6-4, 3-6, 7-9, 8-6, 6-4

Johnston 6-0, 6-2, 7-5

Vincent Richards — Richards 6-3, 6-3, 6-2
Thomas J. Mangan
Charles S. Garland — Garland 6-3, 6-1, 6-4
John A. Magee
— Richards 6-1, 6-2, 7-5

William J. Gallon — Gallon Default
Clifford Lockhorn
Carl Fischer — Fischer Default
John Hennessey
— Fischer 6-1, 6-4, 2-6, 6-2

Richards 6-2, 6-4, 6-1

Frank T. Anderson — Anderson 8-6, 7-5, 8-6
Henry H. Bassford
E. T. Herndon — Herndon 7-5, 6-2, 7-5
Frank A. Fall
— Anderson 4-6, 6-1, 3-6, 9-7, 6-1

Herbert L. Bowman — Bowman 6-1, 9-7, 6-3
E. C. Hall
Thomas C. Leonards — Leonards Default
Ruppert C. Wertheim
— Bowman 6-2, 6-2, 10-8

Bowman 3-6, 6-3, 7-5, 2-6, 8-6

Richards 6-2, 6-3, 6-3

Robert Kinsey — Kinsey 6-0, 6-2, 6-2
I. Biltchik
Edward M. Edwards — Edwards 8-6, 7-5, 7-9, 9-7
John T. Graves, Jr.
— Kinsey 6-2, 6-2, 6-1

Perry S. Osborne — Osborne 6-3, 6-4, 6-2
John W. Dudley
Norman Bramall — Bramall 6-4, 6-2, 8-10, 6-3
E. C. Oelsner
— Osborne 6-1, 6-3, 3-6, 8-6

Kinsey 6-2, 6-1, 6-2

L. E. Williams — Williams 6-0, 6-1, 6-1
Robert F. Norton
Arthur C. Nielsen — Nielsen 2-6, 9-7, 4-6, 6-3, 8-6
J. P. Stockton
— Williams 6-2, 6-1, 6-1

Kirk M. Reid — Reid 3-6, 7-5, 3-6, 6-4, 6-1
Armand L. Bruneau
James O. Anderson — Anderson 6-3, 3-6, 6-2, 6-4
Sidney Thayer, Jr.
— Anderson 6-4, 9-7, 9-7

Anderson 6-4, 6-2, 6-4

Anderson 6-3, 6-3, 2-6, 6-1

Richards 6-4, 6-2, 7-5

William T. Tilden, II — Tilden, II 6-0, 6-2, 6-2
Alexander D. Thayer
George King — King 6-0, 6-1, 6-3
Kenneth Stoddart
— Tilden, II 6-3, 6-3, 6-4

Lyman L. Tremaine — Tremaine 6-1, 7-5, 6-0
Hanson H. Hodge
L. H. Richards — Richards 6-0, 11-9, 2-6, 8-6
Horace R. Hayday
— Tremaine 10-8, 6-1, 6-0

Tilden, II 6-2, 6-0, 6-1

Willis E. Davis — Davis 2-6, 6-3, 2-6, 6-3, 6-4
N. W. Niles
Lyman Tremaine — Tremaine 6-2, 6-4, 6-4
G. A. L. Dionne
— Davis 8-6, 6-2, 6-3

Murray Vernon — Vernon 7-5, 6-3, 6-4
J. M. Vanneman, Jr.
Pat O'Hara Wood — Wood 6-3, 6-4, 6-1
Arthur Mathis
— Wood 6-3, 6-2, 6-1

Wood 6-2, 6-4, 6-4

Tilden II 6-2, 6-3, 6-2

Wallace F. Johnson — Johnson 6-1, 6-0, 6-2
H. R. Hathaway
Charles Watson, III — Watson, III 7-5, 6-4, 6-8, 9-7
E. W. Wilson
— Johnson 6-0, 6-4, 6-1

Andrew S. Morgan — Morgan 6-2, 7-5, 6-1
James S. Merritt
Leon de Turrenne — de Turrenne 5-7, 6-3, 6-4, 7-5
Rowland Evans
— de Turenne 6-2, 6-2, 6-4

Johnson 6-3, 6-2, 6-1

William P. Wear — Wear Default
Dean Mathey
Walter Newell — Nowell 6-3, 6-4, 12-10
J. G. Elliott
— Wear 6-0, 6-4, 6-3

Herman F. Dornheim — Dornheim 6-1, 6-3, 6-2
Dr. William Rosenbaum
Zenzo Shimidzu — Shimidzu 6-4, 7-5, 6-3
Walter Westbrook
— Shimidzu 6-1, 6-1, 6-2

Shimidzu 6-2, 6-0, 6-1

Shimidzu 8-6, 4-6, 6-4, 4-6, 6-4

Tilden, II 6-2, 6-3, 6-1

R. N. Williams — Williams 6-0, 6-2, 4-6, 6-2
I. C. Wright
John F. Whitbeck — Whitbeck 6-0, 6-1, 6-1
C. Stanley Thompson
— Williams 6-4, 7-5, 6-3

Perry E. Hall — Hall 6-2, 6-4, 6-2
Frank F. Wieder
Roy R. Coffin — Coffin 6-1, 6-2, 6-3
R. M. Graham
— Hall 6-2, 6-0, 6-4

Williams 6-3, 6-3, 6-3

P. L. Goldsborough — Goldsborough Default
Philip Neer
Ray D. Johnson — Johnson 6-3, 6-3, 7-5
A. B. Sheridan
— Johnson 3-6, 10-8, 1-6, 8-6, 6-0

H. G. M. Kelleher — Kelleher 6-1, 6-1, 6-3
Manfred Goldman
Elliott H. Binzen — Binzen 6-2, 6-1, 6-3
George W. Wightman
— Binzen 2-6, 6-4, 6-3, 3-6, 7-5

Binzen 6-2, 2-6, 6-4, 6-2

Williams 6-0, 6-2, 6-1

Francis T. Hunter — Hunter 6-1, 6-2, 6-4
R. D. Golden
Samuel B. Gilpin — Gilpin 4-6, 4-6, 10-8, 6-3, 6-2
Walter L. Pate
— Hunter 6-3, 6-0, 7-5

Lawrence B. Rice — Rice 6-0, 6-3, 6-3
Daniel Kiefer, Jr.
Fred C. Baggs — Boggs 4-6, 6-4, 7-5, 6-2
Gerald B. Emerson
— Rice 6-3, 6-4, 4-6, 6-2

Hunter 7-9, 6-3, 3-6, 6-3, 6-3

W. W. Ingraham — Ingraham Default
Arnold W. Jones
Major ....
— Ingraham 4-6, 6-0, 6-3, 5-7, 6-2

Patterson 8-6, 6-1, 7-5

Patterson ....
Hubbell ....
— Patterson 6-0, 6-0, 6-2
— Patterson 6-3, 6-3, 7-5

Patterson 6-3, 6-3, 6-4

Johnston, 8-6, 6-2, 6-1

Tilden, II, 4-6, 3-6, 6-2, 6-3, 6-4

Tilden, II, 4-6, 6-4, 6-3, 6-1

FORTY-SECOND USLTA MEN'S SINGLES CHAMPIONSHIPS
Germantown Cricket Club, Philadelphia, Pa., 1923

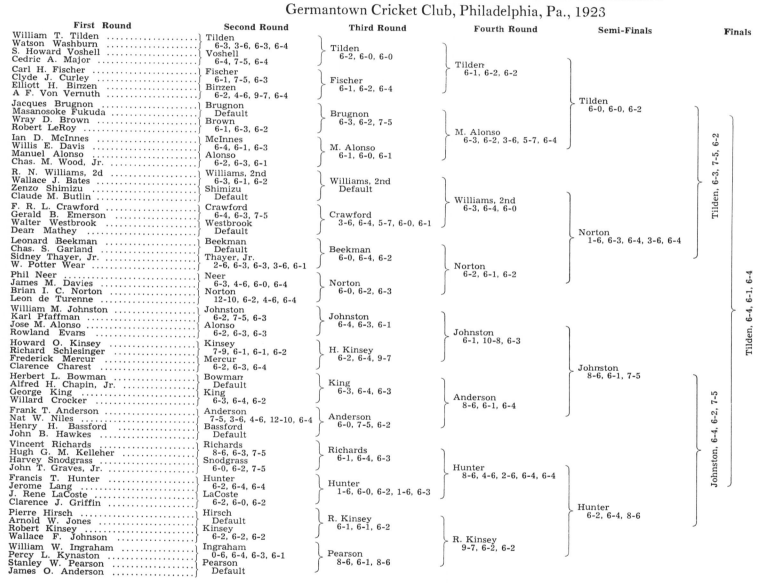

First Round	Second Round	Third Round	Fourth Round	Semi-Finals	Finals
William T. Tilden	Tilden				
Watson Washburn	6-3, 3-6, 6-3, 6-4	Tilden			
S. Howard Voshell	Voshell	6-2, 6-0, 6-0			
Cedric A. Major	6-4, 7-5, 6-4		Tilden		
Carl H. Fischer	Fischer		6-1, 6-2, 6-2		
Clyde J. Curley	6-1, 7-5, 6-3	Fischer			
Elliott H. Binzen	Binzen	6-1, 6-2, 6-4			
A. F. Von Vernuth	6-2, 4-6, 9-7, 6-4			Tilden	
Jacques Brugnon	Brugnon			6-0, 6-0, 6-2	
Masanosoke Fukuda	Default	Brugnon			
Wray D. Brown	Brown	6-3, 6-2, 7-5			
Robert LeRoy	6-1, 6-3, 6-2		M. Alonso		
Ian D. McInnes	McInnes		6-3, 6-2, 3-6, 5-7, 6-4		
Willis E. Davis	6-4, 6-1, 6-3	M. Alonso			
Manuel Alonso	Alonso	6-1, 6-0, 6-1			
Chas. M. Wood, Jr.	6-2, 6-3, 6-1				Tilden, 6-3, 7-5, 6-2
R. N. Williams, 2d	Williams, 2nd				
Wallace J. Bates	6-3, 6-1, 6-2	Williams, 2nd			
Zenzo Shimizu	Shimizu	Default			
Claude M. Butlin	Default		Williams, 2nd		
F. R. L. Crawford	Crawford		6-3, 6-4, 6-0		
Gerald B. Emerson	6-4, 6-3, 7-5	Crawford			
Walter Westbrook	Westbrook	3-6, 6-4, 5-7, 6-0, 6-1			
Dean Mathey	Default			Norton	
Leonard Beekman	Beekman			1-6, 6-3, 6-4, 3-6, 6-4	
Chas. S. Garland	Default	Beekman			
Sidney Thayer, Jr.	Thayer, Jr.	6-0, 6-4, 6-2			
W. Potter Wear	2-6, 6-3, 6-3, 3-6, 6-1		Norton		
Phil Neer	Neer		6-2, 6-1, 6-2		
James M. Davies	6-3, 4-6, 6-0, 6-4	Norton			
Brian I. C. Norton	Norton	6-0, 6-2, 6-3			
Leon de Turenne	12-10, 6-2, 4-6, 6-4				Tilden, 6-4, 6-1, 6-4
William M. Johnston	Johnston				
Karl Pfaffman	6-2, 7-5, 6-3	Johnston			
Jose M. Alonso	Alonso	6-4, 6-3, 6-1			
Rowland Evans	6-2, 6-3, 6-3		Johnston		
Howard O. Kinsey	Kinsey		6-1, 10-8, 6-3		
Richard Schlesinger	7-9, 6-1, 6-1, 6-2	H. Kinsey			
Frederick Mercur	Mercur	6-2, 6-4, 9-7			
Clarence Charest	6-2, 6-3, 6-4			Johnston	
Herbert L. Bowman	Bowman			8-6, 6-1, 7-5	
Alfred H. Chapin, Jr.	Default	King			
George King	King	6-3, 6-4, 6-3			
Willard Crocker	6-3, 6-4, 6-2		Anderson		
Frank T. Anderson	Anderson		8-6, 6-1, 6-4		
Nat W. Niles	7-5, 3-6, 4-6, 12-10, 6-4	Anderson			
Henry H. Bassford	Bassford	6-0, 7-5, 6-2			
John B. Hawkes	Default				Johnston, 6-4, 6-2, 7-5
Vincent Richards	Richards				
Hugh G. M. Kelleher	8-6, 6-3, 7-5	Richards			
Harvey Snodgrass	Snodgrass	6-1, 6-4, 6-3			
John T. Graves, Jr.	6-0, 6-2, 7-5		Hunter		
Francis T. Hunter	Hunter		8-6, 4-6, 2-6, 6-4, 6-4		
Jerome Lang	6-2, 6-4, 6-4	Hunter			
J. Rene LaCoste	LaCoste	1-6, 6-0, 6-2, 1-6, 6-3			
Clarence J. Griffin	6-2, 6-0, 6-2			Hunter	
Pierre Hirsch	Hirsch			6-2, 6-4, 8-6	
Arnold W. Jones	Default	R. Kinsey			
Robert Kinsey	Kinsey	6-1, 6-1, 6-2			
Wallace F. Johnson	6-2, 6-2, 6-2		R. Kinsey		
William W. Ingraham	Ingraham		9-7, 6-2, 6-2		
Percy L. Kynaston	0-6, 6-4, 6-3, 6-1	Pearson			
Stanley W. Pearson	Pearson	8-6, 6-1, 8-6			
James O. Anderson	Default				

FORTY-THIRD USLTA MEN'S SINGLES CHAMPIONSHIPS
West Side Tennis Club, Forest Hills, N.Y. 1924

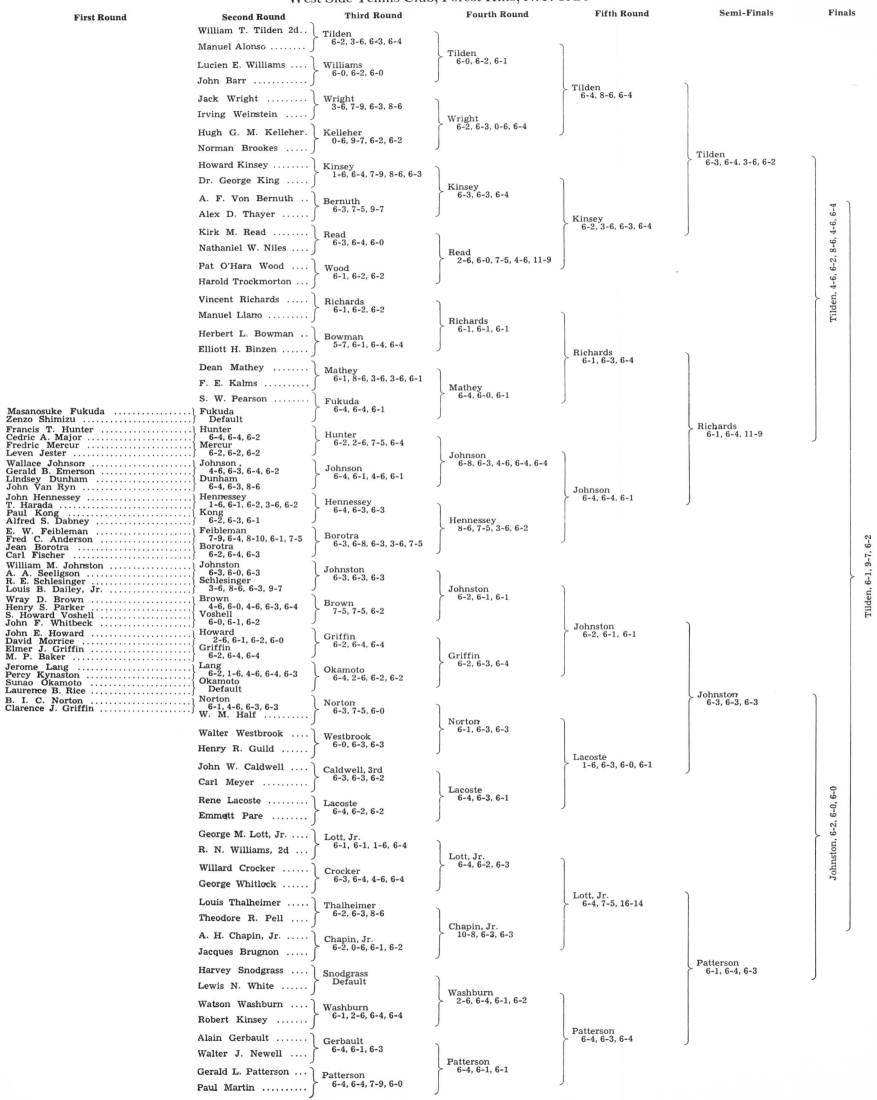

First Round   Second Round   Third Round   Fourth Round   Fifth Round   Semi-Finals   Finals

William T. Tilden 2d..
Manuel Alonso ....
   Tilden 6-2, 3-6, 6-3, 6-4
Lucien E. Williams ....
John Barr ....
   Williams 6-0, 6-2, 6-0
    Tilden 6-0, 6-2, 6-1

Jack Wright ....
Irving Weinstein .....
   Wright 3-6, 7-9, 6-3, 8-6
Hugh G. M. Kelleher.
Norman Brookes .....
   Kelleher 0-6, 9-7, 6-2, 6-2
    Wright 6-2, 6-3, 0-6, 6-4
     Tilden 6-4, 8-6, 6-4

Howard Kinsey ....
Dr. George King .....
   Kinsey 1-6, 6-4, 7-9, 8-6, 6-3
A. F. Von Bernuth ..
Alex D. Thayer ......
   Bernuth 6-3, 7-5, 9-7
    Kinsey 6-3, 6-3, 6-4

Kirk M. Read ....
Nathaniel W. Niles ....
   Read 6-3, 6-4, 6-0
Pat O'Hara Wood ....
Harold Trockmorton ...
   Wood 6-1, 6-2, 6-2
    Read 2-6, 6-0, 7-5, 4-6, 11-9
     Kinsey 6-2, 3-6, 6-3, 6-4
      Tilden 6-3, 6-4, 3-6, 6-2

Vincent Richards .....
Manuel Llano ....
   Richards 6-1, 6-2, 6-2
Herbert L. Bowman ...
Elliott H. Binzen ......
   Bowman 5-7, 6-1, 6-4, 6-4
    Richards 6-1, 6-1, 6-1

Dean Mathey ....
F. E. Kalms ....
   Mathey 6-1, 8-6, 3-6, 3-6, 6-1
S. W. Pearson ....
Fukuda
   Fukuda 6-4, 6-4, 6-1
    Mathey 6-4, 6-0, 6-1
     Richards 6-1, 6-3, 6-4

Masanosuke Fukuda ....
Zenzo Shimizu ....   Fukuda Default
Francis T. Hunter ....
Cedric A. Major ....   Hunter 6-4, 6-4, 6-2
Fredric Mercur ....   Mercur 6-2, 6-2, 6-2
Leven Jester ....
   Hunter 6-2, 2-6, 7-5, 6-4
Wallace Johnson ....   Johnson 4-6, 6-3, 6-4, 6-2
Gerald B. Emerson ....
Lindsey Dunham ....   Dunham 6-4, 6-3, 8-6
John Van Ryn ....
   Johnson 6-4, 6-1, 4-6, 6-1
    Johnson 6-8, 6-3, 4-6, 6-4, 6-4

John Hennessey ....   Hennessey 1-6, 6-1, 6-2, 3-6, 6-2
T. Harada ....
Paul Kong ....   Kong 6-2, 6-3, 6-1
Alfred S. Dabney ....
   Hennessey 6-4, 6-3, 6-3
E. W. Feibleman ....   Feibleman 7-9, 6-4, 8-10, 6-1, 7-5
Fred C. Anderson ....
Jean Borotra ....   Borotra 6-2, 6-4, 6-3
Carl Fischer ....
   Borotra 6-3, 6-8, 6-3, 3-6, 7-5
    Hennessey 8-6, 7-5, 3-6, 6-2
     Johnson 6-4, 6-4, 6-1

William M. Johnston ....   Johnston 6-3, 6-0, 6-3
A. A. Seeligson ....
R. E. Schlesinger ....   Schlesinger 3-6, 8-6, 6-3, 9-7
Louis B. Dailey, Jr. ....
   Johnston 6-3, 6-3, 6-3
Wray D. Brown ....   Brown 4-6, 6-0, 4-6, 6-3, 6-4
Henry S. Parker ....
S. Howard Voshell ....   Voshell 6-0, 6-1, 6-2
John F. Whitbeck ....
   Brown 7-5, 7-5, 6-2
    Johnston 6-2, 6-1, 6-1

John E. Howard ....   Howard 2-6, 6-1, 6-2, 6-0
David Morrice ....
Elmer J. Griffin ....   Griffin 6-2, 6-4, 6-4
M. P. Baker ....
   Griffin 6-2, 6-4, 6-4
Jerome Lang ....   Lang 6-2, 1-6, 4-6, 6-4, 6-3
Percy Kynaston ....
Sunao Okamoto ....   Okamoto Default
Laurence B. Rice ....
   Okamoto 6-4, 2-6, 6-2, 6-2
    Griffin 6-2, 6-3, 6-4
     Johnston 6-2, 6-1, 6-1

B. I. C. Norton ....   Norton 6-1, 4-6, 6-3, 6-3
Clarence J. Griffin ....   W. M. Half ....
   Norton 6-3, 7-5, 6-0
Walter Westbrook ....
Henry R. Guild ......
   Westbrook 6-0, 6-3, 6-3
    Norton 6-1, 6-3, 6-3
     Johnston 6-3, 6-3, 6-3

John W. Caldwell ....
Carl Meyer ....
   Caldwell, 3rd 6-3, 6-3, 6-2
Rene Lacoste ....
Emmett Pare ....
   Lacoste 6-4, 6-2, 6-2
    Lacoste 6-4, 6-3, 6-1
     Lacoste 1-6, 6-3, 6-0, 6-1

George M. Lott, Jr. ....
R. N. Williams, 2d ...
   Lott, Jr. 6-1, 6-1, 1-6, 6-4
Willard Crocker ......
George Whitlock ......
   Crocker 6-3, 6-4, 4-6, 6-4
    Lott, Jr. 6-4, 6-2, 6-3

Louis Thalheimer .....
Theodore R. Pell ....
   Thalheimer 6-2, 6-3, 8-6
A. H. Chapin, Jr. .....
Jacques Brugnon .....
   Chapin, Jr. 6-2, 0-6, 6-1, 6-2
    Chapin, Jr. 10-8, 6-3, 6-3
     Lott, Jr. 6-4, 7-5, 16-14

Harvey Snodgrass ....
Lewis N. White ......
   Snodgrass Default
Watson Washburn ....
Robert Kinsey ....
   Washburn 6-1, 2-6, 6-4, 6-4
    Washburn 2-6, 6-4, 6-1, 6-2
     Patterson 6-1, 6-4, 6-3

Alain Gerbault ......
Walter J. Newell ....
   Gerbault 6-4, 6-1, 6-3
Gerald L. Patterson ...
Paul Martin ....
   Patterson 6-4, 6-4, 7-9, 6-0
    Patterson 6-4, 6-1, 6-1
     Patterson 6-4, 6-3, 6-4

Richards 6-1, 6-4, 11-9

Johnston 6-2, 6-0, 6-0

Tilden, 6-1, 9-7, 6-2

Tilden, 4-6, 6-2, 8-6, 4-6, 6-4

102

FORTY-FOURTH USLTA MEN'S SINGLES CHAMPIONSHIPS
West Side Tennis Club, Forest Hills, N.Y., 1925

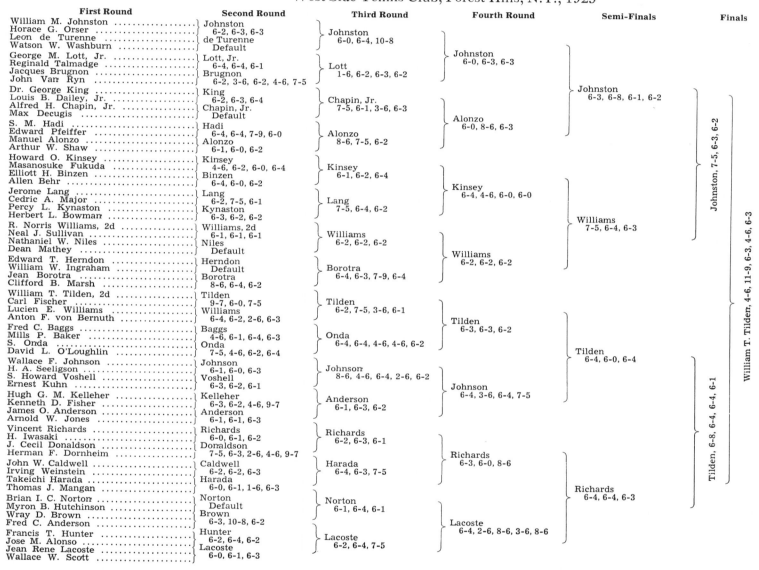

First Round	Second Round	Third Round	Fourth Round	Semi-Finals	Finals
William M. Johnston	Johnston				
Horace G. Orser	6-2, 6-3, 6-3	Johnston			
Leon de Turenne	de Turenne	6-0, 6-4, 10-8			
Watson W. Washburn	Default		Johnston		
George M. Lott, Jr.	Lott, Jr.		6-0, 6-3, 6-3		
Reginald Talmadge	6-4, 6-4, 6-1	Lott			
Jacques Brugnon	Brugnon	1-6, 6-2, 6-3, 6-2			
John Van Ryn	6-2, 3-6, 6-2, 4-6, 7-5			Johnston	
Dr. George King	King			6-3, 6-8, 6-1, 6-2	
Louis B. Dailey, Jr.	6-2, 6-3, 6-4	Chapin, Jr.			
Alfred H. Chapin, Jr.	Chapin, Jr.	7-5, 6-1, 3-6, 6-3			
Max Decugis	Default		Alonzo		
S. M. Hadi	Hadi		6-0, 8-6, 6-3		
Edward Pfeiffer	6-4, 6-4, 7-9, 6-0	Alonzo			
Manuel Alonzo	Alonzo	8-6, 7-5, 6-2			
Arthur W. Shaw	6-1, 6-0, 6-2				Johnston, 7-5, 6-3, 6-2
Howard O. Kinsey	Kinsey				
Masanosuke Fukuda	4-6, 6-2, 6-0, 6-4	Kinsey			
Elliott H. Binzen	Binzen	6-1, 6-2, 6-4			
Allen Behr	6-4, 6-0, 6-2		Kinsey		
Jerome Lang	Lang		6-4, 4-6, 6-0, 6-0		
Cedric A. Major	6-2, 7-5, 6-1	Lang			
Percy L. Kynaston	Kynaston	7-5, 6-4, 6-2			
Herbert L. Bowman	6-3, 6-2, 6-2			Williams	
R. Norris Williams, 2d	Williams, 2d			7-5, 6-4, 6-3	
Neal J. Sullivan	6-1, 6-1, 6-1	Williams			
Nathaniel W. Niles	Niles	6-2, 6-2, 6-2			
Dean Mathey	Default		Williams		
Edward T. Herndon	Herndon		6-2, 6-2, 6-2		
William W. Ingraham	Default	Borotra			
Jean Borotra	Borotra	6-4, 6-3, 7-9, 6-4			
Clifford B. Marsh	8-6, 6-4, 6-2				
William T. Tilden, 2d	Tilden				
Carl Fischer	9-7, 6-0, 7-5	Tilden			
Lucien E. Williams	Williams	6-2, 7-5, 3-6, 6-1			
Anton F. von Bernuth	6-4, 6-2, 2-6, 6-3		Tilden		
Fred C. Baggs	Baggs		6-3, 6-3, 6-2		
Mills P. Baker	4-6, 6-1, 6-4, 6-3	Onda			
S. Onda	Onda	6-4, 6-4, 4-6, 4-6, 6-2			
David L. O'Loughlin	7-5, 4-6, 6-2, 6-4			Tilden	
Wallace F. Johnson	Johnson			6-4, 6-0, 6-4	
H. A. Seeligson	6-1, 6-0, 6-3	Johnson			
S. Howard Voshell	Voshell	8-6, 4-6, 6-4, 2-6, 6-2			
Ernest Kuhn	6-3, 6-2, 6-1		Johnson		
Hugh G. M. Kelleher	Kelleher		6-4, 3-6, 6-4, 7-5		
Kenneth D. Fisher	6-3, 6-2, 4-6, 9-7	Anderson			
James O. Anderson	Anderson	6-1, 6-3, 6-2			Tilden, 6-8, 6-4, 6-4, 6-1
Arnold W. Jones	6-1, 6-1, 6-3				
Vincent Richards	Richards				
H. Iwasaki	6-0, 6-1, 6-2	Richards			
J. Cecil Donaldson	Donaldson	6-2, 6-3, 6-1			
Herman F. Dornheim	7-5, 6-3, 2-6, 4-6, 9-7		Richards		
John W. Caldwell	Caldwell		6-3, 6-0, 8-6		
Irving Weinstein	6-2, 6-2, 6-3	Harada			
Takeichi Harada	Harada	6-4, 6-3, 7-5			
Thomas J. Mangan	6-0, 6-1, 1-6, 6-3			Richards	
Brian I. C. Norton	Norton			6-4, 6-4, 6-3	
Myron B. Hutchinson	Default	Norton			
Wray D. Brown	Brown	6-1, 6-4, 6-1			
Fred C. Anderson	6-3, 10-8, 6-2		Lacoste		
Francis T. Hunter	Hunter		6-4, 2-6, 8-6, 3-6, 8-6		
Jose M. Alonso	6-2, 6-4, 6-2	Lacoste			
Jean Rene Lacoste	Lacoste	6-2, 6-4, 7-5			
Wallace W. Scott	6-0, 6-1, 6-3				

William T. Tilden, 4-6, 11-9, 6-3, 4-6, 6-3

FORTY-FIFTH USLTA MEN'S SINGLES CHAMPIONSHIPS
West Side Tennis Club, Forest Hills, N.Y., 1926

First Round — Second Round — Third Round — Fourth Round — Semi-Finals — Finals

First Round / Second Round

First Round	Second Round
Wiliam T. Tilden, 2d / John Van Ryn	Tilden — 6-4, 3-6, 7-5, 6-2
Neil Sullivan / Louis Thalheimer	Sullivan — 6-3, 6-3, 7-5
Arnold W. Jones / Fritz Mercur	Jones — 6-4, 6-4, 1-6, 7-9, 6-0
Tsumio Tawara / Frank Shields	Tawara — 6-4, 6-2, 7-5
A. H. Chapin, Jr. / Cedric Major	Chapin, Jr. — 7-5, 10-12, 4-6, 6-4, 6-2
Francis T. Hunter / Luis Heyden	Hunter — 6-2, 6-4, 6-3
Elmer Griffin / John Hennessey	Griffin — 6-2, 6-4, 6-2
Henri Cochet / W. W. Ingraham	Cochet — 6-3, 9-7, 6-2
R. Norris Williams / Philip Neer	Williams — 6-3, 6-3, 7-5
Carl Fischer / Fred C. Anderson	Fischer — 6-2, 3-6, 9-7, 7-5
Edward Feibleman / Louis B. Dailey, Jr.	Feibleman — 9-11, 6-2, 6-4, 7-5
Herbert L. Bowman / Jack Wright	Bowman — 7-5, 6-1, 8-6
Manuel Alonzo / Wallace F. Johnson	Alonzo — 6-1, 7-9, 6-1, 6-1
Hugh G. M. Kelleher / Fred C. Baggs	Kelleher — 4-6, 6-2, 6-4, 6-3
Malcolm T. Hill / Nathaniel W. Niles	Hill — 5-7, 8-6, 6-4, 1-6, 8-6
Rene Lacoste / Charles S. Garland	Lacoste — 6-2, 6-1, 6-0
Vincent Richards / Horace Orser	Richards — 6-1, 6-2, 6-1
George M. Lott, Jr. / Elliottt H. Binzen	Lott, Jr. — 6-1, 6-0, 6-1
Kenneth Appel / Kirk Reid	Appel — 4-6, 6-4, 6-2, 7-5
Teizo Toba / Julius Seligson	Toba — 5-7, 6-2, 7-5, 6-3
Takeichi Harada / Percy L. Kynaston	Harada — 6-3, 6-1, 6-3
Dr. George King / Richard Lewis	King — 6-4, 6-3, 6-3
Jerome Lang / Frank Owens	Lang — 6-4, 6-0, 6-3
Jacques Brugnon / John Barr	Brugnon — 6-2, 6-2, 6-3
William M. Johnston / Leon S. Baker	Johnston — 6-2, 6-4, 6-1
Cranston Holman / Lionel Ogden	Holman — Default
Leslie Johnson / John Hubbell	Johnson — 6-4, 3-6, 4-6, 6-4, 6-3
Edward Jacobs / Manuel Liano	Jacobs, 3-6, 6-2, 6-3 — 4-2, default
Edward G. Chandler / Brian Norton	Chandler — 10-8, 3-6, 7-5, 6-1
Lewis S. White / Clifford B. Marsh	White — 6-3, 6-2, 6-3
Watson M. Washburn / S. Howard Voshell	Washburn — 9-7, 1-6, 4-6, 6-4, 6-4
Jean Borotra / Douglas S. Watters	Borotra — 6-3, 6-3, 9-7

Third Round

- Tilden — 4-6, 6-4, 6-2, 6-1
- Jones — 2-6, 6-4, 2-6, 6-3, 6-1
- Hunter — 6-2, 5-7, 8-6, 6-3
- Cochet — 6-0, 6-4, 6-4
- Williams — 6-2, 9-7, 6-1
- Bowman — 5-7, 1-6, 6-1, 8-6, 6-2
- Alonzo — 6-2, 6-2, 8-6
- Lacoste — 6-0, 6-3, 6-4
- Richards — 6-0, 6-2, 4-6, 6-4
- Toba — 6-1, 7-5, 6-3
- King — 6-4, 8-6, 8-6
- Brugnon — 4-6, 11-9, 3-6, 6-4, 6-0
- Johnston, Default
- Jacobs — 11-9, 6-3, 1-6, 1-6, 6-4
- Chandler — 6-4, 6-3, 6-2
- Borotra — 7-9, 6-4, 6-3, 6-3

Fourth Round

- Tilden — 7-9, 7-5, 4-6, 6-1, 6-2
- Cochet — 7-5, 6-3, 0-6, 6-3
- Williams — 4-6, 6-2, 6-3, 6-4
- Lacoste — 6-1, 6-2, 4-6, 6-2
- Richards — 6-0, 6-2, 6-4
- Brugnon — 6-3, 6-2, 7-9, 5-7, 6-1
- Johnston — 6-2, 6-3, 8-6
- Borotra — 6-2, 6-3, 6-2

Semi-Finals

- Cochet — 6-8, 6-1, 6-3, 1-6, 8-6
- Lacoste — 6-0, 6-3, 8-6
- Richards — 6-2, 6-1, 6-2
- Borotra — 3-6, 4-6, 6-3, 6-4, 6-4

Lacoste, 2-6, 4-6, 6-4, 6-4, 6-3

Borotra, 3-6, 6-4, 4-6, 8-6, 6-2

Finals

Lacoste, 6-4, 6-0, 6-4

FORTY-SIXTH USLTA MEN'S SINGLES CHAMPIONSHIPS
West Side Tennis Club, Forest Hills, N.Y., 1927

First Round	Second Round	Third Round	Fourth Round	Semi-Finals	Finals	U.S. Seedings

First Round

WILLIAM T. TILDEN, 2d
Frederick Mercur
H. Holbrook Hyde
Berkeley Bell
Elmer Griffin
John W. Hubbell
Clarence J. Griffin
YOSHIRO OHTA*
JOHN H. DOEG
Kenneth Appel
Jerome Lang
Fred C. Anderson
Samuel B. Gilpin
Louis Thalheimer
Teizo Toba
JEAN BOROTRA*
FRANCIS T. HUNTER
Julius Seligson
Edward Chandler
Wilmer Allison
Weller B. Evans
Harris Coggeshall
Junior Coen
JEAN WASHER*
R. NORRIS WILLIAMS, 2d
E. T. Herndon
Byron A. Baur
John T. Hennessey
Edward W. Fiebleman
Sadakazu Onda
Percy L. Kynaston
HENRI COCHET*
WILLIAM M. JOHNSTON
Dr. George King
Joseph H. Olhausen
C. B. Marsh, Jr.
Lucien E. Williams
C. W. Leslie
Jack Mooney
JACK WRIGHT*
LEWIS N. WHITE
Arnold W. Jones
Carl Fischer
Frank Shields
Donald Strachan
Sidney B. Wood, Jr.
Gregory S. Mangin
JACQUES BRUGNON*
MANUEL ALONSO
J. Gilbert Hall
Watson Washburn
A. L. Weiner, Jr.
JOHN VAN RYN
Wallace F. Johnson
Herbert L. Bowman
RYUKI MIKI*
GEORGE M. LOTT, JR.
Allen Behr
Takeichi Harada
Horace Orser
Gilbert Nunns
Neil J. Sullivan
Frank C. Owens
RENE LACOSTE*

Second Round

TILDEN — 6-3, 10-8, 7-5
Bell — Default
Griffin — 3-6, 8-6, 6-4, 6-4
OHTA — 2-6, 7-5, 6-2, 3-6, 6-3
Appel — 10-8, 6-3, 3-6, 6-2
Lang — 6-1, 4-6, 4-6, 6-0, 6-3
Gilpin — 5-7, 3-6, 6-3, default
BOROTRA — 3-6, 2-6, 6-2, 6-3, 6-0
HUNTER — 6-1, 8-6, 3-6, 6-2
Chandler — Default
Coggeshall — 6-0, 6-1, 6-1
WASHER — Default
Herndon — Default
Hennessey — 6-3, 6-4, 6-2
Fiebleman — 6-4, 6-3, 6-4
COCHET — 6-3, 7-5, 6-3
JOHNSTON — 7-5, 6-3, 7-5
Marsh — 8-6, 9-7, 6-4
Leslie — Default
WRIGHT — 6-0, 6-4, 6-2
Jones — 5-7, 6-3, 6-1, 6-0
Fischer — 6-3, 3-6, 6-2, 6-8, 6-3
Strachan — 4-6, 6-3, 6-4, 6-2
BRUGNON — 6-4, 7-5, 6-3
ALONSO — 5-7, 8-6, 6-4, 6-3
Washburn — 5-7, 6-1, 5-7, 6-0, 6-0
Van Ryn — 6-4, 6-4, 3-6, 6-4
Bowman — 6-4, 6-1, 6-2
Behr — Default
Harada — 6-1, 6-3, 6-1
Nunns — 4-6, 6-4, 3-6, 6-0, 6-3
LACOSTE — 6-4, 6-4, 6-2

Third Round

TILDEN — 6-2, 6-2, 6-2
Griffin — 6-0, 6-2, 6-2
Lang — 8-6, 7-5, 6-0
BOROTRA — 6-4, 8-6, 6-8, 7-5
HUNTER — 6-2, 9-7, 6-4
WASHER — 6-4, 6-0, 6-3
Hennessey — 6-4, 6-1, 6-2
COCHET — 6-4, 8-6, 5-7, 6-0
JOHNSTON — 6-1, 6-4, 7-5
WRIGHT — 7-5, 6-1, 7-9, 6-1
Jones — 6-1, 6-1, 6-2
BRUGNON — 6-0, 6-1, 6-2
ALONSO — 6-2, 4-6, 6-3, 6-2
Van Ryn — 4-6, 6-2, 7-5, 8-6
Harada — 6-3 6-3, 6-2
LACOSTE — 6-0, 6-2, 6-4

Fourth Round

TILDEN — 4-6, 6-1, 11-9, 6-0
BOROTRA — 2-6, 4-6, 6-3, 6-1, 6-3
HUNTER — 7-5, 6-3, 6-3
Hennessey — 6-4, 6-4, 4-6, 3-6, 6-1
JOHNSTON — 6-4, 6-4, 6-4
BRUGNON — 9-7, 4-6, 3-6, 6-1, 6-1
ALONSO — 5-7, 3-6, 6-1, 6-4, 6-0
LACOSTE — 6-3, 6-4, 6-3

Semi-Finals

TILDEN — 6-1, 3-6, 10-8, 6-1
HUNTER — 4-6, 5-7, 6-0, 6-3, 6-4
JOHNSTON — 3-6, 6-2, 6-4, 6-4
LACOSTE — 6-8, 6-4, 6-1, 6-2

Finals

TILDEN, 14-12, 6-1, 4-6, 9-7
LACOSTE, 6-2, 2-6, 6-4, 6-1
RENE LACOSTE, 11-9, 6-3, 11-9

U.S. Seedings
1. Wm. T. Tilden, 2nd
2. W. M. Johnston
3. Manuel Alonso
4. F. T. Hunter
5. George M. Lott
6. R. N Williams, 2nd
7. Lewis White
8. John Doeg

Foreign Seedings
1. Rene Lacoste
2. Henri Cochet
3. Jean Borotra
4. Jacques Brugnon
5. Jean Washer
6. Jack Wright
7. Y. Ohta
8. R. Miki

FORTY-SEVENTH USLTA MEN'S SINGLES CHAMPIONSHIPS
West Side Tennis Club, Forest Hills, N.Y., 1928

First Round | Second Round | Third Round | Fourth Round | Semi-Finals | Finals | U.S. Seedings

First Round

- G. M. LOTT, JR.
- Pierre Landry
- Edward Jacobs
- Elmer Griffin
- H. H. Hyde
- Donald Strachan
- Christian Boussus
- EDGAR F. MOON*
- JOHN DOEG
- R. Tapia, Jr.
- Sadakazu Onda
- W. Aydelotte
- Jack Wright
- Edwards Higgs
- Teizo Toba
- H. W. AUSTIN*
- JOHN VAN RYN
- R. Morales
- A. Unda
- E. T. Herndon
- W. F. Johnson
- B. Gorchakoff
- Sidney Wood, Jr.
- JACK CRAWFORD*
- FRANCIS T. HUNTER
- R. N. Williams, 2d
- Julius Seligson
- James Quick
- Arnold W. Jones
- Donald Cram
- Manuel Alonso
- JEAN BOROTRA*
- J. F. HENNESSEY
- Dr. G. A. King
- P L. Kynaston
- M. Partridge
- Samuel B. Gilpin
- Emmett Page
- Dr. C. G. Fischer
- JACQUES BRUGNON*
- FRANK X. SHIELDS
- H. O. Hopman
- E. W. Feibleman
- I. G. Collins
- H. Coggeshall
- J. Gilbert Hall
- H. L. Bowman
- J. COLIN GREGORY*
- WILMER ALLISON
- Paul de Ricou
- C. S. Garland
- Rene de Buzelet
- Harry C. Brunie
- G. S. Mangin
- Leslie Johnson
- R. O. CUMMINGS*
- FRITZ MERCUR
- E. F. Dawson
- E. McKnight
- German Upmann
- W. M. Washburn
- W. F. Coen, Jr.
- Thomas Wilber
- HENRI COCHET*

Second Round

- LOTT, JR. — 6-2, 3-6, 6-1
- Griffin — 9-11, 6-2, 7-5, 6-4
- Hyde — 2-6, 7-5, 6-3, 6-3
- Boussus — 6-1, 6-4, 6-3
- DOEG — 6-3, 7-5, 6-8, 6-3
- Onda — 7-9, 6-4, 6-4, 4-1
- Wright — 2-6, 6-1, 3-6, 6-3, 6-2
- AUSTIN — 6-1, 3-6, 6-4, 4-6, 6-1
- VAN RYN — 6-0, 6-2, 6-1
- Herndon — 6-0, 6-0, 6-2
- Gorchakoff — 6-3, 6-3, 6-0
- CRAWFORD — 9-7, 7-9, 12-10, 6-4
- HUNTER — 6-1, 6-4, 7-5
- Seligson — 6-4, 6-4, 7-5
- Jones — 4-6, 6-2, 6-3, 6-3
- BOROTRA — Default
- King — 7-5, 6-4, 6-4
- Kynaston — 6-3, 6-1, 1-6, 6-4
- Gilpin — 6-1, 3-6, 6-2, 6-3
- BRUGNON — 6-2, 6-3, 4-6, 8-6
- SHIELDS — 6-1, 6-1, 6-4
- Feibleman — 10-8, 6-4, 6-3
- Coggeshall — 6-2, 1-6, 3-6, 8-6, 6-4
- Bowman — 6-3, 1-6, 6-3, 2-6, 6-2
- ALLISON — 6-3, 8-6, 10-8
- de Buzelet — 7-5, 4-6, 6-3, 6-2
- Mangin — 3-6, 6-1, 6-4, 6-4
- CUMMINGS — 6-2, 6-4, 8-6
- MERCUR — 6-4, 6-3, 6-1
- McKnight — 0-6, 6-2, 6-2, 6-2
- Coen, Jr. — 4-6, 7-9, 6-2, 6-3, 6-4
- COCHET — 6-0, 6-2, 6-1

Third Round

- LOTT, JR. — 6-0, 6-2, 6-3
- Boussus — 7-5, 6-1, 4-6, 6-2
- DOEG — 6-4, 6-4, 1-6, 6-4
- AUSTIN — 3-6, 6-3, 6-3, 6-8, 6-3
- VAN RYN — 6-2, 6-4, 6-4
- CRAWFORD — 6-8, 7-9, 6-3, 7-5, 6-1
- HUNTER — 6-3, 6-3, 7-5
- BOROTRA — 6-2, 6-3, 6-4
- King — 6-3, 6-3, 7-5
- BRUGNON — 6-4, 1-6, 7-5, 6-4
- SHIELDS — 7-5, 6-3, 6-1
- Coggeshall — 6-1, 6-4, 6-4
- deBuzelet — 2-6, 1-6, 6-4, 6-4, 6-1
- Mangin — 6-3, 6-2, 2-6, 6-4
- MERCUR — 3-6, 6-4, 6-0, 7-5
- COCHET — 7-5, 6-3, 6-3

Fourth Round

- LOTT, JR. — 6-2, 6-2, 6-4
- DOEG — 6-4, 5-7, 6-2, 6-8, 6-2
- CRAWFORD — 4-6, 6-4, 1-6, 6-2, 6-3
- HUNTER — 0-6, 5-7, 6-0, 6-4, 6-2
- BRUGNON — 6-2, 4-6, 6-0, 6-3
- SHIELDS — 11-9, 6-2, 6-2
- Mangin — 8-6, 6-2, 3-6, 6-2
- COCHET — 4-6, 11-9, 6-4, 6-4

Semi-Finals

- LOTT, JR. — 6-2, 6-2, 7-5
- HUNTER — 7-5, 3-6, 6-3, 6-4
- SHIELDS — 7-5, 6-1, 6-0
- COCHET — 4-6, 6-3, 6-1, 6-2

Finals

- HUNTER, 6-8, 6-4, 6-3, 6-4
- COCHET, 6-2, 8-6, 6-4

Champion: COCHET, 4-6, 6-4, 3-6, 7-5, 6-3

*Denotes foreign seeding

106

FORTY-EIGHTH USLTA MEN'S SINGLES CHAMPIONSHIPS
West Side Tennis Club, Forest Hills, N.Y., 1929

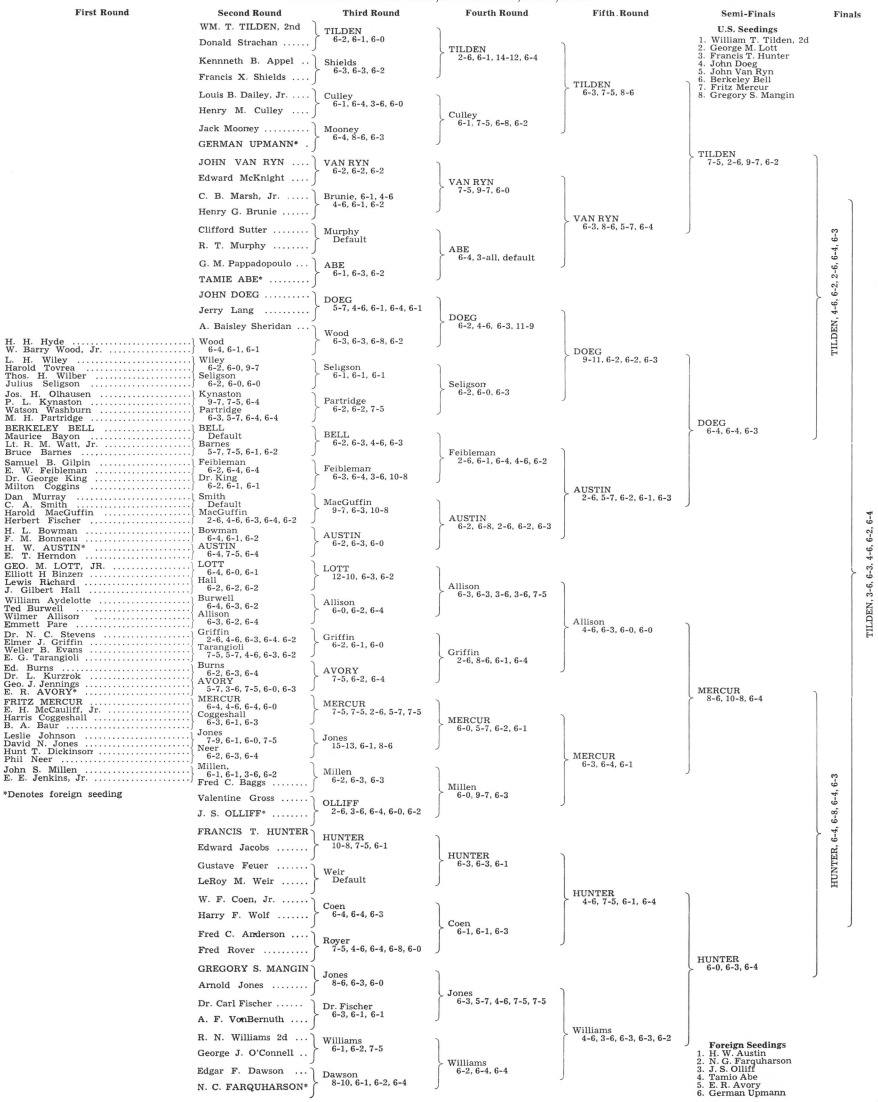

First Round	Second Round	Third Round	Fourth Round	Fifth Round	Semi-Finals	Finals

U.S. Seedings
1. William T. Tilden, 2d
2. George M. Lott
3. Francis T. Hunter
4. John Doeg
5. John Van Ryn
6. Berkeley Bell
7. Fritz Mercur
8. Gregory S. Mangin

*Denotes foreign seeding

Foreign Seedings
1. H. W. Austin
2. N. G. Farquharson
3. J. S. Olliff
4. Tamio Abe
5. E. R. Avory
6. German Upmann

107

FORTY-NINTH USLTA MEN'S SINGLES CHAMPIONSHIPS
West Side Tennis Club, Forest Hills, N.Y., 1930

First Round	Second Round	Third Round	Fourth Round	Fifth Round	Semi-Finals	Final

WILMER ALLISON
Robert Bryan
ALLISON 6-3, 6-3, 6-3

Richard Murphy
Henry M. Culley
Murphy 8-6, 6-1, 6-3

ALLISON 4-6, 6-1, 6-3, 6-3

Frank X. Shields
Edward C. Tarangioli.
Shields 6-1, 6-0, 6-3

Elmer J. Griffin
MARCEL RAINVILLE*
Griffin, 6-4, 0-6, 2-6 6-2, 6-4

Shields 6-4, 6-4, 7-5

Shields 6-4, 4-6, 6-2, 1-6, 6-3

GREG. S. MANGIN
Bertram Hammell
MANGIN 6-1, 6-3, 6-2

Philip Neer
John F. Hennessey
Hennessey 6-2, 6-3, 7-5

MANGIN 6-2, 6-0, 6-1, 6-2

Keith Werner
Watson Washburn
Werner 9-7, 9-7, 6-3

Howard Langlie
J. S. OLLIFF*
OLLIFF Default

OLLIFF 6-4, 6-2, 6-0

MANGIN 6-3, 6-3, 10-8

Shields 3-6, 6-8, 6-2, 6-1, 6-1

SIDNEY B. WOOD, JR.
Weller B. Evans
WOOD 6-1, 6-2, 6-0
Julius Seligson
Jack Tidball
Seligson Default

WOOD 4-6, 2-6, 6-0, 6-1, 6-4

Geo. J. Jennings
Wilbur F. Coen, Jr.
Coen 6-2, 6-3, 6-4
J. Gilbert Hall
Armand L. Bruneau
Hall 6-0, 6-1, 6-2

Coen 6-2, 6-4, 6-8, 6-1

WOOD 6-2, 1-6, 6-1, 6-1

Bryan Grant, Jr.
Cedric A. Major
Grant 6-1, 7-5, 10-8
G. Frederick Roll
David N. Jones
Jones 6-3, 3-6, 8-6, 6-1

Grant 8-6, 6-4, 4-6, 6-2

David R. Morrice
Samuel B. Gilpin, 2d
Gilpin 6-1, 6-2, 6-2
Arthur S. Fowler
L. A. GODFREE*
Fowler 6-1, 6-3, 6-2

Gilpin 6-3, 6-1, 7-5

Gilpin 6-2, 4-6, 11-9, 3-6, 6-4

WOOD 6-3, 6-2, 6-3

CLIFFORD S. SUTTER
Arthur W. MacPherson
SUTTER 5-7, 6-4, 6-2, 2-6, 6-1
J. Emmett Pare
Donald M. Frame
Pare 6-1, 6-1, 6-3

SUTTER 6-2, 6-0, 8-6

Herbert L. Bowman
Dr. Carl Fischer
Bowman 6-0, 6-0, 6-1
Kenneth B. Appel
C. W. Leslie
Leslie 6-1, 3-6, 6-3, 6-3

Bowman 7-9, 7-5, 6-4, 6-3

SUTTER 6-1, 2-6, 4-6, 6-3, 6-3

Donald C. Strachan
Richard D. Lewis
Lewis 6-8, 6-4, 6-0, 6-1
Harold MacGuffin
Louis B. Dailey, Jr.
MacGuffin 6-3, 6-2, 7-5

Lewis 6-3, 6-4, 6-4

Lloyd Nordstrom
Fritz Mercur
Mercur Default
R. Berkeley Bell
JEAN BOROTRA*
Bell 3-6, 6-2, 12-10, 7-5

Bell 6-1, 6-2, 1-6, 6-4

Bell 6-3, 6-4, 13-11

SUTTER 7-9, 6-4, 6-1, 2-6, 8-6

WILLIAM T. TILDEN, 2nd
C. Lincoln Halberstadt
TILDEN 6-1, 6-0, 6-4
Joseph J. Armstrong
Stanley J. Harte
Armstrong Default

TILDEN 6-1, 6-1, 6-0

Jack DeLara
Dr. Herbert Fischer
DeLara 6-3, 6-2, 6-4
Edward W. Feibleman
Robert Considine
Feibleman 6-4, 6-2, 8-6

Feibleman 6-3, 9-7, 6-2

TILDEN 6-1, 6-1, 6-0

H. Ellsworth Vines, Jr.
Ralph M. DeMott
Vines 6-3, 7-5, 6-3
Bruce Barnes
John S. Millen
Barnes 6-2, 6-3, 3-6, 10-8

Vines 12-10, 7-5, 7-5

A. Baisley Sheridan
Edward W. Burns
Burns 2-6, 6-1, 6-1, 6-1
Edward E. Jenkins, Jr.
G. LYTTELTON ROGERS*
ROGERS 6-1, 8-6, 6-3

ROGERS 7-9, 2-6, 7-5, 11-9, 6-2

TILDEN 6-4, 6-1, 6-2

ROGERS 4-6, 4-6, 6-4, 6-1, 6-4

JOHN W. VAN RYN
Arnold W. Jones
VAN RYN 6-0, 6-2, 6-2
William Clines
Kirk M. Reid
Reid 6-3, 6-1, 6-1

VAN RYN 6-1, 6-1, 6-2

Dr. Gerald Bartosh
Percy L. Kynaston
Kynaston Default
Alain Gerbault
Keith E. Gledhill
Gledhill 6-4, 6-1, 6-0

Gledhill 6-1, 6-4, 8-10, 6-3

VAN RYN 6-2, 6-4, 6-1

Edward Jacobs
G. H. Boehmer, Jr.
Jacobs 1-6, 6-3, 6-4, 6-2
Anton F. von Bernuth
Frank W. Bowden
Bowden 6-4, 4-6, 6-4, 6-2

Jacobs 6-1, 6-4, 6-1

Frank N. Bonneau
Sadakazu Onda
Onda 6-1, 6-4, 6-2
FRED. J. PERRY*
PERRY 6-4, 2-6, 6-2, 4-6, 6-4

PERRY 6-2, 6-3, 6-3

VAN RYN 4-6, 6-3, 6-4, 6-1

TILDEN 4-6, 6-2, 6-4, 6-4

*Denotes foreign seeding

GEO. M. LOTT, JR.
R. Norris Williams 2d
Williams 7-9, 7-5, 7-5, 6-1

Harold Blauer
Herman Upmann
Blauer 6-0, 7-5, 3-6, 6-2

Williams 6-4, 6-3, 6-3

Francis T. Hunter
Russell Phillips
Hunter 6-2, 6-0, 6-2

E. H. McCauliff, Jr.
E. R. AVORY*
AVORY 6-1, 6-1 6-1

Hunter 4-6, 8-6, 6-2, 6-2

Hunter 7-5, 6-2, 6-4

JOHN H. DOEG
W. Barry Wood, Jr.
DOEG 6-2, 6-2, 5-7, 4-6, 6-2

Lieut. R. M. Watt Jr.
James Nuthall
Watt 13-11, 4-6, 6-2, 6-4

DOEG 6-4, 4-6, 6-2, 6-4

Jerome Lang
E. Ralph Martin
Lang 5-7, 6-3, 6-3, 6-3

C. Alphonso Smith, Jr.
H. G. N. LEE*
LEE 6-0, 5-7, 6-2, 6-3

LEE 6-3, 6-4, 6-2

DOEG 8-6, 6-1, 6-4

DOEG 11-13, 6-4, 3-6, 6-2, 6-4

SHIELDS, 6-2, 6-3, 4-6, 6-3

JOHN H. DOEG, 10-8, 1-6, 6-4, 16-14

DOEG, 10-3, 6-3, 3-6, 12-10

FIFTIETH USLTA MEN'S SINGLES CHAMPIONSHIPS
West Side Tennis Club, Forest Hills, N.Y., 1931

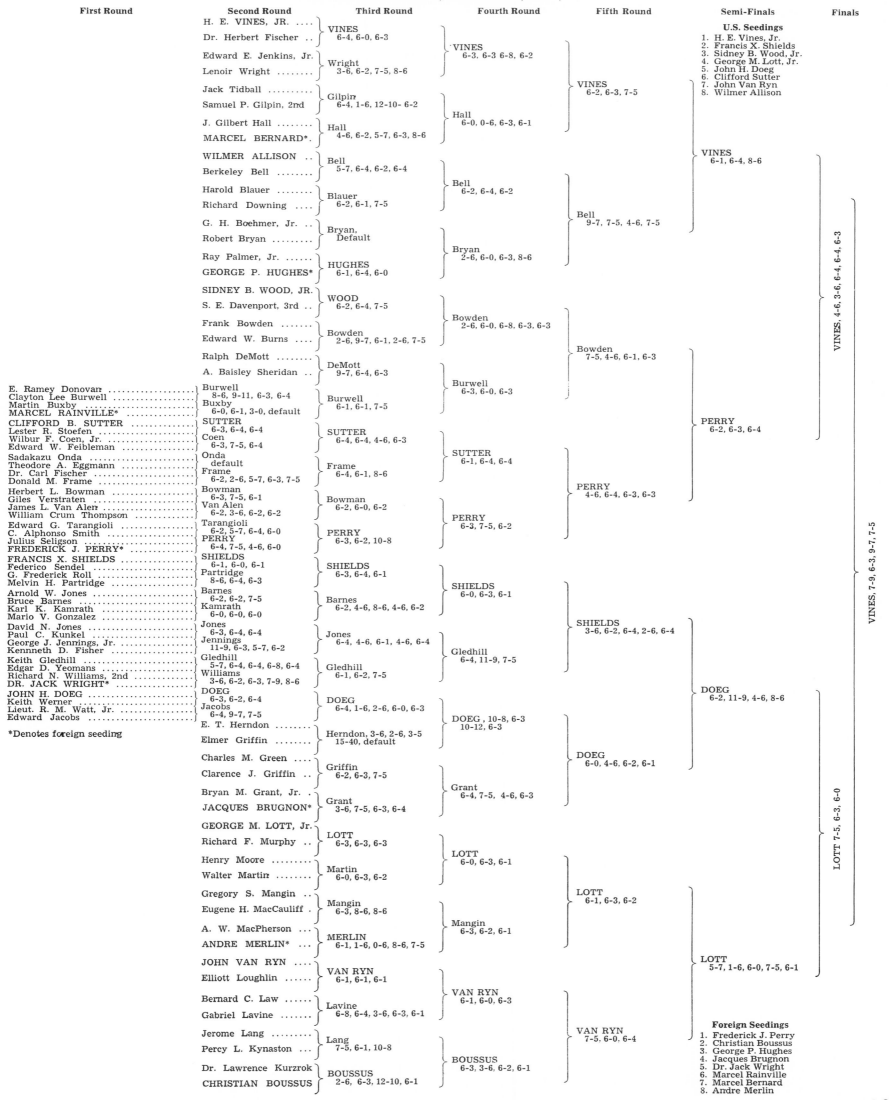

First Round	Second Round	Third Round	Fourth Round	Fifth Round	Semi-Finals	Finals

H. E. VINES, JR. ....
Dr. Herbert Fischer .. — VINES 6-4, 6-0, 6-3

Edward E. Jenkins, Jr.
Lenoir Wright .... — Wright 3-6, 6-2, 7-5, 8-6

VINES 6-3, 6-3 6-8, 6-2

Jack Tidball ....
Samuel P. Gilpin, 2nd — Gilpin 6-4, 1-6, 12-10- 6-2

J. Gilbert Hall ....
MARCEL BERNARD*. — Hall 4-6, 6-2, 5-7, 6-3, 8-6

Hall 6-0, 0-6, 6-3, 6-1

VINES 6-2, 6-3, 7-5

WILMER ALLISON ..
Berkeley Bell .... — Bell 5-7, 6-4, 6-2, 6-4

Harold Blauer ....
Richard Downing .... — Blauer 6-2, 6-1, 7-5

Bell 6-2, 6-4, 6-2

G. H. Boehmer, Jr. ..
Robert Bryan .... — Bryan, Default

Ray Palmer, Jr. ......
GEORGE P. HUGHES* — HUGHES 6-1, 6-4, 6-0

Bryan 2-6, 6-0, 6-3, 8-6

Bell 9-7, 7-5, 4-6, 7-5

VINES 6-1, 6-4, 8-6

U.S. Seedings
1. H. E. Vines, Jr.
2. Francis X. Shields
3. Sidney B. Wood, Jr.
4. George M. Lott, Jr.
5. John H. Doeg
6. Clifford Sutter
7. John Van Ryn
8. Wilmer Allison

SIDNEY B. WOOD, JR.
S. E. Davenport, 3rd — WOOD 6-2, 6-4, 7-5

Frank Bowden ....
Edward W. Burns .... — Bowden 2-6, 9-7, 6-1, 2-6, 7-5

Bowden 2-6, 6-0, 6-8, 6-3, 6-3

Ralph DeMott ....
A. Baisley Sheridan .. — DeMott 9-7, 6-4, 6-3

Bowden 7-5, 4-6, 6-1, 6-3

E. Ramey Donovan ...
Clayton Lee Burwell ... — Burwell 8-6, 9-11, 6-3, 6-4

Martin Buxby ....
MARCEL RAINVILLE* ... — Buxby 6-0, 6-1, 3-0, default

Burwell 6-1, 6-1, 7-5

Burwell 6-3, 6-0, 6-3

CLIFFORD B. SUTTER ...
Lester R. Stoefen ..... — SUTTER 6-3, 6-4, 6-4

Wilbur F. Coen, Jr. ...
Edward W. Feibleman ... — Coen 6-3, 7-5, 6-4

SUTTER 6-4, 6-4, 4-6, 6-3

Sadakazu Onda ....
Theodore A. Eggmann ... — Onda default

Dr. Carl Fischer ......
Donald M. Frame ...... — Frame 6-2, 2-6, 5-7, 6-3, 7-5

Frame 6-4, 6-1, 8-6

SUTTER 6-1, 6-4, 6-4

Herbert L. Bowman ....
Giles Verstraten ...... — Bowman 6-3, 7-5, 6-1

James L. Van Alen .....
William Crum Thompson ... — Van Alen 6-2, 3-6, 6-2, 6-2

Bowman 6-2, 6-0, 6-2

Edward G. Tarangioli ...
C. Alphonso Smith ..... — Tarangioli 6-2, 5-7, 6-4, 6-0

Julius Seligson ....
FREDERICK J. PERRY* ... — PERRY 6-4, 7-5, 4-6, 6-0

PERRY 6-3, 6-2, 10-8

PERRY 6-3, 7-5, 6-2

PERRY 4-6, 6-4, 6-3, 6-3

PERRY 6-2, 6-3, 6-4

FRANCIS X. SHIELDS ...
Federico Sendel .... — SHIELDS 6-1, 6-0, 6-1

G. Frederick Roll .....
Melvin H. Partridge ... — Partridge 8-6, 6-4, 6-3

SHIELDS 6-3, 6-4, 6-1

Arnold W. Jones ....
Bruce Barnes .... — Barnes 6-2, 6-2, 7-5

Karl K. Kamrath ......
Mario V. Gonzalez ..... — Kamrath 6-0, 6-0, 6-0

Barnes 6-2, 4-6, 8-6, 4-6, 6-2

SHIELDS 6-0, 6-3, 6-1

David N. Jones ....
Paul C. Kunkel .... — Jones 6-3, 6-4, 6-4

George J. Jennings, Jr. ...
Kennneth D. Fisher .... — Jennings 11-9, 6-3, 5-7, 6-2

Jones 6-4, 4-6, 6-1, 4-6, 6-4

Keith Gledhill ....
Edgar D. Yeomans ..... — Gledhill 5-7, 6-4, 6-4, 6-8, 6-4

Richard N. Williams, 2nd ...
DR. JACK WRIGHT* ..... — Williams 3-6, 6-2, 6-3, 7-9, 8-6

Gledhill 6-1, 6-2, 7-5

Gledhill 6-4, 11-9, 7-5

SHIELDS 3-6, 6-2, 6-4, 2-6, 6-4

JOHN H. DOEG ....
Keith Werner .... — DOEG 6-3, 6-2, 6-4

Lieut. R. M. Watt, Jr. ...
Edward Jacobs .... — Jacobs 6-4, 9-7, 7-5

DOEG 6-4, 1-6, 2-6, 6-0, 6-3

E. T. Herndon ....
Elmer Griffin .... — Herndon, 3-6, 2-6, 3-5 15-40, default

DOEG , 10-8, 6-3 10-12, 6-3

Charles M. Green ....
Clarence J. Griffin .. — Griffin 6-2, 6-3, 7-5

Bryan M. Grant, Jr. .
JACQUES BRUGNON* — Grant 3-6, 7-5, 6-3, 6-4

Grant 6-4, 7-5, 4-6, 6-3

DOEG 6-0, 4-6, 6-2, 6-1

DOEG 6-2, 11-9, 4-6, 8-6

GEORGE M. LOTT, Jr.
Richard F. Murphy .. — LOTT 6-3, 6-3, 6-3

Henry Moore ....
Walter Martin .... — Martin 6-0, 6-3, 6-2

LOTT 6-0, 6-3, 6-1

Gregory S. Mangin ..
Eugene H. MacCauliff — Mangin 6-3, 8-6, 8-6

A. W. MacPherson ...
ANDRE MERLIN* — MERLIN 6-1, 1-6, 0-6, 8-6, 7-5

Mangin 6-3, 6-2, 6-1

LOTT 6-1, 6-3, 6-2

JOHN VAN RYN ....
Elliott Loughlin ...... — VAN RYN 6-1, 6-1, 6-1

Bernard C. Law ......
Gabriel Lavine .... — Lavine 6-8, 6-4, 3-6, 6-3, 6-1

VAN RYN 6-1, 6-0, 6-3

Jerome Lang ....
Percy L. Kynaston ... — Lang 7-5, 6-1, 10-8

Dr. Lawrence Kurzrok
CHRISTIAN BOUSSUS — BOUSSUS 2-6, 6-3, 12-10, 6-1

BOUSSUS 6-3, 3-6, 6-2, 6-1

VAN RYN 7-5, 6-0, 6-4

LOTT 5-7, 1-6, 6-0, 7-5, 6-1

VINES, 4-6, 3-6, 6-4, 6-4, 6-3

VINES, 7-9, 6-3, 9-7, 7-5

LOTT 7-5, 6-3, 6-0

*Denotes foreign seeding

Foreign Seedings
1. Frederick J. Perry
2. Christian Boussus
3. George P. Hughes
4. Jacques Brugnon
5. Dr. Jack Wright
6. Marcel Rainville
7. Marcel Bernard
8. Andre Merlin

109

FIFTY-FIRST USLTA MEN'S SINGLES CHAMPIONSHIPS
West Side Tennis Club, Forest Hills, N.Y., 1932

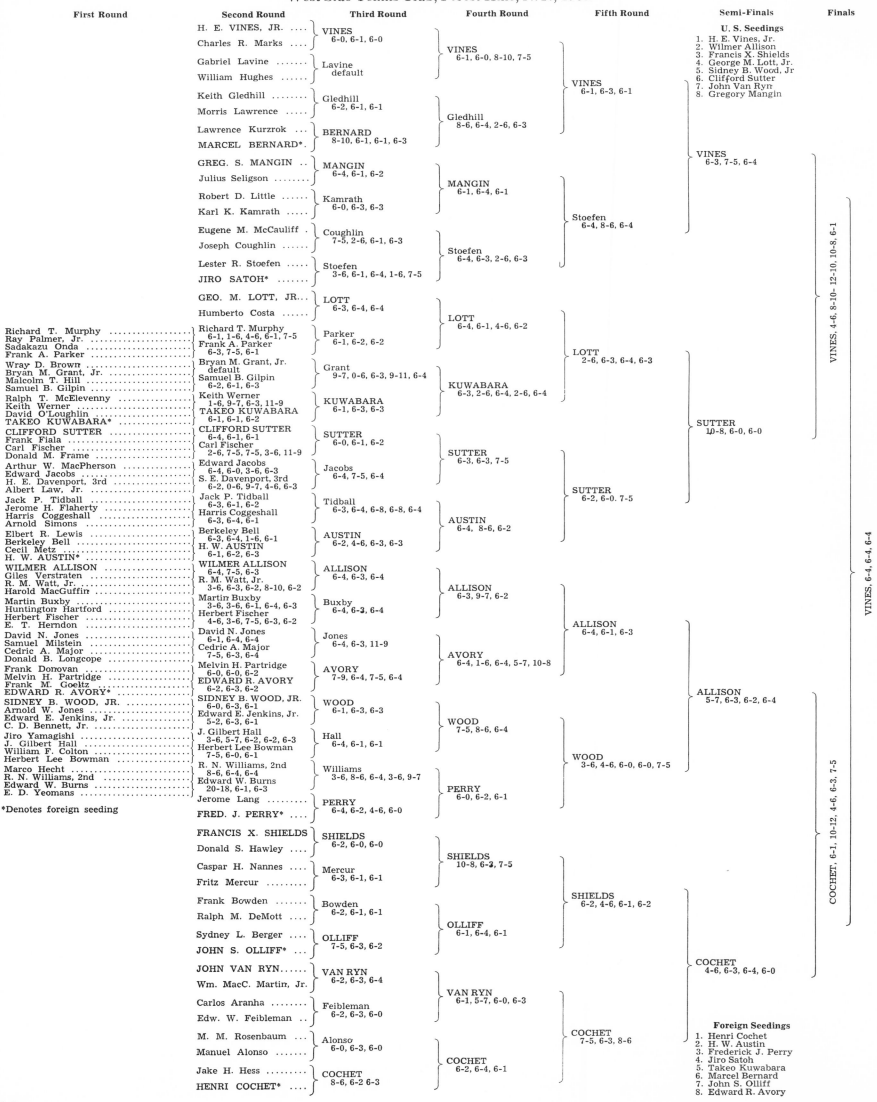

First Round	Second Round	Third Round	Fourth Round	Fifth Round	Semi-Finals	Finals

U. S. Seedings
1. H. E. Vines, Jr.
2. Wilmer Allison
3. Francis X. Shields
4. George M. Lott, Jr.
5. Sidney B. Wood, Jr
6. Clifford Sutter
7. John Van Ryn
8. Gregory Mangin

H. E. VINES, JR. ....
Charles R. Marks ....
VINES 6-0, 6-1, 6-0
Gabriel Lavine ....
William Hughes ......
Lavine default
VINES 6-1, 6-0, 8-10, 7-5

Keith Gledhill ....
Morris Lawrence .....
Gledhill 6-2, 6-1, 6-1
Lawrence Kurzrok ...
MARCEL BERNARD*.
BERNARD 8-10, 6-1, 6-1, 6-3
Gledhill 8-6, 6-4, 2-6, 6-3
VINES 6-1, 6-3, 6-1

GREG. S. MANGIN ..
Julius Seligson ....
MANGIN 6-4, 6-1, 6-2
Robert D. Little ......
Karl K. Kamrath .....
Kamrath 6-0, 6-3, 6-3
MANGIN 6-1, 6-4, 6-1

Eugene M. McCauliff .
Joseph Coughlin ......
Coughlin 7-5, 2-6, 6-1, 6-3
Lester R. Stoefen .....
JIRO SATOH* ....
Stoefen 3-6, 6-1, 6-4, 1-6, 7-5
Stoefen 6-4, 6-3, 2-6, 6-3
Stoefen 6-4, 8-6, 6-4

VINES 6-3, 7-5, 6-4

VINES, 4-6, 8-10, 12-10, 10-8, 6-1

GEO. M. LOTT, JR...
Humberto Costa ......
LOTT 6-3, 6-4, 6-4
Richard T. Murphy ....
Ray Palmer, Jr. ....
Sadakazu Onda ....
Frank A. Parker ....
Richard T. Murphy 6-1, 1-6, 4-6, 6-1, 7-5
Frank A. Parker 6-3, 7-5, 6-1
Parker 6-1, 6-2, 6-2
LOTT 6-4, 6-1, 4-6, 6-2

Wray D. Brown ....
Bryan M. Grant, Jr. ....
Malcolm T. Hill ....
Samuel B. Gilpin ....
Bryan M. Grant, Jr. default
Samuel B. Gilpin 6-2, 6-1, 6-3
Grant 9-7, 0-6, 6-3, 9-11, 6-4
Ralph T. McElevenny ....
Keith Werner ....
David O'Loughlin ....
TAKEO KUWABARA* ....
Keith Werner 1-6, 9-7, 6-3, 11-9
TAKEO KUWABARA 6-1, 6-1, 6-2
KUWABARA 6-1, 6-3, 6-3
LOTT 2-6, 6-3, 6-4, 6-3
KUWABARA 6-3, 2-6, 6-4, 2-6, 6-4

CLIFFORD SUTTER ....
Frank Fiala ....
Carl Fischer ....
Donald M. Frame ....
CLIFFORD SUTTER 6-4, 6-1, 6-1
Carl Fischer 2-6, 7-5, 7-5, 3-6, 11-9
SUTTER 6-0, 6-1, 6-2
Arthur W. MacPherson ....
Edward Jacobs ....
H. E. Davenport, 3rd ....
Albert Law, Jr. ....
Edward Jacobs 6-4, 6-0, 3-6, 6-3
S. E. Davenport, 3rd 6-2, 0-6, 9-7, 4-6, 6-3
Jacobs 6-4, 7-5, 6-4
SUTTER 6-3, 6-3, 7-5

Jack P. Tidball ....
Jerome H. Flaherty ....
Harris Coggeshall ....
Arnold Simons ....
Jack P. Tidball 6-3, 6-1, 6-2
Harris Coggeshall 6-3, 6-4, 6-1
Tidball 6-3, 6-4, 6-8, 6-8, 6-4
Elbert R. Lewis ....
Berkeley Bell ....
Cecil Metz ....
H. W. AUSTIN* ....
Berkeley Bell 6-3, 6-4, 1-6, 6-1
H. W. AUSTIN 6-1, 6-2, 6-3
AUSTIN 6-2, 4-6, 6-3, 6-3
AUSTIN 6-4, 8-6, 6-2
SUTTER 6-2, 6-0. 7-5

SUTTER 10-8, 6-0, 6-0

WILMER ALLISON ....
Giles Verstraten ....
R. M. Watt, Jr. ....
Harold MacGuffin ....
WILMER ALLISON 6-4, 7-5, 6-3
R. M. Watt, Jr. 3-6, 6-3, 6-2, 8-10, 6-2
ALLISON 6-4, 6-3, 6-4
Martin Buxby ....
Huntington Hartford ....
Herbert Fischer ....
E. T. Herndon ....
Martin Buxby 3-6, 3-6, 6-1, 6-4, 6-3
Herbert Fischer 4-6, 3-6, 7-5, 6-3, 6-2
Buxby 6-4, 6-3, 6-4
ALLISON 6-3, 9-7, 6-2

David N. Jones ....
Samuel Milstein ....
Cedric A. Major ....
Donald B. Longcope ....
David N. Jones 6-1, 6-4, 6-4
Cedric A. Major 7-5, 6-3, 6-4
Jones 6-4, 6-3, 11-9
Frank Donovan ....
Melvin H. Partridge ....
Frank M. Goeltz ....
EDWARD R. AVORY* ....
Melvin H. Partridge 6-0, 6-0, 6-2
EDWARD R. AVORY 6-2, 6-3, 6-2
AVORY 7-9, 6-4, 7-5, 6-4
AVORY 6-4, 1-6, 6-4, 5-7, 10-8
ALLISON 6-4, 6-1, 6-3

SIDNEY B. WOOD, JR. ....
Arnold W. Jones ....
Edward E. Jenkins, Jr. ....
C. D. Bennett, Jr. ....
SIDNEY B. WOOD, JR. 6-0, 6-3, 6-1
Edward E. Jenkins, Jr. 5-2, 6-3, 6-1
WOOD 6-1, 6-3, 6-3
Jiro Yamagishi ....
J. Gilbert Hall ....
William F. Colton ....
Herbert Lee Bowman ....
J. Gilbert Hall 3-6, 5-7, 6-2, 6-2, 6-3
Herbert Lee Bowman 7-5, 6-0, 6-1
Hall 6-4, 6-1, 6-1
WOOD 7-5, 8-6, 6-4

Marco Hecht ....
R. N. Williams, 2nd ....
Edward W. Burns ....
E. D. Yeomans ....
R. N. Williams, 2nd 8-6, 6-4, 6-4
Edward W. Burns 20-18, 6-1, 6-3
Williams 3-6, 8-6, 6-4, 3-6, 9-7
Jerome Lang ....
FRED. J. PERRY* ....
PERRY 6-4, 6-2, 4-6, 6-0
PERRY 6-0, 6-2, 6-1
WOOD 3-6, 4-6, 6-0, 6-0, 7-5

ALLISON 5-7, 6-3, 6-2, 6-4

VINES, 6-4, 6-4, 6-4

FRANCIS X. SHIELDS
Donald S. Hawley ....
SHIELDS 6-2, 6-0, 6-0
Caspar H. Nannes ....
Fritz Mercur ....
Mercur 6-3, 6-1, 6-1
SHIELDS 10-8, 6-3, 7-5

Frank Bowden ....
Ralph M. DeMott ....
Bowden 6-2, 6-1, 6-1
Sydney L. Berger ....
JOHN S. OLLIFF* ...
OLLIFF 7-5, 6-3, 6-2
OLLIFF 6-1, 6-4, 6-1
SHIELDS 6-2, 4-6, 6-1, 6-2

JOHN VAN RYN......
Wm. MacC. Martin, Jr.
VAN RYN 6-2, 6-3, 6-4
Carlos Aranha ....
Edw. W. Feibleman ..
Feibleman 6-2, 6-3, 6-0
VAN RYN 6-1, 5-7, 6-0, 6-3

M. M. Rosenbaum ...
Manuel Alonso ....
Alonso 6-0, 6-3, 6-0
Jake H. Hess ....
HENRI COCHET* ....
COCHET 8-6, 6-2 6-3
COCHET 6-2, 6-4, 6-1
COCHET 7-5, 6-3, 8-6

COCHET 4-6, 6-3, 6-4, 6-0

COCHET, 6-1, 10-12, 4-6, 6-3, 7-5

COCHET, 6-1, 10-12, 4-6, 6-3, 7-5

Foreign Seedings
1. Henri Cochet
2. H. W. Austin
3. Frederick J. Perry
4. Jiro Satoh
5. Takeo Kuwabara
6. Marcel Bernard
7. John S. Olliff
8. Edward R. Avory

*Denotes foreign seeding

110

FIFTY-SECOND USLTA MEN'S SINGLES CHAMPIONSHIPS
West Side Tennis Club, Forest Hills, N.Y., 1933

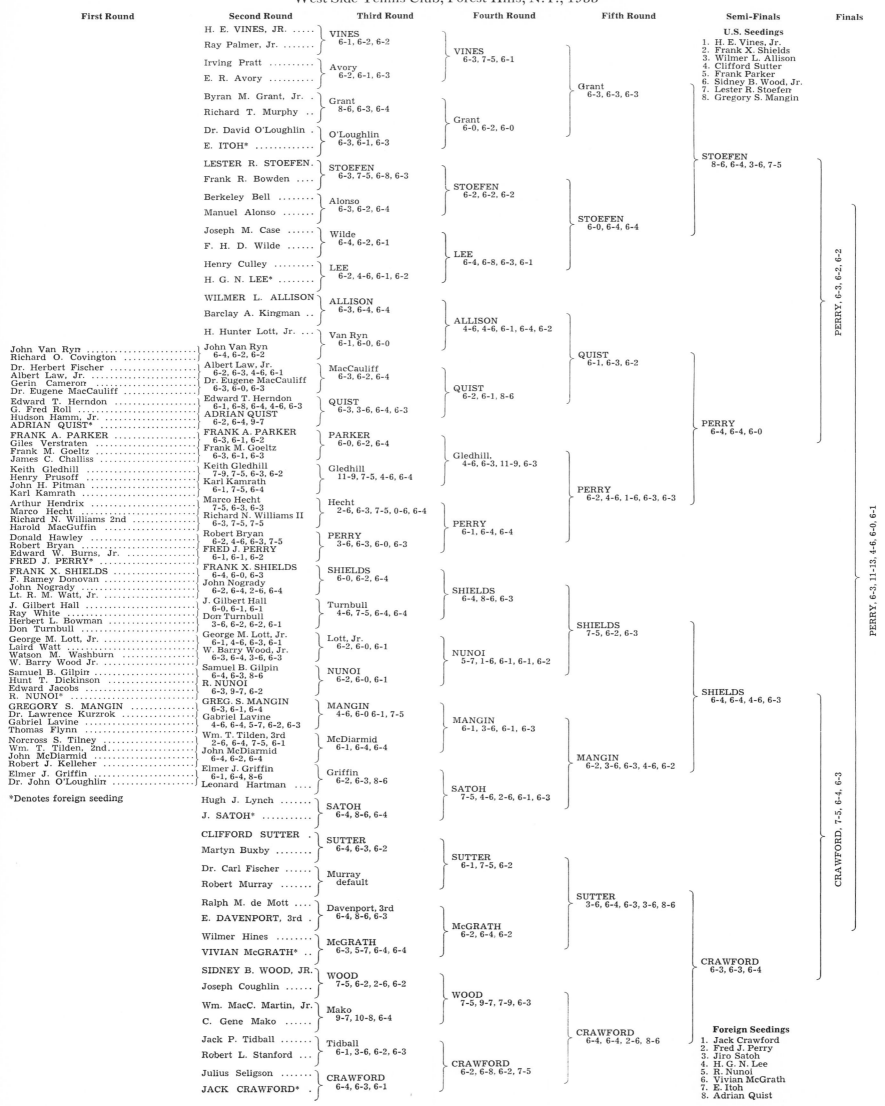

First Round · **Second Round** · **Third Round** · **Fourth Round** · **Fifth Round** · **Semi-Finals** · **Finals**

U.S. Seedings
1. H. E. Vines, Jr.
2. Frank X. Shields
3. Wilmer L. Allison
4. Clifford Sutter
5. Frank Parker
6. Sidney B. Wood, Jr.
7. Lester R. Stoefen
8. Gregory S. Mangin

H. E. VINES, JR.
Ray Palmer, Jr. — VINES 6-1, 6-2, 6-2
Irving Pratt
E. R. Avory — Avory 6-2, 6-1, 6-3
— VINES 6-3, 7-5, 6-1
Byran M. Grant, Jr.
Richard T. Murphy — Grant 8-6, 6-3, 6-4
Dr. David O'Loughlin
E. ITOH* — O'Loughlin 6-3, 6-1, 6-3
— Grant 6-0, 6-2, 6-0
— Grant 6-3, 6-3, 6-3

LESTER R. STOEFEN.
Frank R. Bowden — STOEFEN 6-3, 7-5, 6-8, 6-3
Berkeley Bell
Manuel Alonso — Alonso 6-3, 6-2, 6-4
— STOEFEN 6-2, 6-2, 6-2
Joseph M. Case
F. H. D. Wilde — Wilde 6-4, 6-2, 6-1
Henry Culley
H. G. N. LEE* — LEE 6-2, 4-6, 6-1, 6-2
— LEE 6-4, 6-8, 6-3, 6-1
— STOEFEN 6-0, 6-4, 6-4
— STOEFEN 8-6, 6-4, 3-6, 7-5

WILMER L. ALLISON
Barclay A. Kingman — ALLISON 6-3, 6-4, 6-4
H. Hunter Lott, Jr.
John Van Ryn 6-4, 6-2, 6-2 — Van Ryn 6-1, 6-0, 6-0
— ALLISON 4-6, 4-6, 6-1, 6-4, 6-2

John Van Ryn
Richard O. Covington
Dr. Herbert Fischer
Albert Law, Jr. 6-2, 6-3, 4-6, 6-1 — Albert Law, Jr. / Dr. Eugene MacCauliff 6-3, 6-0, 6-3 — MacCauliff 6-3, 6-2, 6-4
Gerin Cameron
Dr. Eugene MacCauliff
Edward T. Herndon 6-1, 6-8, 6-4, 4-6, 6-3 — Edward T. Herndon / ADRIAN QUIST 6-2, 6-4, 9-7 — QUIST 6-3, 3-6, 6-4, 6-3
G. Fred Roll
Hudson Hamm, Jr.
ADRIAN QUIST*
— QUIST 6-2, 6-1, 8-6
— QUIST 6-1, 6-3, 6-2

FRANK A. PARKER 6-3, 6-1, 6-2
Giles Verstraten
Frank M. Goeltz 6-3, 6-1, 6-3 — Frank M. Goeltz — PARKER 6-0, 6-2, 6-4
James C. Challiss
Keith Gledhill 7-9, 7-5, 6-3, 6-2 — Keith Gledhill / Karl Kamrath 6-1, 7-5, 6-4 — Gledhill 11-9, 7-5, 4-6, 6-4
Henry Prusoff
John H. Pitman
Karl Kamrath
— Gledhill, 4-6, 6-3, 11-9, 6-3
Arthur Hendrix 7-5, 6-3, 6-3 — Marco Hecht / Richard N. Williams II 6-3, 7-5, 7-5 — Hecht 2-6, 6-3, 7-5, 0-6, 6-4
Marco Hecht
Richard N. Williams 2nd
Harold MacGuffin
Donald Hawley 6-2, 4-6, 6-3, 7-5 — Robert Bryan / FRED J. PERRY 6-1, 6-1, 6-2 — PERRY 3-6, 6-3, 6-0, 6-3
Robert Bryan
Edward W. Burns, Jr.
FRED J. PERRY*
— PERRY 6-1, 6-4, 6-4
— PERRY 6-2, 4-6, 1-6, 6-3, 6-3
— PERRY 6-4, 6-4, 6-0

FRANK X. SHIELDS 6-4, 6-0, 6-3
F. Ramey Donovan
John Nogrady 6-2, 6-4, 2-6, 6-4 — John Nogrady — SHIELDS 6-0, 6-2, 6-4
Lt. R. M. Watt, Jr.
J. Gilbert Hall 6-0, 6-1, 6-1 — J. Gilbert Hall / Don Turnbull 3-6, 6-2, 6-2, 6-1 — Turnbull 4-6, 7-5, 6-4, 6-4
Ray White
Herbert L. Bowman
Don Turnbull
— SHIELDS 6-4, 8-6, 6-3
George M. Lott, Jr. 6-1, 4-6, 6-3, 6-1 — George M. Lott, Jr. / W. Barry Wood, Jr. 6-3, 6-4, 3-6, 6-3 — Lott, Jr. 6-2, 6-0, 6-1
Laird Watt
Watson M. Washburn
W. Barry Wood Jr.
Samuel B. Gilpin 6-4, 6-3, 8-6 — Samuel B. Gilpin / R. NUNOI 6-3, 9-7, 6-2 — NUNOI 6-2, 6-0, 6-1
Hunt T. Dickinson
Edward Jacobs
R. NUNOI*
— NUNOI 5-7, 1-6, 6-1, 6-1, 6-2
— SHIELDS 7-5, 6-2, 6-3
— SHIELDS 6-4, 6-4, 4-6, 6-3

GREG. S. MANGIN 6-3, 6-1, 6-4
Dr. Lawrence Kurzrok
Gabriel Lavine 4-6, 6-4, 5-7, 6-2, 6-3 — Gabriel Lavine — MANGIN 4-6, 6-0 6-1, 7-5
Thomas Flynn
Norcross S. Tilney 2-6, 6-4, 7-5, 6-1 — Wm. T. Tilden, 3rd / John McDiarmid 6-4, 6-2, 6-4 — McDiarmid 6-1, 6-4, 6-4
Wm. T. Tilden, 2nd
John McDiarmid
Robert J. Kelleher
— MANGIN 6-1, 3-6, 6-1, 6-3
Elmer J. Griffin 6-1, 6-4, 8-6 — Elmer J. Griffin / Leonard Hartman — Griffin 6-2, 6-3, 8-6
Dr. John O'Loughlin
Hugh J. Lynch
J. SATOH* — SATOH 6-4, 8-6, 6-4
— SATOH 7-5, 4-6, 2-6, 6-1, 6-3
— MANGIN 6-2, 3-6, 6-3, 4-6, 6-2

*Denotes foreign seeding

CLIFFORD SUTTER.
Martyn Buxby — SUTTER 6-4, 6-3, 6-2
Dr. Carl Fischer
Robert Murray — Murray default
— SUTTER 6-1, 7-5, 6-2
Ralph M. de Mott
E. DAVENPORT, 3rd. — Davenport, 3rd 6-4, 8-6, 6-3
Wilmer Hines
VIVIAN McGRATH* — McGRATH 6-3, 5-7, 6-4, 6-4
— McGRATH 6-2, 6-4, 6-2
— SUTTER 3-6, 6-4, 6-3, 3-6, 8-6

SIDNEY B. WOOD, JR.
Joseph Coughlin — WOOD 7-5, 6-2, 2-6, 6-2
Wm. MacC. Martin, Jr.
C. Gene Mako — Mako 9-7, 10-8, 6-4
— WOOD 7-5, 9-7, 7-9, 6-3
Jack P. Tidball
Robert L. Stanford — Tidball 6-1, 3-6, 6-2, 6-3
Julius Seligson
JACK CRAWFORD* — CRAWFORD 6-4, 6-3, 6-1
— CRAWFORD 6-2, 6-8, 6-2, 7-5
— CRAWFORD 6-4, 6-4, 2-6, 8-6
— CRAWFORD 6-3, 6-3, 6-4

PERRY, 6-4, 6-4, 6-0
SHIELDS 6-4, 6-4, 4-6, 6-3

PERRY, 6-3, 6-2, 6-2
CRAWFORD, 7-5, 6-4, 6-3

PERRY, 6-3, 11-13, 4-6, 6-0, 6-1

Foreign Seedings
1. Jack Crawford
2. Fred J. Perry
3. Jiro Satoh
4. H. G. N. Lee
5. R. Nunoi
6. Vivian McGrath
7. E. Itoh
8. Adrian Quist

FIFTY-THIRD USLTA MEN'S SINGLES CHAMPIONSHIPS
West Side Tennis Club, Forest Hills, N.Y., 1934

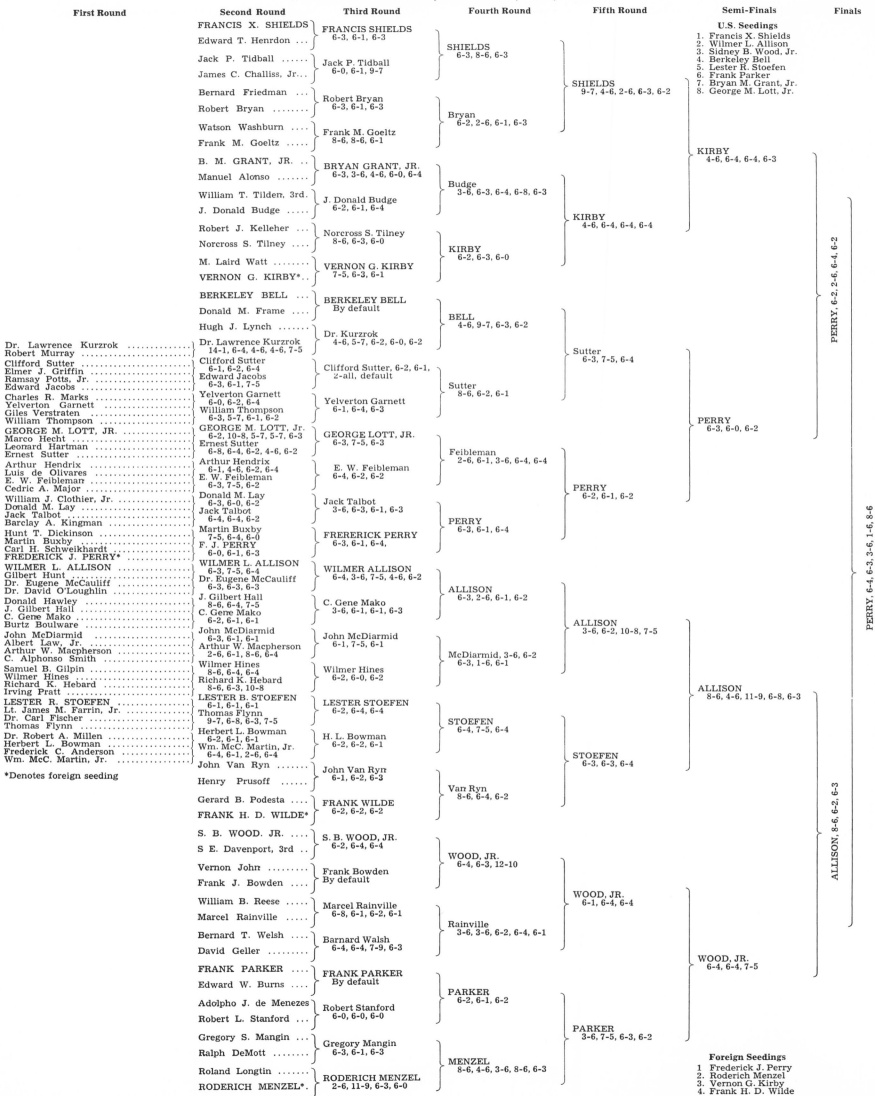

First Round	Second Round	Third Round	Fourth Round	Fifth Round	Semi-Finals	Finals

U.S. Seedings
1. Francis X. Shields
2. Wilmer L. Allison
3. Sidney B. Wood, Jr.
4. Berkeley Bell
5. Lester R. Stoefen
6. Frank Parker
7. Bryan M. Grant, Jr.
8. George M. Lott, Jr.

FRANCIS X. SHIELDS
Edward T. Herndon ...
FRANCIS SHIELDS 6-3, 6-1, 6-3
SHIELDS 6-3, 8-6, 6-3

Jack P. Tidball ......
James C. Challiss, Jr...
Jack P. Tidball 6-0, 6-1, 9-7

SHIELDS 9-7, 4-6, 2-6, 6-3, 6-2

Bernard Friedman ...
Robert Bryan ....
Robert Bryan 6-3, 6-1, 6-3
Bryan 6-2, 2-6, 6-1, 6-3

Watson Washburn ....
Frank M. Goeltz .....
Frank M. Goeltz 8-6, 8-6, 6-1

KIRBY 4-6, 6-4, 6-4, 6-3

B. M. GRANT, JR. ..
Manuel Alonso ......
BRYAN GRANT, JR. 6-3, 3-6, 4-6, 6-0, 6-4
Budge 3-6, 6-3, 6-4, 6-8, 6-3

William T. Tilden, 3rd.
J. Donald Budge .....
J. Donald Budge 6-2, 6-1, 6-4

KIRBY 4-6, 6-4, 6-4, 6-4

Robert J. Kelleher ...
Norcross S. Tilney ....
Norcross S. Tilney 8-6, 6-3, 6-0
KIRBY 6-2, 6-3, 6-0

M. Laird Watt ....
VERNON G. KIRBY*..
VERNON G. KIRBY 7-5, 6-3, 6-1

PERRY, 6-2, 2-6, 6-4, 6-2

BERKELEY BELL ....
Donald M. Frame ....
BERKELEY BELL By default
BELL 4-6, 9-7, 6-3, 6-2

Hugh J. Lynch ....
Dr. Lawrence Kurzrok
14-1, 6-4, 4-6, 4-6, 7-5
Dr. Kurzrok 4-6, 5-7, 6-2, 6-0, 6-2

Sutter 6-3, 7-5, 6-4

Dr. Lawrence Kurzrok
Robert Murray
Clifford Sutter
Clifford Sutter 6-1, 6-2, 6-4
Clifford Sutter, 6-2, 6-1, 2-all, default
Elmer J. Griffin
Ramsay Potts, Jr.
Edward Jacobs 6-3, 6-1, 7-5
Edward Jacobs
Sutter 8-6, 6-2, 6-1

Charles R. Marks
Yelverton Garnett
Yelverton Garnett 6-0, 6-2, 6-4
Yelverton Garnett 6-1, 6-4, 6-3
Giles Verstraten
William Thompson 6-3, 5-7, 6-1, 6-2
William Thompson

PERRY 6-3, 6-0, 6-2

GEORGE M. LOTT, JR.
Marco Hecht
GEORGE M. LOTT, JR. 6-2, 10-8, 5-7, 5-7, 6-3
GEORGE LOTT, JR. 6-3, 7-5, 6-3
Leonard Hartman
Ernest Sutter 6-8, 6-4, 6-2, 4-6, 6-2
Ernest Sutter
Feibleman 2-6, 6-1, 3-6, 6-4, 6-4

Arthur Hendrix
Luis de Olivares 6-1, 4-6, 6-2, 6-4
E. W. Feibleman
E. W. Feibleman 6-3, 7-5, 6-2
E. W. Feibleman 6-4, 6-2, 6-2
Cedric A. Major

PERRY 6-2, 6-1, 6-2

William J. Clothier, Jr.
Donald M. Lay 6-3, 6-0, 6-2
Donald M. Lay
Jack Talbot 6-4, 6-4, 6-2
Jack Talbot 3-6, 6-3, 6-1, 6-3
Jack Talbot
Barclay A. Kingman
PERRY 6-3, 6-1, 6-4

Hunt T. Dickinson
Martin Buxby 7-5, 6-4, 6-0
Martin Buxby
F. J. PERRY 6-0, 6-1, 6-3
FREDERICK PERRY 6-3, 6-1, 6-4,
Carl H. Schweikhardt
FREDERICK J. PERRY*

WILMER L. ALLISON
Gilbert Hunt
WILMER L. ALLISON 6-3, 7-5, 6-4
WILMER ALLISON 6-4, 3-6, 7-5, 4-6, 6-2
Dr. Eugene McCauliff
Dr. David O'Loughlin
Dr. Eugene McCauliff 6-3, 6-3, 6-3
ALLISON 6-3, 2-6, 6-1, 6-2

Donald Hawley
J. Gilbert Hall 8-6, 6-4, 7-5
J. Gilbert Hall
C. Gene Mako 6-2, 6-1, 6-1
C. Gene Mako 3-6, 6-1, 6-1, 6-3
C. Gene Mako
Burtz Boulware

ALLISON 3-6, 6-2, 10-8, 7-5

John McDiarmid
Albert Law, Jr.
John McDiarmid 6-3, 6-1, 6-1
John McDiarmid 6-1, 7-5, 6-1
Arthur W. Macpherson
Arthur W. Macpherson 2-6, 6-1, 8-6, 6-4
C. Alphonso Smith
McDiarmid, 3-6, 6-2, 6-3, 1-6, 6-1

Samuel B. Gilpin
Wilmer Hines 8-6, 6-4, 6-4
Wilmer Hines
Wilmer Hines 6-2, 6-0, 6-2
Richard K. Hebard
Richard K. Hebard 8-6, 6-3, 10-8
Irving Pratt

ALLISON 8-6, 4-6, 11-9, 6-8, 6-3

LESTER R. STOEFEN
Lt. James M. Farrin, Jr.
LESTER B. STOEFEN 6-1, 6-1, 6-1
LESTER STOEFEN 6-2, 6-4, 6-4
Dr. Carl Fischer
Thomas Flynn 9-7, 6-8, 6-3, 7-5
Thomas Flynn
STOEFEN 6-4, 7-5, 6-4

Dr. Robert A. Millen
Herbert L. Bowman 6-2, 6-1, 6-1
Herbert L. Bowman
H. L. Bowman 6-2, 6-2, 6-1
Frederick C. Anderson
Wm. McC. Martin, Jr. 6-4, 6-1, 2-6, 6-4
Wm. McC. Martin, Jr.

STOEFEN 6-3, 6-3, 6-4

John Van Ryn
Henry Prusoff
John Van Ryn 6-1, 6-2, 6-3
Van Ryn 8-6, 6-4, 6-2

Gerard B. Podesta ....
FRANK H. D. WILDE*
FRANK WILDE 6-2, 6-2, 6-2

ALLISON 8-6, 6-2, 6-3

*Denotes foreign seeding

S. B. WOOD. JR. ...
S E. Davenport, 3rd ..
S. B. WOOD, JR. 6-2, 6-4, 6-4
WOOD, JR. 6-4, 6-3, 12-10

Vernon John ....
Frank J. Bowden ....
Frank Bowden By default

WOOD, JR. 6-1, 6-4, 6-4

William B. Reese ....
Marcel Rainville .....
Marcel Rainville 6-8, 6-1, 6-2, 6-1
Rainville 3-6, 3-6, 6-2, 6-4, 6-1

Bernard T. Welsh ....
David Geller ....
Barnard Walsh 6-4, 6-4, 7-9, 6-3

WOOD, JR. 6-4, 6-4, 7-5

FRANK PARKER ....
Edward W. Burns ....
FRANK PARKER By default
PARKER 6-2, 6-1, 6-2

Adolpho J. de Menezes
Robert L. Stanford ...
Robert Stanford 6-0, 6-0, 6-0

PARKER 3-6, 7-5, 6-3, 6-2

Gregory S. Mangin ...
Ralph DeMott ....
Gregory Mangin 6-3, 6-1, 6-3
MENZEL 8-6, 4-6, 3-6, 8-6, 6-3

Roland Longtin ......
RODERICH MENZEL*.
RODERICH MENZEL 2-6, 11-9, 6-3, 6-0

PERRY, 6-4, 6-3, 3-6, 1-6, 8-6

ALLISON, 8-6, 2-6, 6-3

Foreign Seedings
1 Frederick J. Perry
2. Roderich Menzel
3. Vernon G. Kirby
4. Frank H. D. Wilde

FIFTY-FOURTH USLTA MEN'S SINGLES CHAMPIONSHIPS
West Side Tennis Club, Forest Hills, N.Y., 1935

First Round	Second Round	Third Round	Fourth Round	Fifth Round	Semi-Finals	Finals

U. S. Seedings
1. Wilmer L. Allison
2. J. Donald Budge
3. Francis X. Shields
4. Sidney B. Wood, Jr.
5. Bryan M. Grant, Jr.
6. Frank A. Parker
7. Berkeley Bell
8. Gregory S. Mangin

J. DONALD BUDGE
Donald Hawley
— J. DONALD BUDGE 6-1, 6-0, 6-1

Wilmer Hines
A. Y. P. Garnet, Jr.
— Wilmer Hines 6-0, 6-1, 9-7

— J. DONALD BUDGE 9-7, 6-1, 7-5

John Van Ryn
John Ronald Behr
— John Van Ryn 6-2, 6-0, 6-1

Richard T. Willis
A. M. LEGEAY
— A. MARTIN LEGEAY 6-2, 6-1, 6-2

— John Van Ryn 6-0, 6-3, 6-3

— J. DONALD BUDGE 8-6, 6-4, 8-6

B. M. GRANT, JR.
Wm. J. Clothier, 2nd
— B. M. GRANT, JR. 6-3, 6-1, 6-4

D. Lawrence Nelson
Robert Murray
— Robert Murray 6-4, 6-3, 6-2

— B. M. GRANT, JR. 6-1, 6-2, 6-2

Wilbur E. Hess
John Nogrady
— Wilbur E. Hess 6-1, 6-1, 6-2

Marco Hecht
Robert Harmon
— Robert Harmon 6-1, 6-1, 6-0

— Wilbur E. Hess 7-5, 6-2, 5-7, 2-6, 6-4

— B. M. GRANT, JR. 7-5, 5-7, 6-1, 6-4

— B M. GRANT, JR. 6-4, 6-4, 5-7, 6-3

Robert Harmon
CHRISTIAN BOUSSUS*
— Robert Harmon 6-4, 3-6, 7-5, 6-1

SIDNEY. B. WOOD, JR.
William B. Reese
— SIDNEY B. WOOD, JR. 1-6, 6-2, 6-3, 6-2

J. Gilbert Hall
Dr. Carl Fischer
— J. Gilbert Hall 6-0, 6-4, 6-3

— S. B. WOOD, JR. 3-6, 3-6, 6-4, 6-4, 6-4

Edward W. Fiebleman
John Walter Ruckert
— Edward W. Feibleman 4-6, 6-3, 6-2, 6-2

Watson Washburn
Frederic Mercur
— Frederic Mercur 6-3, 6-4, 10-8

— E. W. Feibleman 1-6, 6-4, 6-3, 3-6, 10-8

— S B. WOOD, JR. 6-3, 6-2, 6-1

George L. Seewagen
Percy L. Kynaston
— George L. Seewagen 6-0, 6-2, 6-2

John McDiarmid
William Robertson
— John McDiarmid 6-4, 1-6, 7-5, 6-3

— John McDiarmid 6-2, 6-3, 6-2

Ramsay D. Potts, Jr.
Martin Buxby
— Martin Buxby 4-6, 2-6, 6-1, 6-1, 6-3

Frank Broida
ESKELL D. ANDREWS*
— Eskell D. Andrews 6-3, 6-4, 6-3

— Martin Buxby 5-7, 5-7, 6-3, 6-4, 6-4

— John McDiarmid 7-5, 1-6, 6-8, 6-3

— S. B. WOOD, JR. 6-2, 6-3, 4-6, 6-1

GREGORY S. MANGIN
G. Price Colvin
— GREGORY S. MANGIN 6-4, 6-4, 6-1

Clayton L. Burwell
Dr. Herbert Fischer
— Clayton L. Burwell 6-2, 5-7, 6-2, 6-3

— G. S. Mangin 6-3, 6-4, 6-4

Hunter Lott, Jr.
Robert L. Stanford
— Hunter Lott, Jr. 6-4, 6-4, 6-2

Dave Geller
Dr. Lawrence Kurzrok
— Dr. Lawrence Kurzrok 6-2, 8-10, 6-2, 6-1

— Dr. L. Kurzrok 7-5, 6-1, 6-4

— G. S. Mangin 6-4, 6-1, 6-0

Richard Keith Hebard
Robert J. Kelleher
— Robert J. Kelleher 7-9, 7-5, 6-3, 6-4

M. Laird Watt
Lt. R. M. Watt, Jr.
— M. Laird Watt 7-9, 6-8, 8-6, 8-6, 6-2

— M. Laird Watt 6-4, 6-0, 6-4

Richard N. Williams, 2nd
Barnard T. Welsh
— R. N. Williams, 2nd 3-6, 4-6, 6-1, 7-5, 7-5

Norcross Tilney
RODERICH MENZEL*
— RODERICH MENZEL 7-5, 6-3, 4-6, 6-2

— RODERICH MENZEL 6-2, 6-2 6-0

— RODERICH MENZEL 6-4, 6-2, 6-3

— G. S. MANGIN 6-1, 9-7, 6-2

WILLMER ALLISON
Henry C. Brunie
— W. L. ALLISON 6-0, 6-2, 6-2

Donald M. Lay, Jr.
Thomas Flynn
— Thomas Flynn 9-7, 6-3, 6-1

— W. L. Allison 6-2, 6-2, 6-1

Dr. D. L. O'Loughlin
E. T. Herndon
— Dr. D. L. O'Loughlin 6-3, 8-6, 6-2

Henry N. Culley
William Lurie
— Henry N. Culley 6-3, 6-1, 5-7, 6-0

— Henry N. Culley 6-3, 6-3, 6-4

— W. L. ALLISON 3-6, 6-4, 6-2, 6-3

Clifford Sutter
Edward J. DeGray
— Clifford Sutter 6-3, 6-3, 6-2

Jess Millman
Albert Law, Jr.
— Jess Millman 6-1, 6-0, 6-2

— Clifford Sutter 7-9, 6-3, 6-2, 6-4

Gabriel Lavine
Robert L. Madden
— Gabriel Lavine 6-3, 6-4, 2-6, 6-2

C. Gene Mako
JACQUES BRUGNON*
— C. Gene Mako 0-6, 6-2, 7-5, 6-1

— C. Gene Mako 4-6, 6-3, 6-3, 6-4

— C. G. Mako 4-6, 3-6, 6-3, 6-2, 6-4

— WILMER L. ALLISON 6-2, 6-0, 7-5

BERKELEY BELL
Manuel Alonso
Robert Little
Samuel Lee
— Manuel Alonso 6-4, 7-9, 6-8, 7-5, 6-4
— Robert Little By default
— Manuel Alonso 6-3, 6-4, 8-6

Donald M. Frame
Peter Lauck
— Donald M. Frame 6-1, 6-3, 6-0

Frank A. Thompson
Gilbert Hunt, Jr.
— Gilbert Hunt, Jr. 7-5, 6-1, 4-6, 14-12

— Gilbert Hunt, Jr. 6-4, 7-5, 3-6, 6-3

— Manuel Alonso 6-8, 6-2, 6-1, 6-4

Herbert Lee Bowman
Leonard S. Patterson
— Herbert Lee Bowman 4-6, 8-6, 6-4, 6-1

Guy Cheng
Samuel B. Gilpin
— Guy Cheng 0-6, 6-2, 6-3, 4-6, 6-2

— H. L. Bowman 6-8, 5-7, 7-5, 6-4, 6-4

Robert Underwood
Hal Surface, Jr.
— Hal Surface, Jr. 6-1, 6-3, 6-0

E. Ramsey Donovan
ENRIQUE MAIER*
— ENRIQUE MAIER 6-2, 6-1, 6-3

— ENRIQUE MAIER 6-3, 6-8, 6-0, 6-4

— ENRIQUE MAIER 6-2, 6-2, 6-4

— ENRIQUE MAIER 6-1, 6-2, 8-6

— WILMER L. ALLISON 6-2, 6-4, 6-4

FRANCIS X. SHIELDS
Henri Paul Emard
— F. X. SHIELDS 6-0, 6-3, 6-1
— Ernest Sutter
— F. X. SHIELDS 6-2, 6-0, 6-0

Henry Justin Prusoff
S. E. Davenport, 3rd
— Henry J. Prusoff 3-6, 4-6, 6-1, 6-4, 6-1

— F. X. SHIELDS 7-5, 7-5, 2-6, 7-5

Charles R. Harris
Frank J. Bowden
— F. J. Bowden 8-6, 6-1, 6-4

Burtz Boulware
Frank M. Goeltz
— Burtz Boulware 4-6, 5-7, 6-4, 7-5, 10-8

— F. J. Bowden 6-1, 6-3, 6-4

— F. X. SHIELDS 6-1, 6-4, 6-2

FRANK A. PARKER
William Thompson
— FRANK A. PARKER 6-0, 6-0, 4-6, 6-2

Robert Bryan
John S. Tilney
— Robert Bryan 6-0, 6-2, 6-2

— F. A. PARKER 6-1, 6-1, 7-5

Wm. T. Tilden, 3rd
Leonard Hartman
— Leonard Hartman 6-3, 6-2, 3-6, 6-4

Arthur S. Fowler
F. J. PERRY*
— F. J. PERRY 6-3, 6-2, 6-1

— F. J. PERRY 6-4, 6-3, 7-5

— F. J. PERRY 6-4, 6-2, 6-0

— FREDERICK J. PERRY 6-4, 4-6, 8-6, 6-0

— SIDNEY B. WOOD, Jr. 6-2, 4-6, 12-10, 6-2

— WILMER L. ALLISON, 6-2, 6-2, 6-3

— WILMER L. ALLISON, 7-5, 6-3, 6-3

*Denotes foreign seeding

Foreign Seedings
1. Frederick J. Perry
2. Roderich Menzel
3. Christian Boussus
4. Enrique Maier
5. A. Martin Legeay
6. Jacques Brugnon
7. Eskell D. Andrews

113

FIFTY-FIFTH USLTA MEN'S SINGLES CHAMPIONSHIPS
West Side Tennis Club, Forest Hills, N.Y., 1936

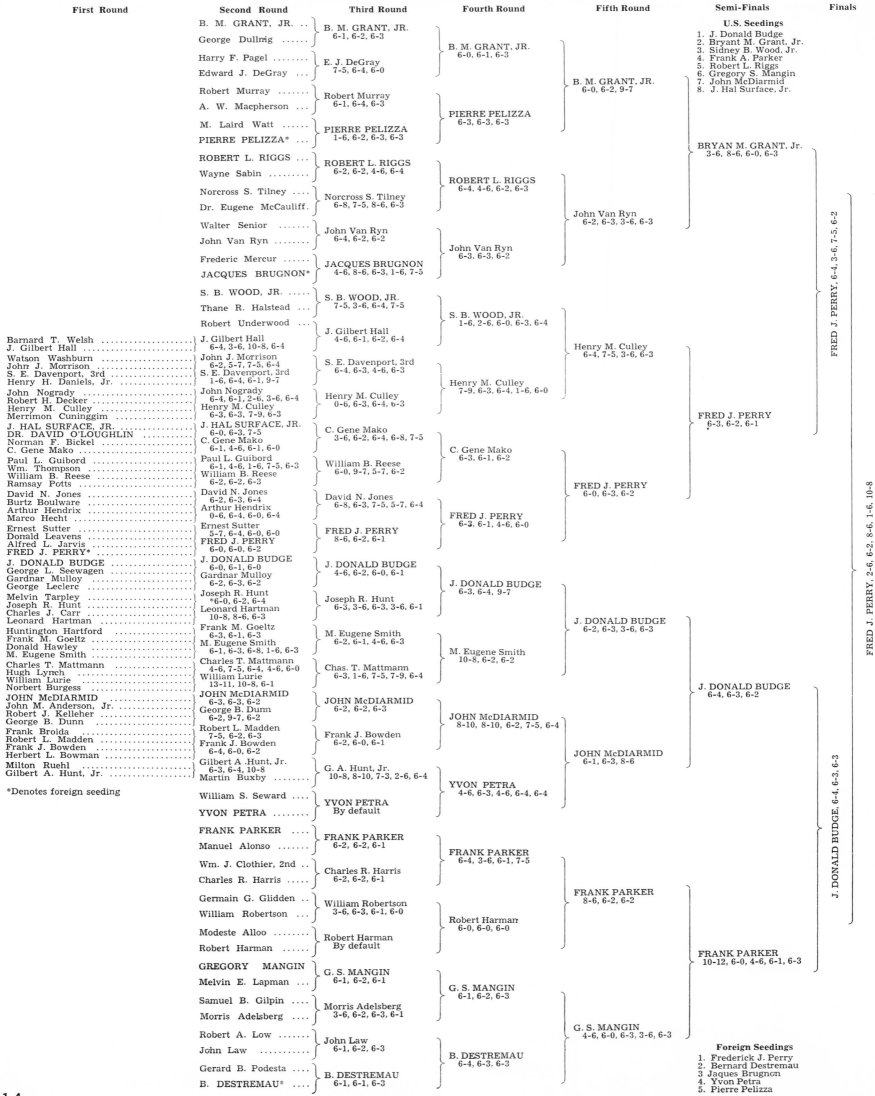

First Round	Second Round	Third Round	Fourth Round	Fifth Round	Semi-Finals	Finals

U.S. Seedings
1. J. Donald Budge
2. Bryant M. Grant, Jr.
3. Sidney B. Wood, Jr.
4. Frank A. Parker
5. Robert L. Riggs
6. Gregory S. Mangin
7. John McDiarmid
8. J. Hal Surface, Jr.

B. M. GRANT, JR.
George Dulling

B. M. GRANT, JR.
6-1, 6-2, 6-3

Harry F. Pagel
Edward J. DeGray

E. J. DeGray
7-5, 6-4, 6-0

B. M. GRANT, JR.
6-0, 6-1, 6-3

Robert Murray
A. W. Macpherson

Robert Murray
6-1, 6-4, 6-3

M. Laird Watt
PIERRE PELIZZA*

PIERRE PELIZZA
1-6, 6-2, 6-3, 6-3

PIERRE PELIZZA
6-3, 6-3, 6-3

B. M. GRANT, JR.
6-0, 6-2, 9-7

ROBERT L. RIGGS
Wayne Sabin

ROBERT L. RIGGS
6-2, 6-2, 4-6, 6-4

Norcross S. Tilney
Dr. Eugene McCauliff.

Norcross S. Tilney
6-8, 7-5, 8-6, 6-3

ROBERT L. RIGGS
6-4, 4-6, 6-2, 6-3

Walter Senior
John Van Ryn

John Van Ryn
6-4, 6-2, 6-2

John Van Ryn
6-3, 6-3, 6-2

Frederic Mercur
JACQUES BRUGNON*

JACQUES BRUGNON
4-6, 8-6, 6-3, 1-6, 7-5

John Van Ryn
6-2, 6-3, 3-6, 6-3

BRYAN M. GRANT, Jr.
3-6, 8-6, 6-0, 6-3

S. B. WOOD, JR.
Thane R. Halstead

S. B. WOOD, JR.
7-5, 3-6, 6-4, 7-5

Robert Underwood
J. Gilbert Hall

J. Gilbert Hall
4-6, 6-1, 6-2, 6-4

S. B. WOOD, JR.
1-6, 2-6, 6-0, 6-3, 6-4

Barnard T. Welsh
J. Gilbert Hall

J. Gilbert Hall
6-4, 3-6, 10-8, 6-4

Watson Washburn
John J. Morrison

John J. Morrison
6-2, 5-7, 7-5, 6-4

S. E. Davenport, 3rd
Henry H. Daniels, Jr.

S. E. Davenport, 3rd
1-6, 6-4, 6-1, 9-7

S. E. Davenport, 3rd
6-4, 6-3, 4-6, 6-3

John Nogrady
Robert H. Decker

John Nogrady
6-4, 6-1, 2-6, 3-6, 6-4

Henry M. Culley
Merrimon Cuninggim

Henry M. Culley
6-3, 6-3, 7-9, 6-3

Henry M. Culley
0-6, 6-3, 6-4, 6-3

Henry M. Culley
7-9, 6-3, 6-4, 1-6, 6-0

Henry M. Culley
6-4, 7-5, 3-6, 6-3

J. HAL SURFACE, JR.
DR. DAVID O'LOUGHLIN
Norman F. Bickel
C. Gene Mako

J. HAL SURFACE, JR.
6-0, 6-3, 7-5

C. Gene Mako
6-1, 4-6, 6-1, 6-0

C. Gene Mako
3-6, 6-2, 6-4, 6-8, 7-5

Paul L. Guibord
Wm. Thompson
William B. Reese
Ramsay Potts

Paul L. Guibord
6-1, 4-6, 1-6, 7-5, 6-3

William B. Reese
6-2, 6-2, 6-3

William B. Reese
6-0, 9-7, 5-7, 6-2

C. Gene Mako
6-3, 6-1, 6-2

David N. Jones
Burtz Boulware
Arthur Hendrix
Marco Hecht

David N. Jones
6-2, 6-3, 6-4

Arthur Hendrix
0-6, 6-4, 6-0, 6-4

David N. Jones
6-8, 6-3, 7-5, 5-7, 6-4

FRED J. PERRY
6-0, 6-3, 6-2

Ernest Sutter
Donald Leavens
Alfred L. Jarvis
FRED J. PERRY*

Ernest Sutter
5-7, 6-4, 6-0, 6-0

FRED J. PERRY
6-0, 6-0, 6-2

FRED J. PERRY
8-6, 6-2, 6-1

FRED J. PERRY
6-3, 6-1, 4-6, 6-0

FRED J. PERRY
6-3, 6-2, 6-1

J. DONALD BUDGE
George L. Seewagen
Gardnar Mulloy
George Leclerc

J. DONALD BUDGE
6-0, 6-1, 6-0

Gardnar Mulloy
6-2, 6-3, 6-2

J. DONALD BUDGE
4-6, 6-2, 6-0, 6-1

Melvin Tarpley
Joseph R. Hunt
Charles J. Carr
Leonard Hartman

Joseph R. Hunt
*6-0, 6-2, 6-4

Leonard Hartman
10-8, 8-6, 6-3

Joseph R. Hunt
6-3, 3-6, 6-3, 3-6, 6-1

J. DONALD BUDGE
6-3, 6-4, 9-7

Huntington Hartford
Frank M. Goeltz
Donald Hawley
M. Eugene Smith

Frank M. Goeltz
6-3, 6-1, 6-3

M. Eugene Smith
6-1, 6-3, 6-8, 1-6, 6-3

M. Eugene Smith
6-2, 6-1, 4-6, 6-3

J. DONALD BUDGE
6-2, 6-3, 3-6, 6-3

Charles T. Mattmann
Hugh Lynch
William Lurie
Norbert Burgess

Charles T. Mattmann
4-6, 7-5, 6-4, 4-6, 6-0

William Lurie
13-11, 10-8, 6-1

Chas. T. Mattmann
6-3, 1-6, 7-5, 7-9, 6-4

M. Eugene Smith
10-8, 6-2, 6-2

JOHN McDIARMID
John M. Anderson, Jr.
Robert J. Kelleher
George B. Dunn

JOHN McDIARMID
6-3, 6-3, 6-2

George B. Dunn
6-2, 9-7, 6-2

JOHN McDIARMID
6-2, 6-2, 6-3

Frank Broida
Robert L. Madden
Frank J. Bowden
Herbert L. Bowman

Robert L. Madden
7-5, 6-2, 6-3

Frank J. Bowden
6-4, 6-0, 6-2

Frank J. Bowden
6-2, 6-0, 6-1

JOHN McDIARMID
8-10, 8-10, 6-2, 7-5, 6-4

Milton Ruehl
Gilbert A. Hunt, Jr.

Gilbert A. Hunt, Jr.
6-3, 6-4, 10-8

G. A. Hunt, Jr.
10-8, 8-10, 7-3, 2-6, 6-4

Martin Buxby

JOHN McDIARMID
6-1, 6-3, 8-6

J. DONALD BUDGE
6-4, 6-3, 6-2

*Denotes foreign seeding

William S. Seward
YVON PETRA

YVON PETRA
By default

YVON PETRA
4-6, 6-3, 4-6, 6-4, 6-4

FRANK PARKER
Manuel Alonso

FRANK PARKER
6-2, 6-2, 6-1

Wm. J. Clothier, 2nd
Charles R. Harris

Charles R. Harris
6-2, 6-2, 6-1

FRANK PARKER
6-4, 3-6, 6-1, 7-5

Germain G. Glidden
William Robertson

William Robertson
3-6, 6-3, 6-1, 6-0

Modeste Alloo
Robert Harman

Robert Harman
By default

Robert Harman
6-0, 6-0, 6-0

FRANK PARKER
8-6, 6-2, 6-2

GREGORY MANGIN
Melvin E. Lapman

G. S. MANGIN
6-1, 6-2, 6-1

Samuel B. Gilpin
Morris Adelsberg

Morris Adelsberg
3-6, 6-2, 6-3, 6-1

G. S. MANGIN
6-1, 6-2, 6-3

FRANK PARKER
10-12, 6-0, 4-6, 6-1, 6-3

Robert A. Low
John Law

John Law
6-1, 6-2, 6-3

B. DESTREMAU
6-4, 6-3, 6-3

G. S. MANGIN
4-6, 6-0, 6-3, 3-6, 6-3

Gerard B. Podesta
B. DESTREMAU*

B. DESTREMAU
6-1, 6-1, 6-3

Foreign Seedings
1. Frederick J. Perry
2. Bernard Destremau
3. Jaques Brugnon
4. Yvon Petra
5. Pierre Pelizza

FRED J. PERRY, 6-4, 3-6, 7-5, 6-2

FRED J. PERRY, 2-6, 6-2, 8-6, 1-6, 10-8

J. DONALD BUDGE, 6-4, 6-3, 6-3

FIFTY-SIXTH USLTA MEN'S SINGLES CHAMPIONSHIPS
West Side Tennis Club, Forest Hills, N.Y., 1937

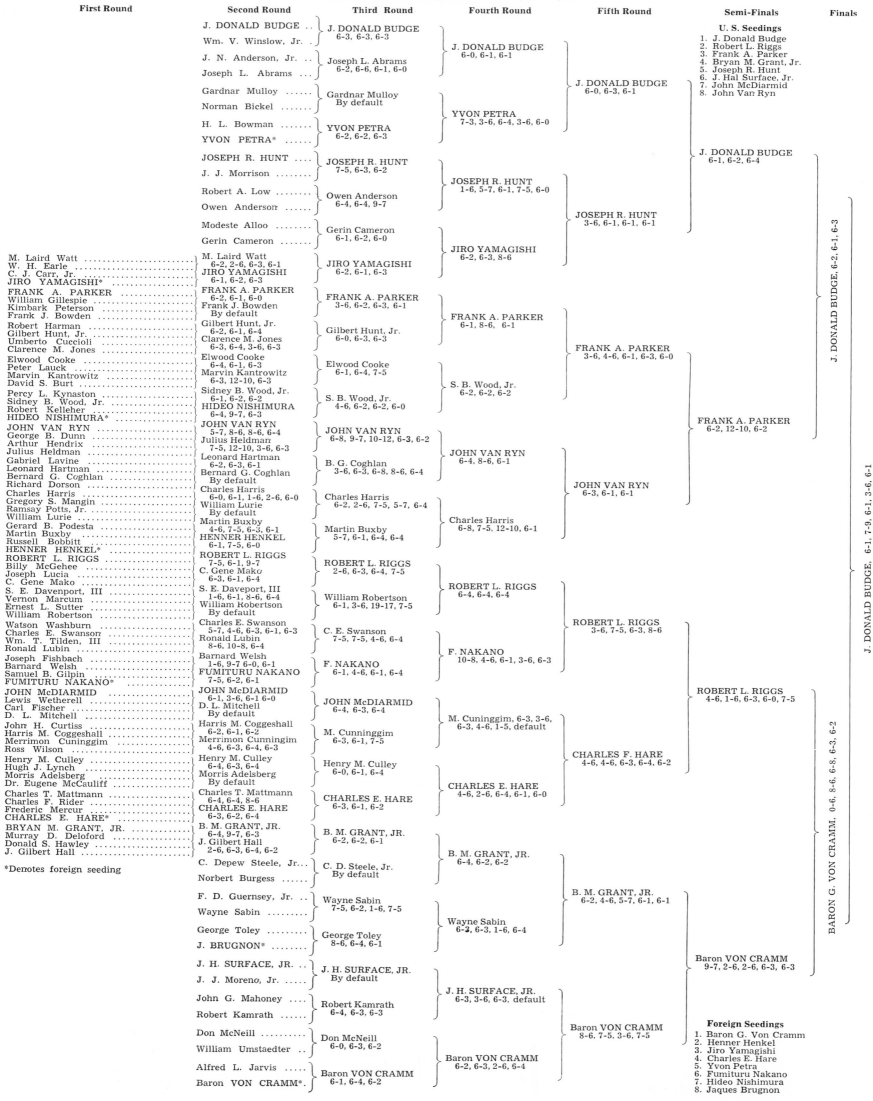

First Round | Second Round | Third Round | Fourth Round | Fifth Round | Semi-Finals | Finals

U. S. Seedings
1. J. Donald Budge
2. Robert L. Riggs
3. Frank A. Parker
4. Bryan M. Grant, Jr.
5. Joseph R. Hunt
6. J. Hal Surface, Jr.
7. John McDiarmid
8. John Van Ryn

J. DONALD BUDGE ..
Wm. V. Winslow, Jr. .
— J. DONALD BUDGE 6-3, 6-3, 6-3
J. N. Anderson, Jr. ..
Joseph L. Abrams ...
— Joseph L. Abrams 6-2, 6-6, 6-1, 6-0
— J. DONALD BUDGE 6-0, 6-1, 6-1
Gardnar Mulloy ......
Norman Bickel ....
— Gardnar Mulloy By default
H. L. Bowman ....
YVON PETRA* ......
— YVON PETRA 6-2, 6-2, 6-3
— YVON PETRA 7-3, 3-6, 6-4, 3-6, 6-0
— J. DONALD BUDGE 6-0, 6-3, 6-1

JOSEPH R. HUNT ....
J. J. Morrison ....
— JOSEPH R. HUNT 7-5, 6-3, 6-2
Robert A. Low ....
Owen Anderson ......
— Owen Anderson 6-4, 6-4, 9-7
— JOSEPH R. HUNT 1-6, 5-7, 6-1, 7-5, 6-0
Modeste Alloo ....
Gerin Cameron ....
— Gerin Cameron 6-1, 6-2, 6-0
— JIRO YAMAGISHI 6-2, 6-3, 8-6
— JOSEPH R. HUNT 3-6, 6-1, 6-1, 6-1

M. Laird Watt
W. H. Earle
C. J. Carr, Jr.
JIRO YAMAGISHI*
— M. Laird Watt 6-2, 2-6, 6-3, 6-1
— JIRO YAMAGISHI 6-1, 6-2, 6-3
— JIRO YAMAGISHI 6-2, 6-1, 6-3

— J. DONALD BUDGE 6-1, 6-2, 6-4

FRANK A. PARKER
William Gillespie
Kimbark Peterson
Frank J. Bowden
— FRANK A. PARKER 6-2, 6-1, 6-0
— Frank J. Bowden By default
— FRANK A. PARKER 3-6, 6-2, 6-3, 6-1
Robert Harman
Gilbert Hunt, Jr.
Umberto Cuccioli
Clarence M. Jones
— Gilbert Hunt, Jr. 6-2, 6-1, 6-4
— Clarence M. Jones 6-3, 6-4, 3-6, 6-3
— Gilbert Hunt, Jr. 6-0, 6-3, 6-3
— FRANK A. PARKER 6-1, 8-6, 6-1

Elwood Cooke
Peter Lauck
Marvin Kantrowitz
David S. Burt
— Elwood Cooke 6-4, 6-1, 6-3
— Marvin Kantrowitz 6-3, 12-10, 6-3
— Elwood Cooke 6-1, 6-4, 7-5
Percy L. Kynaston
Sidney B. Wood, Jr.
Robert Kelleher
HIDEO NISHIMURA*
— Sidney B. Wood, Jr. 6-1, 6-2, 6-2
— HIDEO NISHIMURA 6-4, 9-7, 6-3
— S. B. Wood, Jr. 4-6, 6-2, 6-2, 6-0
— S. B. Wood, Jr. 6-2, 6-2, 6-2
— FRANK A. PARKER 3-6, 4-6, 6-1, 6-3, 6-0

JOHN VAN RYN
George B. Dunn
Arthur Hendrix
Julius Heldman
— JOHN VAN RYN 5-7, 8-6, 8-6, 6-4
— Julius Heldman 7-5, 12-10, 3-6, 6-3
— JOHN VAN RYN 6-8, 9-7, 10-12, 6-3, 6-2
Gabriel Lavine
Leonard Hartman
Bernard G. Coghlan
Richard Dorson
— Leonard Hartman 6-2, 6-3, 6-1
— Bernard G. Coghlan By default
— B. G. Coghlan 3-6, 6-3, 6-8, 8-6, 6-4
— JOHN VAN RYN 6-4, 8-6, 6-1
— FRANK A. PARKER 6-2, 12-10, 6-2

Charles Harris
Gregory S. Mangin
Ramsay Potts, Jr.
William Lurie
— Charles Harris 6-0, 6-1, 1-6, 2-6, 6-0
— William Lurie By default
— Charles Harris 6-2, 2-6, 7-5, 5-7, 6-4
Gerard B. Podesta
Martin Buxby
Russell Bobbitt
HENNER HENKEL*
— Martin Buxby 4-6, 7-5, 6-3, 6-1
— HENNER HENKEL 6-1, 7-5, 6-0
— Martin Buxby 5-7, 6-1, 6-4, 6-4
— Charles Harris 6-8, 7-5, 12-10, 6-1
— JOHN VAN RYN 6-3, 6-1, 6-1

ROBERT L. RIGGS
Billy McGehee
Joseph Lucia
C. Gene Mako
— ROBERT L. RIGGS 7-5, 6-1, 9-7
— C. Gene Mako 6-3, 6-1, 6-4
— ROBERT L. RIGGS 2-6, 6-3, 6-4, 7-5
S. E. Davenport, III
Vernon Marcum
Ernest L. Sutter
William Robertson
— S. E. Davenport, III 1-6, 6-1, 8-6, 6-4
— William Robertson By default
— William Robertson 6-1, 3-6, 19-17, 7-5
— ROBERT L. RIGGS 6-4, 6-4, 6-4

Watson Washburn
Charles E. Swanson
Wm. T. Tilden, III
Ronald Lubin
— Charles E. Swanson 5-7, 4-6, 6-3, 6-1, 6-3
— Ronald Lubin 8-6, 10-8, 6-4
— C. E. Swanson 7-5, 7-5, 4-6, 6-4
Joseph Fishbach
Barnard Welsh
Samuel B. Gilpin
FUMITURU NAKANO*
— Barnard Welsh 1-6, 9-7 6-0, 6-1
— FUMITURU NAKANO 7-5, 6-2, 6-1
— F. NAKANO 6-1, 4-6, 6-1, 6-4
— F. NAKANO 10-8, 4-6, 6-1, 3-6, 6-3
— ROBERT L. RIGGS 3-6, 7-5, 6-3, 8-6

JOHN McDIARMID
Lewis Wetherell
Carl Fischer
D. L. Mitchell
— JOHN McDIARMID 6-1, 3-6, 6-1 6-0
— D. L. Mitchell By default
— JOHN McDIARMID 6-4, 6-3, 6-4
John H. Curtiss
Harris M. Coggeshall
Merrimon Cuninggim
Ross Wilson
— Harris M. Coggeshall 6-2, 6-1, 6-2
— Merrimon Cuninggim 4-6, 6-3, 6-4, 6-3
— M. Cuninggim 6-3, 6-1, 7-5
— M. Cuninggim, 6-3, 3-6, 6-3, 4-6, 1-5, default

Henry M. Culley
Hugh J. Lynch
Morris Adelsberg
Dr. Eugene McCauliff
— Henry M. Culley 6-4, 6-3, 6-4
— Morris Adelsberg By default
— Henry M. Culley 6-0, 6-1, 6-4
Charles T. Mattmann
Charles F. Rider
Frederic Mercur
CHARLES E. HARE*
— Charles T. Mattmann 6-4, 6-4, 8-6
— CHARLES E. HARE 6-3, 6-2, 6-4
— CHARLES E. HARE 6-3, 6-1, 6-2
— CHARLES E. HARE 4-6, 2-6, 6-4, 6-1, 6-0
— CHARLES F. HARE 4-6, 4-6, 6-3, 6-4, 6-2

BRYAN M. GRANT, JR.
Murray D. Deloford
Donald S. Hawley
J. Gilbert Hall
— B. M. GRANT, JR. 6-4, 9-7, 6-3
— J. Gilbert Hall 2-6, 6-3, 6-4, 6-2
— B. M. GRANT, JR. 6-2, 6-2, 6-1
C. Depew Steele, Jr...
Norbert Burgess ......
— C. D. Steele, Jr. By default
— B. M. GRANT, JR. 6-4, 6-2, 6-2
— ROBERT L. RIGGS 4-6, 1-6, 6-3, 6-0, 7-5

F. D. Guernsey, Jr. ..
Wayne Sabin ....
— Wayne Sabin 7-5, 6-2, 1-6, 7-5
George Toley ....
J. BRUGNON* ....
— George Toley 8-6, 6-4, 6-1
— Wayne Sabin 6-3, 6-3, 1-6, 6-4
— B. M. GRANT, JR. 6-2, 4-6, 5-7, 6-1, 6-1

J. H. SURFACE, JR. ..
J. J. Moreno, Jr. .....
— J. H. SURFACE, JR. By default
John G. Mahoney ....
Robert Kamrath ......
— Robert Kamrath 6-4, 6-3, 6-3
— J. H. SURFACE, JR. 6-3, 3-6, 6-3, default

Don McNeill ....
William Umstaedter ..
— Don McNeill 6-0, 6-3, 6-2
Alfred L. Jarvis .....
Baron VON CRAMM*.
— Baron VON CRAMM 6-1, 6-4, 6-2
— Baron VON CRAMM 6-2, 6-3, 2-6, 6-4
— Baron VON CRAMM 8-6, 7-5, 3-6, 7-5

— Baron VON CRAMM 9-7, 2-6, 2-6, 6-3, 6-3

J. DONALD BUDGE, 6-2, 6-1, 6-3

J. DONALD BUDGE, 6-1, 7-9, 6-1, 3-6, 6-1

BARON G. VON CRAMM, 0-6, 8-6, 6-8, 6-3, 6-2

*Denotes foreign seeding

FIFTY-SEVENTH USLTA MEN'S SINGLES CHAMPIONSHIPS
West Side Tennis Club, Forest Hills, N.Y., 1938

First Round	Second Round	Third Round	Fourth Round	Fifth Round	Semi-Finals	Finals

U. S. Seedings
1. J. Donald Budge
2. Robert L. Riggs
3. Joseph R. Hunt
4. Sidney B. Wood, Jr.
5. Elwood T. Cooke
6. Frank Kovacs
7. Frank Parker
8. Bryan M. Grant, Jr.

Foreign Seedings
1. J. E. Bromwich
2. A. K Quist
3. Franjo Pupcec
4. Bernard Destremau
5. Yvon Petra
6. Franjo Kukuljevic
7. Fumiteru Nakana
8. Charles E. Hare

J. DONALD BUDGE ..
Welby Van Horn .....
J. DONALD BUDGE — 6-0, 6-0, 6-1

Robert Kamrath ......
Jack Kramer ....
Robert Kamrath — 6-1, 6-0, 6-1

J. DONALD BUDGE — 6-3, 7-5, 9-7

Bian Finnigan ....
Frank Farrell ....
Frank Farrell — 5-7, 6-0, 6-4, 6-4

Leonard A. Schwartz .
CHARLES E. HARE*.
C. E. HARE, 6-4, 7-5, 10-12, 5-7, 10-8

CHARLES E. HARE — 6-3, 6-2, 6-1

J. D. BUDGE — 6-3, 6-4, 6-0

ELWOOD T. COOKE .
George Godsell ....
ELWOOD T. COOKE — 6-2, 7-5, 6-0

Harry C. Hopman ....
Martin Buxby ....
Harry C. Hopman — 6-3, 7-5, 6-4

Harry C. Hopman — 6-2, 4-6, 6-4, 10-8

Eugene McCauliff ....
George Toley ....
George Toley — 4-2, default

Leonard Hartman — 7-5, 4-6, 6-2, 6-3
Don McNeill — 6-2, 4-6, 6-1, 6-3
Don McNeill — 7-5, 6-3, 6-1

Don McNeill — 6-1, 6-4, 6-1

Harry C. Hopman — 6-4, 6-3, 7-5

J. D. BUDGE — 6-3, 6-1, 6-3

George Lowman ....
Leonard Hartman ....
Don McNeill ....
BERNARD DESTREMAU* ....

SIDNEY B. WOOD, JR.
Billy McGehee ....
S. E. Davenport, 3rd ....
J. Gilbert Hall ....
SIDNEY B. WOOD, Jr. — 6-4, 6-1, 6-4
J. Gilbert Hall — 6-1, 8-6, 6-4

S. B. WOOD, JR. — 9-7, 4-6, 1-6, 6-4, 6-4

Gardnar Mulloy ......
P. Morey Lewis ......
Donald Lay ......
Robert Low ......
Gardnar Mulloy — 7-5, 6-1, 6-4
Robert Low — 6-2, 6-0, 6-0
Gardnar Mulloy — 7-5, 6-3, 6-1

SIDNEY B. WOOD, JR. — 6-4, 6-1, 4-6, 6-8, 6-2

William Gillespie ......
Jack Bushman ......
Gabriel Lavine ......
William Robertson ......
William Gillespie — 6-4, 4-6, 2-6, 6-4, 6-4
William Robertson — 6-4, 4-6, 7-5, 6-3
William Gillespie — 6-3, 2-6, 6-0, 2-6, 6-3

Jacques Brugnon ......
Hal Surface, Jr. ......
Arthur Prochaska ......
FRANJO KUKULJEVIC ......
Hal Surface, Jr. — 6-1, 6-1, 6-2
F. KUKULJEVIC — 7-5, 6-1, 6-0
F. KUKULJEVIC — 6-1, 6-3, 6-1

F. KUKULJEVIC — 6-2, 6-2, 6-1

S. B. WOOD, JR. — 8-6, 6-4, 6-3

BRYAN M. GRANT, JR.
Harris Everett ......
Charles Mattmann ......
Phil Harman ......
B. M. GRANT, JR. — 6-4, 9-7, 6-4
Charles Mattmann — By Default
B. M. GRANT, JR. — 6-2, 6-2, 6-2

Frank Bowden ......
Archie Henderson ......
Owen Anderson ......
Wilson Rood ......
Archie Henderson — 6-3, 6-4, 5-7, 9-7
Owen Anderson — 6-4, 6-4, 4-6, 6-2
Owen Anderson — 6-1, 6-3, 8-6

B. M. GRANT, JR. — 6-3, 6-1, 4-6, 6-1

J. N. Anderson, Jr. ......
Isadore Bellis ......
Mort Ballagh ......
David Burt ......
Isadore Bellis — 3-6, 4-6, 6-4, 6-0, 7-5
Mort Ballagh — 6-2, 7-5, 6-2
Mort Ballagh — 8-6, 13-11, 6-2

William Umstaedter ......
David Johnsen ......
Frank Broida ......
ADRIAN K. QUIST ......
William Umstaedter — 6-4, 6-4, 5-7, 6-2
ADRIAN K. QUIST — 6-2, 6-1, 6-1
ADRIAN K. QUIST — 6-3, 6-1, 6-0

ADRIAN K. QUIST — 3-6, 6-2, 6-4, 6-4

B. M. GRANT, JR. — 6-1, 4-6, 6-1, 7-5

ROBERT L. RIGGS ......
Peter Lauck ......
A. Ronald Lubin ......
Frank Guernsey, Jr. ......
ROBERT L. RIGGS — 5-7, 6-3, 6-4, 6-4
Frank Guernsey, Jr. — 6-2, 6-1, 6-3
ROBERT L. RIGGS — 5-7, 6-2, 6-3, 6-4

R. A. Shayes ......
Robert Mouvet ......
Edward DeGray ......
Russell Bobbitt ......
R. A. Shayes — 6-4, 6-1, 6-2
Russell Bobbitt — 6-2, 6-4, 6-4
R. A. Shayes — 6-3, 4-6, 6-4, 6-4

ROBERT L. RIGGS — 6-3, 6-3, 4-6, 1-6, 6-4

Alfred Jarvis ......
Joseph Abrams ......
J. A. Baldwin ......
William Talbert ......
Alfred Jarvis — 6-1, 4-6, 6-3, 6-1
William Talbert — 6-1, 6-3, 6-3
Alfred Jarvis — 4-6, 3-6, 6-4, 6-2, 6-2

William Murphy ......
Gilbert A. Hunt, Jr. ......
Lewis Wetherell ......
FUMITERU NAKANO* ......
Gilbert A. Hunt, Jr. — 6-4, 4-6, 6-4, 5-7, 6-4
FUMITERU NAKANO — 3-6, 6-3, 3-6, 6-2, 6-2
Gilbert A. Hunt, Jr. — 6-8, 1-6, 6-3, 6-3, 6-3

Gilbert A. Hunt, Jr. — 6-3, 6-2, 6-2

Gilbert A. Hunt, Jr. — 6-2, 0-6, 9-7, 0-6, 6-4

FRANK KOVACS ......
E. J. Filby ......
Yasumine Kuramitsu ......
Verne Hughes ......
FRANK KOVACS — 6-1, 6-3, 9-7
Y. Kuramitsu — 7-5, 3-6, 6-2, 6-2
FRANK KOVACS — 6-3, 4-6, 3-6, 6-4, 7-5

C. Gene Mako ......
Gerard Podesta ......
John Foreman ......
Howard Stephens, Jr. ......
C. Gene Mako — 6-1, 6-2, 6-2
John Foreman — By default
C. Gene Mako — 6-2, 6-1, 18-16

C. Gene Mako — 6-0, 6-2, 8-6

Mervyn Weston ......
Gregory Mangin ......
Hugh Lynch ......
Wm. Freisenbruch ......
Mervyn Weston — 6-1, 6-4, 7-9, 5-7, 8-6
Hugh Lynch — 6-0, 6-1, 6-3
Mervyn Weston — 6-4, 6-3, 4-6, 7-5

Robert Kerdasha ......
Javier F. Lamas ......
Roger Durivage ......
FRANJO PUNCEC* ......
Robert Kerdasha — 6-0, 6-2, 6-1
FRANJO PUNCEC — 6-1, 4-6, 6-1, 6-3
FRANJO PUNCEC — 6-2, 6-0, 6-2

FRANJO PUNCEC — 6-0, 6-2, 6-2

C. Gene Mako — 6-2, 6-4, 9-7

C. Gene Mako — 7-5, 1-6, 8-6, 6-0

JOSEPH R. HUNT ......
Tamto Abe ......
JOSEPH R. HUNT — 6-1, 4-6, 6-1, 6-3
Wayne Sabin ......
JOSEPH R. HUNT — 6-1, 8-6, 6-3

Chauncey Steele, Jr. ...
George Dunn ....
George Dunn — 6-2, 6-3, 6-4

JOSEPH R. HUNT — 6-2, 6-3, 6-4

Chester Murphy ......
Joseph Fishbach .....
Joseph Fishbach — 6-3, 4-6, 4-6, 7-5, 6-4

Charles E. Swanson ...
YVON PETRA* ......
YVON PETRA — 6-4, 7-5, 6-1

YVON PETRA — 6-2, 6-4, 6-3

JOSEPH R. HUNT — 6-4, 4-6, 6-4, 9-7

FRANK PARKER ....
William Lurie ....
FRANK PARKER — 6-2, 6-1, 6-3

Donald Hawley ....
Carlton Rood ......
Carlton Rood — 6-4, 6-2, 10-8

FRANK PARKER — 6-2, 6-1, 6-3

FRANK PARKER — 6-2, 6-4, 7-5

Frank Shields ....
Ernest Sutter ....
Frank Shields — 6-3, 6-3, 8-6

August Ganzenmuller .
J. E. BROMWICH ...
J. E. BROMWICH — 6-1, 6-0, 6-1

J. E. BROMWICH, 1-6, 10-12, 10-8, 6-2, 6-2

J. E. BROMWICH — 6-2, 6-3, 6-2

J. E. BROMWICH — 6-1, 9-11, 6-3, 6-4

J. DONALD BUDGE, 6-3, 6-3, 6-3

J. DONALD BUDGE, 6-3, 6-8, 6-2, 6-1

C. Gene Mako, 6-3, 7-5, 6-4

FIFTY-EIGHTH USLTA MEN'S SINGLES CHAMPIONSHIPS
West Side Tennis Club, Forest Hills, N.Y., 1939

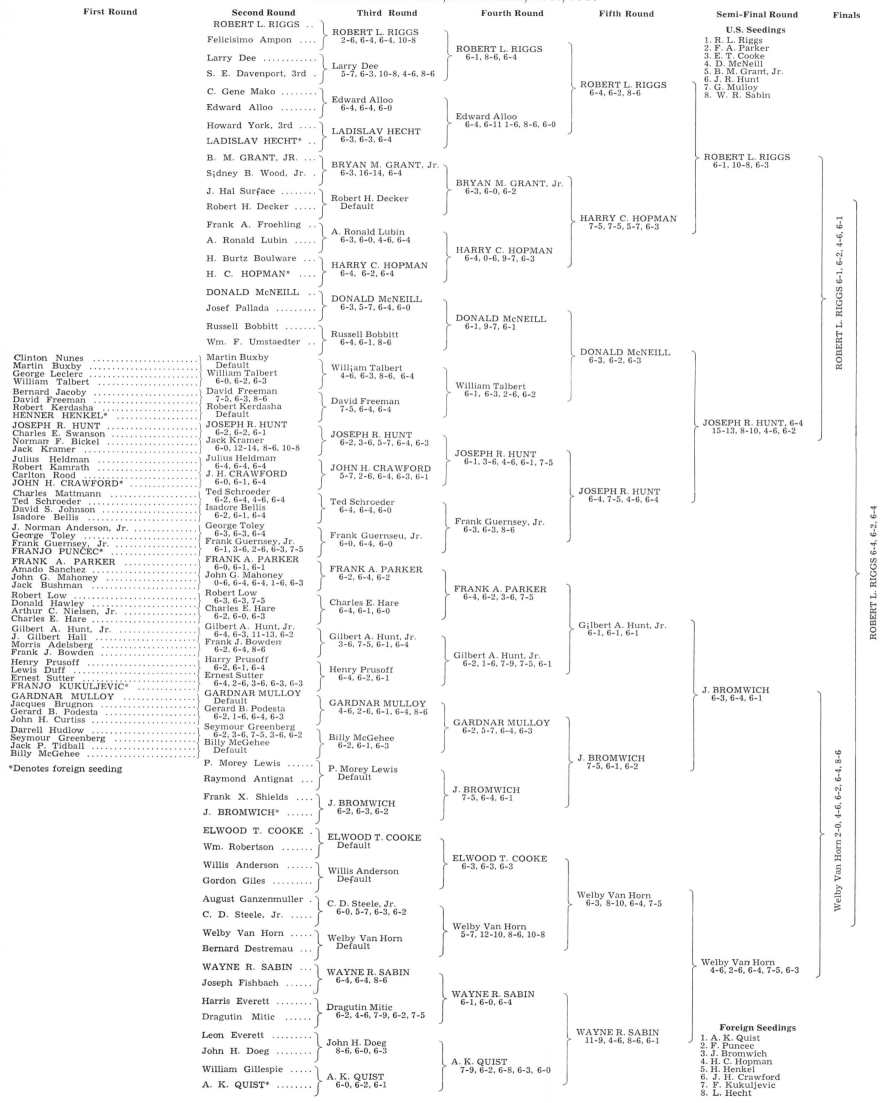

First Round	Second Round	Third Round	Fourth Round	Fifth Round	Semi-Final Round	Finals

ROBERT L. RIGGS ..
Felicisimo Ampon ...

ROBERT L. RIGGS
2-6, 6-4, 6-4, 10-8

Larry Dee ....
S. E. Davenport, 3rd .

Larry Dee
5-7, 6-3, 10-8, 4-6, 8-6

ROBERT L. RIGGS
6-1, 8-6, 6-4

C. Gene Mako ....
Edward Alloo ....

Edward Alloo
6-4, 6-4, 6-0

Howard York, 3rd ....
LADISLAV HECHT* ..

LADISLAV HECHT
6-3, 6-3, 6-4

Edward Alloo
6-4, 6-11 1-6, 8-6, 6-0

ROBERT L. RIGGS
6-4, 6-2, 8-6

B. M. GRANT, JR. ...
Sidney B. Wood, Jr. .

BRYAN M. GRANT, Jr.
6-3, 16-14, 6-4

J. Hal Surface ....
Robert H. Decker .....

Robert H. Decker
Default

BRYAN M. GRANT, Jr.
6-3, 6-0, 6-2

Frank A. Froehling ..
A. Ronald Lubin .....

A. Ronald Lubin
6-3, 6-0, 4-6, 6-4

H. Burtz Boulware ...
H. C. HOPMAN* ....

HARRY C. HOPMAN
6-4, 6-2, 6-4

HARRY C. HOPMAN
6-4, 0-6, 9-7, 6-3

HARRY C. HOPMAN
7-5, 7-5, 5-7, 6-3

ROBERT L. RIGGS
6-1, 10-8, 6-3

DONALD McNEILL ..
Josef Pallada ....

DONALD McNEILL
6-3, 5-7, 6-4, 6-0

Russell Bobbitt ....
Wm. F. Umstaedter ..

Russell Bobbitt
6-4, 6-1, 8-6

DONALD McNEILL
6-1, 9-7, 6-1

Clinton Nunes ....
Martin Buxby ....
George Leclerc ....
William Talbert ....

Martin Buxby
Default
William Talbert
6-0, 6-2, 6-3

William Talbert
4-6, 6-3, 8-6, 6-4

DONALD McNEILL
6-3, 6-2, 6-3

Bernard Jacoby ....
David Freeman ....
Robert Kerdasha ....
HENNER HENKEL* ....

David Freeman
7-5, 6-3, 8-6
Robert Kerdasha
Default

David Freeman
7-5, 6-4, 6-4

William Talbert
6-1, 6-3, 2-6, 6-2

JOSEPH R. HUNT ....
Charles E. Swanson ....
Norman F. Bickel ....
Jack Kramer ....

JOSEPH R. HUNT
6-2, 6-2, 6-1
Jack Kramer
6-0, 12-14, 8-6, 10-8

JOSEPH R. HUNT
6-2, 3-6, 5-7, 6-4, 6-3

JOSEPH R. HUNT, 6-4
15-13, 8-10, 4-6, 6-2

Julius Heldman ....
Robert Kamrath ....
Carlton Rood ....
JOHN H. CRAWFORD* ....

Julius Heldman
6-4, 6-4, 6-4
J. H. CRAWFORD
6-0, 6-1, 6-4

JOHN H. CRAWFORD
5-7, 2-6, 6-4, 6-3, 6-1

JOSEPH R. HUNT
6-1, 3-6, 4-6, 6-1, 7-5

Charles Mattmann ....
Ted Schroeder ....
David S. Johnson ....
Isadore Bellis ....

Ted Schroeder
6-2, 6-4, 4-6, 6-4
Isadore Bellis
6-2, 6-1, 6-4

Ted Schroeder
6-4, 6-4, 6-0

JOSEPH R. HUNT
6-4, 7-5, 4-6, 6-4

J. Norman Anderson, Jr. ....
George Toley ....
Frank Guernsey, Jr. ....
FRANJO PUNCEC* ....

George Toley
6-3, 6-3, 6-4
Frank Guernsey, Jr.
6-1, 3-6, 2-6, 6-3, 7-5

Frank Guernseu, Jr.
6-0, 6-4, 6-0

Frank Guernsey, Jr.
6-3, 6-3, 8-6

FRANK A. PARKER ....
Amado Sanchez ....
John G. Mahoney ....
Jack Bushman ....

FRANK A. PARKER
6-0, 6-1, 6-1
John G. Mahoney
0-6, 6-4, 6-4, 1-6, 6-3

FRANK A. PARKER
6-2, 6-4, 6-2

Robert Low ....
Donald Hawley ....
Arthur C. Nielsen, Jr. ....
Charles E. Hare ....

Robert Low
6-3, 6-3, 7-5
Charles E. Hare
6-2, 6-0, 6-3

Charles E. Hare
6-4, 6-1, 6-0

FRANK A. PARKER
6-4, 6-2, 3-6, 7-5

Gilbert A. Hunt, Jr. ....
J. Gilbert Hall ....
Morris Adelsberg ....
Frank J. Bowden ....

Gilbert A. Hunt, Jr.
6-4, 6-3, 11-13, 6-2
Frank J. Bowden
6-2, 6-4, 8-6

Gilbert A. Hunt, Jr.
3-6, 7-5, 6-1, 6-4

Gilbert A. Hunt, Jr.
6-1, 6-1, 6-1

Henry Prusoff ....
Lewis Duff ....
Ernest Sutter ....
FRANJO KUKULJEVIC* ....

Harry Prusoff
6-2, 6-1, 6-4
Ernest Sutter
6-4, 2-6, 3-6, 6-3, 6-3

Henry Prusoff
6-4, 6-2, 6-1

Gilbert A. Hunt, Jr.
6-2, 1-6, 7-9, 7-5, 6-1

GARDNAR MULLOY ....
Jacques Brugnon ....
Gerard B. Podesta ....
John H. Curtiss ....

GARDNAR MULLOY
Default
Gerard B. Podesta
6-2, 1-6, 6-4, 6-3

GARDNAR MULLOY
4-6, 2-6, 6-1, 6-4, 8-6

J. BROMWICH
6-3, 6-4, 6-1

Darrell Hudlow ....
Seymour Greenberg ....
Jack P. Tidball ....
Billy McGehee ....

Seymour Greenberg
6-2, 3-6, 7-5, 3-6, 6-2
Billy McGehee
Default

Billy McGehee
6-2, 6-1, 6-3

GARDNAR MULLOY
6-2, 5-7, 6-4, 6-3

*Denotes foreign seeding

P. Morey Lewis ......
Raymond Antignat ...

P. Morey Lewis
Default

J. BROMWICH
7-5, 6-1, 6-2

Frank X. Shields ....
J. BROMWICH* ......

J. BROMWICH
6-2, 6-3, 6-2

J. BROMWICH
7-5, 6-4, 6-1

ELWOOD T. COOKE .
Wm. Robertson ....

ELWOOD T. COOKE
Default

Willis Anderson ......
Gordon Giles ....

Willis Anderson
Default

ELWOOD T. COOKE
6-3, 6-3, 6-3

August Ganzenmuller .
C. D. Steele, Jr. .....

C. D. Steele, Jr.
6-0, 5-7, 6-3, 6-2

Welby Van Horn
5-7, 12-10, 8-6, 10-8

Welby Van Horn .....
Bernard Destremau ...

Welby Van Horn
Default

Welby Van Horn
6-3, 8-10, 6-4, 7-5

WAYNE R. SABIN ...
Joseph Fishbach ......

WAYNE R. SABIN
6-4, 6-4, 8-6

Harris Everett ....
Dragutin Mitic ......

Dragutin Mitic
6-2, 4-6, 7-9, 6-2, 7-5

WAYNE R. SABIN
6-1, 6-0, 6-4

Welby Van Horn
4-6, 2-6, 6-4, 7-5, 6-3

Leon Everett ....
John H. Doeg ......

John H. Doeg
8-6, 6-0, 6-3

WAYNE R. SABIN
11-9, 4-6, 8-6, 6-1

William Gillespie .....
A. K. QUIST* ....

A. K. QUIST
6-0, 6-2, 6-1

A. K. QUIST
7-9, 6-2, 6-8, 6-3, 6-0

ROBERT L. RIGGS 6-1, 6-2, 4-6, 6-1

ROBERT L. RIGGS 6-4, 6-2, 6-4

Welby Van Horn 2-0, 4-6, 6-2, 6-4, 8-6

FIFTY-NINTH USLTA MEN'S SINGLES CHAMPIONSHIPS
West Side Tennis Club, Forest Hills, N.Y., 1940

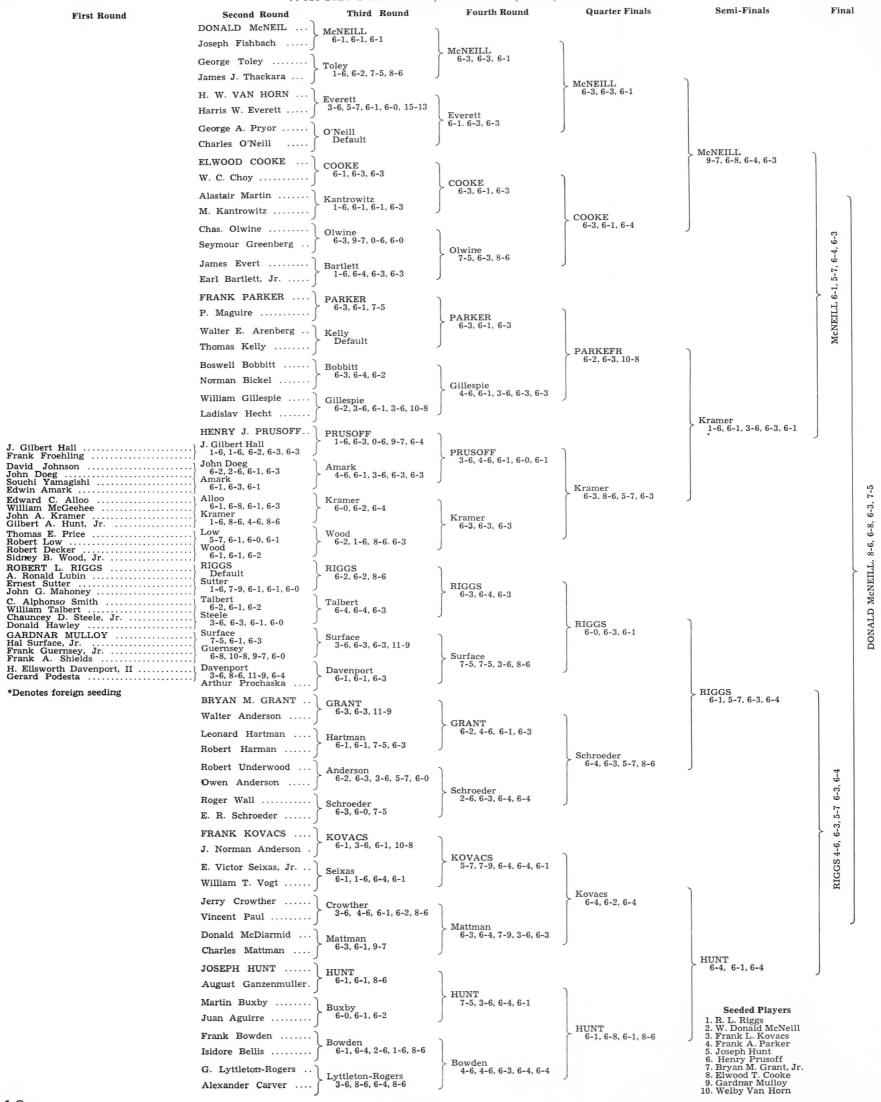

First Round | Second Round | Third Round | Fourth Round | Quarter Finals | Semi-Finals | Final

DONALD McNEIL ...
Joseph Fishbach .....
McNEILL 6-1, 6-1, 6-1

George Toley ....
James J. Thackara ...
Toley 1-6, 6-2, 7-5, 8-6

McNEILL 6-3, 6-3, 6-1

H. W. VAN HORN ...
Harris W. Everett .....
Everett 3-6, 5-7, 6-1, 6-0, 15-13

George A. Pryor ......
Charles O'Neill .....
O'Neill Default

Everett 6-1, 6-3, 6-3

McNEILL 6-3, 6-3, 6-1

ELWOOD COOKE ...
W. C. Choy ....
COOKE 6-1, 6-3, 6-3

Alastair Martin ....
M. Kantrowitz ....
Kantrowitz 1-6, 6-1, 6-1, 6-3

COOKE 6-3, 6-1, 6-3

Chas. Olwine ....
Seymour Greenberg ..
Olwine 6-3, 9-7, 0-6, 6-0

James Evert ....
Earl Bartlett, Jr. .....
Bartlett 1-6, 6-4, 6-3, 6-3

Olwine 7-5, 6-3, 8-6

COOKE 6-3, 6-1, 6-4

McNEILL 9-7, 6-8, 6-4, 6-3

FRANK PARKER ....
P. Maguire ....
PARKER 6-3, 6-1, 7-5

Walter E. Arenberg ..
Thomas Kelly ....
Kelly Default

PARKER 6-3, 6-1, 6-3

Boswell Bobbitt ......
Norman Bickel ....
Bobbitt 6-3, 6-4, 6-2

William Gillespie .....
Ladislav Hecht ....
Gillespie 6-2, 3-6, 6-1, 3-6, 10-8

Gillespie 4-6, 6-1, 3-6, 6-3, 6-3

PARKEFR 6-2, 6-3, 10-8

HENRY J. PRUSOFF..
J. Gilbert Hall ....
Frank Froehling ....
PRUSOFF 1-6, 6-3, 0-6, 9-7, 6-4

David Johnson ....
John Doeg ....
Souchi Yamagishi ....
Edwin Amark ....
Amark 4-6, 6-1, 3-6, 6-3, 6-3

PRUSOFF 1-6, 1-6, 6-2, 6-3, 6-3
J. Gilbert Hall 6-2, 2-6, 6-1, 6-3
John Doeg

PRUSOFF 3-6, 4-6, 6-1, 6-0, 6-1

Kramer 1-6, 6-1, 3-6, 6-3, 6-1

Edward C. Alloo ....
William McGeehee ....
John A. Kramer ....
Gilbert A. Hunt, Jr. ....
Alloo 6-1, 6-8, 6-1, 6-3
Kramer 1-6, 8-6, 4-6, 8-6

Kramer 6-0, 6-2, 6-4

Thomas E. Price ....
Robert Low ....
Robert Decker ....
Sidney B. Wood, Jr. ....
Low 5-7, 6-1, 6-0, 6-1
Wood 6-1, 6-1, 6-2

Wood 6-2, 1-6, 8-6. 6-3

Kramer 6-3, 6-3, 6-3

Kramer 6-3, 8-6, 5-7, 6-3

ROBERT L. RIGGS ....
A. Ronald Lubin ....
Ernest Sutter ....
John G. Mahoney ....
RIGGS Default
Sutter 1-6, 7-9, 6-1, 6-1, 6-0

RIGGS 6-2, 6-2, 8-6

C. Alphonso Smith ....
William Talbert ....
Chauncey D. Steele, Jr. ....
Donald Hawley ....
Talbert 6-2, 6-1, 6-2
Steele 3-6, 6-3, 6-1, 6-0

Talbert 6-4, 6-4, 6-3

RIGGS 6-3, 6-4, 6-3

GARDNAR MULLOY ....
Hal Surface, Jr. ....
Frank Guernsey, Jr. ....
Frank A. Shields ....
Surface 7-5, 6-1, 6-3
Guernsey 6-8, 10-8, 9-7, 6-0

Surface 3-6, 6-3, 6-3, 11-9

RIGGS 6-0, 6-3, 6-1

H. Ellsworth Davenport, II ....
Gerard Podesta ....
Davenport 3-6, 8-6, 11-9, 6-4
Davenport 6-1, 6-1, 6-3
Arthur Prochaska ....

Surface 7-5, 7-5, 3-6, 8-6

*Denotes foreign seeding

BRYAN M. GRANT ..
Walter Anderson .....
GRANT 6-3, 6-3, 11-9

Leonard Hartman .....
Robert Harman ....
Hartman 6-1, 6-1, 7-5, 6-3

GRANT 6-2, 4-6, 6-1, 6-3

Robert Underwood ...
Owen Anderson ......
Anderson 6-2, 6-3, 3-6, 5-7, 6-0

Roger Wall ....
E. R. Schroeder ......
Schroeder 6-3, 6-0, 7-5

Schroeder 2-6, 6-3, 6-4, 6-4

Schroeder 6-4, 6-3, 5-7, 8-6

RIGGS 6-1, 5-7, 6-3, 6-4

FRANK KOVACS ....
J. Norman Anderson .
KOVACS 6-1, 3-6, 6-1, 10-8

E. Victor Seixas, Jr. ...
William T. Vogt ......
Seixas 6-1, 1-6, 6-4, 6-1

KOVACS 5-7, 7-9, 6-4, 6-4, 6-1

Jerry Crowther ......
Vincent Paul ....
Crowther 3-6, 4-6, 6-1, 6-2, 8-6

Donald McDiarmid ...
Charles Mattman ....
Mattman 6-3, 6-1, 9-7

Mattman 6-3, 6-4, 7-9, 3-6, 6-3

Kovacs 6-4, 6-2, 6-4

JOSEPH HUNT ......
August Ganzenmuller.
HUNT 6-1, 6-1, 8-6

Martin Buxby ....
Juan Aguirre ....
Buxby 6-0, 6-1, 6-2

HUNT 7-5, 3-6, 6-4, 6-1

Frank Bowden ....
Isidore Bellis ....
Bowden 6-1, 6-4, 2-6, 1-6, 8-6

G. Lyttleton-Rogers ..
Alexander Carver ....
Lyttleton-Rogers 3-6, 8-6, 6-4, 8-6

Bowden 4-6, 4-6, 6-3, 6-4, 6-4

HUNT 6-1, 6-8, 6-1, 8-6

HUNT 6-4, 6-1, 6-4

DONALD McNEILL, 8-6, 6-8, 6-3, 7-5

McNEILL 6-1, 5-7, 6-4, 6-3

RIGGS 4-6, 6-3, 5-7 6-3, 6-4

Seeded Players
1. R. L. Riggs
2. W. Donald McNeill
3. Frank L. Kovacs
4. Frank A. Parker
5. Joseph Hunt
6. Henry Prusoff
7. Bryan M. Grant, Jr.
8. Elwood T. Cooke
9. Gardnar Mulloy
10. Welby Van Horn

SIXTIETH USLTA MEN'S SINGLES CHAMPIONSHIPS
West Side Tennis Club, Forest Hills, N.Y., 1941

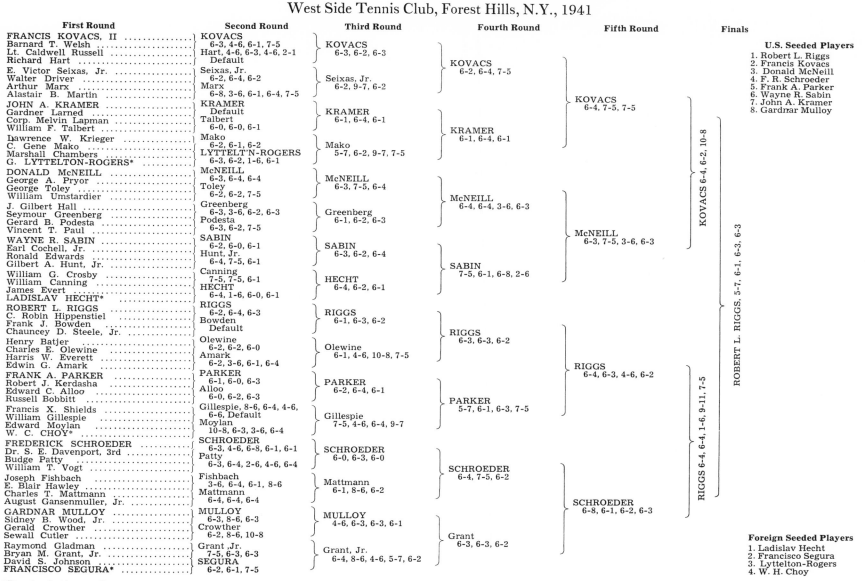

First Round

FRANCIS KOVACS, II
Barnard T. Welsh
Lt. Caldwell Russell
Richard Hart
E. Victor Seixas, Jr.
Walter Driver
Arthur Marx
Alastair B. Martin
JOHN A. KRAMER
Gardner Larned
Corp. Melvin Lapman
William F. Talbert
Lawrence W. Krieger
C. Gene Mako
Marshall Chambers
G. LYTTELTON-ROGERS*
DONALD McNEILL
George A. Pryor
George Toley
William Umstardier
J. Gilbert Hall
Seymour Greenberg
Gerard B. Podesta
Vincent T. Paul
WAYNE R. SABIN
Earl Cochell, Jr.
Ronald Edwards
Gilbert A. Hunt, Jr.
William G. Crosby
William Canning
James Evert
LADISLAV HECHT*
ROBERT L. RIGGS
C. Robin Hippenstiel
Frank J. Bowden
Chauncey D. Steele, Jr.
Henry Batjer
Charles E. Olewine
Harris W. Everett
Edwin G. Amark
FRANK A. PARKER
Robert J. Kerdasha
Edward C. Alloo
Russell Bobbitt
Francis X. Shields
William Gillespie
Edward Moylan
W. C. CHOY*
FREDERICK SCHROEDER
Dr. S. E. Davenport, 3rd
Budge Patty
William T. Vogt
Joseph Fishbach
E. Blair Hawley
Charles T. Mattmann
August Gansenmuller, Jr.
GARDNAR MULLOY
Sidney B. Wood, Jr.
Gerald Crowther
Sewall Cutler
Raymond Gladman
Bryan M. Grant, Jr.
David S. Johnson
FRANCISCO SEGURA*

Second Round

KOVACS
6-3, 4-6, 6-1, 7-5
Hart, 4-6, 6-3, 4-6, 2-1
Default
Seixas, Jr.
6-2, 6-4, 6-2
Marx
6-8, 3-6, 6-1, 6-4, 7-5
KRAMER
Default
Talbert
6-0, 6-0, 6-1
Mako
6-2, 6-1, 6-2
LYTTELT'N-ROGERS
6-3, 6-2, 1-6, 6-1
McNEILL
6-3, 6-4, 6-4
Toley
6-2, 6-2, 7-5
Greenberg
6-3, 3-6, 6-2, 6-3
Podesta
6-3, 6-2, 7-5
SABIN
6-2, 6-0, 6-1
Hunt, Jr.
6-4, 7-5, 6-1
Canning
7-5, 7-5, 6-1
HECHT
6-4, 1-6, 6-0, 6-1
RIGGS
6-2, 6-4, 6-3
Bowden
Default
Olewine
6-2, 6-2, 6-0
Amark
6-2, 3-6, 6-1, 6-4
PARKER
6-1, 6-0, 6-3
Alloo
6-0, 6-2, 6-3
Gillespie, 8-6, 6-4, 4-6,
6-6, Default
Moylan
10-8, 6-3, 3-6, 6-4
SCHROEDER
6-3, 4-6, 6-8, 6-1, 6-1
Patty
6-3, 6-4, 2-6, 4-6, 6-4
Fishbach
3-6, 6-4, 6-1, 8-6
Mattmann
6-4, 6-4, 6-4
MULLOY
6-3, 8-6, 6-3
Crowther
6-2, 8-6, 10-8
Grant, Jr.
7-5, 6-3, 6-3
SEGURA
6-2, 6-1, 7-5

Third Round

KOVACS
6-3, 6-2, 6-3
Seixas, Jr.
6-2, 9-7, 6-2
KRAMER
6-1, 6-4, 6-1
Mako
5-7, 6-2, 9-7, 7-5
McNEILL
6-3, 7-5, 6-4
Greenberg
6-1, 6-2, 6-3
SABIN
6-3, 6-2, 6-4
HECHT
6-4, 6-2, 6-1
RIGGS
6-1, 6-3, 6-2
Olewine
6-1, 4-6, 10-8, 7-5
PARKER
6-2, 6-4, 6-1
Gillespie
7-5, 4-6, 6-4, 9-7
SCHROEDER
6-0, 6-3, 6-0
Mattmann
6-1, 8-6, 6-2
MULLOY
4-6, 6-3, 6-3, 6-1
Grant, Jr.
6-4, 8-6, 4-6, 5-7, 6-2

Fourth Round

KOVACS
6-2, 6-4, 7-5
KRAMER
6-1, 6-4, 6-1
McNEILL
6-4, 6-4, 3-6, 6-3
SABIN
7-5, 6-1, 6-8, 2-6
RIGGS
6-3, 6-3, 6-2
PARKER
5-7, 6-1, 6-3, 7-5
SCHROEDER
6-4, 7-5, 6-2
Grant
6-3, 6-3, 6-2

Fifth Round

KOVACS
6-4, 7-5, 7-5
McNEILL
6-3, 7-5, 3-6, 6-3
RIGGS
6-4, 6-3, 4-6, 6-2
SCHROEDER
6-8, 6-1, 6-2, 6-3

Finals

KOVACS 6-4, 6-2, 10-8

RIGGS 6-4, 6-4, 1-6, 9-11, 7-5

ROBERT L. RIGGS, 5-7, 6-1, 6-3, 6-3

U.S. Seeded Players
1. Robert L. Riggs
2. Francis Kovacs
3. Donald McNeill
4. F. R. Schroeder
5. Frank A. Parker
6. Wayne R. Sabin
7. John A. Kramer
8. Gardnar Mulloy

Foreign Seeded Players
1. Ladislav Hecht
2. Francisco Segura
3. Lyttelton-Rogers
4. W. H. Choy

*Denotes foreign seeding

SIXTY-FIRST USLTA MEN'S SINGLES CHAMPIONSHIPS
West Side Tennis Club, Forest Hills, N.Y., 1942

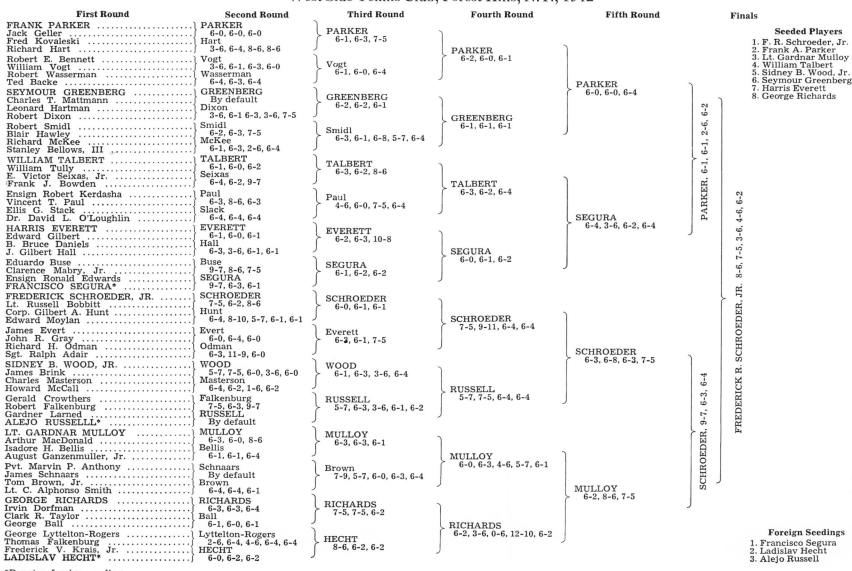

First Round

FRANK PARKER
Jack Geller
Fred Kovaleski
Richard Hart
Robert E. Bennett
William Vogt
Robert Wasserman
Ted Backe
SEYMOUR GREENBERG
Charles M. Mattmann
Leonard Hartman
Robert Dixon
Robert Smidl
Blair Hawley
Richard McKee
Stanley Bellows, III
WILLIAM TALBERT
William Tully
E. Victor Seixas, Jr.
Frank J. Bowden
Ensign Robert Kerdasha
Vincent T. Paul
Ellis G. Stack
Dr. David L. O'Loughlin
HARRIS EVERETT
Edward Gilbert
B. Bruce Daniels
J. Gilbert Hall
Eduardo Buse
Clarence Mabry, Jr.
Ensign Ronald Edwards
FRANCISCO SEGURA*
FREDERICK SCHROEDER, JR.
Lt. Russell Bobbitt
Corp. Gilbert A. Hunt
Edward Moylan
James Evert
John R. Gray
Richard H. Odman
Sgt. Ralph Adair
SIDNEY B. WOOD, JR.
James Brink
Charles Masterson
Howard McCall
Gerald Crowthers
Robert Falkenburg
Gardner Larned
ALEJO RUSSELL*
LT. GARDNAR MULLOY
Arthur MacDonald
Isadore H. Bellis
August Ganzenmuller, Jr.
Pvt. Marvin P. Anthony
James Schnaars
Tom Brown, Jr.
Lt. C. Alphonso Smith
GEORGE RICHARDS
Irvin Dorfman
Clark R. Taylor
George Ball
George Lyttelton-Rogers
Thomas Falkenburg
Frederick V. Krais, Jr.
LADISLAV HECHT*

Second Round

PARKER
6-0, 6-0, 6-0
Hart
3-6, 6-4, 8-6, 8-6
Vogt
3-6, 6-1, 6-3, 6-0
Wasserman
6-4, 6-3, 6-4
GREENBERG
By default
Dixon
3-6, 6-1 6-3, 3-6, 7-5
Smidl
6-2, 6-3, 7-5
McKee
6-1, 6-3, 2-6, 6-4
TALBERT
6-1, 6-0, 6-2
Seixas
6-4, 6-2, 9-7
Paul
6-3, 8-6, 6-3
Slack
6-4, 6-4, 6-4
EVERETT
6-1, 6-0, 6-1
Hall
6-3, 3-6, 6-1, 6-1
Buse
9-7, 8-6, 7-5
SEGURA
9-7, 6-3, 6-1
SCHROEDER
7-5, 6-2, 8-6
Hunt
6-4, 8-10, 5-7, 6-1, 6-1
Evert
6-0, 6-4, 6-0
Odman
6-3, 11-9, 6-0
WOOD
5-7, 7-5, 6-0, 3-6, 6-0
Masterson
6-4, 6-2, 1-6, 6-2
Falkenburg
7-5, 6-3, 9-7
RUSSELL
By default
MULLOY
6-3, 6-0, 8-6
Bellis
6-1, 6-1, 6-4
Schnaars
By default
Brown
6-4, 6-4, 6-1
RICHARDS
6-3, 6-3, 6-4
Ball
6-1, 6-0, 6-1
Lyttelton-Rogers
2-6, 6-4, 4-6, 6-4, 6-4
HECHT
6-0, 6-2, 6-2

Third Round

PARKER
6-1, 6-3, 7-5
Vogt
6-1, 6-0, 6-4
GREENBERG
6-2, 6-2, 6-1
Smidl
6-3, 6-1, 6-8, 5-7, 6-4
TALBERT
6-3, 6-2, 8-6
Paul
4-6, 6-0, 7-5, 6-4
EVERETT
6-2, 6-3, 10-8
SEGURA
6-1, 6-2, 6-2
SCHROEDER
6-0, 6-1, 6-1
Everett
6-3, 6-1, 7-5
WOOD
6-1, 6-3, 3-6, 6-4
RUSSELL
5-7, 6-3, 3-6, 6-1, 6-2
MULLOY
6-3, 6-3, 6-1
Brown
7-9, 5-7, 6-0, 6-3, 6-4
RICHARDS
7-5, 7-5, 6-2
HECHT
8-6, 6-2, 6-2

Fourth Round

PARKER
6-2, 6-0, 6-1
GREENBERG
6-1, 6-1, 6-1
TALBERT
6-3, 6-2, 6-4
SEGURA
6-0, 6-1, 6-2
SCHROEDER
7-5, 9-11, 6-4, 6-4
RUSSELL
5-7, 7-5, 6-4, 6-4
MULLOY
6-0, 6-3, 4-6, 5-7, 6-1
RICHARDS
6-2, 3-6, 0-6, 12-10, 6-2

Fifth Round

PARKER
6-0, 6-0, 6-4
SEGURA
6-4, 3-6, 6-2, 6-4
SCHROEDER
6-3, 6-8, 6-3, 7-5
MULLOY
6-2, 8-6, 7-5

Finals

PARKER, 6-1, 6-1, 2-6, 6-2

SCHROEDER, 9-7, 6-3, 6-4

FREDERICK R. SCHROEDER, JR. 8-6, 7-5, 3-6, 4-6, 6-2

Seeded Players
1. F. R. Schroeder, Jr.
2. Frank A. Parker
3. Lt. Gardnar Mulloy
4. William Talbert
5. Sidney B. Wood, Jr.
6. Seymour Greenberg
7. Harris Everett
8. George Richards

Foreign Seedings
1. Francisco Segura
2. Ladislav Hecht
3. Alejo Russell

*Denotes foreign seeding

SIXTY-SECOND USLTA MEN'S SINGLES CHAMPIONSHIPS
West Side Tennis Club, Forest Hills, N.Y., 1943

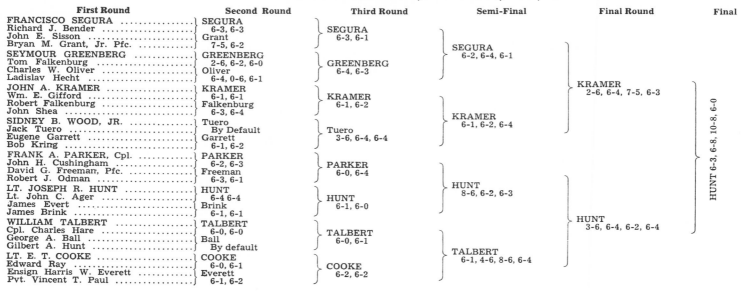

First Round	Second Round	Third Round	Semi-Final	Final Round	Final
FRANCISCO SEGURA	SEGURA				
Richard J. Bender	6-3, 6-3	SEGURA			
John E. Sisson	Grant	6-3, 6-1			
Bryan M. Grant, Jr. Pfc.	7-5, 6-2		SEGURA		
SEYMOUR GREENBERG	GREENBERG		6-2, 6-4, 6-1		
Tom Falkenburg	2-6, 6-2, 6-0	GREENBERG			
Charles W. Oliver	Oliver	6-4, 6-3			
Ladislav Hecht	6-4, 0-6, 6-1			KRAMER	
JOHN A. KRAMER	KRAMER			2-6, 6-4, 7-5, 6-3	
Wm. E. Gifford	6-1, 6-1	KRAMER			
Robert Falkenburg	Falkenburg	6-1, 6-2			
John Shea	6-3, 6-4		KRAMER		
SIDNEY B. WOOD, JR.	Tuero		6-1, 6-2, 6-4		
Jack Tuero	By Default	Tuero			
Eugene Garrett	Garrett	3-6, 6-4, 6-4			HUNT 6-3, 6-8, 10-8, 6-0
Bob Kring	6-1, 6-2				
FRANK A. PARKER, Cpl.	PARKER				
John H. Cushingham	6-2, 6-3	PARKER			
David G. Freeman, Pfc.	Freeman	6-0, 6-4			
Robert J. Odman	6-3, 6-1		HUNT		
LT. JOSEPH R. HUNT	HUNT		8-6, 6-2, 6-3		
Lt. John C. Ager	6-4 6-4	HUNT			
James Evert	Brink	6-1, 6-0			
James Brink	6-1, 6-1			HUNT	
WILLIAM TALBERT	TALBERT			3-6, 6-4, 6-2, 6-4	
Cpl. Charles Hare	6-0, 6-0	TALBERT			
George A. Ball	Ball	6-0, 6-1			
Gilbert A. Hunt	By default		TALBERT		
LT. E. T. COOKE	COOKE		6-1, 4-6, 8-6, 6-4		
Edward Ray	6-0, 6-1	COOKE			
Ensign Harris W. Everett	Everett	6-2, 6-2			
Pvt. Vincent T. Paul	6-1, 6-2				

SIXTY-THIRD USLTA MEN'S SINGLES CHAMPIONSHIPS
West Side Tennis Club, Forest Hills, N.Y., 1944

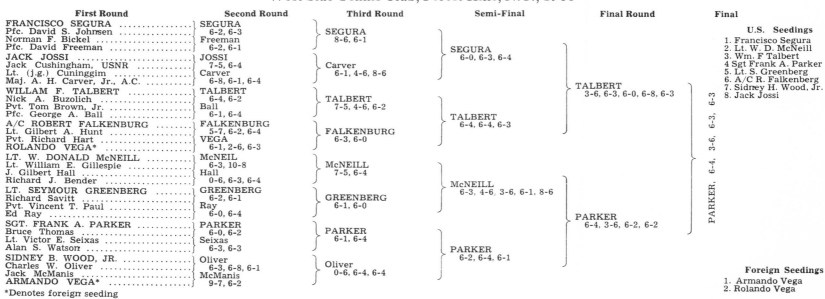

First Round	Second Round	Third Round	Semi-Final	Final Round	Final
FRANCISCO SEGURA	SEGURA				
Pfc. David S. Johnsen	6-2, 6-3	SEGURA			
Norman F. Bickel	Freeman	8-6, 6-1			
Pfc. David Freeman	6-2, 6-1		SEGURA		
JACK JOSSI	JOSSI		6-0, 6-3, 6-4		
Jack Cushingham, USNR	7-5, 6-4	Carver			
Lt. (j.g.) Cuninggim	Carver	6-1, 4-6, 8-6			
Maj. A. H. Carver, Jr., A.C.	6-8, 6-1, 6-4			TALBERT	
WILLAM F. TALBERT	TALBERT			3-6, 6-3, 6-0, 6-8, 6-3	
Nick A. Buzolich	6-4, 6-2	TALBERT			
Pvt. Tom Brown, Jr.	Ball	7-5, 4-6, 6-2			
Pfc. George A. Ball	6-1, 6-4		TALBERT		
A/C ROBERT FALKENBURG	FALKENBURG		6-4, 6-4, 6-3		
Lt. Gilbert A. Hunt	5-7, 6-2, 6-4	FALKENBURG			
Pvt. Richard Hart	VEGA	6-3, 6-0			
ROLANDO VEGA*	6-1, 2-6, 6-3				PARKER, 6-4, 3-6, 6-3, 6-3
LT. W. DONALD McNEILL	McNEIL				
Lt. William E. Gillespie	6-3, 10-8	McNEILL			
J. Gilbert Hall	Hall	7-5, 6-4			
Richard J. Bender	0-6, 6-3, 6-4		McNEILL		
LT. SEYMOUR GREENBERG	GREENBERG		6-3, 4-6, 3-6, 6-1, 8-6		
Richard Savitt	6-2, 6-1	GREENBERG			
Pvt. Vincent T. Paul	Ray	6-1, 6-0			
Ed Ray	6-0, 6-4			PARKER	
SGT. FRANK A. PARKER	PARKER			6-4, 3-6, 6-2, 6-2	
Bruce Thomas	6-0, 6-2	PARKER			
Lt. Victor E. Seixas	Seixas	6-1, 6-4			
Alan S. Watson	6-3, 6-3		PARKER		
SIDNEY B. WOOD, JR.	Oliver		6-2, 6-4, 6-1		
Charles W. Oliver	6-3, 6-8, 6-1	Oliver			
Jack McManis	McManis	0-6, 6-4, 6-4			
ARMANDO VEGA*	9-7, 6-2				

*Denotes foreign seeding

U.S. Seedings
1. Francisco Segura
2. Lt. W. D. McNeill
3. Wm. F Talbert
4 Sgt Frank A. Parker
5. Lt. S. Greenberg
6. A/C R. Falkenburg
7. Sidney H. Wood, Jr.
8. Jack Jossi

Foreign Seedings
1. Armando Vega
2. Rolando Vega

SIXTY-FOURTH USLTA MEN'S SINGLES CHAMPIONSHIPS
West Side Tennis Club, Forest Hills, N.Y., 1945

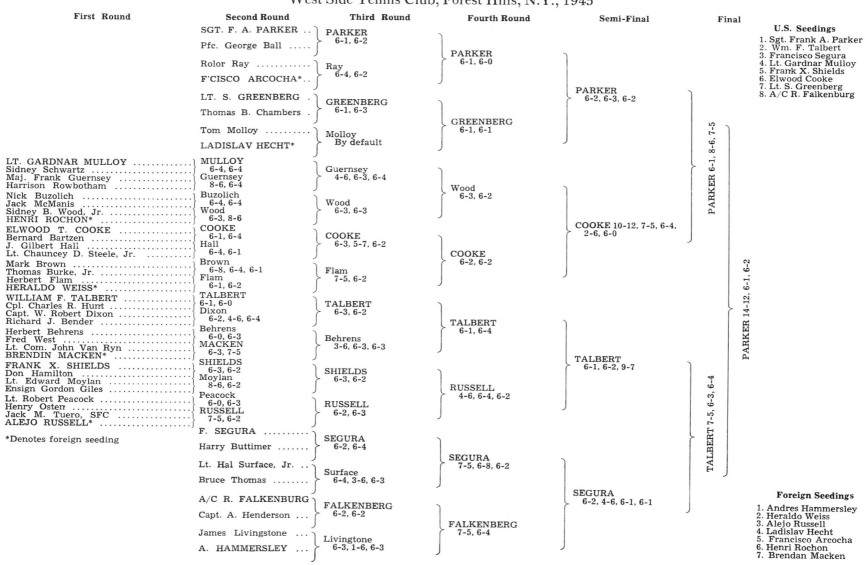

First Round	Second Round	Third Round	Fourth Round	Semi-Final	Final

First Round ... **Second Round** ... **Third Round** ... **Fourth Round** ... **Semi-Final** ... **Final**

SGT. F. A. PARKER ..
Pfc. George Ball .....
— PARKER 6-1, 6-2

Rolor Ray ....
F'CISCO ARCOCHA*..
— Ray 6-4, 6-2

PARKER 6-1, 6-0

LT. S. GREENBERG .
Thomas B. Chambers .
— GREENBERG 6-1, 6-3

Tom Molloy ....
LADISLAV HECHT*
— Molloy By default

GREENBERG 6-1, 6-1

PARKER 6-2, 6-3, 6-2

LT. GARDNAR MULLOY ....
Sidney Schwartz ....
— MULLOY 6-4, 6-4
Maj. Frank Guernsey ....
Harrison Rowbotham ....
— Guernsey 8-6, 6-4

Guernsey 4-6, 6-3, 6-4

Nick Buzolich ....
Jack McManis ....
— Buzolich 6-4, 6-4
Sidney B. Wood, Jr. ....
HENRI ROCHON* ....
— Wood 6-3, 8-6

Wood 6-3, 6-3

Wood 6-3, 6-2

ELWOOD T. COOKE ....
Bernard Bartzen ....
— COOKE 6-1, 6-4
J. Gilbert Hall ....
Lt. Chauncey D. Steele, Jr. ....
— Hall 6-4, 6-1

COOKE 6-3, 5-7, 6-2

Mark Brown ....
Thomas Burke, Jr. ....
— Brown 6-8, 6-4, 6-1
Herbert Flam ....
HERALDO WEISS* ....
— Flam 6-1, 6-2

Flam 7-5, 6-2

COOKE 6-2, 6-2

COOKE 10-12, 7-5, 6-4, 2-6, 6-0

WILLIAM F. TALBERT ....
Cpl. Charles R. Hunt ....
— TALBERT 6-1, 6-0
Capt. W. Robert Dixon ....
Richard J. Bender ....
— Dixon 6-2, 4-6, 6-4

TALBERT 6-3, 6-2

Herbert Behrens ....
Fred West ....
— Behrens 6-0, 6-3
Lt. Com. John Van Ryn ....
BRENDIN MACKEN* ....
— MACKEN 6-3, 7-5

Behrens 3-6, 6-3, 6-3

TALBERT 6-1, 6-4

FRANK X. SHIELDS ....
Don Hamilton ....
— SHIELDS 6-3, 6-2
Lt. Edward Moylan ....
Ensign Gordon Giles ....
— Moylan 8-6, 6-2

SHIELDS 6-3, 6-2

Lt. Robert Peacock ....
Henry Oster ....
— Peacock 6-0, 6-3
Jack M. Tuero, SFC ....
ALEJO RUSSELL* ....
— RUSSELL 7-5, 6-2

RUSSELL 6-2, 6-3

RUSSELL 4-6, 6-4, 6-2

TALBERT 6-1, 6-2, 9-7

F. SEGURA ....
Harry Buttimer ....
— SEGURA 6-2, 6-4

Lt. Hal Surface, Jr. ...
Bruce Thomas ....
— Surface 6-4, 3-6, 6-3

SEGURA 7-5, 6-8, 6-2

A/C R. FALKENBURG
Capt. A. Henderson ...
— FALKENBERG 6-2, 6-2

James Livingstone ...
A. HAMMERSLEY ...
— Livingtone 6-3, 1-6, 6-3

FALKENBERG 7-5, 6-4

SEGURA 6-2, 4-6, 6-1, 6-1

TALBERT 7-5, 6-3, 6-4

PARKER 6-1, 8-6, 7-5

PARKER 14-12, 6-1, 6-2

*Denotes foreign seeding

U.S. Seedings
1. Sgt. Frank A. Parker
2. Wm. F. Talbert
3. Francisco Segura
4. Lt. Gardnar Mulloy
5. Frank X. Shields
6. Elwood Cooke
7. Lt. S. Greenberg
8. A/C R. Falkenburg

Foreign Seedings
1. Andres Hammersley
2. Heraldo Weiss
3. Alejo Russell
4. Ladislav Hecht
5. Francisco Arcocha
6. Henri Rochon
7. Brendan Macken

SIXTY-FIFTH USLTA MEN'S SINGLES CHAMPIONSHIPS
West Side Tennis Club, Forest Hills, N.Y., 1946

First Round	Second Round	Third Round	Fourth Round	Quarter-Finals	Semi-Finals	Final

JOHN A. KRAMER ..
J. Gilbert Hall ......
KRAMER 7-5, 6-0, 6-3

Alastair B. Martin ....
DEREK BARTON* ......
BARTON 4-6, 6-2, 9-7, 3-6, 6-2

KRAMER 6-1, 6-0, 6-3

F. D. GUERNSEY, Jr. ..
Emery Neale ....
GUERNSEY, JR. 6-4, 6-3, 6-4

Edward Moylan .....
PHILLIPPE WASHER* ..
Moylan 7-5, 6-1, 6-1

Moylan 1-6, 3-6, 6-3, 6-4, 6-3

KRAMER 6-4, 6-4, 6-4

W. DON McNEILL ..
Don McDiarmid .....
McNEILL 6-3, 6-2, 6-4

Andres Hammersley ..
Cesar Carmona ....
Hammersley 6-3, 6-4, 7-5

McNEILL 6-3, 6-3, 6-3

Robert H. Perez .....
Harris Everett ....
Everett 6-4, 8-6, 6-2

Jan Staubo
Chauncey D. Steele, Jr. ....
PIERRE PELLIZZA* ....
PELLIZZA 6-3, 6-3, 6-2

PELLIZZA 6-1, 6-1, 3-6, 8-6

McNEILL 4-6, 14-12, 6-1, 6-8, 7-5

PELLIZZA 6-3, 6-4, 6-2

KRAMER 6-3, 6-2, 1-6, 6-2

WILLIAM F. TALBERT ....
William T. Vogt ....
Amado J. Sanchez ....
Charles H. Samson ....
TALBERT 7-5, 6-2, 7-5

TALBERT 6-0, 6-2, 6-2

Robert Kimbrell ....
Jack Rodgers ....
Richard Savitt ....
Herbert Behrens ....
Kimbrell 6-2, 7-5, 6-8, 6-1
Savitt 6-2, 6-3, 6-2
Savitt 6-4, 6-2, 2-6, 4-6, 6-4

TALBERT 6-2, 6-2, 6-0

Isadore H. Bellis ....
Earl H. Cochell ....
James A. Schnaars ....
Jack Cushingham ....
Cochell 7-5, 6-1, 6-0
Schnarrs By default
Cochell 6-1, 6-2, 6-1

T. Elwood Cooke ....
Nick Carter ....
Alexander Carver, Jr. ....
HARRY HOPMAN* ....
Cooke 6-3, 8-6, 2-6, 6-3, 13-11
HOPMAN 7-5, 6-3, 6-4
Cooke 6-1, 9-7, 8-6

Cochell 11-9, 6-1, 8-6, 6-1

TALBERT 6-4, 6-4, 8-6

ROBERT FALKENBURG ....
Enrique Buse ....
MacDonald Mathey ....
Bernard Bartzen ....
FALKENBURG 6-1, 6-3, 6-8, 6-1
Bartzen 6-0, 6-1, 6-1
FALKENBURG 7-5, 6-4, 6-2

Lt. Com. Gene Holbrook ....
Sam Match ....
Richard T. Hart ....
Edgar D. Yeomans ....
Match 3-6, 7-5, 6-3, 6-4
Hart 6-4, 7-5, 4-6, 6-2
Match 6-1, 6-2, 6-3

FALKENBURG 5-7, 2-6, 7-5, 6-1, 6-2

R. Philip Hanna ....
Chas. F. Masterson ....
William L. Canning ....
Tony Mottram ....
Masterson 6-2, 2-6, 6-1, 11-9
Canning 6-3, 6-3, 7-9, 9-7
Canning 6-0, 6-3, 6-3

Irvin Dorfman ....
Budge Patty ....
Hal Burrows ....
YVON PETRA* ....
Patty 6-3, 6-4, 6-1
PETRA 6-4, 6-1, 6-4
Patty 6-4, 9-7, 6-4

Patty 3-6, 6-3, 6-3, 6-2

FALKENBURG 6-4, 6-4, 6-2

FRANK A. PARKER ....
Brendan Macken ....
James Brink ....
Leonard L. Steiner ....
PARKER 6-1, 6-1, 6-3
Brink 7-5, 6-4, 6-4
PARKER 6-2, 6-1, 6-3

Lt. Robert Kerdasha ....
Bruce Thomas ....
Harry E. Likas, Jr. ....
ENRIQUE MOREA* ....
Thomas 6-0, 6-1, 6-2
Likas 4-6, 8-6, 6-2, 6-4
Likas 4-6, 6-2, 11-9, 6-4

PARKER 6-0, 6-2, 6-3

SEYMOUR GREENBERG ....
Tom Molloy ....
Jacques Van den Eynde ....
Jack Tuero ....
GREENBERG 6-2, 6-4, 4-6, 3-6, 6-2
Tuero 6-4, 6-4, 7-5
GREENBERG 6-0, 6-4, 6-4

Dean W. Mathey ....
Morey Lewis ....
Gardner E. Larned ....
BERNARD DESTREMAU* ....
Lewis 6-3, 6-4, 6-3
Larned 6-4, 6-4, 12-10
Larned 2-6, 6-4, 6-3, 6-3

GREENBERG 3-6, 6-1, 6-2, 4-6, 6-3

PARKER 6-3, 6-3, 6-2

TOM BROWN, JR. ....
Fred Kovaleski ....
Philippe Neff ....
Thomas Falkenburg ....
BROWN 7-5, 6-2, 12-10
Falkenburg 6-4, 7-5, 10-8
BROWN 6-4, 4-6, 6-1

John C. Ager ....
Sidney Schwartz ....
Bryan M. Grant, Jr. ....
Henri Rochon ....
Schwartz 6-2, 3-6, 4-6, 7-5, 6-2
Grant 6-4, 7-5, 6-2
Grant 6-4, 7-5, 6-3

BROWN 6-1, 6-2, 6-2

Lt. Richard Hainline ....
Herbert Flam ....
Heige Plougmann ....
Glenn Gardner ....
Flam 6-4, 6-2, 4-6, 1-6, 6-4
Gardner By default
Flam 6-4, 6-2, 7-5

George Pero ....
Sidney B. Wood, Jr. ....
Noel Brown ....
FELICISIMO AMPON* ....
Pero 6-3, 6-4, 6-3
AMPON 6-1, 6-3, 6-1
AMPON 8-6, 6-3, 6-1

Flam 6-4, 3-6, 6-1, 8-6

BROWN 6-3, 6-4, 6-2

BROWN 6-3, 6-4, 6-8, 3-6, 6-1

GARDNAR MULLOY ....
Capt. W. T. Anderson ....
MULLOY 6-0, 6-0, 6-1
Frank J. Bowden .....
MULLOY 6-2, 6-3, 7-5

E. Victor Seixas, Jr. ...
Ted Avory ....
Seixas 4-6, 6-2, 6-3, 8-6

MULLOY 6-3, 6-3, 6-2

Gayle Kellogg ....
Norman K. Brooks ....
Brooks 9-7, 7-5, 6-4

Jim Macken ....
ROBERT BARNES* ...
BARNES 6-2, 6-3, 6-1

Brooks 6-4, 6-3, 7-5

MULLOY 7-5, 6-2, 7-5

FRANCISCO SEGURA.
Mark Brown ....
SEGURA 6-2, 6-2, 6-2

Dennis H. Slack ......
Jean Marois ....
Slack 5-7, 2-6, 6-4, 6-2, 7-5

SEGURA 6-2, 6-0, 6-2

Alan S. Watson ......
Raymond Deyro ......
Deyro 6-2, 6-3, 6-4

Raymond F. Antignat .
ALEJO D. RUSSELL*.
RUSSELL 6-3, 1-6, 7-5, 6-4

RUSSELL 4-6, 6-0, 6-1, 3-6, 6-3

SEGURA 6-2, 6-2, 5-7, 6-4

MULLOY 4-6, 6-4, 12-10, 6-3

BROWN 6-4, 6-2, 6-4

KRAMER 6-0, 6-4, 6-4

KRAMER 9-7, 6-3, 6-0

*Denotes foreign seeding

SIXTY-SIXTH USLTA MEN'S SINGLES CHAMPIONSHIPS
West Side Tennis Club, Forest Hills, N.Y., 1947

First Round	Second Round	Third Round	Fourth Round	Quarter-Finals	Semi-Finals	Final

U. S. Seeding
1. Jack Kramer
2. Frank Parker
3. Thomas Brown, Jr.
4. Gardnar Mulloy
5. William Talbert
6. Francisco Segura
7. Robert Falkenberg
8. Edward Moylan
9. Victor Seixas
10. Earl Cochell

JACK KRAMER ...... — KRAMER 6-0, 6-3, 6-1
Edward McGrath .....

Brendan Macken ...... — MOREA 6-0, 3-6, 6-2, 6-4
ENRIQUE MOREA* ...

KRAMER 6-1, 6-1, 6-4

James Brink .... — Brink 6-4, 6-0, 6-2
Charles Masterson .....

R. S. McKenzie .... — CERNIK 8-6, 6-4, 6-2
C. CERNIK* ....

Brink 6-2, 3-6, 4-6, 6-2, 6-3

KRAMER 6-1, 3-6, 9-7, 7-5

ROBERT FALKENBURG ...... — FALKENBURG 6-1, 6-3, 6-4
Leonard Steiner ....

Gardner Larned .... — Likas By default
Harry Likas ....

FALKENBURG 4-6, 6-2, 6-3, 4-6, 6-4

Alastair Martin .... — Balbiers 4-6, 10-8, 6-2, 6-1
Ricardo Balbiers ......

Fred Fisher .... Mouledous 6-3, 7-5, 6-2
Richard Mouledous ....
Howe Atwater .... LONG 6-2, 6-3, 6-4
COLIN LONG* ....

LONG 6-2, 6-2, 6-4

FALKENBURG 4-6, 6-8, 6-3, 6-2, 6-4

LONG 6-4, 6-2, 6-4

KRAMER 6-2, 7-5, 6-1

THOMAS P BROWN, JR. .... BROWN, JR. 10-8, 4-6, 6-1, 6-2
Chauncey D. Steele
Joe Davis .... Hart 6-0, 6-0, 6-1
Richard Hart ....

BROWN, JR. 7-5, 6-0, 6-2

Dennis Slack .... Kovaleski 6-0, 6-4, 6-4
Fred Kovaleski ....
Francis X. Shields .... Shields 6-3, 6-4, 6-4
A. J. Mottram ....

Kovaleski 13-11, 3-6, 4-6, 6-3, 6-4

BROWN, JR. 6-4, 6-0, 6-8, 6-2

EARL COCHELL .... Dorfman 6-3, 3-6, 6-3, 7-5
Irvin Dorfman
Sidney B. Wood .... Heldman 4-0, 6-4, 6-4, 6-2
Dr. Julius D. Heldman ...

Dorfman 6-4, 6-4, 3-6, 6-4

James Macken .... Vogt 6-3, 6-2, 6-4
William T. Vogt
Kenneth E. McCarthy .... BROWN 6-4, 6-1, 6-3
GEOFFREY BROWN* ....

BROWN 6-4, 9-7, 7-5

BROWN 6-1, 6-3, 7-9, 4-6, 6-2

BROWN, JR. 7-5, 4-6, 10-8, 6-1

WILLIAM F. TALBERT .... Flam By default, 9-11, 1-0
Herbert Flam
Man Mohan .... Mattmann 6-2, 6-0, 6-1
Charles T. Mattmann ....

Flam 6-1, 6-1, 6-3

Cpl. Tom Molloy .... Molloy 6-4, 1-6, 6-1, 6-3
Vincent T. Paul
Alexander H. Carver .... Match 6-1, 6-3, 7-5
Sam Match ....

Match 6-2, 0-6, 6-4, 6-3

Flam 6-1, 6-2 2-6, 6-2

Alexander T. Hetzeck .... Vieira 6-3, 6-1, 6-0
Armando Vieira
Macdonald Mathey .... Behrens 9-7, 6-0, 5-7, 6-3
Herbert Behrens ....

Behrens 4-6, 6-2, 2-6, 9-7, 6-4

Frank J. Bowden .... Bowden 3-6, 6-4, 6-1, 6-3
James T. Thackara
Clayton Benham .... DROBNY 9-7, 6-4, 7-5
JAROSLAV DROBNY* ....

DROBNY 6-4, 6-4, 6-3

DROBNY 6-2, 8-6, 6-1

DROBNY 2-6, 6-2, 6-1, 6-4

DROBNY 7-5, 6-3, 6-4

FRANK PARKER .... PARKER 6-2, 6-1
Clark R. Taylor
Rolando Vega .... Hecht By default
Ladislav Hecht ....

PARKER 6-2, 6-4, 6-4

J. H. Crawford .... Paish 6-0, 6-1, 6-4
G. L. Paish
Pfc. Hugh Stewart .... DESTREMAU 3-6, 6-4, 8-6, 6-3
BERNARD DESTREMAU* ....

DESTREMAU 6-4, 3-6, 6-4, 6-2

PARKER 6-0, 6-2, 6-3

E. VICTOR SEIXAS .... SEIXAS 6-4, 6-0, 7-5
Jack Tuero
Sam Daniel .... Beisser 6-2, 7-5, 6-2
Arnold Beisser ....

SEIXAS 6-3, 6-2, 6-2

R. Philip Hanna .... Paton 7-5, 7-5, 13-11
Andy Paton
Koon Hong Ip .... SIDWELL 6-0, 6-0, 6-2
BILLY SIDWELL* ....

SIDWELL 7-5, 6-3, 6-2

SEIXAS 3-6, 6-3, 4-6, 6-0, 6-4

PARKER 6-1, 4-6, 6-3, 6-4

FRANCISCO SEGURA .... SEGURA 6-2, 6-1, 6-3
Joseph Fishbach
Richard Savitt .... Savitt 1-6, 6-3, 6-4, 3-6, 6-4
Sidney Schwartz ....

SEGURA 6-3, 6-1, 6-2

J. Gilbert Hall .... Mehta 6-4, 6-4, 6-1
Jimmy Mehta
Bernard Bartzen .... Bartzen 6-4, 6-2, 6-1
A. L. Hollander, Jr. ....

Bartzen 6-4, 6-4, 6-1

SEGURA 6-8, 6-1, 6-3, 6-3

Harold M. Burrows .... Burrows 3-6, 6-0, 6-4, 6-3
Barney Welsh
Clarence Carter .... Carter 4-6, 4-6, 7-5, 6-0, 6-2
Thomas J. Burke ....

Carter 6-2, 6-3, 6-1

Dean Mathey .... Rurac 6-3, 6-4, 6-2
Vinicius Rurac
James Evert .... PAILS 6-3, 6-2, 6-1
DINNY PAILS* ....

PAILS 6-1, 6-4, 6-3

PAILS 6-1, 7-5, 6-2

SEGURA 1-6, 6-1, 6-2, 7-5

PARKER 6-3, 11-9, 6-4

GARDNAR MULLOY .... MULLOY 6-3, 6-4, 6-1
Bryan M. Grant
Richard A. Gonzales .... Gonzales 6-3, 6-0, 6-3
Derek Barton ....

MULLOY 6-3, 6-2, 2-6, 9-11, 6-4

John Olliff .... Misra 6-1, 2-6, 6-0, 9-7
Sumant Misra ....

MULLOY 6-3, 6-2, 9-7

Seymour Greenberg ... Greenberg By default
Armando Vega ....

Jack Geller .... JOHANSSON 9-7, 6-4, 6-0
TORSTEN JOHANSSON* ....

JOHANSSON 6-3, 6-3, 1-6, 6-1

MULLOY 6-3, 6-2, 6-3

EDWARD MOYLAN ... MOYLAN 9-7, 6-4, 6-1
Robert Abdesselam ....

Oliver Roddey .... Roddey 6-2, 6-1, 6-2
W. Robert Dixon ....

MOYLAN 6-1, 6-1, 6-1

Henri Rochon .... Rochon 6-2, 6-3, 7-5
Jacques Peten ....

George Pero .... BROMWICH 7-5, 6-3, 6-1
JOHN BROMWICH* ...

BROMWICH 6-1, 6-0, 6-1

BROMWICH 6-2, 6-1, 6-2

BROMWICH 7-5, 6-1, 6-1

KRAMER 3-6, 6-3, 6-0, 6-1

KRAMER 4-6, 2-6, 6-1, 6-0, 6-3

PARKER 6-3, 4-6, 6-3, 6-8, 8-6

*Denotes foreign seeding

Foreign Seedings
1. John Bromwich
2. Jaroslov Drobny
3. Dennis Pails
4. Colin Long
5. Torsten Johansson
6. Geoffrey Brown
7. Billy Sidwell
8. C. Cernik
9. Enrique Morea
10. Bernard Destremau

SIXTY-SEVENTH USLTA MEN'S SINGLES CHAMPIONSHIPS
West Side Tennis Club, Forest Hills, N.Y., 1948

First Round | Second Round | Third Round | Fourth Round | Quarter Finals | Semi-Finals | Final

Foreign Seeding
1. Adrian Quist
2. Jaroslav Drobny
3. Billy Sidwell
4. Geoff Brown
5. Eric W. Sturgess
6. Colin Long
7. Frank A. Sedgman
8. Enrique Morea

FRANK A. PARKER ..
Gilbert A. Bogley ....
PARKER 6-2, 6-1, 6-0

Gustavo Palafox ....
John E. Lohstoeter, Jr..
Lohstoeter Default

PARKER 6-0, 6-1, 6-0

Wm. Andrew Paton, Jr.
James Bicknell ....
Paton 6-4, 5-7, 3-6, 6-3, 6-2

E. Raymond Morris ....
FRANK A. SEDGMAN*
SEDGMAN 6-4, 6-2, 6-2

SEDGMAN 6-2, 13-11, 6-2

PARKER 6-4, 7-5, 6-3

RICHARD A. GONZALES ....
Ladislav Hecht ....
GONZALES 8-6, 6-3, 6-1

Wally Bostick ....
August Ganzenmuller, Jr. ....
Ganzenmuller 6-8, 6-3, 4-6, 8-6, 8-6

GONZALES 6-3, 6-2, 6-3

Arthur D. Larsen ......
Tom Molloy ....
Larsen 7-5, 2-6, 3-6, 6-4, 7-5

Sverre Lie ....
BILLY SIDWELL* ....
SIDWELL 6-0, 6-3, 6-3

Larsen 4-6, 6-2, 8-6, 6-4

GONZALES 6-2, 2-6, 3-6, 6-3, 6-2

GONZALES 8-6, 2-6, 7-5, 6-3

ROBERT FALKENBERG ......
George Richards ......
FALKENBURG 6-4, 1-6, 6-3, 6-3

J. Edward (Budge) Patty ....
Anthony J. Mottram ....
Patty 6-4, 6-8, 6-1, 6-3

Harold M. Burrows, Jr. ....
Arnold Saul ....
Saul 8-6, 8-6, 6-3

Patty 6-3, 6-4, 6-3

FALKENBURG 6-1, 4-6, 3-6, 6-4, 10-8

Alexander H. Carver, Jr. ....
Clarence Carter ....
Carter 6-1, 6-3, 6-4

Charles T. Mattmann ....
Henri Rochon ....
Rochon 6-3, 8-6, 6-3

Carter 6-3, 7-5, 6-0

Thomas P. Brown, Jr. ....
James Brink ....
Brown 6-3, 6-8, 6-3, 6-2

Diehl Mateer, Jr. ....
COLIN LONG* ....
LONG 6-3, 8-6, 6-4

Brown 6-2, 6-3, 6-4

Carter 6-4, 6-3, 6-4

FALKENBURG 8-6, 6-3, 6-4

E. VICTOR SEIXAS, JR. ....
Edward McGrath ....
SEIXAS 6-2, 6-3, 6-1

Samuel Match ....
Vinicius Rurac ....
Match 6-0, 6-0, 6-3

SEIXAS 6-3, 6-0, 6-4

Oliver F. Roddey ....
John E. Lynch, Jr. ....
Roddey 6-2, 6-1, 6-1

William T. Vogt ....
Herbert Behrens ....
Vogt 6-4, 8-6, 6-4

Vogt 9-7, 3-6, 6-3, 6-4

SEIXAS 6-3, 6-8, 6-3, 5-7, 9-7

Sidney Schwartz ....
Isadore H. Bellis ....
Schwartz 6-0, 0-6, 6-4, 5-7, 6-2

Gilbert J. Shea, Jr. ....
Harry Hoffman ....
Shea 3-6, 14-16, 6-3, 6-3, 6-1

Shea 6-4, 5-7, 7-5, 6-3

Irvin Dorfman ....
Bernard J. Bartzen ....
Bartzen 6-0, 6-2, 6-4

Tony Vincent ....
JAROSLAV DROBNY* ....
DROBNY 6-1, 6-1, 6-0

DROBNY 6-3, 6-2, 6-4

DROBNY 5-7, 6-4, 6-2, 8-6

WILLIAM F. TALBERT ....
Bernard T. Welsh ....
TALBERT 6-2, 6-1, 4-6, 6-1

Ricardo Balbiers ....
G. Dever Hobbs ....
Balbiers 6-2, 6-2, 3-6, 6-2

TALBERT 7-5, 6-2, 6-3

William Tully ....
Eugene Garrett ....
Garrett 6-3, 7-5, 6-2

Thomas Boys ....
Vladimir Cernik ....
Cernik 6-2, 6-2, 6-4

Garrett 6-4, 6-3, 4-6, 6-2

TALBERT 6-3, 6-2, 6-4

Jack Geller ....
Richard Savitt ....
Savitt 6-1, 6-3, 6-3

Brendan Macken ....
Harry C. Hopman ....
Hopman 6-2, 6-4, 3-6, 6-3

Savitt 6-4, 6-0, 6-2

Bruce Thomas ....
Capt. C. R. Hippenstiel ....
Thomas 6-3, 3-6, 6-4, 6-3

Clark Taylor ....
ERIC W. STURGESS* ....
STURGESS 6-0, 6-1, 6-2

STURGESS 6-0, 6-4, 6-2

STURGESS 6-3, 6-4, 6-2

STURGESS 5-7, 6-4, 6-2, 1-6, 6-4

DROBNY 8-6, 6-1, 6-3

EARL H. COCHELL ....
Edward Moylan ....
COCHELL 6-4, 6-3, 4-6, 6-2

Richard Mouledous ....
Fred Kovaleski ....
Kovaleski 6-3, 6-1, 6-3

COCHELL 4-6, 8-6, 4-6, 6-4, 6-3

J. Gilbert Hall ....
Chauncey D. Steele, Jr. ....
Steele 6-4, 6-2, 4-6, 6-4

Tony Trabert ....
Robert J. Kerdasha ....
Trabert 6-1, 6-4, 8-6

Trabert 6-3, 5-7, 4-6, 6-3, 6-4

COCHELL 6-0, 6-3, 3-6, 6-4

Juan Weiss ....
Alexander T. Hetzeck ....
Weiss 6-2, 6-3, 4-6, 6-3

MacDonald Mathey ....
Weiss 3-6, 4-6, 6-2, 6-1, 6-4

Felicisimo Ampon .....
GEOFF BROWN* .....
Ampon 6-1, 6-4, 3-6, 7-5

Ampon 6-3, 6-2, 6-4

COCHELL 6-2, 6-0, 6-2

STURGESS 6-2, 8-6, 3-6, 5-7, 6-3

*Denotes foreign seeding

GARDNAR MULLOY .
Paul R. Massey ....
MULLOY 6-2, 6-2, 6-3

Charles F. Masterson ..
Sidney B. Wood, Jr. ...
Wood 7-5, 1-6, 6-3, 9-7

MULLOY 8-6, 6-4, 10-8

Francisco Galvan .....
Herbert Flam ....
Flam 6-3, 6-2, 6-3

Leonard Steiner ....
ENRIQUE MOREA* ...
MOREA 6-3, 9-7, 6-0

Flam 6-3, 3-6, 6-1, 2-6, 6-0

Flam 6-4, 7-5, 3-6, 4-6, 6-3

HARRY E. LIKAS, JR. .
Robert Abdesselam ....
LIKAS 6-3, 6-2, 7-5

Alastair B. Martin ....
R. Phillip Hanna ......
Martin 6-0, 6-4, 6-4

LIKAS 6-2, 6-4, 6-4

Straight Clark ....
Grant Golden ....
Clark 2-6, 9-7, 6-1, 6-4

Francis X. Shields ....
ADRIAN QUIST* ......
QUIST 6-2, 6-1, 2-6, 6-4

QUIST 7-5, 8-6, 6-3

LIKAS 6-2, 6-3, 4-6, 6-4

Flam 2-6, 6-4, 6-1, 6-0

STURGESS 9-7, 6-3, 6-2

GONZALES 8-10, 11-9, 6-0, 6-3

GONZALES 6-2, 6-3, 14-12

U. S. Seeding
1. Frank A. Parker
2. William F. Talbert
3. Gardnar Mulloy
4. Robert Falkenburg
5. Earl Cochell
6. Harry E. Likas, Jr.
7. E. Victor Seixas, Jr.
8. Richard Gonzales

124

SIXTY-EIGHTH USLTA MEN'S SINGLES CHAMPIONSHIPS
West Side Tennis Club, ForestHills, N.Y., 1949

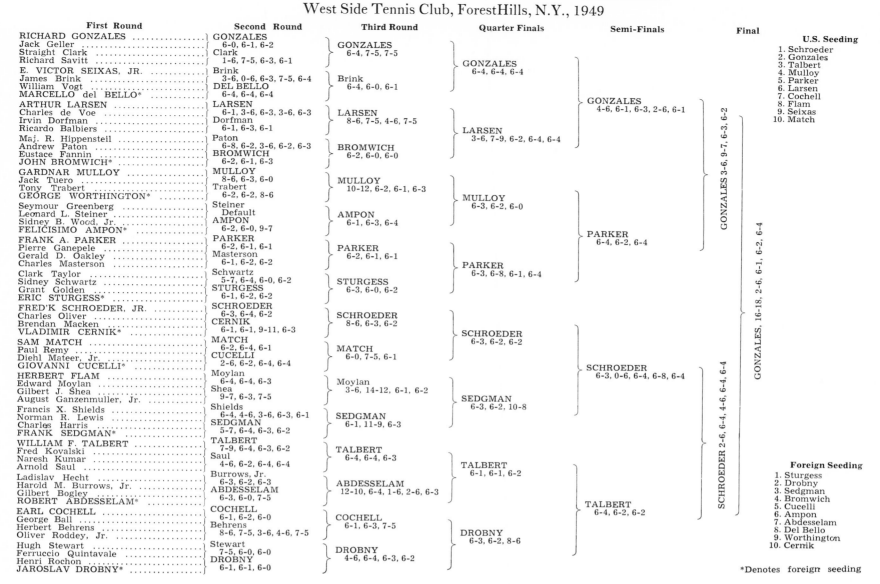

First Round	Second Round
RICHARD GONZALES	GONZALES 6-0, 6-1, 6-2
Jack Geller	
Straight Clark	Clark 1-6, 7-5, 6-3, 6-1
Richard Savitt	
E. VICTOR SEIXAS, JR.	Brink 3-6, 0-6, 6-3, 7-5, 6-4
James Brink	
William Vogt	DEL BELLO 6-4, 6-4, 6-4
MARCELLO del BELLO*	
ARTHUR LARSEN	LARSEN 6-1, 3-6, 6-3, 3-6, 6-3
Charles de Voe	
Irvin Dorfman	Dorfman 6-1, 6-3, 6-1
Ricardo Balbiers	
Maj. R. Hippensteil	Paton 6-8, 6-2, 3-6, 6-2, 6-3
Andrew Paton	
Eustace Fannin	BROMWICH 6-2, 6-1, 6-3
JOHN BROMWICH*	
GARDNAR MULLOY	MULLOY 8-6, 6-3, 6-0
Jack Tuero	
Tony Trabert	Trabert 6-2, 6-2, 8-6
GEORGE WORTHINGTON*	
Seymour Greenberg	Steiner Default
Leonard L. Steiner	
Sidney B. Wood, Jr.	AMPON 6-2, 6-0, 9-7
FELICISIMO AMPON*	
FRANK A. PARKER	PARKER 6-2, 6-1, 6-1
Pierre Ganepele	
Gerald D. Oakley	Masterson 6-1, 6-2, 6-2
Charles Masterson	
Clark Taylor	Schwartz 5-7, 6-4, 6-0, 6-2
Sidney Schwartz	
Grant Golden	STURGESS 6-1, 6-2, 6-2
ERIC STURGESS*	
FRED'K SCHROEDER, JR.	SCHROEDER 6-3, 6-4, 6-2
Charles Oliver	
Brendan Macken	CERNIK 6-1, 6-1, 9-11, 6-3
VLADIMIR CERNIK*	
SAM MATCH	MATCH 6-2, 6-4, 6-1
Paul Remy	
Diehl Mateer, Jr.	CUCELLI 2-6, 6-2, 6-4, 6-4
GIOVANNI CUCELLI*	
HERBERT FLAM	Moylan 6-4, 6-4, 6-3
Edward Moylan	
Gilbert J. Shea	Shea 9-7, 6-3, 7-5
August Ganzenmuller, Jr.	
Francis X. Shields	Shields 6-4, 4-6, 3-6, 6-3, 6-1
Norman R. Lewis	
Charles Harris	SEDGMAN 5-7, 6-4, 6-3, 6-2
FRANK SEDGMAN*	
WILLIAM F. TALBERT	TALBERT 7-9, 6-4, 6-3, 6-2
Fred Kovalski	
Naresh Kumar	Saul 4-6, 6-2, 6-4, 6-4
Arnold Saul	
Ladislav Hecht	Burrows, Jr. 6-3, 6-2, 6-3
Harold M. Burrows, Jr.	
Gilbert Bogley	ABDESSELAM 6-3, 6-0, 7-5
ROBERT ABDESSELAM*	
EARL COCHELL	COCHELL 6-1, 6-2, 6-0
George Ball	
Herbert Behrens	Behrens 8-6, 7-5, 3-6, 4-6, 7-5
Oliver Roddey, Jr.	
Hugh Stewart	Stewart 7-5, 6-0, 6-0
Ferruccio Quintavale	
Henri Rochon	DROBNY 6-1, 6-1, 6-0
JAROSLAV DROBNY*	

Third Round:
GONZALES 6-4, 7-5, 7-5 — Brink 6-4, 6-0, 6-1 — LARSEN 8-6, 7-5, 4-6, 7-5 — BROMWICH 6-2, 6-0, 6-0 — MULLOY 10-12, 6-2, 6-1, 6-3 — AMPON 6-1, 6-3, 6-4 — PARKER 6-2, 6-1, 6-1 — STURGESS 6-3, 6-0, 6-2 — SCHROEDER 8-6, 6-3, 6-2 — MATCH 6-0, 7-5, 6-1 — Moylan 3-6, 14-12, 6-1, 6-2 — SEDGMAN 6-1, 11-9, 6-3 — TALBERT 6-4, 6-4, 6-3 — ABDESSELAM 12-10, 6-4, 1-6, 2-6, 6-3 — COCHELL 6-1, 6-3, 7-5 — DROBNY 4-6, 6-4, 6-3, 6-2

Quarter Finals:
GONZALES 6-4, 6-4, 6-4 — LARSEN 3-6, 7-9, 6-2, 6-4, 6-4 — MULLOY 6-3, 6-2, 6-0 — PARKER 6-3, 6-8, 6-1, 6-4 — SCHROEDER 6-3, 6-2, 6-2 — SEDGMAN 6-3, 6-2, 10-8 — TALBERT 6-1, 6-1, 6-2 — DROBNY 6-3, 6-2, 8-6

Semi-Finals:
GONZALES 4-6, 6-1, 6-3, 2-6, 6-1 — PARKER 6-4, 6-2, 6-4 — SCHROEDER 6-3, 0-6, 6-4, 6-8, 6-4 — TALBERT 6-4, 6-2, 6-2

Final:
GONZALES 3-6, 9-7, 6-3, 6-2 — SCHROEDER 2-6, 6-4, 4-6, 6-4, 6-4

GONZALES, 16-18, 2-6, 6-1, 6-2, 6-4

U.S. Seeding
1. Schroeder
2. Gonzales
3. Talbert
4. Mulloy
5. Parker
6. Larsen
7. Cochell
8. Flam
9. Seixas
10. Match

Foreign Seeding
1. Sturgess
2. Drobny
3. Sedgman
4. Bromwich
5. Cucelli
6. Ampon
7. Abdesselam
8. Del Bello
9. Worthington
10. Cernik

*Denotes foreign seeding

SIXTY-NINTH USLTA MEN'S SINGLES CHAMPIONSHIPS
West Side Tennis Club, Forest Hills, N.Y., 1950

First Round	Second Round
HERBERT FLAM	FLAM 3-6, 6-4, 6-1, 6-4
Gilbert A. Bogley	
George Ball	WASHER 8-6, 6-3, 6-4
PHILIPPE WASHER*	
JAMES BRINK	BRINK 6-1, 7-5, 5-7, 3-6, 6-4
Jean Ducos	
August Ganzenmuller	MOTTRAM 6-0, 6-4, 6-3
TONY MOTTRAM*	
E. VICTOR SEIXAS, JR.	SEIXAS, JR. 6-1, 6-0, 6-1
Andy Paton	
Ricardo Balbiers	Balbiers 6-3, 6-3, 6-2
Alastair B. Martin	
WILLIAM F. TALBERT	TALBERT 6-1, 3-6, 6-1, 6-2
Francis X. Shields	
W. Donald McNeill	McNeill 9-7, 3-6, 6-4, 6-1
KENNETH McGREGOR*	
GARDNAR MULLOY	MULLOY 6-4, 6-0, 6-1
Tony Vincent	
Hugh Stewart	Stewart 6-3, 3-6, 5-7, 6-2, 6-1
Gilbert J. Shea, Jr.	
Hamilton Richardson	Richardson 6-3, 1-6, 6-3, 6-3
Herbert Behrens	
Richard Gaines	JOHANSSON 6-3, 6-3, 6-8, 6-2
TORSTEN JOHANSSON*	
EARL COCHELL	COCHELL 6-1, 6-3, 6-0
Fred Fisher	
Harry E. Likas, Jr.	Likas, Jr. 6-4, 6-2, 7-5
Charles Masterson	
Straight Clark	Clark 10-8, 6-3, 6-1
J. Brichant	
Harold M. Burrows, Jr.	SEDGMAN 3-6, 6-3, 7-5, 10-8
FRANK SEDGMAN*	
BUDGE PATTY	DeVoe Default
Charles De Voe	
Sidney Schwartz	Schwartz 6-2, 6-4, 6-4
GUSTAVO PALAFOX*	
Sam Match	Match 6-2, 6-2, 6-4
Aake Eliason	
Lorne Main	AMPON 5-7, 6-3, 7-5, 6-4
FELICISIMO AMPON*	
RICHARD SAVITT	SAVITT Default
Arnold Saul	
George Richards	Rose 5-7, 6-3, 6-3, 7-5
Mervyn Rose	
Brendan Macken	Moylan 6-2, 7-5, 6-1
Edward Moylan	
Tony Trabert	BROMWICH 6-4, 6-0, 6-1
JOHN BROMWICH*	
THOMAS P. BROWN, JR.	BROWN, JR. 1-6, 6-4, 6-1, 6-.4
Jack Tuero	
Grant Golden	Golden 6-4, 6-4, 9-7
Robert Abdesselam	
Leonard Brose	Rochon 6-2, 6-4, 6-1
Henri Rochon	
Malcolm Fox	WORTHINGTON 6-2, 6-2, 6-0
GEORGE WORTHINGTON*	
ARTHUR LARSEN	LARSEN 6-3, 6-4, 6-3
John A. T. Horn	
Sven Davidsson	Davidsson 6-4, 4-6, 6-4, 13-11
Whitney Reed	
Harry Hopman	Hopman 10-12, 1-6, 6-1, 7-5, 6-2
Bernard Schreiber	
Dr. Arnold Beisser	DROBNY 5-7, 9-7, 11-9, 6-2
JARSOLAV DROBNY*	

Third Round:
FLAM 6-1, 6-4, 6-8, 6-4 — BRINK 6-4, 4-6, 6-3, 4-6, 6-3 — SEIXAS, JR. 6-3, 6-2, 6-3 — TALBERT 6-1, 4-6, 7-5, 6-0 — MULLOY 6-1, 6-2, 6-1 — JOHANSSON 7-5, 4-6, 6-4, 6-3 — COCHELL 6-0, 6-1, 6-2 — SEDGMAN 4-6, 6-3, 7-5, 3-6, 7-5 — Schwartz 6-4, 21-19, 6-3 — AMPON 6-2, 6-4, 6-1 — SAVITT 6-4, 6-2, 6-4 — BROMWICH 6-3, 6-4, 1-6, 6-4 — BROWN, JR. 6-3, 6-3, 6-2 — WORTHINGTON 3-6, 3-6, 6-0, 10-8, 7-5 — LARSEN 6-4, 6-4, 4-6, 6-4 — DROBNY 9-7, 6-3, 6-1

Quarter-Finals:
FLAM 6-4, 6-3, 6-3 — TALBERT 6-1, 2-6, 3-6, 6-2, 6-3 — MULLOY 6-4, 6-2, 6-2 — COCHELL 7-5, 5-7, 1-6, 6-2, 6-2 — Schwartz 4-6, 6-2, 10-8, 7-5 — SAVITT 3-6, 6-0, 4-6, 6-2, 6-3 — BROWN, JR. 6-2, 1-6, 6-1, 7-5 — LARSEN 6-3, 2-6, 6-1, 6-4

Semi-Finals:
FLAM 9-7, 6-4, 6-3 — MULLOY 6-3, 7-5, 6-2 — SAVITT 8-6, 6-2, 2-6, 6-3 — LARSEN 6-3, 2-6, 6-1, 6-4

Final:
FLAM 2-6, 6-2, 9-11, 6-3 — LARSEN 6-3, 4-6, 5-7, 6-4, 6-3

LARSEN 6-2, 10-8, 7-9, 6-2

U.S. Seeding
1. Patty
2. Flam
3. Mulloy
4. Brown, Jr.
5. Seixas
6. Larsen
7. Cochell
8. Savitt
9. Talbert
10. Brink

Foreign Seeding
1. Sedgman
2. Drobny
3. Bromwich
4. McGregor
5. Johansson
6. Ampon
7. Worthington
8. Mottram
9. Washer
10. Palafox

SEVENTIETH USLTA MEN'S SINGLES CHAMPIONSHIPS
West Side Tennis Club, Forest Hills, N.Y., 1951

First Round	Second Round	Third Round	Fourth Round	Quarter Finals	Semi-Finals	Final

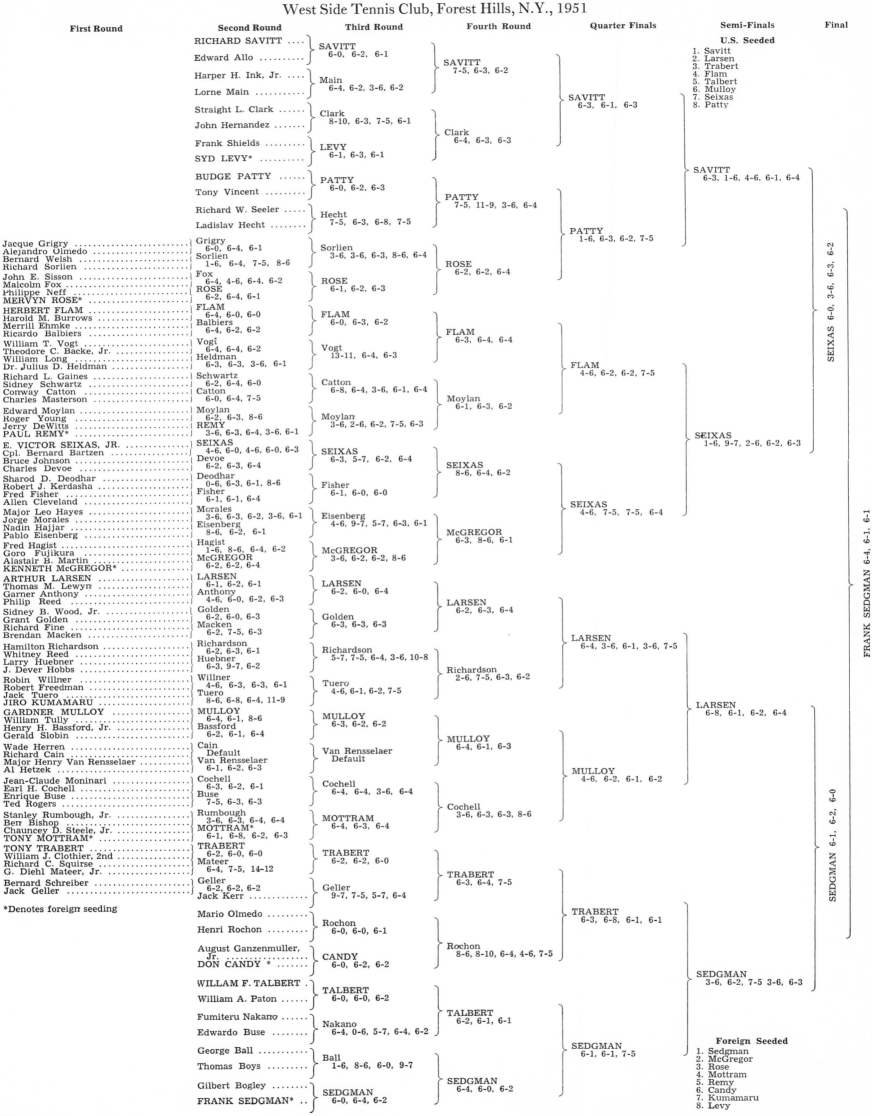

U.S. Seeded
1. Savitt
2. Larsen
3. Trabert
4. Flam
5. Talbert
6. Mulloy
7. Seixas
8. Patty

RICHARD SAVITT ....
Edward Allo ....
SAVITT 6-0, 6-2, 6-1

Harper H. Ink, Jr. ....
Lorne Main ....
Main 6-4, 6-2, 3-6, 6-2

SAVITT 7-5, 6-3, 6-2

Straight L. Clark ......
John Hernandez ....
Clark 8-10, 6-3, 7-5, 6-1

Frank Shields ....
SYD LEVY* ....
LEVY 6-1, 6-3, 6-1

Clark 6-4, 6-3, 6-3

SAVITT 6-3, 6-1, 6-3

BUDGE PATTY ......
Tony Vincent ....
PATTY 6-0, 6-2, 6-3

Richard W. Seeler .....
Ladislav Hecht ....
Hecht 7-5, 6-3, 6-8, 7-5

PATTY 7-5, 11-9, 3-6, 6-4

SAVITT 6-3, 1-6, 4-6, 6-1, 6-4

Jacque Grigry — Grigry 6-0, 6-4, 6-1
Alejandro Olmedo
Bernard Welsh — Sorlien 1-6, 6-4, 7-5, 8-6
Richard Sorlien
Sorlien 3-6, 3-6, 6-3, 8-6, 6-4

John E. Sisson — Fox 6-4, 4-6, 6-4, 6-2
Malcolm Fox
Philippe Neff — ROSE 6-2, 6-4, 6-1
MERVYN ROSE*
ROSE 6-1, 6-2, 6-3

ROSE 6-2, 6-2, 6-4

PATTY 1-6, 6-3, 6-2, 7-5

HERBERT FLAM — FLAM 6-4, 6-0, 6-0
Harold M. Burrows
Merrill Ehmke — Balbiers 6-4, 6-2, 6-2
Ricardo Balbiers
FLAM 6-0, 6-3, 6-2

William T. Vogt — Vogt 6-4, 6-4, 6-2
Theodore C. Backe, Jr.
William Long — Heldman 6-3, 6-3, 3-6, 6-1
Dr. Julius D. Heldman
Vogt 13-11, 6-4, 6-3

FLAM 6-3, 6-4, 6-4

Richard L. Gaines — Schwartz 6-2, 6-4, 6-0
Sidney Schwartz
Conway Catton — Catton 6-0, 6-4, 7-5
Charles Masterson
Catton 6-8, 6-4, 3-6, 6-1, 6-4

Edward Moylan — Moylan 6-2, 6-3, 8-6
Roger Young
Jerry DeWitts — REMY 3-6, 6-3, 6-4, 3-6, 6-1
PAUL REMY*
Moylan 3-6, 2-6, 6-2, 7-5, 6-3

Moylan 6-1, 6-3, 6-2

FLAM 4-6, 6-2, 6-2, 7-5

E. VICTOR SEIXAS, JR. — SEIXAS 4-6, 6-0, 4-6, 6-0, 6-3
Cpl. Bernard Bartzen
Bruce Johnson — Devoe 6-2, 6-3, 6-4
Charles Devoe
SEIXAS 6-3, 5-7, 6-2, 6-4

Sharod D. Deodhar — Deodhar 0-6, 6-3, 6-1, 8-6
Robert J. Kerdasha
Fred Fisher — Fisher 6-1, 6-1, 6-4
Allen Cleveland
Fisher 6-1, 6-0, 6-0

SEIXAS 8-6, 6-4, 6-2

Major Leo Hayes — Morales 3-6, 6-3, 6-2, 3-6, 6-1
Jorge Morales
Nadin Hajjar — Eisenberg 8-6, 6-2, 6-1
Pablo Eisenberg
Eisenberg 4-6, 9-7, 5-7, 6-3, 6-1

Fred Hagist — Hagist 1-6, 8-6, 6-4, 6-2
Goro Fujikura
Alastair B. Martin — McGREGOR 6-2, 6-2, 6-4
KENNETH McGREGOR*
McGREGOR 3-6, 6-2, 6-2, 8-6

McGREGOR 6-3, 8-6, 6-1

SEIXAS 4-6, 7-5, 7-5, 6-4

SEIXAS 1-6, 9-7, 2-6, 6-2, 6-3

ARTHUR LARSEN — LARSEN 6-1, 6-2, 6-1
Thomas M. Lewyn
Garner Anthony — Anthony 4-6, 6-0, 6-2, 6-3
Philip Reed
LARSEN 6-2, 6-0, 6-4

Sidney B. Wood, Jr. — Golden 6-2, 6-0, 6-3
Grant Golden
Richard Fine — Macken 6-2, 7-5, 6-3
Brendan Macken
Golden 6-3, 6-3, 6-3

LARSEN 6-2, 6-3, 6-4

Hamilton Richardson — Richardson 6-2, 6-3, 6-1
Whitney Reed
Larry Huebner — Huebner 6-3, 9-7, 6-2
J. Dever Hobbs
Richardson 5-7, 7-5, 6-4, 3-6, 10-8

Robin Willner — Willner 4-6, 6-3, 6-3, 6-1
Robert Freedman
Jack Tuero — Tuero 8-6, 6-8, 6-4, 11-9
JIRO KUMAMARU
Tuero 4-6, 6-1, 6-2, 7-5

Richardson 2-6, 7-5, 6-3, 6-2

LARSEN 6-4, 3-6, 6-1, 3-6, 7-5

GARDNER MULLOY — MULLOY 6-4, 6-1, 8-6
William Tully
Henry H. Bassford, Jr. — Bassford 6-2, 6-1, 6-4
Gerald Slobin
MULLOY 6-3, 6-2, 6-2

Wade Herren — Cain Default
Richard Cain
Major Henry Van Rensselaer — Van Rensselaer 6-1, 6-2, 6-3
Al Hetzek
Van Rensselaer Default

MULLOY 6-4, 6-1, 6-3

Jean-Claude Moninari — Cochell 6-3, 6-2, 6-1
Earl H. Cochell
Enrique Buse — Buse 7-5, 6-3, 6-3
Ted Rogers
Cochell 6-4, 6-4, 3-6, 6-4

Stanley Rumbough, Jr. — Rumbough 3-6, 6-3, 6-4, 6-4
Ben Bishop
Chauncey D. Steele, Jr. — MOTTRAM* 6-1, 6-8, 6-2, 6-3
TONY MOTTRAM*
MOTTRAM 6-4, 6-3, 6-4

Cochell 3-6, 6-3, 6-3, 8-6

MULLOY 4-6, 6-2, 6-1, 6-2

LARSEN 6-8, 6-1, 6-2, 6-4

TONY TRABERT — TRABERT 6-2, 6-0, 6-0
William J. Clothier, 2nd
Richard C. Squirse — Mateer 6-4, 7-5, 14-12
G. Diehl Mateer, Jr.
TRABERT 6-2, 6-2, 6-0

Bernard Schreiber — Geller 6-2, 6-2, 6-2
Jack Geller
Jack Kerr — Geller 9-7, 7-5, 5-7, 6-4

TRABERT 6-3, 6-4, 7-5

Mario Olmedo — Rochon 6-0, 6-0, 6-1
Henri Rochon
Rochon 8-6, 8-10, 6-4, 4-6, 7-5

August Ganzenmuller, Jr. — CANDY 6-0, 6-2, 6-2
DON CANDY*

TRABERT 6-3, 6-8, 6-1, 6-1

WILLAM F. TALBERT . — TALBERT 6-0, 6-0, 6-2
William A. Paton
TALBERT 6-2, 6-1, 6-1

Fumiteru Nakano — Nakano 6-4, 0-6, 5-7, 6-4, 6-2
Edwardo Buse

George Ball — Ball 1-6, 8-6, 6-0, 9-7
Thomas Boys
SEDGMAN 6-4, 6-0, 6-2

Gilbert Bogley — SEDGMAN 6-0, 6-4, 6-2
FRANK SEDGMAN*

SEDGMAN 6-1, 6-1, 7-5

SEDGMAN 3-6, 6-2, 7-5, 3-6, 6-3

SEIXAS 6-0, 3-6, 6-3, 6-2

SEDGMAN 6-1, 6-2, 6-0

FRANK SEDGMAN 6-4, 6-1, 6-1

*Denotes foreign seeding

Foreign Seeded
1. Sedgman
2. McGregor
3. Rose
4. Mottram
5. Remy
6. Candy
7. Kumamaru
8. Levy

126

SEVENTY-FIRST USLTA MEN'S SINGLES CHAMPIONSHIPS
West Side Tennis Club, Forest Hills, N.Y., 1952

First Round	Second Round	Third Round	Fourth Round	Quarter Finals	Semi-Finals	Final

U. S. Seeded
1. Seixas
2. Savitt
3. Larsen
4. Flam
5. Talbert
6. Mulloy
7. Richardson
8. Bartzen

Foreign Seeded
1. Sedgman
2. McGregor
3. Rose
4. Washer
5. Nielsen
6. Ampon
7. Rosewall
8. Hoad

Top half

- E. VICTOR SEIXAS, JR. — SEIXAS
- Frank A. Okey — 6-3, 6-1, 6-0
- Ralph J. Wickel — Wood
- Sidney B. Wood, Jr. — 6-0, 6-2, 6-4
  - SEIXAS 7-5, 6-3, 7-5
- Jack Tuero — Tuero
- Frank A. Thompson — 6-4, 6-3, 3-6, 6-4
- Gustavo Rueda — Bishop
- Ben Bishop — 6-3, 6-2, 7-9, 7-5
  - Tuero 6-3, 7-5, 6-4
    - SEIXAS 7-5, 7-5, 15-0, Default
- Sidney Schwartz — Schwartz
- William J. Clothier, 2nd — 6-2, 6-3, 6-4
- Andrew J. Stern — Thompson
- Donald Thompson — 9-11, 6-3, 9-7, 6-2
  - Schwartz 6-2, 6-2, 6-0
- Arthur Edis — Edis
- Roy Wilder — 6-3, 11-9, 3-6, 6-3
- Clint Nettleton — ROSEWALL
- KEN ROSEWALL* — 6-2, 6-3, 6-3
  - ROSEWALL 6-1, 6-2, 6-2
    - ROSEWALL 6-4, 6-1, 6-3
      - ROSEWALL 3-6, 6-2, 7-5, 5-7, 6-3

- GARDNER MULLOY — MULLOY
- Louis Riefkohl — 6-0, 6-2, 6-1
- Hugh Ditzler — Ditzler
- F. R. Mott-Trille — 6-3, 6-3, 9-7
  - MULLOY 6-1, 6-1, 6-1
- Don Eisenberg — Eisenberg
- James A. Schnaars — 6-4, 6-3, 6-1
- Robert J. Kerdasha — Palafox
- Gustavo Palafox — 7-5, 6-2, 6-4
  - Palafox 6-0, 6-4, 6-2
    - MULLOY 6-2, 5-7, 3-6, 6-3, 6-4
- Larry Huebner — Huebner
- Herschel Hyde, Jr. — 6-1, 6-1, 6-2
- Calhoun Dickson — Dickson
- Keith Self — 1-6, 17-19, 8-6, 6-4, 6-1
  - Huebner 6-3, 6-2, 6-2
- Jacque R. Grigry — Grigry
- Roger Young — 6-1, 6-4, 6-1
- J. W. Nicholson — WASHER
- PHILLIPPE WASHER* — 6-1, 6-0, 6-2
  - WASHER, 6-4, 6-4 9-11, 11-13, 12-10
    - WASHER 6-1, 6-1, 6-0
      - MULLOY 9-7, 6-1, 6-3
        - MULLOY 6-4, 3-6, 4-6, 7-5, 7-5

- HERBERT FLAM — FLAM
- Wladinir Lerque — 6-2, 6-3, 6-3
- Thomas M. Lewyn — Lewyn
- Henry H. Bassford, Jr. — 6-4, 6-0, 6-3
  - FLAM 6-4, 6-4, 6-2
- Dean Mathey — Longshore
- Leslie Longshore — 2-6, 6-3, 6-2, 3-6, 6-1
- Nadin Hajjar — Perry
- Robert Perry — 6-4, 6-1, 6-4
  - Perry 6-3, 6-4, 6-2
    - FLAM 6-1, 6-2, 6-0
- Straight Clark — Clark
- William E. Davis — 4-6, 6-1, 6-0, 6-0
- Chauncey D. Steele, Jr. — Rochon
- Henri Rochon — 2-6, 3-6, 6-4, 6-0, 6-2
  - Clark 6-1, 7-5, 6-4
- Ricardo Balbiers — Balbiers
- Edward Alloo — 6-3, 6-2, 6-4
- Richard Macatee — NIELSEN
- KURT NIELSEN* — 6-2, 6-2, 6-3
  - NIELSEN 6-3, 4-6, 6-4, 6-4
    - Clark 6-2, 2-6, 4-6, 6-2, 7-5
      - Clark 4-6, 6-1, 4-6, 6-4, 7-5

- HAMILTON RICHARDSON — RICHARDSON
- Tony Vincent — 6-2, 7-5, 6-0
- William Lurie — Arcocha
- Pancho Arcocha — 4-6, 6-4, 3-6, 6-2, 6-3
  - RICHARDSON 6-0, 6-0, 6-0
- J. E. Barrett — Barrett
- R. Phillip Hanna — 7-5, 6-2, 3-6, 6-3
- David Rodriquez — Ayala
- Luis Ayala — 6-0, 6-3, 6-1
  - Ayala 8-6, 5-7, 2-6, 7-5, 6-3
    - RICHARDSON 6-0, 6-4, 6-3
- Ted Rogers — Rogers Default
- Linn Rockwood —
- Franklin W. Pierce — Mayne
- Clifton P. Mayne — 4-6, 6-1, 6-4, 9-7
  - Mayne 4-6, 9-7, 6-1, 4-6, 6-4
- Charles F. Masterson — Masterson
- George H. Bostwick, Jr. — 6-0, 6-1, 6-4
- Calvin D. MacCracken — MacCracken
- KENNETH McGREGOR* — 3-6, 4-6, 6-5, Default
  - Masterson 6-2, 7-5, 6-2
    - RICHARDSON 6-1, 9-7, 6-2
      - RICHARDSON 6-8, 11-9, 5-7, 8-6, 6-4

Bottom half

- RICHARD SAVITT — SAVITT
- Morton Stern — 6-2, 6-1, 6-3
- William R. Stucki — Stucki
- Dr. Reginald S. Weir — 11-9, 5-7, 8-6, 6-1
  - SAVITT 6-0, 6-3, 6-0
- Samuel Giammalva — Giammalva
- Raefael Ortega — 6-8, 6-4, 6-2, 7-5
- Ricardo S. Lopez — Kovaleski
- Frederick Kovaleski — 6-3, 6-1, 6-4
  - Kovaleski 6-1, 6-1, 6-4
    - SAVITT 7-5, 6-3, 6-4
- Frederick Hagist — Hagist
- Robert J. Freedman — 6-2, 6-2, 10-8
- Bernard Gerhardt — Frost
- Jack Frost — 6-4, 6-2, 1-6, 6-4
  - Hagist 9-7, 6-4, 6-2
- I. A. McDonald — McDonald
- John E. Sisson — 6-4, 6-2, 2-6, 6-1
- Alexander H. Carver — AMPON
- FELICISIMO H. AMPON — 6-2, 7-5, 6-0
  - AMPON 6-3, 6-1, 6-1
    - AMPON 6-3, 6-4, 6-4
      - SAVITT 8-6, 6-0, 6-0

- BERNARD J. BARTZEN — BARTZEN
- George Stewart — 6-3, 9-7, 6-0
- William T. Vogt — Tully
- William J. Tully — 4-6, 8-6, Default
  - BARTZEN 6-0, 6-1, 3-6, 6-2
- G. Dever Hobbs — Hobbs
- J. G. H. Hirsch — 6-1, 6-4, 7-5
- Richard G. Sorlien — Brichant
- Jacques Brichant — 3-6, 6-2, 6-0, 4-6, 6-2
  - Brichant 6-1, 6-3, 7-5
    - BARTZEN 4-6, 4-6, 6-4, 6-1, 6-4
- Steve Potts — Potts
- Jose A. Cortes — 6-0, 6-1, 6-1
- Gilbert Shea — Shea
- Atsushi Miyagi — 6-4, 6-3, 7-5
  - Shea 7-5, 6-1, 8-6
- W. Donald McNeill — Dailey
- Edward G. Dailey — 7-5, 6-4, 7-5
- Richard L. Gaines — ROSE
- MERVYN ROSE* — 6-2, 6-2, 7-5
  - ROSE 6-0, 6-1, 6-1
    - ROSE 6-2, 7-5, 6-3
      - ROSE 6-0, 6-2, 6-1
        - ROSE 6-3, 8-6, 8-6

- ARTHUR LARSON — LARSEN
- William Long — 6-2, 6-4, 6-4
- Ladislav Hecht — Hecht
- Alastair B. Martin — 6-3, 5-7, 6-4, 7-5
  - LARSEN 6-1, 6-0, 8-10, 6-3
- Ellis Slack — Slack
- Andy Paton — 7-5, 3-6, 6-2, 6-3
- P. M. M. DeWet — Backe, Jr.
- Theodore C. Backe, Jr. — 3-6, 6-4, 6-3, 11-9
  - Slack 6-1, 8-6, 6-2
    - LARSEN 1-6, 6-3, 7-5, 6-2
- Grant Golden — Golden
- Don Flye — 6-2, 6-2, 6-1
- G. D. Oakley — Oakley
- Richard Fine — 6-3, 6-4, 6-3
  - Oakley 5-7, 6-3, 6-3, 6-1
- Frank Shields — Likas
- Harry Likas — 6-4, 6-4, 6-2
- Lorne Main — HOAD
- LEWIS HOAD — 416, 6-0, 6-2, 6-3
  - HOAD 4-6, 6-2, 6-8, 6-1, 6-4
    - HOAD 6-2, 6-3, 6-4
      - HOAD 6-3, 6-4, 6-4

- WILLIAM F. TALBERT — TALBERT
- Pablo Eisenberg — 6-2, 6-4, 6-3
- Rudolfo May — May
- Thomas F. Curtin — 6-2, 6-4, 6-2
  - TALBERT 6-3, 6-0, 6-1
- William E. Cranston — Cranston
- Angelmo Puente — 3-6, 6-3, 6-3, 6-2
- Joaquin Reyes — Macken
- Brendan Macken — 6-0, 6-3, 6-2
  - Macken 6-4, 6-2, 8-6
    - TALBERT 6-4, 6-2, 6-4
- Dr. Jack Geller — Quillian
- William Quillian — 3-6, 6-3, 6-3, 6-2
- Harold M. Burrows — Burrows
- James W. Read — 6-4, 6-3, 6-3
  - Burrows 6-2, 6-3, 6-0
- Alan Fischl — Boys
- Thomas Boys — 6-3, 8-6, 6-2
- Alvin W. Bunis — SEDGMAN
- FRANK SEDGMAN* — 6-1, 6-0, 6-0
  - SEDGMAN 6-2, 6-0, 6-0
    - SEDGMAN 6-2, 6-2, 6-4
      - SEDGMAN 6-1, 6-3, 6-3
        - SEDGMAN 6-2, 6-1, 6-3

Semi-Finals / Final:
- MULLOY 10-8, 6-0, 8-6
- SEDGMAN 6-3, 6-3, 6-4
- FRANK SEDGMAN 6-1, 6-2, 6-3

*Denotes foreign seeding

127

SEVENTY-SECOND USLTA MEN'S SINGLES CHAMPIONSHIPS
West Side Tennis Club, Forest Hills, N.Y., 1953

First Round	Second Round	Third Round	Fourth Round	Quarter Finals	Semi-Finals	Final

TONY TRABERT
TRABERT 6-2, 6-2, 6-1
Dan Sullivan

Donald Fontana
Peterson, Jr. 6-4, 6-3, 8-6
Seth Peterson, Jr.

TRABERT 6-3, 6-2, 6-0

Jack Frost
Frost 6-3, 9-7, 3-6, 6-2

Kalmon (Buzzy) Hettleman
Pierce 6-2, 6-8, 2-6, 6-3, 6-4
Franklin W. Pierce

AYRE 6-4, 14-12, 6-0

Gordon Warden, Jr.
Warden, Jr. Default
Jules A. Cohen

AYRE 6-1, 6-0, 6-0

Ubert C. Vincent
AYRE 6-3, 6-3, 6-4
IAN AYRE

TRABERT 6-2, 7-5, 6-2

BUDGE PATTY
PATTY 6-1, 6-2, 6-1
Wm. J. Clothier, 2nd

PATTY 7-9, 2-6, 6-4, 6-3, 6-1

James A. Schulze
Mayne 6-2, 6-3, 6-4
Clifton P. Mayne

Leslie C. Longshore, Jr.
Masterson 6-8, 7-5, 6-3, 7-5
Charles F. Masterson

PATTY 6-2, 6-3, 6-3

Ted Rogers
Wood, Jr. 3-6, 6-2, 6-4, 9-7
Sidney B. Wood, Jr.

Masterson 4-6, 6-1, 6-4, 7-5

Alastair B. Martin
Main 7-5, 6-1, 7-5
Lorne Main

TRABERT 6-4, 6-4, 6-2

Chauncey D. Steele, Jr.
Browne Jr. 2-6, 5-7, 6-3, 6-2, 6-4
Herbert H. Browne

Main 6-0, 6-3, 6-4

Francisco Contreras
Schwartz 6-3, 4-6, 11-9, 8-6
Sidney Schwartz

ROSE 6-2, 9-7, 6-2

Allen Morris
ROSE 8-10, 7-9, 6-3, 6-2, 6-2
MERVYN ROSE*

ROSE 6-3, 6-4, 6-1

PATTY 7-9, 6-4, 6-2, 6-3

ARTHUR D. LARSEN
LARSEN 6-1, 6-1, 10-8
Mario Llamas

LARSEN 6-2, 1-6, 6-2, 8-6

Clive Wilderspin
Wilderspin 6-4, 10-8, 3-6, 6-4
Atsushi Miyagi

Philip Seymour
Shea 6-1, 7-5, 6-3
Gilbert J. Shea

LARSEN 9-7, 11-9, 6-4

Ladislav Hecht
Schnaars 6-4, 6-2, 6-8, 6-2
James A. Schnaars

Shea 6-3, 6-1, 6-1

Edward M. Kauder
Kauder 6-2, 6-2, 6-1
Glenn Land

DAVIDSON 1-6, 3-6, 6-1, 6-4, 6-4

Alan S. Englander
Gaines 6-4, 6-4, 6-3
Richard L. Gaines

Kauder 6-3, 6-4, 6-2

Charles Warden
Moss 6-0, 8-6, 6-3
Gerald Moss

DAVIDSON 6-1, 6-3, 6-3

Brendan Macken
DAVIDSON 6-2, 6-2, 6-2
SVEN DAVIDSON*

DAVIDSON 6-3, 3-6, 2-6, 6-4, 6-3

THOMAS P. BROWN, JR.
BROWN, JR. 6-4, 6-4, 6-4
Donald Flye

BROWN, JR. 6-4, 6-0, 6-3

Luis Ayala
Ayala 6-1, 6-2, 6-1
Jeffrey H. Arnold

Barry MacKay
Garrett 6-2, 6-4, 6-3
Gene Garrett

BROWN, JR. 8-6, 6-3, 6-2

Kosei Kamo
Kamo 5-7, 6-3, 6-2, 6-3
Calvin D. MacCracken

Garrett 6-2, 10-8, 1-6, 6-2

Norman J. MacDonald
Reyes 6-4, 6-4, 6-1
Joaquin Reyes

ROSEWALL 9-7, 7-5, 6-2

Francis X. Shields
Sorlien 7-5, 12-10, 1-6, 4-6, 7-5
Richard C. Sorlein

Reyes 6-3, 7-5, 4-6, 6-3

Henri Rochon
Rochon 6-3, 8-6, 6-3
Blair Hawley

ROSEWALL 6-4, 4-6, 6-1, 5-2

Bernard J. Bartzen
ROSEWALL 6-0, 6-4, 6-2
KEN ROSEWALL*

ROSEWALL 8-6, 6-3, 6-2

ROSEWALL 6-0, 8-10, 2-6, 6-0, 11-9

E. VICTOR SEIXAS, JR.
SEIXAS, JR. 6-2, 6-2, 6-1
Morton N. Stern

SEIXAS, JR. 6-2, 9-7, 6-1

Pablo Eisenberg
Grigry 6-3, 6-4, 6-4
Jacque Grigry

Bernard Gerhardt
Willey 6-2, 6-1, 6-0
Paul Willey

SEIXAS, JR. 6-2, 6-4, 3-6, 6-3

Donald Kaiser
Golden 6-1, 6-4, 6-2
Grant Golden

Golden 6-4, 6-3, 6-2

Ricardo Balbiers
Balbiers 6-4, 2-6, 6-3, 6-2
Richard H. Raskind

SEIXAS, JR. 6-2, 6-0, 6-0

Rafael Ortega
Quillian 6-2, 3-6, 5-7, 6-4, 6-2
William Quillian

Quillian 6-1, 6-2, 10-12, 6-3

Don Thompson
Talbert 6-2, 6-1, 6-1
William F. Talbert

Talbert 6-2, 6-3, 6-3

Robin Wilner
HARTWIG 11-9, 6-3, 6-4
REX HARTWIG*

Talbert 5-7, 6-2, 6-4, 6-4

SEIXAS, JR. 6-3, 7-9, 8-6, 6-4

L. STRAIGHT CLARK
CLARK 4-6, 6-1, 6-1, 6-3
Stephen D. Potts

Clark 6-4, 6-3, 1-6, 7-5

Harry E. Likas, Jr.
Perry 6-4, 7-5, 6-4
Robert M. Perry

Thomas A. Bradford, Jr.
Kovaleski 7-5, 7-5, 9-7
Fred T. Kovaleski

Kovaleski 6-3, 9-11, 7-5, 7-5

William Cranston
Cranston 6-3, 6-2, 6-2
Charles Pasarell

Kovaleski 6-4, 6-0, 6-3

Andrew Stern
Bedard 6-4, 3-6, 6-4, 7-5
Robert Bedard

NIELSEN 6-3, 5-7, 4-6, 6-4, 6-4

Dixon Osburn
Paton 5-7, 6-2, 6-2, 7-5
Andy Paton

Paton 3-6, 7-9, 12-10, 6-2, 6-3

Herbert Flam
Flam 6-3, 6-4, 7-5
Leonard L. Steiner

NIELSEN 2-6, 6-3, 6-4, 2-6, 6-4

George Ball
NIELSEN 7-5, 6-2, 6-2
KURT NIELSEN*

NIELSEN 6-4, 6-4, 10-8

GARDNAR MULLOY
MULLOY 6-4, 7-5, 6-4
Hugh West Sweeney

MULLOY 6-2, 6-3, 6-1

Richard C. Squires
Squires 6-2, 6-3, 6-1
Gerard A. Alleyne

J. E. Barrett
Barrett 6-2, 6-1, 3-6, 4-6, 7-5
Art Anderson

MULLOY 6-4, 6-3, 6-1

Stanley Drobac
Drobac 6-3, 6-3, 6-3
Jordan Bentley

Barrett 2-6, 9-7, 6-1, 6-4

Enrique Vijande
Dailey 6-2, 6-2, 6-3
Edward G. Dailey

MULLOY 3-6, 6-3, 7-5, 6-2

Thomas L. Boys
Stewart 4-6, 6-4, 6-3, 8-10, 7-5
George Stewart

Dailey 11-9, 6-3, 6-4

Harold M. Burrows, Jr.
Ulrich 4-6, 6-4, 7-5, 6-0
Torben Ulrich

Ulrich 6-4, 6-4, 6-2

Masanobu Kimura
MOREA 6-1, 7-5, 9-7
ENRIQUE MOREA*

Ulrich 7-5, 6-2, 6-4

HOAD 6-4, 6-2, 11-9

HAMILTON RICHARDSON
RICHARDSON 7-5, 6-3, 6-4
Roger Becker

RICHARDSON 6-1, 9-7, 3-6, 6-1

William J. Tully
Stewart 6-4, 6-1, 6-1
Hugh W. Stewart

RICHARDSON 6-4, 6-1, 6-1

John Been
Doss 9-7, 6-3, 8-10, 6-4
Richard Doss

Dorfman 11-9, 6-3, 6-3

Irving Dorfman

HOAD 6-3, 6-4, 6-4

Joe Davis
Davis, 6-8, 7-9, 6-3, 6-4, 6-4
Oscar Johnson

HOAD 6-3, 6-2, 6-3

Frederick Hagist
HOAD 6-3, 6-1, 9-7
LEWIS HOAD*

*Denotes foreign seeding

TRABERT 7-5, 6-3, 6-3

TONY TRABERT 6-3, 6-2, 6-3

SEIXAS, JR. 7-5, 6-4, 6-4

SEVENTY-THIRD USLTA MEN'S SINGLES CHAMPIONSHIPS
West Side Tennis Club, Forest Hills, N.Y., 1954

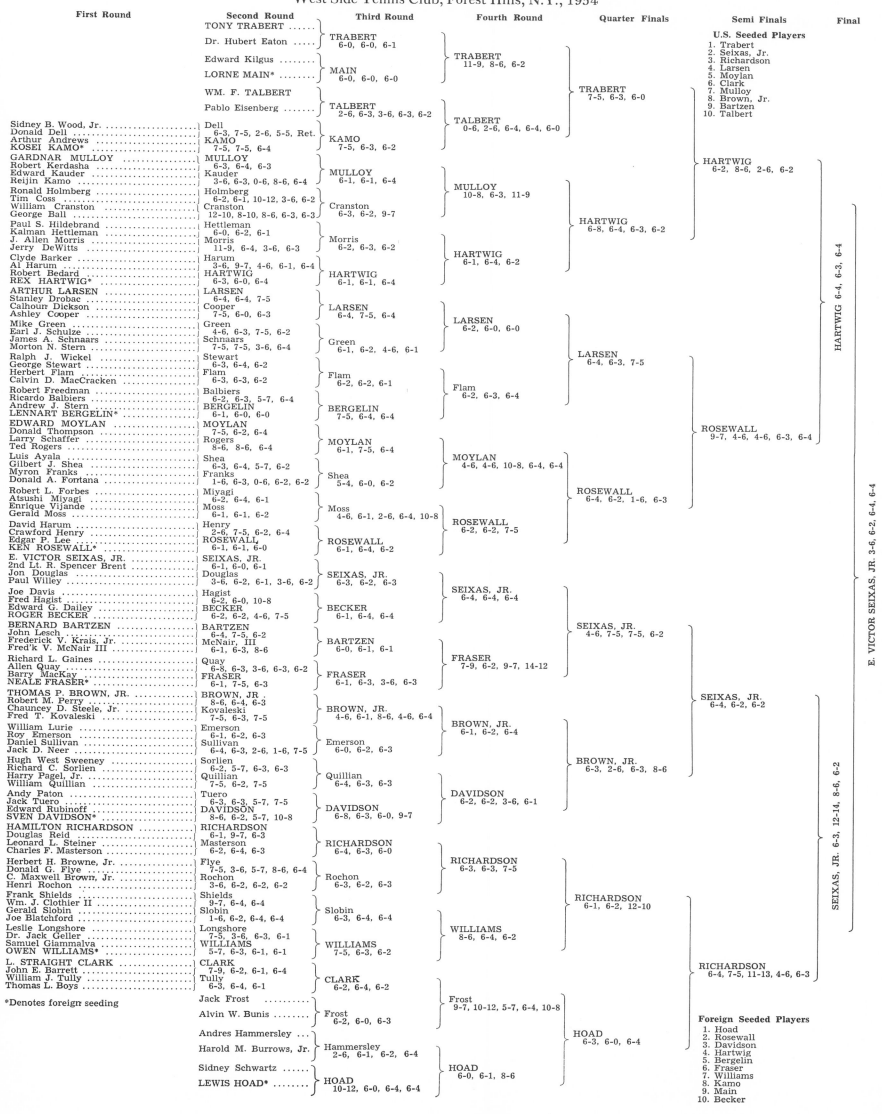

First Round	Second Round	Third Round	Fourth Round	Quarter Finals	Semi Finals	Final

U.S. Seeded Players
1. Trabert
2. Seixas, Jr.
3. Richardson
4. Larsen
5. Moylan
6. Clark
7. Mulloy
8. Brown, Jr.
9. Bartzen
10. Talbert

TONY TRABERT
Dr. Hubert Eaton
TRABERT 6-0, 6-0, 6-1
Edward Kilgus
LORNE MAIN*
MAIN 6-0, 6-0, 6-0
TRABERT 11-9, 8-6, 6-2
WM. F. TALBERT
Pablo Eisenberg
TALBERT 2-6, 6-3, 3-6, 6-3, 6-2
TRABERT 7-5, 6-3, 6-0
Sidney B. Wood, Jr.
Donald Dell — Dell 6-3, 7-5, 2-6, 5-5, Ret.
Arthur Andrews
KOSEI KAMO* — KAMO 7-5, 7-5, 6-4
KAMO 7-5, 6-3, 6-2
TALBERT 0-6, 2-6, 6-4, 6-4, 6-0
GARDNAR MULLOY — MULLOY 6-3, 6-4, 6-3
Robert Kerdasha
Edward Kauder — Kauder 3-6, 6-3, 0-6, 8-6, 6-4
Reijin Kamo
MULLOY 6-1, 6-1, 6-4
HARTWIG 6-2, 8-6, 2-6, 6-2
Ronald Holmberg — Holmberg 6-2, 6-1, 10-12, 3-6, 6-2
Tim Coss
William Cranston — Cranston 12-10, 8-10, 8-6, 6-3, 6-3
George Ball
Cranston 6-3, 6-2, 9-7
MULLOY 10-8, 6-3, 11-9
Paul S. Hildebrand — Hettleman 6-0, 6-2, 6-1
Kalman Hettleman
J. Allen Morris — Morris 11-9, 6-4, 3-6, 6-3
Jerry DeWitts
Morris 6-2, 6-3, 6-2
HARTWIG 6-8, 6-4, 6-3, 6-2
Clyde Barker — Harum 3-6, 9-7, 4-6, 6-1, 6-4
Al Harum
Robert Bedard — HARTWIG 6-3, 6-0, 6-4
REX HARTWIG*
HARTWIG 6-1, 6-1, 6-4
HARTWIG 6-1, 6-4, 6-2
ARTHUR LARSEN — LARSEN 6-4, 6-4, 7-5
Stanley Drobac
Calhoun Dickson — Cooper 7-5, 6-0, 6-3
Ashley Cooper
LARSEN 6-4, 7-5, 6-4
HARTWIG 6-4, 6-3, 6-4
Mike Green — Green 4-6, 6-3, 7-5, 6-2
Earl J. Schulze
James A. Schnaars — Schnaars 7-5, 7-5, 3-6, 6-4
Morton N. Stern
Green 6-1, 6-2, 4-6, 6-1
LARSEN 6-2, 6-0, 6-0
Ralph J. Wickel — Stewart 6-3, 6-4, 6-2
George Stewart
Herbert Flam — Flam 6-3, 6-3, 6-2
Calvin D. MacCracken
Flam 6-2, 6-2, 6-1
LARSEN 6-4, 6-3, 7-5
Robert Freedman — Balbiers 6-2, 6-3, 5-7, 6-4
Ricardo Balbiers
Andrew J. Stern — BERGELIN 6-1, 6-0, 6-0
LENNART BERGELIN*
BERGELIN 7-5, 6-4, 6-4
Flam 6-2, 6-3, 6-4
EDWARD MOYLAN — MOYLAN 7-5, 6-2, 6-4
Donald Thompson
Larry Schaffer — Rogers 8-6, 8-6, 6-4
Ted Rogers
MOYLAN 6-1, 7-5, 6-4
ROSEWALL 9-7, 4-6, 4-6, 6-3, 6-4
Luis Ayala — Shea 6-3, 6-4, 5-7, 6-2
Gilbert J. Shea
Myron Franks — Franks 1-6, 6-3, 0-6, 6-2, 6-2
Donald A. Fontana
Shea 5-4, 6-0, 6-2
MOYLAN 4-6, 4-6, 10-8, 6-4, 6-4
Robert L. Forbes — Miyagi 6-2, 6-4, 6-1
Atsushi Miyagi
Enrique Vijande — Moss 6-1, 6-1, 6-2
Gerald Moss
Moss 4-6, 6-1, 2-6, 6-4, 10-8
ROSEWALL 6-4, 6-2, 1-6, 6-3
David Harum — Henry 2-6, 7-5, 6-2, 6-4
Crawford Henry
Edgar P. Lee — ROSEWALL 6-1, 6-1, 6-0
KEN ROSEWALL*
ROSEWALL 6-1, 6-4, 6-2
ROSEWALL 6-2, 6-2, 7-5
E. VICTOR SEIXAS, JR. — SEIXAS, JR. 6-1, 6-0, 6-1
2nd Lt. R. Spencer Brent
Jon Douglas — Douglas 3-6, 6-2, 6-1, 3-6, 6-2
Paul Willey
SEIXAS, JR. 6-3, 6-2, 6-3
SEIXAS, JR. 6-4, 6-4, 6-4
Joe Davis — Hagist 6-2, 6-0, 10-8
Fred Hagist
Edward G. Dailey — BECKER 6-2, 6-2, 4-6, 7-5
ROGER BECKER
BECKER 6-1, 6-4, 6-4
SEIXAS, JR. 4-6, 7-5, 7-5, 6-2
BERNARD BARTZEN — BARTZEN 6-4, 7-5, 6-2
John Lesch
Frederick V. Krais, Jr. — McNair, III 6-1, 6-3, 8-6
Fred'k V. McNair III
BARTZEN 6-0, 6-1, 6-1
SEIXAS, JR. 6-4, 6-2, 6-2
Richard L. Gaines — Quay 6-8, 6-3, 3-6, 6-3, 6-2
Allen Quay
Barry MacKay — FRASER 6-1, 7-5, 6-3
NEALE FRASER*
FRASER 6-1, 6-3, 3-6, 6-3
FRASER 7-9, 6-2, 9-7, 14-12
THOMAS P. BROWN, JR. — BROWN, JR. 8-6, 6-4, 6-3
Robert M. Perry
Chauncey D. Steele, Jr. — Kovaleski 7-5, 6-3, 7-5
Fred T. Kovaleski
BROWN, JR. 4-6, 6-1, 8-6, 4-6, 6-4
SEIXAS, JR. 6-3, 2-6, 6-3, 8-6
William Lurie — Emerson 6-1, 6-2, 6-3
Roy Emerson
Daniel Sullivan — Sullivan 6-4, 6-3, 2-6, 1-6, 7-5
Jack D. Neer
Emerson 6-0, 6-2, 6-3
BROWN, JR. 6-1, 6-2, 6-4
Hugh West Sweeney — Sorlien 6-2, 5-7, 6-3, 6-3
Richard C. Sorlien
Harry Pagel, Jr. — Quillian 7-5, 6-2, 7-5
William Quillian
Quillian 6-4, 6-3, 6-3
BROWN, JR. 6-3, 2-6, 6-3, 8-6
Andy Paton — Tuero 6-3, 6-3, 5-7, 7-5
Jack Tuero
Edward Rubinoff — DAVIDSON 8-6, 6-2, 5-7, 10-8
SVEN DAVIDSON*
DAVIDSON 6-8, 6-3, 6-0, 9-7
DAVIDSON 6-2, 6-2, 3-6, 6-1
HAMILTON RICHARDSON — RICHARDSON 6-1, 9-7, 6-3
Douglas Reid
Leonard L. Steiner — Masterson 6-2, 6-4, 6-3
Charles F. Masterson
RICHARDSON 6-4, 6-3, 6-0
RICHARDSON 6-3, 6-3, 7-5
Herbert H. Browne, Jr. — Flye 7-5, 3-6, 5-7, 8-6, 6-4
Donald G. Flye
C. Maxwell Brown, Jr. — Rochon 3-6, 6-2, 6-2, 6-2
Henri Rochon
Rochon 6-3, 6-2, 6-3
RICHARDSON 6-1, 6-2, 12-10
Frank Shields — Shields 9-7, 6-4, 6-4
Wm. J. Clothier II
Gerald Slobin — Slobin 1-6, 6-2, 6-4, 6-4
Joe Blatchford
Slobin 6-3, 6-4, 6-4
WILLIAMS 8-6, 6-4, 6-2
Leslie Longshore — Longshore 7-5, 3-6, 6-3, 6-1
Dr. Jack Geller
Samuel Giammalva — WILLIAMS 5-7, 6-3, 6-1, 6-1
OWEN WILLIAMS*
WILLIAMS 7-5, 6-3, 6-2
RICHARDSON 6-4, 7-5, 11-13, 4-6, 6-3
L. STRAIGHT CLARK — CLARK 7-9, 6-2, 6-1, 6-4
John E. Barrett
William J. Tully — Tully 6-3, 6-4, 6-1
Thomas L. Boys
CLARK 6-2, 6-4, 6-2
Jack Frost
Alvin W. Bunis — Frost 6-2, 6-0, 6-3
Frost 9-7, 10-12, 5-7, 6-4, 10-8
HOAD 6-3, 6-0, 6-4
Andres Hammersley
Harold M. Burrows, Jr. — Hammersley 2-6, 6-1, 6-2, 6-4
HOAD 6-3, 6-0, 6-4
Sidney Schwartz
LEWIS HOAD* — HOAD 10-12, 6-0, 6-4, 6-4
HOAD 6-0, 6-1, 8-6

HARTWIG 6-4, 6-3, 6-4

E. VICTOR SEIXAS, JR. 3-6, 6-2, 6-4, 6-4

SEIXAS, JR. 6-3, 12-14, 8-6, 6-2

*Denotes foreign seeding

Foreign Seeded Players
1. Hoad
2. Rosewall
3. Davidson
4. Hartwig
5. Bergelin
6. Fraser
7. Williams
8. Kamo
9. Main
10. Becker

129

SEVENTY-FOURTH USLTA MEN'S SINGLES CHAMPIONSHIPS
West Side Tennis Club, Forest Hills, N.Y., 1955

First Round	Second Round	Third Round	Fourth Round	Quarter Finals	Semi Finals	Final

U. S. Seeded Players
1. Trabert
2. Seixas
3. Richardson
4. Shea
5. Moylan
6. Larsen
7. Bartzen
8. Flam

E. VICTOR SEIXAS, JR.
John E. Barrett ....
SEIXAS 6-2, 6-2, 6-4

Yves Thieullent .... Moss 6-0, 6-3, 6-1
Gerald Moss
Clifton P. Mayne .... Mayne 6-1, 6-2, 6-0
Harold Freeman
Mayne 6-4, 6-3, 6-2

SEIXAS 6-2, 6-3, 6-3

Barry MacKay .... MacKay 6-4, 7-5, 9-7
Richard C. Sorlien .... Raskind 6-1, 6-4, 6-4
Richard H. Raskind
Juan Jose
MacKay 6-1, 6-4, 6-8, 6-4

Ralph J. Wickel .... Falkenburg 8-6, 6-1, 5-7, 6-0
Robert Falkenburg
Calvin MacCracken .... FRASER 6-3, 6-3, 3-6, 6-2
NEALE FRASER*
FRASER 6-3, 7-9, 6-4, 6-4

FRASER 6-4, 6-4, 6-2

SEIXAS 7-5, 6-4, 6-2

BERNARD BARTZEN .... BARTZEN 6-1, 6-3, 6-1
Crawford Henry
Jose Aguero .... Aguero 6-1, 3-6, 7-5, 6-4
Kalman Hettleman
BARTZEN 6-2, 6-1, 6-1

Phillipe Chatrier .... Gaines 6-0, 6-4, 4-6, 6-0
Richard L. Gaines
Ramundo Deyro .... Deyro 7-5, 6-3, 5-7, 6-3
Andres Hammersley
Deyro 6-2, 6-4, 6-4

BARTZEN 6-4, 6-1, 6-4

Wm. J. Clothier, 2nd .... Burrows 6-3, 6-1, 6-2
Harold M. Burrows, Jr.
Donald F. Platt .... Platt 4-6, 6-2, 6-3, 6-3
Barry Walraven
Burrows, Jr. 6-3, 6-4, 6-4

Alastair B. Martin .... Olmedo 6-3, 6-2, 10-12, 6-4
Alejandro Olmedo
Franklin W. Pierce .... Nielsen 6-0, 6-0, 7-5
KURT NIELSEN*
NIELSEN 6-1, 6-2, 4-6, 1-6, 10-8

Burrows, Jr. 6-3, 3-6, 2-6, 6-4, 8-6

BARTZEN 6-0, 6-1, 6-2

HAMILTON RICHARDSON .... RICHARDSON 6-2, 3-6, 9-11, 10-8, 6-0
Edward Kauder
Edward G. Dailey .... Barker 7-5, 7-5, 7-5
Clyde F. Barker
RICHARDSON 6-3, 6-1, 6-1

Tim Coss .... Coss 6-3, 6-3, 1-6, 10-8
Ben Sobieraj
David Freishtat .... Freishtat 6-4, 6-3, 5-7, 6-3
William Cullen
Coss 9-8, 7-5, 2-6, 6-2

RICHARDSON 6-3, 6-2, 6-2

Donald Thompson .... Cohen 12-10, 8-6, 6-4
Jules A. Cohen
Whitney R. Reed .... Reed 7-5, 6-8, 6-3, 6-1
William Quillian
Reed 6-3, 6-4, 6-2

Robert H. Stuckert .... Green 6-3, 8-6, 6-2
Mike Green
Richard Moody .... PIETRANGELI 6-4, 6-4, 6-3
NICOLA PIETRANGELI*
PIETRANGELI 6-1, 6-4, 6-4

Reed 11-13, 4-6, 6-4, 6-4, 7-5

RICHARDSON 6-3, 6-4, 3-6, 6-4

EDWARD MOYLAN .... MOYLAN 6-1, 9-7, 6-1
Gregory Grant
Donald Walraven .... Longshore, Jr. 4-6, 7-5, 6-1, 6-2
Leslie C. Longshore, Jr.
MOYLAN 6-1, 6-1, 9-7

Henri Rochon .... Quay 1-6, 7-5, 3-6, 8-6, 8-6
Allen Quay
Thomas L. Boys .... Boys 8-6, 6-2, 6-3
Guillermo Garcia
Quay 6-1, 6-2, 6-1

MOYLAN 6-3, 8-6, 7-5

Paul Cranis .... Cranis 8-6, 6-8, 6-4, 6-4
John Powless
David Harum .... Harum 4-6, 6-3, 6-1, 6-3
Jerry R. Dalrymple, Jr.
Harum 6-1, 15-13, 6-3

Ronald Holmberg .... Willner 4-6, 6-8, 8-6, 6-3
Robin Willner
Donald Dell .... ROSEWALL 6-4, 6-4, 6-4
KEN ROSEWALL*
ROSEWALL 7-6, 6-3, 6-2

ROSEWALL 6-2, 8-6, 6-3

ROSEWALL 6-2, 6-2, 6-3

ROSEWALL 6-4, 9-7, 2-6, 6-3

TONY TRABERT .... TRABERT 6-0, 6-4, 6-1
Roger Becker
Stanley Drobac .... Miyagi 6-3, 8-6, 6-2
Atsushi Miyagi
TRABERT 6-4, 6-1, 6-1

J. Allen Morris, Jr. .... Morris 6-0, 6-0, 6-3
Ubert C. Vincent
A. L. Hollander, Jr. .... Ball 11-9, 4-6, 5-7, 8-6, 6-1
Geo. H. Ball
Morris 6-0, 6-0, 6-1

TRABERT 6-4, 6-4, 6-1

Alan S. Englander .... Cooper 6-1, 6-2, 6-4
Ashley Cooper
Irvin Dorfman .... Dorfman 6-4, 6-3, 6-1
William J. Tully
Cooper 6-2, 3-6, 6-3, 6-4

Arthur Andrews .... Andrews 2-6, 6-3, 6-2, 6-2
C. Maxwell Brown, Jr.
Geoffrey Radford .... MOREA 6-1, 6-4, 6-2
ENRIQUE MOREA*
MOREA 6-4, 6-2, 6-3

MOREA 1-6, 7-5, 13-11, 6-3

TRABERT 6-3, 6-1, 6-3

HERBERT FLAM .... FLAM 6-0, 8-6, 8-6
Earl Baumgardner
Andre Najar .... Davis 4-6, 6-2, 6-2, 6-2
Wilbert Davis
FLAM 6-0, 6-1, 6-2

Gardnar Mulloy .... Mulloy 6-3, 6-1, 6-3
Edgar A. Neely III
William Demas .... Brown 6-4, 11-9, 6-0
Thomas P. Brown, Jr.
Brown 6-3, 6-4, 3-6, 6-4

FLAM 6-3, 3-6, 5-7, 11-9, 9-7

Renato Gori .... Gori 8-6, 6-1, 6-1
Eduardo Garcia
Chauncey D. Steele, Jr. .... Geller 0-6, 6-1, 6-4, 4-6, 6-2
Dr. Jack Geller
Geller 7-5, 6-2, 6-8, 6-4

Robert J. Kerdasha .... Stewart 6-2, 9-7, 6-4
Hugh Stewart
Nadin Hajjar .... HARTWIG 6-1, 6-1, 6-3
REX HARTWIG*
HARTWIG 7-5, 6-4, 2-6, 15-13

HARTWIG 6-2, 6-3, 6-3

FLAM 6-4, 6-2, 6-2

TRABERT 6-2, 6-3, 6-4

GILBERT J. SHEA .... Golden 6-4, 3-6, 3-6, 7-5, 6-2
Grant Golden
Alvin W. Bunis .... Schwartz 6-2, 6-2, 6-4
Sidney Schwartz
Schwartz 1-6, 6-3, 8-6, 6-3

Robert J. Freedman .... Harum 6-3, 6-2, 7-5
Albert E. Harum, Jr.
Robert M. Perry .... Perry 6-1, 6-3, 6-3
Robert H. Ryland
Perry 6-2, 6-4, 6-4

Schwartz 6-3, 7-5, 8-6

Robert K. Wilson .... Wilson 6-1, 6-4, 6-1
Guiseppe Merlo
Laurence Schaffer .... Giammalva 6-2, 6-1, 6-2
Samuel Giammalva
Giammalva 6-4, 6-4, 6-3

Malcolm Anderson .... Anderson 6-4, 6-2, 6-4
Donald A. Fontana
Clyde Freeman .... KAMO 6-1, 6-0, 6-0
KOSEI KAMO*
Anderson 8-6, 11-13, 4-6, 8-6, 8-6

Giammalva 6-4, 6-2, 1-6, 6-4

Giammalva 6-3, 6-2, 2-6, 6-4

HOAD 6-3, 6-2, 5-7, 6-3

ARTHUR D. LARSEN .... LARSEN 8-6, 6-4, 7-5
Henry Van Rensselaer
Lawrence Barclay .... Barclay 9-7, 6-3, 4-6, 6-2
J. Edward Meyer, III
LARSEN 7-5, 6-2, 8-6

William J. Rose .... Main 6-0, 7-5, 6-2
Lorne Main
Johann F. Kupferburger .... Kupferburger
Ronald Moreira .... Default
Kupferburger 6-2, 7-5, 6-4

LARSEN 6-3, 6-3, 4-6, 6-3

Robert Bedard .... Bedard 3-6, 6-1, 6-4, 2-6, 6-1
Leslie Dodson
William J. Beale, Jr. .... Beale 11-9, 2-6, 8-6, 6-1
Robert M. Barker
Bedard 7-5, 4-6, 6-3, 6-4

HOAD 6-2, 6-4, 6-2

Roger Pharr ....
LEWIS HOAD* ......
HOAD 6-2, 6-3, 6-4
HOAD 6-4, 6-4, 6-4

*Denotes foreign seeding

Foreign Seeded Players
1. Rosewall
2. Hoad
3. Neilsen
4. Hartwig
5. Pietrangeli
6. Morea
7. Fraser
8. Kamo

ROSEWALL 6-4, 6-4, 7-5

TONY TRABERT 9-7, 6-3, 6-3

TRABERT 6-4, 6-2, 6-1

SEVENTY-FIFTH USLTA MEN'S SINGLES CHAMPIONSHIPS
West Side Tennis Club, Forest Hills, N.Y., 1956

First Round	Second Round	Third Round	Fourth Round	Quarter Finals	Semi Finals	Finals

KENNETH ROSEWALL — ROSEWALL
Jeffry J. E. Robinson — 6-1, 6-0, 6-1
Paul Remy — Remy
Gene Land — 6-0, 6-2, 6-2
  ROSEWALL 6-1, 6-4, 6-2

Arthur D. Larsen — Larsen
Robert Mark — 3-6, 6-2, 6-1, 7-5
William J. Kurross — Kurross
John Leach — 6-2, 9-2, 6-1
  Larsen 6-2, 6-4, 14-12
    ROSEWALL 6-3, 6-2, 6-2

Geoffry D. Owen — Cullen
John C. Cullen — 6-4, 7-5, 6-4
Morton Stern — Stewart
Hugh W. Stewart — 6-2, 6-4, 7-5
  Stewart 6-3, 6-3, 6-1

Robert J. Freedman — Bedard
Robert Bedard — 6-0, 6-1, 7-5
Clifton P. Mayne — Mayne
Arthur W. Andrews — 6-3, 6-4, 7-5
  Bedard 4-6, 6-4, 9-7, 6-3
    Stewart 9-11, 6-2, 6-4, 6-4
      ROSEWALL 2-6, 9-7, 6-1, 6-2

RICHARD SAVITT — SAVITT
David W. Snyder — 1-6, 6-1, 6-1, 6-0
Leslie C. Longshore, Jr. — Harum
David Harum — 6-3, 6-3, 7-5
  SAVITT 6-0, 6-1, 6-0

Tim Coss — Coss
Richard M. Ogden — 6-1, 6-2, 6-4, 6-2
Richard C. Sorlien — Sorlien
Jack Ter Borg — 6-4, 6-1, 6-4
  Coss 2-6, 6-4, 4-6, 6-3, 9-7
    SAVITT 6-1, 6-2, 6-3

Pancho Contreras — Contreras
William J. Tully — 4-6, 6-3, 10-8, 7-5
Sidney B. Wood, III — Barker
Robert M. Barker — 8-6, 6-2, 0-6, 6-3
  Contreras 6-2, 6-1, 6-2

Pedro Bueno Neto — Steele, Jr.
Chauncey D. Steele, Jr. — 6-1, 6-2, 8-6
Anthony J. Clayton — Reed
Whitney Reed — 4-6, 6-3, 6-3, 4-6, 6-2
  Reed 6-8, 6-0, 6-3, 6-2
    Contreras 6-4, 3-6, 7-5, 6-3
      SAVITT 6-3, 6-2, 6-2
        ROSEWALL 6-4, 7-5, 4-6, 8-10, 6-1

E. VICTOR SEIXAS, JR. — SEIXAS, JR.
Michael G. Davies — 6-3, 3-6, 8-10, 6-3, 7-5
Wladimir Lerque — Darmon
Pierre Darmon — 6-1, 6-1, 6-2
  SEIXAS, JR. 6-3, 6-3, 3-6, 7-5

Luis Ayala — Ayala
Thomas L. Boys — 6-0, 6-3, 6-3
Armando Vieira — Vieira
Richard H. Raskind — 3-6, 6-3, 6-2, 6-2
  Ayala 6-2, 6-4, 6-1
    SEIXAS, JR. 8-6, 4-6, 3-6, 12-10, 8-6

Albert E. Harum, Jr. — Harum, Jr.
Clyde C. Freeman — 6-2, 6-3, 6-4
Reynaldo Garrido — Garrido
Henry C. Van Rensselaer — 4-6, 7-5, 6-3, 10-8
  Garrido 14-12, 6-3, 4-6, 6-4

Carl Eltzholtz — Ulrich
Torben Ulrich — 6-2, 9-7, 6-2
Norman Perry — Perry
C. Maxwell Brown, Jr. — 7-5, 6-8, 3-6, 6-4, 6-2
  Ulrich 6-1, 6-1, 6-1
    Ulrich 6-4, 6-3, 6-1
      SEIXAS, JR. 3-6, 6-3, 6-4, 6-3

ASHLEY COOPER — COOPER
Edward G. Dailey — 6-3, 6-3, 6-2
Bernard Bartzen — Bartzen
Andy Paton — 6-3, 6-2, 6-3
  COOPER 9-7, 6-3, 8-10, 6-4

Myron J. Franks — Franks
Carl M. Noble, Jr. — 4-6, 10-8, 6-0, 6-3
Samuel V. Schoonmaker, III — Davis
Wilbert Davis — 3-6, 6-3, 9-7, 6-1
  Franks 3-6, 6-2, 6-1, 6-1
    COOPER 4-6, 6-3, 6-4, 5-7, 6-4

Lonnie C. Jorden, Jr. — Schwartz
Sidney Schwartz — 6-2, 9-7, 6-3
Harold P. Freeman — Geller
Dr. Jack Geller — 6-0, 6-2, 6-4
  Schwartz 6-1, 6-2, 2-6, 6-1

Samuel Giammalva — Giammalva
Ronald Holmberg — 6-4, 6-4, 6-2
Crawford Henry — Henry
Donald Walraven — 6-2, 6-4, 6-3
  Giammalva 6-4, 6-2, 9-11, 7-5
    Giammalva 7-5, 6-1, 6-4
      COOPER 3-6, 3-6, 6-4, 6-3, 7-5
        SEIXAS, JR. 9-7, 3-6, 9-7, 10-12, 6-4

LEWIS HOAD — HOAD
Barry Walraven — 6-0, 6-2, 6-0
Leslie E. Dodson — Dodson
Jimmy (Gan Koen Hie) Gan — 6-2, 6-0, 6-2
  HOAD 3-6, 6-0, 6-3, 6-1

Gregory Grant — Moylan
Edward Moylan — 6-0, 6-1, 5-7, 6-3
Gardner Mulloy — Mulloy
Chris Crawford — 6-2, 6-2, 6-3
  Moylan 6-3, 6-3, 6-4
    HOAD 11-9, 6-3, 6-4

Frederick V. Krais, Jr. — Moss
Gerald Moss — 6-0, 6-2, 4-6, 6-3
Edgar A. (Ned) Neely, III — Schmidt
James Schmidt — 6-1, 6-4, 7-5
  Moss 7-5, 2-6, 7-9, 9-7, 6-2

Grant Golden — Golden
Val Harit — 6-0, 6-1, 6-1
Pvt. Paul L. Cranis — Clark
L. Straight Clark — 6-4, 6-4, 6-1
  Golden 6-1, 9-11, 6-2, 6-4
    Golden 7-5, 6-3, 1-6, 6-2
      HOAD 6-3, 6-2, 7-5

ULF SCHMIDT — SCHMIDT
J. Allen Morris — 6-3, 6-2, 6-4
Pvt. John M. Cranston — Cranston
Donald Platt — 6-1, 6-3, 6-3
  SCHMIDT 6-2, 6-3, 6-1

Earl Buchholz, Jr. — Segal
Abe Segal — 6-3, 6-1, 6-4
James S. Farrin — Perry
Robert J. Perry — 6-4, 6-1, 8-10, 6-1
  Segal 6-2, 6-1, 7-5
    Segal 8-6, 9-7, 5-7, 7-5

Donald Dell — Knight
William A. Knight — 5-7, 3-6, 10-8, 6-3, 13-11
Roy Emerson — Emerson
Donald Thompson — 6-2, 6-1, 6-4
  Emerson 3-6, 6-4, 6-3, 8-6

Allen Fox — Fontana
Donald A. Fontana — 3-6, 6-3, 6-4, 6-3
Robert Haillet — Flam
Herbert Flam — 6-4, 6-2, 6-4
  Flam 6-1, 6-2, 6-1
    Emerson 6-1, 6-1, 3-6, 7-5
      Emerson 9-11, 7-5, 6-2, 6-1
        HOAD 8-6, 6-3, 7-5

HAMILTON RICHARDSON — RICHARDSON
Rodney Laver — 6-1, 6-2, 6-3
Roger Becker — Becker
Lorne Main — 6-0, 6-3, 6-1
  RICHARDSON 6-2, 6-0, 6-4

Wm. W. Quillian — Quillian
Guillermo Garcia — 9-7, 6-3, 6-3
Barry MacKay — MacKay
Richard M. Leslie — 6-1, 6-2, 6-1
  Quillian 4-6, 6-4, 6-3, 6-2
    RICHARDSON 4-6, 6-2, 6-2, 6-2

George Ball — Quay
Allen A. Quay — 6-8, 3-6, 6-2, 6-1, 6-3
Alejandro Olmedo — Olmedo
Renato Gori — 8-6, 6-1, 6-0
  Olmedo 8-6, 6-1, 6-2

John Powless — Llamas
Mario Llamas — 7-5, 6-2, 6-1
Malcolm Anderson — Green
Michael E. Green — 6-3, 6-4, 6-2
  Green 6-3, 6-4, 6-1
    Olmedo 6-3, 6-4, 6-4
      RICHARDSON 7-5, 6-2, 6-0

NEALE FRASER — FRASER
Calvin D. MacCracken — 6-2, 6-4, 6-2
Johann Kupferburger — Kupferburger
Sidney B. Wood, Jr. — 6-4, 6-3, 6-0
  FRASER 6-3, 7-5, 6-8, 7-5

Ubert C. Vincent — Dorfman
Irvin Dorfman — 6-0, 6-0, 6-3
Richard L. Gaines — Gaines
Oscar Furlong — 6-2, 8-6, 6-4
  Dorfman 6-4, 7-5, 6-0
    FRASER 6-4, 6-4, 6-4

John W. Frost — Frost
Henri Rochon — 6-2, 6-1, 6-2
Edward J. Meyer, III — Meyer, III
Vernon Morgan — 6-3, 6-1, 3-6, 7-9, 6-4
  Frost 6-2, 6-2, 6-1

Gilbert J. Shea — Shea
Clarence Edward Sledge, Jr. — 6-3, 6-3, 6-1
C. Graham Daniels — Mandel
George Mandel — 6-2, 7-5, 6-4
  Shea 6-2, 6-3, 6-1
    Shea 6-3, 10-8, 6-3
      FRASER 5-7, 6-3, 6-3, 10-8
        FRASER 3-6, 6-3, 6-2, 6-4

HOAD 15-13, 6-2, 6-4

KENNETH ROSEWALL 4-6, 6-2, 6-3, 6-3

ROSEWALL 10-8, 6-0, 6-3

SEEDED PLAYERS
1. Lewis Hoad
2. Kenneth Rosewall
3. Hamilton Richardson
4. E. Victor Seixas, Jr.
5. Neale Fraser
6. Ashley Cooper
7. Ulf Schmidt
8. Richard Savitt

131

SEVENTY-SIXTH USLTA MEN'S SINGLES CHAMPIONSHIPS
West Side Tennis Club, Forest Hills, N.Y., 1957

First Round	Second Round	Third Round	Fourth Round	Quarter Finals	Semi Finals	Finals

ASHLEY J. COOPER .... COOPER 6-4, 6-3, 6-4
John Brownlow
Peter Lyman .... Dorfman 6-1, 6-2, 6-1
Irvin Dorfman
COOPER 6-1, 6-1, 6-3
Bernard Bartzen .... Bartzen 6-0, 6-0, 6-2
John A. Harris
Ronald Holmberg .... Holmberg 6-2, 6-2, 6-2
Jon D. Erickson
Holmberg 9-7, 5-7, 6-3, 6-8, 6-3
COOPER 12-10, 6-3, 7-5

Sidney B. Wood, III .... McKinley 7-5, 4-6, 6-4, 6-3
Charles McKinley
William S. McClung .... Vincent 7-5, 6-2, 6-2
Tony Vincent
Vincent 6-3, 6-3, 6-0
Norman J. Perry .... Perry 3-6, 7-5, 6-3, 4-6, 6-1
Pfc. Paul L. Cranis
Pvt. Tim Coss .... Coss 6-2, 6-2, 6-3
William J. Scarlett
Coss 6-4, 7-5, 2-6, 4-6, 6-4
Vincent 7-5, 6-0, 6-4
COOPER 6-3, 6-2, 6-2

BUDGE PATTY .... PATTY 6-4, 6-3, 6-4
Laurence Schaffer
Richard Moody .... Moody 7-5, 10-8, 6-3
Forrest Stewart
PATTY 6-4, 6-2, 6-3
Grant Golden .... Golden Default
Pvt. John A. Been
Lawrence Nagler .... Nagler 6-4, 8-10, 3-6, 6-2, 7-5
Roger S. Werksman
Golden 6-2, 6-4, 6-2
PATTY 6-3, 8-10, 4-6, 6-3, 8-6

Samuel P. Howe, III .... Raskind 7-5, 6-2, 6-2
Richard H. Raskind
Donald A. Fontana .... Fontana 6-4, 6-2, 6-4
Thomas L. Boys
Fontana 6-1, 4-6, 7-5, 7-5
L. Straight Clark .... Clark 6-4, 6-1, 6-3
Leslie C. Longshore, Jr.
Edward J. Atkinson .... Farrin 1-6, 6-3, 6-2, 6-0
James S. Farrin
Farrin 6-3, 6-4, 2-6, 6-2
Fontana 7-5, 6-4, 6-3
PATTY 6-4, 6-2, 9-7

E. VICTOR SEIXAS, Jr. .... SEIXAS, JR. 6-2, 6-2, 6-0
Alan Roberts
Whitney Reed .... Reed 6-3, 6-0, 6-4
Frederick V. McNair, III
SEIXAS, JR. 6-4, 3-6, 4-6, 6-2, 6-3
Eugene L. Scott .... Reyes 3-6, 6-2, 6-0, 6-3
Joaquin Reyes
Armando Vieira .... Vieira 6-4, 8-6, 5-7, 6-2
Vernon Morgan
Vieira 6-3, 8-6, 6-2
SEIXAS, JR. 6-4, 6-4, 6-1

Gabriel Dubitzky .... Leslie 6-4, 6-3, 7-5
Richard M. Leslie
Robert Alger .... Emerson 6-1, 6-2, 6-2
Roy Emerson
Emerson 6-2, 6-3, 6-1
Roger A. Gould .... Gould Default
Ed Foster
Robert H. R. Delgado .... Schwartz 11-13, 8-6, 15-17, 6-0, 6-3
Sidney Schwartz
Schwartz 6-1, 6-0, 6-0
Emerson 6-0, 6-4, 6-1
SEIXAS, JR. 6-3, 6-2, 6-4

HERBERT FLAM .... FLAM 6-4, 11-9, 1-6, 6-0
Alejandro Olmedo
Allen Fox .... Fox 7-5, 6-2, 6-3
John F. Mangan
FLAM 6-1, 6-3, 6-3
C. Maxwell Brown, Jr. .... Green 11-9, 6-3, 6-3
Michael E. Green
Morton N. Stern .... Mulloy 6-4, 6-1, 6-3
Gardner Mulloy
Green 6-0, 6-4, 7-5
FLAM 8-6, 2-6, 6-1, 7-5

John M. Cranston .... Cranston 6-2, 3-6, 6-1, 5-7, 6-4
George H. Ball
Chris Crawford .... Giammalva 9-7, 6-1, 6-2
James E. Shakespeare
Cranston 3-6, 4-6, 13-11, 7-5, 6-3
Robert N. Howe .... Howe 6-2, 6-2, 6-1
Michael Davies
Robert S. Bowditch, Jr. .... Davies 10-8, 5-7, 6-1, 6-2
Howe 7-5, 1-6, 6-2, 4-6, 6-1
Howe 6-4, 7-5, 6-3
FLAM 6-4, 6-4, 6-4

RICHARD SAVITT .... SAVITT 6-1, 6-0, 6-4
Calvin D. MacCracken
Johann F. Kupferburger .... Kupferburger 6-2, 6-1, 6-1
Wilbert Davis
SAVITT 6-3, 6-3, 6-3
Harry R. Hoffman, Jr. .... Hoffman, Jr. 4-6, 3-6, 8-6, 6-1, 8-6
William C. Cullen
David Harum .... Krishnan 6-4, 6-3, 6-1
Ramanathan Krishnan
Krishnan 6-1, 6-1, 6-0
SAVITT 6-1, 8-6, 7-5

Henry C. Van Rensselaer .... Van Rensselaer 8-6, 6-2, 8-6
Patricio Rodriguez
Kosei Kamo .... Anderson 9-7, 6-3, 6-2
Malcolm J. Anderson
Anderson 6-2, 6-2, 6-2
Gregory Grant .... Grant 6-1, 7-5, 6-2
Robert M. Barker
Samuel V. Schoonmaker, III .... Corley 8-6, 6-2, 6-3
Douglass Corley
Grant 6-8, 6-3, 6-1, 6-4
Anderson 6-4, 6-0, 6-3
Anderson 6-4, 6-3, 6-1

HAMILTON RICHARDSON .... RICHARDSON 6-0, 6-0, 6-2
Stephen Gottlieb
Kurt Nielsen .... Nielsen 6-4, 7-5, 6-2
Crawford Henry
Nielsen 3-6, 4-6, 13-11, 7-5, 6-3
David M. Nelson .... Franks 6-4, 6-1, 6-3
Myron J. Franks
Edward G. Dailey .... Dailey 7-5, 5-7, 6-4, 6-4
William J. Tully
Franks 6-3, 6-4, 6-4
Nielsen 8-10, 6-0, 8-6, 6-3

Hugh Tierney .... Buchholz 6-3, 6-0, 6-1
Earl Buchholz, Jr.
Gilbert J. Shea .... Shea 6-2, 6-3, 6-1
Barry Walraven
Shea 9-7, 6-4, 3-6, 6-3
Robert Potthast .... Potthast 6-4, 6-1, 4-6, 6-4
Stephen Bank
Richard C. Sorlien .... Ayala 6-3, 6-2, 6-4
Luis Ayala
Ayala 6-2, 7-5, 6-2
Ayala 5-7, 6-4, 6-1, 6-2
Ayala 6-4, 6-4, 8-6

SVEN DAVIDSON .... DAVIDSON 6-1, 6-1, 9-7
Charles F. Masterson
Don Walraven .... Quillian 8-6, 6-1, 6-3
Pfc. William Quillian
DAVIDSON 4-6, 7-5, 6-4, 11-13, 6-4
Henri Rochon .... Rochon 6-3, 9-7, 8-6
C. Edward Sledge, Jr.
Donald L. Dell .... Dell 6-3, 6-4, 6-2
Richard Ogden
Dell 6-1, 6-2, 6-1
DAVIDSON 6-4, 6-2, 6-2

Robert Mark .... Mark 6-1, 6-1, 6-2
Clyde Freeman
Barry MacKay .... MacKay 6-3, 6-1, 6-1
Don Rubell
MacKay 6-2, 7-5, 6-3
Robert Wilson .... Wilson 5-7, 6-2, 6-4, 6-2
Paul Willey
Dever Hobbs .... Lesch 6-3, 6-3, 6-4
John J. Lesch
Wilson 6-1, 3-6, 6-1 6-4
Wilson 7-5, 10-12, 6-3, 12-10
DAVIDSON 5-7, 7-5, 6-3, 6-2

NEALE FRASER .... FRASER 6-1, 6-0, 6-0
Peter Estin
Arthur W. Andrews .... Bedard 6-3, 4-6, 6-2, 7-5
Robert Bedard
FRASER 3-6, 6-3, 6-4, 6-2
2nd Lt. Clifton P. Mayne .... Mayne 7-5, 6-2, 6-0
George Mandel
David Brechner .... Brechner 6-3, 6-2, 6-0
J. Edward Meyer, III
Mayne 6-1, 6-4, 6-2
Mayne 6-3, 9-7, 6-4

James Shaffer .... Shaffer 6-3, 6-1, 6-3
Lloyd Moglen
Carl M. Noble, Jr. .... Noble, Jr. 6-3, 6-4, 6-1
Val Harit
Shaffer 6-8, 8-6, 6-3, 6-3
Pvt. Donald V. Thompson .... Thompson 6-1, 6-1, 8-6
Harold P. Freeman
George Stewart .... Stewart 6-3, 6-3, 6-1
Hal Trevenen
Thompson 7-5, 6-3, 6-4
Thompson 7-5, 8-10, 6-4, 6-4
Mayne 7-5, 6-3, 6-4

DAVIDSON 3-6, 6-3, 7-5, 6-4

Anderson 6-1, 6-3, 6-1

FLAM 6-4, 3-6, 6-4, 4-6, 6-1

COOPER 6-3, 6-3, 6-1

COOPER 6-1, 7-5, 6-4

Anderson, 5-7, 6-2, 4-6, 6-3, 6-4

MALCOLM J. ANDERSON 10-8, 7-5, 6-4

SEEDED PLAYERS
1. Ashley J. Cooper
2. Richard Savitt
3. Sven Davidson
4. E. Victor Seixas, Jr.
5. Neale Fraser
6. Hamilton Richardson
7. Budge Patty
8. Herbert Flam

SEVENTY-SEVENTH USLTA MEN'S SINGLES CHAMPIONSHIPS
West Side Tennis Club, Forest Hills, N.Y., 1958

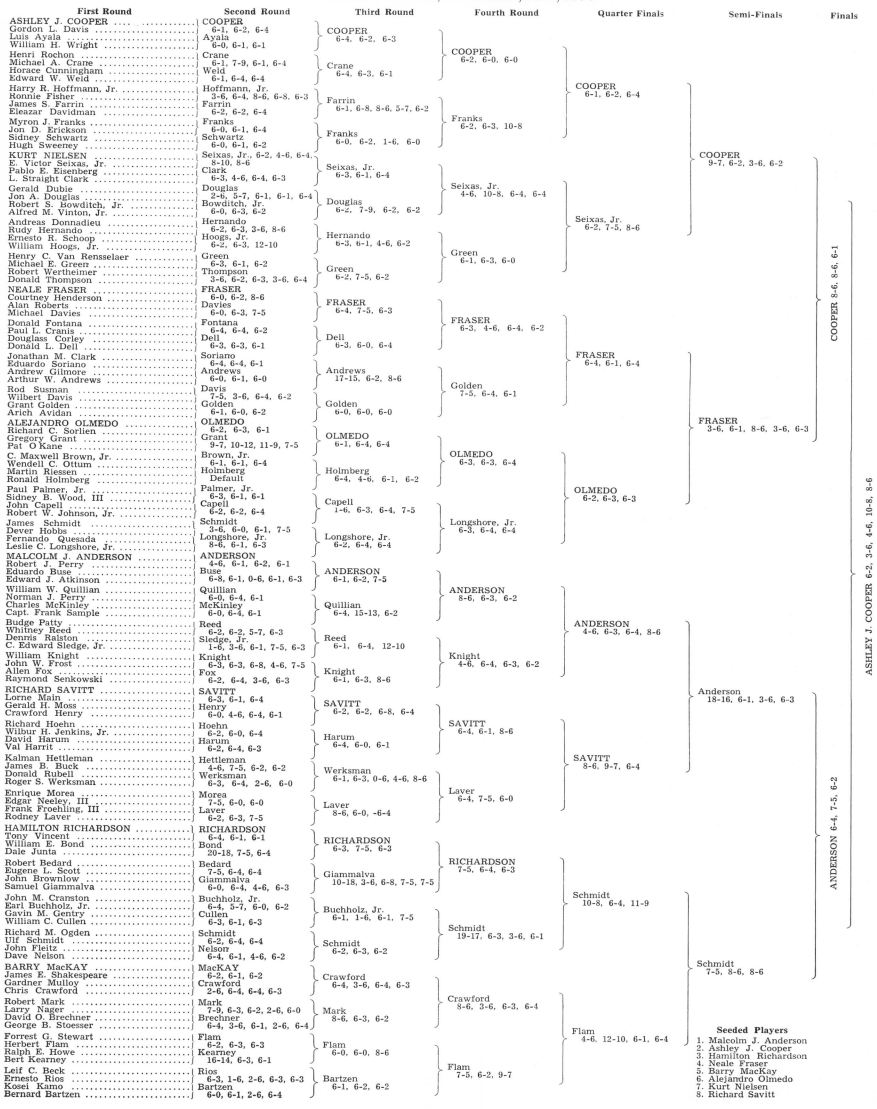

First Round	Second Round	Third Round	Fourth Round	Quarter Finals	Semi-Finals	Finals
ASHLEY J. COOPER	COOPER					
Gordon L. Davis	6-1, 6-2, 6-4	COOPER				
Luis Ayala	Ayala	6-4, 6-2, 6-3				
William H. Wright	6-0, 6-1, 6-1		COOPER			
Henri Rochon	Crane		6-2, 6-0, 6-0			
Michael A. Crane	6-1, 7-9, 6-1, 6-4	Crane				
Horace Cunningham	Weld	6-4, 6-3, 6-1				
Edward W. Weld	6-1, 6-4, 6-4			COOPER		
Harry R. Hoffmann, Jr.	Hoffmann, Jr.			6-1, 6-2, 6-4		
Ronnie Fisher	3-6, 6-4, 8-6, 6-8, 6-3	Farrin				
James S. Farrin	Farrin	6-1, 6-8, 8-6, 5-7, 6-2				
Eleazar Davidman	6-2, 6-2, 6-4		Franks			
Myron J. Franks	Franks		6-2, 6-3, 10-8			
Jon D. Erickson	6-0, 6-1, 6-4	Franks				
Sidney Schwartz	Schwartz	6-0, 6-2, 1-6, 6-0				
Hugh Sweeney	6-0, 6-1, 6-2				COOPER	
KURT NIELSEN	Seixas, Jr., 6-2, 4-6, 6-4,				9-7, 6-2, 3-6, 6-2	
E. Victor Seixas, Jr.	8-10, 8-6	Seixas, Jr.				
Pablo E. Eisenberg	Clark	6-3, 6-1, 6-4				
L. Straight Clark	6-3, 4-6, 6-4, 6-3		Seixas, Jr.			
Gerald Dubie	Douglas		4-6, 10-8, 6-4, 6-4			
Jon A. Douglas	2-6, 5-7, 6-1, 6-1, 6-4	Douglas				
Robert S. Bowditch, Jr.	Bowditch, Jr.	6-2, 7-9, 6-2, 6-2				
Alfred M. Vinton, Jr.	6-0, 6-3, 6-2			Seixas, Jr.		
Andreas Donnadieu	Hernando			6-2, 7-5, 8-6		
Rudy Hernando	6-2, 6-3, 3-6, 8-6	Hernando				
Ernesto R. Schoop	Hoogs, Jr.	6-3, 6-1, 4-6, 6-2				
William Hoogs, Jr.	6-2, 6-3, 12-10		Green			
Henry C. Van Rensselaer	Green		6-1, 6-3, 6-0			
Michael E. Green	6-3, 6-1, 6-2	Green				
Robert Wertheimer	Thompson	6-2, 7-5, 6-2				
Donald Thompson	3-6, 6-2, 6-3, 3-6, 6-4					COOPER 8-6, 8-6, 6-1
NEALE FRASER	FRASER					
Courtney Henderson	6-0, 6-2, 8-6	FRASER				
Alan Roberts	Davies	6-4, 7-5, 6-3				
Michael Davies	6-0, 6-3, 7-5		FRASER			
Donald Fontana	Fontana		6-3, 4-6, 6-4, 6-2			
Paul L. Cranis	6-4, 6-4, 6-2	Dell				
Douglass Corley	Dell	6-3, 6-0, 6-4				
Donald L. Dell	6-3, 6-3, 6-1			FRASER		
Jonathan M. Clark	Soriano			6-4, 6-1, 6-4		
Eduardo Soriano	6-4, 6-4, 6-1	Andrews				
Andrew Gilmore	Andrews	17-15, 6-2, 8-6				
Arthur W. Andrews	6-0, 6-1, 6-0		Golden			
Rod Susman	Davis		7-5, 6-4, 6-1			
Wilbert Davis	7-5, 3-6, 6-4, 6-2	Golden				
Grant Golden	Golden	6-0, 6-0, 6-0				
Arich Avidan	6-1, 6-0, 6-2				FRASER	
ALEJANDRO OLMEDO	OLMEDO				3-6, 6-1, 8-6, 3-6, 6-3	
Richard C. Sorlien	6-2, 6-3, 6-1	OLMEDO				
Gregory Grant	Grant	6-1, 6-4, 6-4				
Pat O'Kane	9-7, 10-12, 11-9, 7-5		OLMEDO			
C. Maxwell Brown, Jr.	Brown, Jr.		6-3, 6-3, 6-4			
Wendell C. Ottum	6-1, 6-1, 6-4	Holmberg				
Martin Riessen	Holmberg	6-4, 4-6, 6-1, 6-2				
Ronald Holmberg	Default			OLMEDO		
Paul Palmer, Jr.	Palmer, Jr.			6-2, 6-3, 6-3		
Sidney B. Wood, III	6-3, 6-1, 6-1	Capell				
John Capell	Capell	1-6, 6-3, 6-4, 7-5				
Robert W. Johnson, Jr.	6-2, 6-2, 6-4		Longshore, Jr.			
James Schmidt	Schmidt		6-3, 6-4, 6-4			
Dever Hobbs	3-6, 6-0, 6-1, 7-5	Longshore, Jr.				
Fernando Quesada	Longshore, Jr.	6-2, 6-4, 6-4				
Leslie C. Longshore, Jr.	8-6, 6-1, 6-3					
MALCOLM J. ANDERSON	ANDERSON					
Robert J. Perry	4-6, 6-1, 6-2, 6-1	ANDERSON				
Eduardo Buse	Buse	6-1, 6-2, 7-5				
Edward J. Atkinson	6-8, 6-1, 0-6, 6-1, 6-3		ANDERSON			
William W. Quillian	Quillian		8-6, 6-3, 6-2			
Norman J. Perry	6-0, 6-4, 6-1	Quillian				
Charles McKinley	McKinley	6-4, 15-13, 6-2				
Capt. Frank Sample	6-0, 6-4, 6-1			ANDERSON		
Budge Patty	Reed			4-6, 6-3, 6-4, 8-6		
Whitney Reed	6-2, 6-2, 5-7, 6-3	Reed				
Dennis Ralston	Sledge, Jr.	6-1, 6-4, 12-10				
C. Edward Sledge, Jr.	1-6, 3-6, 6-1, 7-5, 6-3		Knight			
William Knight	Knight		4-6, 6-4, 6-3, 6-2			
John W. Frost	6-3, 6-3, 6-8, 4-6, 7-5	Knight				
Allen Fox	Fox	6-1, 6-3, 8-6				
Raymond Senkowski	6-2, 6-4, 3-6, 6-3				ANDERSON	
RICHARD SAVITT	SAVITT				4-6, 6-3, 6-4, 8-6	
Lorne Main	6-3, 6-1, 6-4	SAVITT				
Gerald H. Moss	Henry	6-2, 6-2, 6-8, 6-4				
Crawford Henry	6-0, 4-6, 6-4, 6-1		SAVITT			
Richard Hoehn	Hoehn		6-4, 6-1, 8-6			
Wilbur H. Jenkins, Jr.	6-2, 6-0, 6-4	Harum				
David Harum	Harum	6-4, 6-0, 6-1				
Val Harrit	6-2, 6-4, 6-3			SAVITT		
Kalman Hettleman	Hettleman			8-6, 9-7, 6-4		
James B. Buck	4-6, 7-5, 6-2, 6-2	Werksman				
Donald Rubell	Werksman	6-1, 6-3, 0-6, 4-6, 8-6				
Roger S. Werksman	6-3, 6-4, 2-6, 6-0		Laver			
Enrique Morea	Morea		6-4, 7-5, 6-0			
Edgar Neeley, III	7-5, 6-0, 6-0	Laver				
Frank Froehling, III	Laver	8-6, 6-0, -6-4				
Rodney Laver	6-2, 6-3, 7-5					ASHLEY J. COOPER 6-2, 3-6, 4-6, 10-8, 8-6
HAMILTON RICHARDSON	RICHARDSON					
Tony Vincent	6-4, 6-1, 6-1	RICHARDSON				
William E. Bond	Bond	6-3, 7-5, 6-3				
Dale Junta	20-18, 7-5, 6-4		RICHARDSON			
Robert Bedard	Bedard		7-5, 6-4, 6-3			
Eugene L. Scott	7-5, 6-4, 6-4	Giammalva				
John Brownlow	Giammalva	10-18, 3-6, 6-8, 7-5, 7-5				
Samuel Giammalva	6-0, 6-4, 4-6, 6-3			Schmidt		
John M. Cranston	Buchholz, Jr.			10-8, 6-4, 11-9		
Earl Buchholz, Jr.	6-4, 5-7, 6-0, 6-2	Buchholz, Jr.				
Gavin M. Gentry	Cullen	6-1, 1-6, 6-1, 7-5				
William C. Cullen	6-3, 6-1, 6-3		Schmidt			
Richard M. Ogden	Schmidt		19-17, 6-3, 3-6, 6-1			
Ulf Schmidt	6-2, 6-4, 6-4	Schmidt				
John Fleitz	Nelson	6-2, 6-3, 6-2				
Dave Nelson	6-4, 6-1, 4-6, 6-2				Schmidt	
BARRY MacKAY	MacKAY				7-5, 8-6, 8-6	
James E. Shakespeare	6-2, 6-1, 6-2	Crawford				
Gardner Mulloy	Crawford	6-4, 3-6, 6-4, 6-3				
Chris Crawford	2-6, 6-4, 6-4, 6-3		Crawford			
Robert Mark	Mark		8-6, 3-6, 6-3, 6-4			
Larry Nager	7-9, 6-3, 6-2, 2-6, 6-0	Mark				
David O. Brechner	Brechner	8-6, 6-3, 6-2				
George B. Stoesser	6-4, 3-6, 6-1, 2-6, 6-4			Flam		
Forrest G. Stewart	Flam			4-6, 12-10, 6-1, 6-4		
Herbert Flam	6-2, 6-3, 6-3	Flam				
Ralph E. Howe	Kearney	6-0, 6-0, 8-6				
Bert Kearney	16-14, 6-3, 6-1		Flam			
Leif C. Beck	Rios		7-5, 6-2, 9-7			
Ernesto Rios	6-3, 1-6, 2-6, 6-3, 6-3	Bartzen				
Kosei Kamo	Bartzen	6-1, 6-2, 6-2				
Bernard Bartzen	6-0, 6-1, 2-6, 6-4					

ANDERSON 6-4, 7-5, 6-2 (QF)

Anderson 18-16, 6-1, 3-6, 6-3 (semi)

Seeded Players
1. Malcolm J. Anderson
2. Ashley J. Cooper
3. Hamilton Richardson
4. Neale Fraser
5. Barry MacKay
6. Alejandro Olmedo
7. Kurt Nielsen
8. Richard Savitt

SEVENTY-EIGHTH USLTA MEN'S SINGLES CHAMPIONSHIPS
West Side Tennis Club, Forest Hills, N.Y., 1959

First Round	Second Round	Third Round	Fourth Round	Quarter Finals	Semi-Finals	Finals

First Round / Second Round / Third Round / Fourth Round / Quarter Finals / Semi-Finals / Finals

NEALE FRASER — FRASER 5-7, 7-5, 6-1, 6-3
Edgar Neeley, IIII
Ronnie Fisher — Green 6-3, 6-3, 6-3
Michael E. Green
→ FRASER 8-6, 6-4, 6-1

Dennis Ralston — Wilson 6-4, 6-0, 6-3
Robert Wilson
Ralph E. Howe — Lal 6-4, 1-6, 6-8, 6-1, 6-2
Premjit Lal
→ Wilson 6-3, 6-4, 6-2
⇒ FRASER 6-2, 6-4, 6-4

John Bassett — Bassett 6-1, 6-4, 6-3
Thomas L. Boys
Donald L. Kierbow — Hernando 1-6, 6-1, 6-2, 4-6, 6-0
Rudy Hernando
→ Hernando 6-4, 6-2, 1-6, 6-1

Martin Mulligan — Nagler 6-3, 2-6, 6-4,6-2
Lawrence Nagler
J. Allen Morris — Morris 6-3, 6-2, 6-2
Leslie C. Longshore, Jr.
→ Nagler 6-4, 6-4, 4-6, 3-6, 9-7
⇒ Hernando 7-5, 6-4, 4-6, 6-4
⟹ FRASER 6-0, 6-2, 6-3

LUIS AYALA — AYALA 6-2, 8-6, 6-2
Lt. Henry Jungle
Sidney B. Wood, III — Stewart 4-6, 6-4, 4-6, 6-3, 6-4
Forrest Stewart
→ AYALA 6-2, 6-4, 6-0

Richard A. Razzetti — Aubone 6-4, 6-4, 4-6, 6-3
Robert Aubone
Orlando Garrido — Bedard 9-7, 6-1, 6-2
Robert Bedard
→ Bedard 6-4, 6-3, 6-0
⇒ AYALA 8-6, 7-5, 6-2

Wade L. Herren — Buchholz 7-5, 6-1, 7-5
Clifford Buchholz
Edward G. Dailey — Dailey 6-4, 6-3, 7-5
Wilbert Davis
→ Dailey 6-2, 6-1, 6-3

Gilbert J. Shea — Shea 16-14, 8-6, 2-6, 16-14
Iyo Pimental
Robert M. Barker — Hettleman 4-6, 6-3, 6-2, 5-7, 6-2
Kalman Hettleman
→ Hettleman 7-5, 2-6, 6-3, 1-6, 6-4
⇒ Dailey 6-4, 11-9, 1-6, 2-6, 6-4
⟹ AYALA 6-1, 6-3, 6-2

⟹⟹ FRASER 6-3, 6-4, 6-4

BARRY MacKAY — MacKAY 6-2, 6-2, 6-2
Gerard Alleyne
Gardnar Mulloy — Mulloy 3-6, 5-7, 6-2, 6-4, 6-3
Sidney Schwartz
→ MacKAY 6-2, 6-3, 6-4

Crawford Henry — Henry 9-7, 6-1, 11-9
Pvt. Tom Coss
Pvt. Lawrence B. Sears — Farrin 6-2, 6-2, 6-1
James S. Farrin
→ Henry 12-10, 6-4, 6-2
⇒ MacKAY 6-3, 8-6, 7-5

Sergio Tacchini — Barnes 7-5, 7-5, 8-10, 4-6, 6-0
Ronald Barnes
John Powless — Powless 6-3, 6-4, 7-5
Leif C. Beck
→ Barnes 16-14, 6-2, 11-9

Robert F Greene — Mark 6-1, 6-2, 6-2
Robert Mark
Donald E. Ralph — Soriano 6-2, 2-6, 6-1, 6-4
Eduardo Soriano
→ Mark 6-1, 6-3, 6-2
⇒ Mark 6-4, 6-2, 6-4
⟹ MacKAY 6-4, 6-4, 9-7

RAMANATHAN KRISHNAN — KRISHNAN 6-2, 6-1, 6-1
James P. Biggs
Wilbur H. Jenkins, Jr. — Bennett 6-1, 6-1, 6-3
Reginald D. Bennett
→ KRISHNAN 6-4, 7-5, 6-2

E. Victor Seixas, Jr. — Seixas, Jr. 7-5, 6-3, 6-4
Allen Fox
John M. Cranston — Cranston 6-1, 7-5, 5-7, 6-4
Arthur W. Andrews
→ Seixas, Jr. 6-3, 4-6, 6-0, 5-7, 6-2
⇒ Seixas, Jr 6-3, 6-4, 6-2

Alan Roberts — Roberts 5-7, 6-3, 6-4, 6-2
William Lenoir
Bernard Bartzen — Bartzen 6-4, 6-2, 6-1
Doyle Perkins
→ Bartzen 6-0, 6-0, 6-2

Pfc. Carl E. Eltzholtz — Crawford 6-2, 6-1, 6-3
Chris Crawford
G. Clyde Buck — Fontana 6-1, 6-2, 8-6
Donald Fontana
→ Crawford 6-3, 6-2, 6-4
⇒ Bartzen 6-2, 6-4, 6-3
⟹ Bartzen 6-3, 6-1, 2-6, 8-10, 6-0

⟹⟹ Bartzen 6-3, 6-4, 6-4

ALEJANDRO OLMEDO — OLMEDO 6-0, 6-1, 6-1
Gerald Dubie
Ernest R. Schopp — Flam 6-3, 6-1, 6-2
Herbert Flam
→ OLMEDO 7-5, 6-4, 6-3, 6-2

Roger S. Werksman — Werksman 6-1 4-6, 6-2, 6-1
Herbert S. Fitzgibbon, II
Raymond Senkowski — Clark 2-6, 6-4, 6-2, 6-0
L. Straight Clark
→ Clark 6-3, 6-1, 6-1
⇒ OLMEDO 3-6, 6-4, 6-1, 6-2

Douglass Corley — Harit 6-4, 6-3, 7-5
Val Harit
Francisco Castillo — Palafox 6-2, 6-3, 6-4
Antonio Palafox
→ Palafox 6-1, 6-2, 6-2

Eugene L. Scott — Scott 11-9, 14-12, 10-8
C. Edward Sledge, Jr.
William H. Wright — McKinley 6-2, 6-3, 6-3
Charles McKinley
→ McKinley 6-2, 6-4, 6-2
⇒ McKinley 6-3, 4-6, 10-12, 6-4, 6-4
⟹ OLMEDO 6-3, 6-2, 6-4

ROY EMERSON — EMERSON 12-10, 6-1, 6-1
John C. Skogstad
J. A. Pickard — Pickard 6-4, 6-1, 6-4
Juan Jose Hermosilla
→ EMERSON 6-2, 6-2, 6-2

Paul Sullivan — Sullivan 6-4, 6-0, 3-6, 13-11
Juan Notz
Harry R. Hoffmann, Jr. — Hoffmann, Jr. 6-0, 6-1, 6-1
Stephen Gottlieb
→ Hoffman, Jr. 6-4, 6-1, 6-2
⇒ EMERSON 6-2, 6-0, 6-0

Pfc. Robert A. Potthast — Gomez 6-1, 7-5, 6-0
Adolfo Gomez
Paul Palmer, Jr. — Nelson 6-3, 6-4, 6-4
David M. Nelson
→ Nelson 6-4, 6-1, 4-6, 6-0

Williams Hoogs, Jr. — Bond 6-4, 8-6, 6-3
William E. Bond
William S. McClung — Godbout 6-3, 8-6, 6-4
Francois Godbout
→ Bond 6-4, 6-4, 8-6
⇒ Bond 6-3, 6-4, 6-4
⟹ EMERSON 6-2, 13-11, 6-2

⟹⟹ OLMEDO 6-4, 3-6, 6-2, 6-3

ROD LAVER — LAVER 6-2, 7-5, 6-2
Arthur Ashe, Jr.
Donald Thompson — Froehling, III 6-1, 6-4, 2-6, 7-5
Frank Froehling, III
→ LAVER 6-4, 6-0, 6-2

Charles F. Masterson — Masterson 8-6, 5-7, 6-2, 6-1
Dr. Jack Geller
Oscar Perez — Siska 6-0, 6-0, 6-2
Robert Siska
→ Siska 6-3, 6-2, 6-4
⇒ LAVER 7-5, 9-7, 4-6, 6-4

Donald Rubell — Lambert 2-6, 6-1, 11-9, 2-6, 6-3
Capt. Kingman B. Lambert
Al Driscole — Hobbs 6-3, 6-4, 8-6
Dever Hobbs
→ Lambert 5-7, 6-1, 6-3, 7-5

Manuel Santana — Santana 6-4, 6-3, 6-2
William J. Tully
Whitney Reed — Reed 6-2, 6-1, 7-5
Omar Pabst
→ Reed 3-6, 6-3, 6-4, 6-3
⇒ Reed 6-2, 6-1, 6-4
⟹ LAVER 6-1, 6-4, 5-7, 6-4

EARL BUCHHOLZ, JR. — BUCHHOLZ, JR. 9-7, 6-3, 6-3
Robert S. Bowditch, Jr.
John Karabasz — Fletcher 6-3, 6-1, 2-6, 6-4
Kenneth Fletcher
→ BUCHHOLZ, JR. 6-4, 6-1, 10-8

Donald L. Dell — Dell 6-2, 6-3, 6-1
Michael A. Crane
Ramsey Earnheart — Van Rensselaer 6-3, 2-6, 6-4, 3-6, 6-2
Henry C. Van Rensselaer
→ Dell 6-1, 6-1, 6-1
⇒ BUCHHOLZ, Jr 6-4, 6-4, 6-4

Gustavo Palafox — Eisenberg 2-6, 6-4, 6-4, 6-4, 6-4
Pablo S. Eisenberg
Richard Savitt — Savitt 8-6, 6-0, 6-1
Martin C. Riessen
→ Savitt 9-7, 6-0, 6-2

Ronald Holmberg — Holmberg 6-3, 6-2, 6-0
F. Stan Ellis
Ensign John J. Lesch — Susman 6-3, 3-6, 6-3, 1-6, 6-2
Rod Susman
→ Holmberg 6-3, 6-1, 6-0
⇒ Holmberg 1-6, 6-4, 7-5, 2-6, 9-7
⟹ Holmberg 6-3, 7-5, 8-10, 5-7, 6-3

⟹⟹ Holmberg 6-8, 7-5, 6-0, 6-3

Semi-Finals: FRASER 6-3, 6-2, 6-2 — OLMEDO 15-13, 6-4, 3-6, 6-1

Finals: NEALE FRASER 6-3, 5-7, 6-2, 6-4

Seeded Players
1. Alejandro Olmedo
2. Neale Fraser
3. Barry MacKay
4. Rod Laver
5. Ramanathan Krishnan
6. Luis Ayala
7. Earl Buchholz, Jr.
8. Roy Emerson

SEVENTY-NINTH USLTA MEN'S SINGLES CHAMPIONSHIPS
West Side Tennis Club, Forest Hills, N.Y., 1960

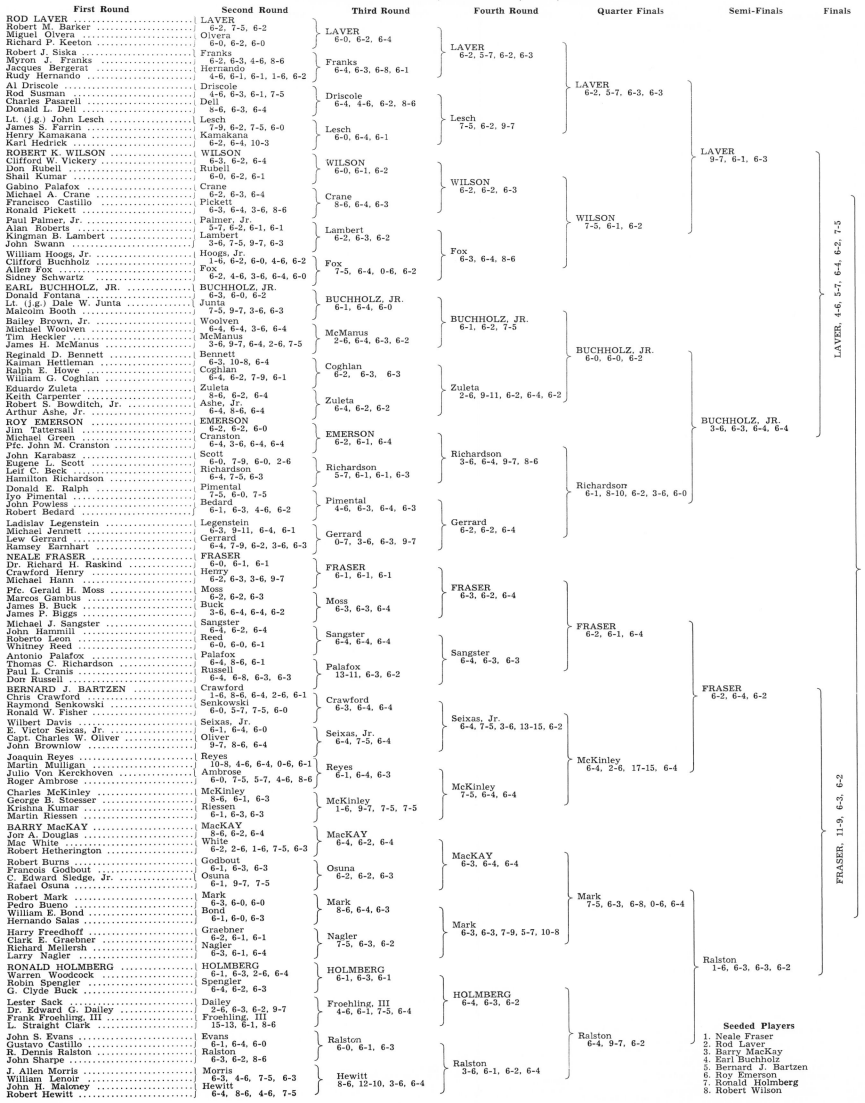

First Round	Second Round	Third Round	Fourth Round	Quarter Finals	Semi-Finals	Finals

ROD LAVER
Robert M. Barker — LAVER 6-2, 7-5, 6-2
Miguel Olvera — Olvera
Richard P. Keeton — 6-0, 6-2, 6-0
LAVER 6-0, 6-2, 6-4
Robert J. Siska — Franks
Myron J. Franks — 6-2, 6-3, 4-6, 8-6
Jacques Bergerat — Hernando
Rudy Hernando — 4-6, 6-1, 1-6, 6-2
Franks 6-4, 6-3, 6-8, 6-1
LAVER 6-2, 5-7, 6-2, 6-3
Al Driscole — Driscole
Rod Susman — 4-6, 6-3, 6-1, 7-5
Charles Pasarell — Dell
Donald L. Dell — 8-6, 6-3, 6-4
Driscole 6-4, 4-6, 6-2, 8-6
Lt. (j.g.) John Lesch — Lesch
James S. Farrin — 7-9, 6-2, 7-5, 6-0
Henry Kamakana — Kamakana
Karl Hedrick — 6-2, 6-4, 10-3
Lesch 6-0, 6-4, 6-1
Lesch 7-5, 6-2, 9-7
LAVER 6-2, 5-7, 6-3, 6-3

ROBERT K. WILSON
Clifford W. Vickery — WILSON 6-3, 6-2, 6-4
Don Rubell — Rubell
Shail Kumar — 6-0, 6-2, 6-1
WILSON 6-0, 6-1, 6-2
Gabino Palafox — Crane
Michael A. Crane — 6-2, 6-3, 6-4
Francisco Castillo — Pickett
Ronald Pickett — 6-3, 6-4, 3-6, 8-6
Crane 8-6, 6-4, 6-3
WILSON 6-2, 6-2, 6-3
Paul Palmer, Jr. — Palmer, Jr.
Alan Roberts — 5-7, 6-2, 6-1, 6-1
Kingman B. Lambert — Lambert
John Swann — 3-6, 7-5, 9-7, 6-3
Lambert 6-2, 6-3, 6-2
William Hoogs, Jr. — Hoogs, Jr.
Clifford Buchholz — 1-6, 6-2, 6-0, 4-6, 6-2
Allen Fox — Fox
Sidney Schwartz — 6-2, 4-6, 3-6, 6-4, 6-0
Fox 7-5, 6-4, 0-6, 6-2
Fox 6-3, 6-4, 8-6
WILSON 7-5, 6-1, 6-2
LAVER 9-7, 6-1, 6-3

EARL BUCHHOLZ, JR.
Donald Fontana — BUCHHOLZ, JR. 6-3, 6-0, 6-2
Lt. (j.g.) Dale W. Junta — Junta
Malcolm Booth — 7-5, 9-7, 3-6, 6-3
BUCHHOLZ, JR. 6-1, 6-4, 6-0
Bailey Brown, Jr. — Woolven
Michael Woolven — 6-4, 6-4, 3-6, 6-4
Tim Heckler — McManus
James H. McManus — 3-6, 9-7, 6-4, 2-6, 7-5
McManus 2-6, 6-4, 6-3, 6-2
BUCHHOLZ, JR. 6-1, 6-2, 7-5
Reginald D. Bennett — Bennett
Kalman Hettleman — 6-3, 10-8, 6-4
Ralph E. Howe — Coghlan
William G. Coghlan — 6-4, 6-2, 7-9, 6-1
Coghlan 6-2, 6-3, 6-3
Eduardo Zuleta — Zuleta
Keith Carpenter — 8-6, 6-2, 6-4
Robert S. Bowditch, Jr. — Ashe, Jr.
Arthur Ashe, Jr. — 6-4, 8-6, 6-4
Zuleta 6-4, 6-2, 6-2
Zuleta 2-6, 9-11, 6-2, 6-4, 6-2
BUCHHOLZ, JR. 6-0, 6-0, 6-2

ROY EMERSON
Jim Tattersall — EMERSON 6-2, 6-2, 6-0
Michael Green — Cranston
Pfc. John M. Cranston — 6-4, 3-6, 6-4, 6-4
EMERSON 6-2, 6-1, 6-4
John Karabasz — Scott
Eugene L. Scott — 6-0, 7-9, 6-0, 2-6
Leif C. Beck — Richardson
Hamilton Richardson — 6-4, 7-5, 6-3
Richardson 5-7, 6-1, 6-1, 6-3
Richardson 3-6, 6-4, 9-7, 8-6
Donald E. Ralph — Pimental
Iyo Pimental — 7-5, 6-0, 7-5
John Powless — Bedard
Robert Bedard — 6-1, 6-3, 4-6, 6-2
Pimental 4-6, 6-3, 6-4, 6-3
Ladislav Legenstein — Legenstein
Michael Jennett — 6-3, 9-11, 6-4, 6-1
Lew Gerrard — Gerrard
Ramsey Earnhart — 6-4, 7-9, 6-2, 3-6, 6-3
Gerrard 0-7, 3-6, 6-3, 9-7
Gerrard 6-2, 6-2, 6-4
Richardson 6-1, 8-10, 6-2, 3-6, 6-0
BUCHHOLZ, JR. 3-6, 6-3, 6-4, 6-4

NEALE FRASER
Dr. Richard H. Raskind — FRASER 6-0, 6-1, 6-1
Crawford Henry — Henry
Michael Hann — 6-2, 6-3, 3-6, 9-7
FRASER 6-1, 6-1, 6-1
Pfc. Gerald H. Moss — Moss
Marcos Gambus — 6-2, 6-2, 6-3
James B. Buck — Buck
James P. Biggs — 3-6, 6-4, 6-4, 6-2
Moss 6-3, 6-3, 6-4
FRASER 6-3, 6-2, 6-4
Michael J. Sangster — Sangster
John Hammill — 6-4, 6-2, 6-4
Roberto Leon — Reed
Whitney Reed — 6-0, 6-0, 6-1
Sangster 6-4, 6-4, 6-4
Antonio Palafox — Palafox
Thomas C. Richardson — 6-4, 8-6, 6-1
Paul L. Cranis — Russell
Don Russell — 6-4, 6-8, 6-3, 6-3
Palafox 13-11, 6-3, 6-2
Sangster 6-4, 6-3, 6-3
FRASER 6-2, 6-1, 6-4

BERNARD J. BARTZEN
Chris Crawford — Crawford 1-6, 8-6, 6-4, 2-6, 6-1
Raymond Senkowski — Senkowski
Ronald W. Fisher — 6-0, 5-7, 7-5, 6-0
Crawford 6-3, 6-4, 6-4
Wilbert Davis — Seixas, Jr.
E. Victor Seixas, Jr. — 6-1, 6-4, 6-0
Capt. Charles W. Oliver — Oliver
John Brownlow — 9-7, 8-6, 6-4
Seixas, Jr. 6-4, 7-5, 6-4
Seixas, Jr. 6-4, 7-5, 3-6, 13-15, 6-2
Joaquin Reyes — Reyes 10-8, 4-6, 6-4, 0-6, 6-1
Martin Mulligan — Ambrose
Julio Von Kerckhoven — 6-0, 7-5, 5-7, 4-6, 8-6
Roger Ambrose —
Reyes 6-1, 6-4, 6-3
Charles McKinley — McKinley
George B. Stoesser — 8-6, 6-1, 6-3
Krishna Kumar — Riessen
Martin Riessen — 6-1, 6-3, 6-3
McKinley 1-6, 9-7, 7-5, 7-5
McKinley 7-5, 6-4, 6-4
McKinley 6-4, 2-6, 17-15, 6-4
FRASER 6-2, 6-4, 6-2

BARRY MacKAY
Jon A. Douglas — MacKAY 8-6, 6-2, 6-4
Mac White — White
Robert Hetherington — 6-2, 2-6, 1-6, 7-5, 6-3
MacKAY 6-4, 6-2, 6-4
Robert Burns — Godbout
Francois Godbout — 6-1, 6-3, 6-3
C. Edward Sledge, Jr. — Osuna
Rafael Osuna — 6-1, 9-7, 7-5
Osuna 6-2, 6-2, 6-3
MacKAY 6-3, 6-4, 6-4
Robert Mark — Mark
Pedro Bueno — 6-3, 6-0, 6-0
William E. Bond — Bond
Hernando Salas — 6-1, 6-0, 6-3
Mark 8-6, 6-4, 6-3
Harry Freedhoff — Graebner
Clark E. Graebner — 6-2, 6-1, 6-1
Richard Mellersh — Nagler
Larry Nagler — 6-3, 6-1, 6-4
Nagler 7-5, 6-3, 6-2
Mark 6-3, 6-3, 7-9, 5-7, 10-8
Mark 7-5, 6-3, 6-8, 0-6, 6-4

RONALD HOLMBERG
Warren Woodcock — HOLMBERG 6-1, 6-3, 2-6, 6-4
Robin Spengler — Spengler
G. Clyde Buck — 6-4, 6-2, 6-3
HOLMBERG 6-1, 6-3, 6-1
Lester Sack — Dailey
Dr. Edward G. Dailey — 2-6, 6-3, 6-2, 9-7
Frank Froehling, III — Froehling, III
L. Straight Clark — 15-13, 6-1, 8-6
Froehling, III 4-6, 6-1, 7-5, 6-4
HOLMBERG 6-4, 6-3, 6-2
John S. Evans — Evans
Gustavo Castillo — 6-1, 6-4, 6-0
R. Dennis Ralston — Ralston
John Sharpe — 6-3, 6-2, 8-6
Ralston 6-0, 6-1, 6-3
J. Allen Morris — Morris
William Lenoir — 6-3, 4-6, 7-5, 6-3
John H. Maloney — Hewitt
Robert Hewitt — 6-4, 8-6, 4-6, 7-5
Hewitt 8-6, 12-10, 3-6, 6-4
Ralston 3-6, 6-1, 6-2, 6-4
Ralston 6-4, 9-7, 6-2
Ralston 1-6, 6-3, 6-3, 6-2

LAVER, 4-6, 5-7, 6-4, 6-2, 7-5

FRASER, 11-9, 6-3, 6-2

Seeded Players
1. Neale Fraser
2. Rod Laver
3. Barry MacKay
4. Earl Buchholz
5. Bernard J. Bartzen
6. Roy Emerson
7. Ronald Holmberg
8. Robert Wilson

135

EIGHTIETH USLTA MEN'S SINGLES CHAMPIONSHIPS
West Side Tennis Club, Forest Hills, N.Y., 1961

First Round — Second Round — Third Round — Fourth Round — Quarter Finals — Semi-Finals — Final

RODNEY LAVER
Chauncey D. Steele, III
LAVER 6-3, 6-1, 6-0
Allen Tong
Andy Lloyd
Lloyd 6-1, 6-3, 5-7, 6-2
LAVER 6-1, 6-2, 6-2

Eduardo Zuleta — Zuleta 6-1, 7-5, 6-1
Adrian Bey — Bey 6-3, 6-1, 6-4
Vernon Morgan
Bey 7-5, 3-6, 6-1, 6-1
Robert Barker — Barker 3-6, 6-12, 3-6, 6-0, 6-3
William Wright — Crawford 6-2, 6-1, 6-2
John Mangan
Christopher Crawford
Crawford 8-6, 6-2, 6-4
Crawford 6-1, 6-2, 6-3
LAVER 6-3, 6-4, 6-3

FRANK FROEHLING, III — FROEHLING, III 6-2, 6-2, 6-0
Dever Hobbs
Rod Susman — Pasarell 6-2, 6-2, 3-6, 6-4
Charles M. Pasarell
FROEHLING, III 6-3, 6-4, 6-4
Donald Dell — Dell 7-5, 6-0, 6-4
Michael Carpenter
John Harrison — Dailey 6-4, 6-2, 6-4
Dr. Edward Dailey
Dell 6-3, 6-2, 6-3
Dell 11-9, 10-8, 6-1
LAVER 6-4, 7-9, 6-3, 6-4

Arthur Ashe — Ashe 6-2, 6-2, 9-7
John Karabasz
Robert Sherman — Godbout 6-4, 7-5, 1-6, 8-6
Francois Godbout
Godbout 6-3, 7-5, 7-5
Henry Kamakana — Sharpe 3-6, 6-3, 6-4, 6-4
John Sharpe
Robert Potthast — Potthast 6-2, 6-1, 6-3
Donald Thompson
Sharpe 4-6, 4-6, 9-7, 6-1, 7-5
Sharpe 8-6, 6-4, 3-6, 6-2
Dell 7-9, 6-3, 6-2, 8-6

MICHAEL SANGSTER — SANGSTER 6-2, 3-6, 6-3, 6-4
Lt. Norman Perry
Karl Hedrick — Higgins, Jr. 6-2, 6-1, 6-3
William C. Higgins, Jr.
SANGSTER 6-3, 6-1, 6-3
Kingman B. Lambert — Lambert 6-2, 6-8, 6-2, 6-2
Hugh Quinn, Jr.
James McManus — McManus 6-1, 6-0, 6-0
Robert Davis
Lambert 6-3, 3-6, 4-6, 6-4, 6-3
SANGSTER 6-3, 7-9, 6-2, 6-4

William Bond — Bond 6-0, 6-0, 6-2
John Powless
Mac White — White 6-3, 6-2, 7-5
Harry Fauquier
Bond 6-3, 6-3, 6-3
Antonio Palafox — Palafox 6-2, 6-2, 6-2
Roger S. Werksman
Fred Vanderbilt — Nagler 6-2, 6-3, 6-3
Lawrence Nagler
Palafox 15-13, 6-1, 6-4
Palafox 6-3, 4-6, 6-3, 6-4
SANGSTER 21-19, 8-10, 6-3, 6-4

CPL. JON DOUGLAS — DOUGLAS 3-6, 6-2, 10-8, 6-1
Hamilton Richardson
Ray Senkowski — Senkowski 6-3, 6-0, 6-2
Jaime Musalem
DOUGLAS 6-3, 7-9, 6-3, 6-3
E. Victor Seixas, Jr. — Seixas 7-5, 6-4, 6-0
Dennis P. Lynch
Robert Siska — Siska 6-0, 6-2, 6-4
Hugh Lynch, III
Seixas 6-4, 10-8, 6-3
DOUGLAS 6-4, 2-6, 2-6, 9-7, 6-4

Gerald Moss — Henry 9-7, 6-4, 6-4
Crawford Henry
Eliseo Sanhueza — Sullivan 6-1, 6-2, 6-1
Paul W. Sullivan
Henry 6-4, 6-3, 6-4
John C. Botts, III — Biggs 6-3, 6-4, 3-6, 6-2
James P. Biggs
Donald E. Ralph — Bedard 6-3, 6-1, 6-3
Robert Bedard
Bedard 9-7, 6-2, 6-2
Henry 5-7, 11-13, 6-1, 6-4, 6-2
DOUGLAS 3-6, 6-3, 7-5, 8-6

CHARLES McKINLEY — McKINLEY 7-5, 6-2, 6-2
George Stoesser
Robert W. Johnson — Beck 6-2, 6-0, 6-4
Leif Beck
McKINLEY 7-5, 6-1, 6-1
Ralph E. Howe — Reed 6-4, 8-6, 7-5
Whitney Reed
David R. Reed — Hernandez 4-6, 4-6, 6-2, 8-6, 6-4
Guillermo Hernandez
Reed 7-5, 7-5, 7-5
Reed 6-3, 9-7, 3-6, 6-3

M. Radoslav Herceg — Olvera 6-0, 6-0, 6-0
Miguel Olvera
John Harris — Fox 6-2, 6-1, 6-1
Allen Fox
Fox 6-2, 10-8, 9-11, 6-3
Allan Lane — Lane 6-2, 9-7, 6-3
L. Straight Clark
Al Hill, Jr. — Hill, Jr. 5-7, 6-4, 2-6, 6-0, 6-2
Robin Spengler
Lane 6-2, 6-1, 6-4
Fox 6-2, 6-0, 8-10, 3-6, 6-1
Reed 8-6, 6-3, 4-6, 6-3

ROBERT MARK — MARK 6-2, 6-1, 6-0
Herbert S. FitzGibbon, II
Gabino Palafox — Palafox 6-4, 6-1, 6-2
Clyde Buck
MARK 6-2, 6-2, 6-2
Mike Belkin — Taylor 6-4, 6-2, 6-2
Roger Taylor
Ronald W. Fisher — Fisher 3-6, 6-2, 6-3, 6-2
Thomas Richardson
Fisher 4-6, 6-3, 8-6, 3-6, 7-5
MARK 6-4, 6-4, 6-2

Patricio Gasman — Shaffer 6-1, 6-2, 6-2
James A. Shaffer
Rafael Osuna — Osuna 6-2, 6-3, 6-3
Peter P. Barizon
Osuna 12-10, 6-2, 9-7
Eugene Scott — Scott 11-9, 6-3, 3-6, 6-3
Al Driscole
Donald Rubell — Sokol 7-9, 3-6, 6-3, 6-2, 8-6
George J. Sokol
Scott 4-6, 6-3, 6-2, 5-2 Retired
Osuna 11-13, 6-4, 6-8, 17-15, 6-0
Osuna 6-3, 6-4, 8-6

Osuna 6-8, 6-3, 6-3, 6-2

ROY EMERSON — EMERSON 6-2, 6-1, 6-0
Ed Rubinoff
Ronald Goldman — Brown, Jr. 6-3, 7-5, 6-1
Bailey Brown, Jr.
EMERSON 6-1, 6-0, 6-1
William Lenoir — Lenoir 6-0, 6-3, 6-1
Keith Carpenter
Edward Hoehn — Buchholz 16-14, 5-7, 6-1, 11-9
Clifford Buchholz
Buchholz 1-6, 6-2, 6-3, 6-3
EMERSON 6-3, 6-3, 6-1

Harry R. Hoffmann, Jr. — Hoffmann, Jr. 6-0, 6-2, 6-3
Edward Greer
Don Fontana — Fontana 3-6, 7-5, 8-6, 6-4
Richard C. Sorlein
Hoffmann, Jr. 10-8, 4-6, 6-3, 7-5
David Dickinson — Earnhart 6-3, 6-2, 6-0
Ramsey V. Earnhart
Wilbert Davis — Davis 8-6, 6-4, 9-7
Bruce Sylvia
Davis 4-6, 6-2, 1-0, Default
Hoffmann, Jr. 6-3, 6-2, 6-1
EMERSON 6-1, 6-2, 6-2

RON HOLMBERG — HOLMBERG 6-4, 6-4, 7-5
Michael Green
John Hammill — Farrin 8-6, 7-5, 4-6, 6-1
James S. Farrin
HOLMBERG 7-5, 6-1, 6-2
Martin Riessen — Riessen 6-4, 8-6, 6-0
Butch Newman
Hugh Sweeney — Snyder 6-4, 6-2, 6-3
David Snyder
Riessen 6-0, 8-6, 6-2
HOLMBERG 7-5, 6-4, 6-2

Clark E. Graebner
William H. Hoogs, Jr.
Hoogs, Jr. 7-5, 1-6, 6-3, 6-4
John W. Frost
Robert Hetherington
Frost 6-1, 6-2, 6-1
Frost 6-1, 6-4, 6-2
HOLMBERG 6-2, 7-9, 6-4, 6-1

EMERSON 6-4, 6-2, 7-5

LAVER 6-4, 7-9, 6-3, 6-4

SANGSTER 6-4, 7-5, 6-1

EMERSON 6-3, 6-2, 3-6, 5-7, 9-7

LAVER, 13-11, 7-5, 6-4

ROY EMERSON, 7-5, 6-3, 6-2

Seeded Players
1. Rodney Laver
2. Charles McKinley
3. Roy Emerson
4. Michael Sangster
5. Robert Mark
6. Frank Froehling, III
7. Jon Douglas
8. Ron Holmberg

EIGHTY-FIRST USLTA MEN'S SINGLES CHAMPIONSHIPS
West Side Tennis Club, Forest Hills, N.Y., 1962

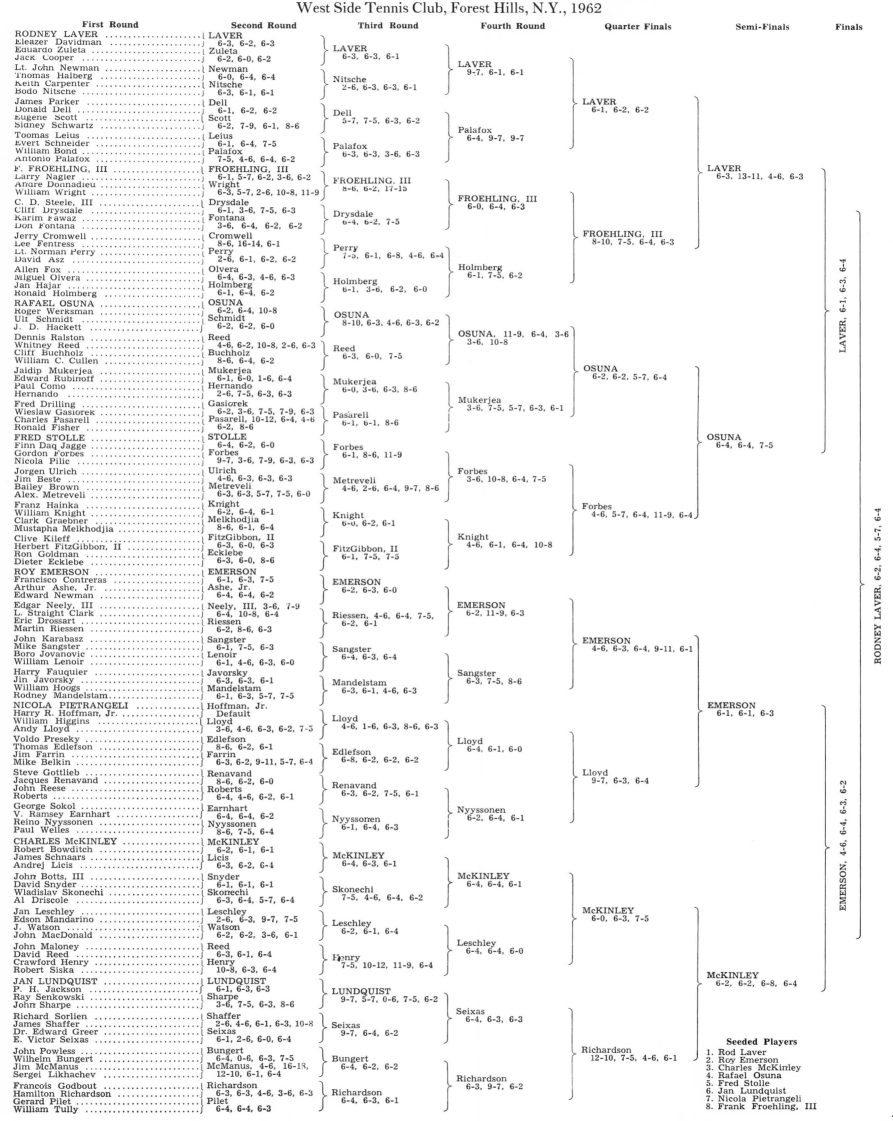

First Round	Second Round	Third Round	Fourth Round	Quarter Finals	Semi-Finals	Finals

RODNEY LAVER — LAVER 6-3, 6-2, 6-3
Eleazer Davidman
Eduardo Zuleta — Zuleta 6-2, 6-0, 6-2
Jack Cooper
— LAVER 6-3, 6-3, 6-1
Lt. John Newman — Newman 6-0, 6-4, 6-4
Thomas Halberg
Keith Carpenter — Nitsche 6-3, 6-1, 6-1
Bodo Nitsche
— Nitsche 2-6, 6-3, 6-3, 6-1
— LAVER 9-7, 6-1, 6-1
James Parker — Dell 6-1, 6-2, 6-2
Donald Dell
Eugene Scott — Scott 6-2, 7-9, 6-1, 8-6
Sidney Schwartz
— Dell 5-7, 7-5, 6-3, 6-2
Toomas Leius — Leius 6-1, 6-4, 7-5
Evert Schneider
William Bond — Palafox 7-5, 4-6, 6-4, 6-2
Antonio Palafox
— Palafox 6-3, 6-3, 3-6, 6-3
— Palafox 6-4, 9-7, 9-7
— LAVER 6-1, 6-2, 6-2

F. FROEHLING, III — FROEHLING, III 6-1, 5-7, 6-2, 3-6, 6-2
Larry Nagler
Andre Donnadieu — Wright 6-3, 5-7, 2-6, 10-8, 11-9
William Wright
— FROEHLING, III 8-6, 6-2, 17-15
C. D. Steele, III — Drysdale 6-1, 3-6, 7-5, 6-3
Cliff Drysdale
Karim Fawaz — Fontana 3-6, 6-4, 6-2, 6-2
Don Fontana
— Drysdale 6-4, 6-2, 7-5
— FROEHLING, III 6-0, 6-4, 6-3
Jerry Cromwell — Cromwell 8-6, 16-14, 6-1
Lee Fentress
Lt. Norman Perry — Perry 2-6, 6-1, 6-2, 6-2
David Asz
— Perry 7-5, 6-1, 6-8, 4-6, 6-4
Allen Fox — Olvera 6-4, 6-3, 4-6, 6-3
Miguel Olvera
Jan Hajar — Holmberg 6-1, 6-4, 6-2
Ronald Holmberg
— Holmberg 6-1, 3-6, 6-2, 6-0
— Holmberg 6-1, 7-5, 6-2
— FROEHLING, III 8-10, 7-5, 6-4, 6-3

RAFAEL OSUNA — OSUNA 6-2, 6-4, 10-8
Roger Werksman
Ult Schmidt — Schmidt 6-2, 6-2, 6-0
J. D. Hackett
— OSUNA 8-10, 6-3, 4-6, 6-3, 6-2
Dennis Ralston — Reed 4-6, 6-2, 10-8, 2-6, 6-3
Whitney Reed
Cliff Buchholz — Buchholz 8-6, 6-4, 6-2
William C. Cullen
— Reed 6-3, 6-0, 7-5
— OSUNA, 11-9, 6-4, 3-6, 3-6, 10-8
Jaidip Mukerjea — Mukerjea 6-1, 6-0, 1-6, 6-4
Edward Rubinoff
Paul Como — Hernando 2-6, 7-5, 6-3, 6-3
Hernando
— Mukerjea 6-0, 3-6, 6-3, 8-6
Fred Drilling — Gasiorek 6-2, 3-6, 7-5, 7-9, 6-3
Wieslaw Gasiorek
Charles Pasarell — Pasarell 10-12, 6-4, 4-6
Ronald Fisher
— Pasarell 6-1, 6-1, 8-6
— Mukerjea 3-6, 7-5, 5-7, 6-3, 6-1
— OSUNA 6-2, 6-2, 5-7, 6-4

FRED STOLLE — STOLLE 6-4, 6-2, 6-0
Finn Dag Jagge
Gordon Forbes — Forbes 9-7, 3-6, 7-9, 6-3, 6-3
Nicola Pilic
— Forbes 6-1, 8-6, 11-9
Jorgen Ulrich — Ulrich 4-6, 6-3, 6-3, 6-3
Jim Beste
Bailey Brown — Metreveli 6-3, 6-3, 5-7, 7-5, 6-0
Alex. Metreveli
— Metreveli 4-6, 2-6, 6-4, 9-7, 8-6
— Forbes 3-6, 10-8, 6-4, 7-5
Franz Hainka — Knight 6-2, 6-4, 6-1
William Knight
Clark Graebner — Melkhodjia 8-6, 6-1, 6-4
Mustapha Melkhodjia
— Knight 6-0, 6-2, 6-1
Clive Kileff — FitzGibbon, II 6-3, 6-0, 6-3
Herbert FitzGibbon, II
Ron Goldman — Ecklebe 6-3, 6-0, 8-6
Dieter Ecklebe
— FitzGibbon, II 6-1, 7-5, 7-5
— Knight 4-6, 6-1, 6-4, 10-8
— Forbes 4-6, 5-7, 6-4, 11-9, 6-4

ROY EMERSON — EMERSON 6-1, 6-3, 7-5
Francisco Contreras
Arthur Ashe, Jr. — Ashe, Jr. 6-4, 6-4, 6-2
Edward Newman
— EMERSON 6-2, 6-3, 6-0
Edgar Neely, III — Neely, III, 3-6, 7-9, 6-4, 10-8, 6-4
L. Straight Clark
Eric Drossart — Riessen 6-2, 8-6, 6-3
Martin Riessen
— Riessen, 4-6, 6-4, 7-5, 6-2, 6-1
— EMERSON 6-2, 11-9, 6-3
John Karabasz — Sangster 6-1, 7-5, 6-3
Mike Sangster
Boro Jovanovic — Lenoir 6-1, 4-6, 6-3, 6-0
William Lenoir
— Sangster 6-4, 6-3, 6-4
Harry Fauquier — Javorsky 6-3, 6-3, 6-1
Jin Javorsky
William Hoogs — Mandelstam 6-1, 6-3, 5-7, 7-5
Rodney Mandelstam
— Mandelstam 6-3, 6-1, 4-6, 6-3
— Sangster 6-3, 7-5, 8-6
— EMERSON 4-6, 6-3, 6-4, 9-11, 6-1

NICOLA PIETRANGELI — Hoffman, Jr. Default
Harry R. Hoffman, Jr.
William Higgins — Lloyd 3-6, 4-6, 6-3, 6-2, 7-5
Andy Lloyd
— Lloyd 4-6, 1-6, 6-3, 8-6, 6-3
Voldo Preseky — Edlefson 8-6, 6-2, 6-1
Thomas Edlefson
Jim Farrin — Farrin 6-3, 6-2, 9-11, 5-7, 6-4
Mike Belkin
— Edlefson 6-8, 6-2, 6-2, 6-2
— Lloyd 6-4, 6-1, 6-0
Steve Gottlieb — Renavand 8-6, 6-2, 6-0
Jacques Renavand
John Reese — Roberts 6-4, 4-6, 6-2, 6-1
Roberts
— Renavand 6-3, 6-2, 7-5, 6-1
George Sokol — Earnhart 6-4, 6-4, 6-2
V. Ramsey Earnhart
Reino Nyyssonen — Nyyssonen 8-6, 7-5, 6-4
Paul Welles
— Nyyssonen 6-1, 6-4, 6-3
— Nyyssonen 6-2, 6-4, 6-1
— Lloyd 9-7, 6-3, 6-4

CHARLES McKINLEY — McKINLEY 6-2, 6-1, 6-1
Robert Bowditch
James Schnaars — Licis 6-3, 6-2, 6-4
Andrej Licis
— McKINLEY 6-4, 6-3, 6-1
John Botts, III — Snyder 6-1, 6-1, 6-1
David Snyder
Wladislav Skonechi — Skonechi 6-3, 6-4, 5-7, 6-4
Al Driscole
— Skonechi 7-5, 4-6, 6-4, 6-2
— McKINLEY 6-4, 6-4, 6-1
Jan Leschley — Leschley 2-6, 6-3, 9-7, 7-5
Edson Mandarino
J. Watson — Watson 6-2, 6-2, 3-6, 6-1
John MacDonald
— Leschley 6-2, 6-1, 6-4
John Maloney — Reed 6-3, 6-1, 6-4
David Reed
Crawford Henry — Henry 10-8, 6-3, 6-4
Robert Siska
— Henry 7-5, 10-12, 11-9, 6-4
— Leschley 6-4, 6-4, 6-0
— McKINLEY 6-0, 6-3, 7-5

JAN LUNDQUIST — LUNDQUIST 6-1, 6-3, 6-3
P. H. Jackson
Ray Senkowski — Sharpe 3-6, 7-5, 6-3, 8-6
John Sharpe
— LUNDQUIST 9-7, 5-7, 0-6, 7-5, 6-2
Richard Sorlien — Shaffer 2-6, 4-6, 6-1, 6-3, 10-8
James Shaffer
Dr. Edward Greer — Seixas 6-1, 2-6, 6-0, 6-4
E. Victor Seixas
— Seixas 9-7, 6-4, 6-2
— Seixas 6-4, 6-3, 6-3
— McKINLEY 6-2, 6-2, 6-8, 6-4
John Powless — Bungert 6-4, 0-6, 6-3, 7-5
Wilhelm Bungert
Jim McManus — McManus, 4-6, 16-18, 12-10, 6-1, 6-4
Sergei Likhachev
— Bungert 6-4, 6-2, 6-2
Francois Godbout — Richardson 6-3, 6-3, 4-6, 3-6, 6-3
Hamilton Richardson
Gerard Pilet — Pilet 6-4, 6-4, 6-3
William Tully
— Richardson 6-4, 6-3, 6-1
— Richardson 6-3, 9-7, 6-2
— Richardson 12-10, 7-5, 4-6, 6-1

LAVER, 6-1, 6-3, 6-4

RODNEY LAVER, 6-2, 6-4, 5-7, 6-4

EMERSON, 4-6, 6-4, 6-3, 6-2

Seeded Players
1. Rod Laver
2. Roy Emerson
3. Charles McKinley
4. Rafael Osuna
5. Fred Stolle
6. Jan Lundquist
7. Nicola Pietrangeli
8. Frank Froehling, III

EIGHTY-SECOND USLTA MEN'S SINGLES CHAMPIONSHIPS
West Side Tennis Club, Forest Hills, N.Y., 1963

First Round	Second Round	Third Round	Fourth Round	Quarter Finals	Semi-Finals	Final

CHARLES McKINLEY — McKINLEY
Eduardo Zuleta, Ecuador — 4-6, 3-6, 8-6, 6-3, 6-1
Jiri Javorski, Czechoslovakia — Javorski
Michio Fujii, Japan — 7-5, 6-1, 7-9, 6-2
→ McKINLEY 6-2, 6-4, 6-3

A. T. Woods, S. Africa — Wood
John Powless — 8-6, 6-2, 6-4
Dieter Ecklebe, Germany — Ecklebe
Robert J. Siska — 8-6, 6-2, 6-3
→ Wood 7-5, 6-4, 9-7
→→ McKINLEY 6-4, 6-4, 8-6

James McManus — McManus
Claude deGronckel, Belgium — 4-6, 6-2, 6-3, 6-2
E. Victor Seixas — Seixas
Robert Bowditch — 13-15, 6-4, 6-0, 6-0
→ Seixas 7-5, 7-9, 8-6, 6-4

Lee Fentress — Fentress
Carl Hedelund, Denmark — 6-0, 6-2, 6-2
Aly Mohammed U.A.R. — Nagler
Lawrence Nagler — 6-3, 6-3, 6-1
→ Nagler 6-3, 6-1, 6-0
→→ Nagler 6-3, 1-6, 11-13, 14-12, 6-1
→→→ McKINLEY 5-7, 6-4, 6-4, 6-2

EUGENE SCOTT — SCOTT
Jack Jackson — 6-4, 6-4, 6-2
Paul Sullivan — Dell
Donald Dell — 4-6, 7-9, 6-2, 6-4, 6-0
→ SCOTT 4-6, 7-5, 6-3, 7-5

Robert Bedard, Canada — Bedard
Willie Hernandez, Philippines — 6-4, 6-1, 5-7, 7-5
Thomas Koch, Brazil — Koch
Harry Hoffmann, Jr. — 6-4, 4-6, 7-9, 6-3, 6-1
→ Koch 6-4, 9-7, 6-2
→→ Koch 4-6, 6-4, 6-3, 6-4

Joe Williams — Sammis
Jessie Sammis — Default
Fred Sherriff, Australia — Higgins, Jr.
William C. Higgins, Jr. — 6-2, 6-4, 6-4
→ Higgins, Jr. 6-0, 6-3, 6-1

Istvan Gulyas, Hungary — Gulyas
William Tully — 6-2, 3-6, 6-4, 6-3
Keith Jennings — Skogstad
John Skogstad — 6-4, 6-2, 4-6, 6-3
→ Gulyas 2-6, 6-3, 6-3, 4-6, 6-4
→→ Gulyas 7-5, 6-4, 6-3
→→→ Koch 7-5, 6-3, 6-3

RAFAEL OSUNA, Mexico — OSUNA
Jean Rouver, France — 6-1, 6-1, 8-6
Fred Drilling — Beste
Jim Beste — 6-4, 6-4, 6-3
→ OSUNA 6-2, 6-4, 13-11

Roger Werksman — Roche
Tony Roche, Australia — 6-1, 6-1, 8-6
Osamu Ishiguro, Japan — Ishiguro
Lester Sack — 6-1, 6-1, 6-0
→ Roche 6-0, 6-4, 6-4
→→ OSUNA 3-6, 6-1, 6-2, 6-2

William Wright, Jr. — Nyyssonen
Reino Nyyssonen, Finland — 7-5, 6-2, 7-5
Keith Carpenter, Canada — Scholl
Peter Scholl, Germany — 8-6, 10-8, 6-3
→ Nyyssonen 1-6, 6-4, 1-6, 6-0, 6-1

Clifford Drysdale, S. Africa — Drysdale
Don Fontana, Canada — 6-1, 6-4, 6-2
Ian Crookendon, New Zealand — Darmon 13-15,
Pierre Darmon, France — 3-6, 8-6, 6-1, 10-8
→ Darmon, 7-9, 6-2, 6-8, 6-0, 5-2, Default
→→ Darmon 6-3, 6-1, 6-2
→→→ OSUNA 6-4, 6-2, 4-6, 3-6, 6-2

HAMILTON RICHARDSON — RICHARDSON
Tony Lieberman — 6-3, 6-1, 6-1
Eric Drossart, Belgium — Drossart
Sidney Schwartz — 1-6, 6-3, 3-6, 6-2, 6-2
→ RICHARDSON 6-2, 6-2, 6-2

Alan Mills, England — Mills
George Seewagen — 6-2, 6-1, 6-1
Antonio Maggi, Italy — Sanderlin
David Sanderlin — 1-6, 5-7, 7-5, 6-1, 6-1
→ Sanderlin 5-7, 6-1, 6-3, 3-6, 6-3
→→ Sanderlin 1-6, 8-6, 4-6, 6-3, 6-3

Alphonso Ochoa, Mexico — Ashe, Jr.
Arthur Ashe, Jr. — 6-4, 5-7, 6-4, 6-4
Norman Perry — Perry
Mike Belkin — 6-4, 6-4, 6-2
→ Ashe, Jr. 3-6, 7-5, 6-2, 6-3

Martin Riessen — Riessen
James Buck — 7-5, 8-6, 6-4
Ronnie Fisher — Fisher
Peter Strobl, Czechoslovakia — 6-4, 4-6, 6-3, 6-2
→ Riessen 1-6, 6-4, 3-6, 6-1, 6-2
→→ Riessen 6-3, 8-6, 2-6, 8-6
→→→ Riessen 6-4, 6-2, 6-4

Roger Taylor, England — Taylor
William Lenoir — 6-3, 3-6, 6-3, 7-5
John McDonald, New Zealand — McDonald
Robert Abdesselam, France — 6-4, 6-4, 6-3
→ Taylor 6-2, 6-4, 6-0

Tony Ryan, South Africa — Ryan
Andy Lloyd — 6-1, 3-6, 6-4, 6-4
Pierre Barthes, France — Barthes
Ed Rubinoff — 6-3, 6-2, 3-6, 6-8, 8-6
→ Barthes 2-6, 7-5, 10-8, 0-6, 6-1
→→ Taylor 6-1, 6-4, 3-6, 4-6, 6-1

Paul Speicher — Barnes
Ronald Barnes, Brazil — 6-4, 6-2, 6-2
Tom Edlefsen — Edlefsen
Andres Donnadieu, Mexico — 6-2, 6-3, 6-4
→ Barnes 2-6, 6-1, 3-6, 6-3, 6-4

Ronald Holmberg — Holmberg
Lancelot Lumsden, Jamaica — Default
Premjit Lall, India — FLETCHER
KEN FLETCHER, Australia — 9-7, 4-6, 6-1, 14-12
→ FLETCHER 7-5, 9-7, 7-9, 4-6, 6-3
→→ Barnes 6-8, 6-2, 2-6, 6-4, 7-5
→→→ Barnes 7-5, 2-6, 7-9, 7-5, 8-6

Michael Hahn, England — Phillips
Dave Phillips, South Africa — 7-5, 6-3, 7-5
Rudy Hernando — Newcombe
John Newcombe, Australia — 6-4, 7-5, 7-5
→ Newcombe 9-7, 8-6, 6-2

Fritz Schunk — Schunk
Clive Kileff, Rhodesia — 6-1, 7-5, 7-5
Jean Baker, Haiti — Rosello
Pedro Rosello, Puerto Rico — Default
→ Schunk 16-14, 6-4, 6-4
→→ Newcombe 8-6, 6-1, 6-4

Mickey Schad — Hajar
Jan Hajar, Holland — 6-3, 6-4, 2-6, 10-8
Thomas Hallberg, Sweden — Davidson
Owen Davidson, Australia — 6-3, 6-4, 6-4
→ Davidson 6-3, 3-6, 6-3, 6-2

Richard Sorlein — Sorlein
N. Bari, Turkey — 6-3, 6-4, 6-3
Walter Johnson — RALSTON
DENNIS RALSTON — 6-1, 6-2, 6-2
→ RALSTON 6-2, 8-10, 6-1, 7-5
→→ RALSTON 6-4, 6-2, 6-8, 6-8, 6-4
→→→ RALSTON 6-3, 6-4, 3-6, 7-5

Jack Cooper — Sokol
George Sokol — 6-3, 6-1, 6-2
Gerald Slobin — Neely
Ned Neely, III — 8-6, 6-4, 6-4
→ Neely, III 8-6, 6-2, 6-2

Cliff Buchholz — Buchholz
Leif Beck — 6-1, 6-1, 7-5
Keith Stoneman, Jr. — Power
David Power — 6-4, 3-6, 6-8, 8-6, 9-7
→ Buchholz 7-9, 6-2, 6-4, 6-3
→→ Buchholz 6-4, 6-4, 5-7, 6-4

Allen Fox — Parasell
Charles Pasarell, Puerto Rico — 8-10, 6-4, 6-4, 6-3
Clark E. Graebner — Graebner
Jan Parker — 6-2, 9-7, 7-5
→ Pasarell 6-3, 6-3, 6-8, 7-5

William A. Tym — Newman
Butch Newman — 7-9, 7-5, 6-2, 6-4
James Schnaars — WILSON
BOBBY WILSON, England — 6-4, 6-3, 6-2
→ WILSON 6-4, 5-7, 7-5, 6-4
→→ WILSON 7-5, 8-6, 14-12
→→→ WILSON 6-3, 6-0, 6-1

Hugh Sweeney — Froehling
Frank Froehling, III — 6-1, 6-3, 6-2
John Isaacs — Reed
David Reed — 6-1, 8-6, 6-4
→ Froehling, III 7-9, 8-6, 6-3, 6-4

Vernon Morgan — Godbout
Francois Godbout, Canada — 6-1, 7-5, 6-0
Ed Turville — Palafox
Antonio Palafox, Mexico — 6-1, 6-3, 6-2
→ Palafox 7-5, 6-4, 7-5
→→ Froehling, III 6-4, 6-1, 6-4

John W. Harrison — Harrison
Herbert FitzGibbon, II — 2-6, 7-5, 3-6, 6-4, 14-12
David Cohen, Portugal — Baxter
C. V. Baxter, Scotland — 6-3, 6-4, 7-5
→ Harrison 4-6, 6-2, 6-2, 6-1

James Osborne — Richey
Cliff Richey — 6-2, 6-8, 5-7, 6-2, 6-4
Chauncey D. Steele, III — EMERSON
ROY EMERSON, Australia — 6-1, 6-4, 6-2
→ EMERSON 6-3, 6-2, 7-5
→→ EMERSON 6-4, 6-2, 6-0
→→→ Froehling, III 6-4, 4-6, 9-7, 6-2

Quarter Finals / Semi-Finals / Final:
McKINLEY 6-4, 4-6, 4-6, 8-6, 6-4
OSUNA 3-6, 9-7, 6-3, 6-3
OSUNA 6-4, 6-4, 10-8
Froehling, III 6-3, 6-1, 6-4
Froehling, III 6-8, 4-6, 6-3, 6-3, 9-7
RAFAEL OSUNA, 7-5, 6-4, 6-2

Seeded Players
1. Charles McKinley
2. Roy Emerson
3. R. Dennis Ralston
4. Rafael Osuna
5. Ken Fletcher
6. Bobby Wilson
7. Eugene Scott
8. Hamilton Richardson

EIGHTY-THIRD USLTA MEN'S SINGLES CHAMPIONSHIPS
West Side Tennis Club, Forest Hills, N.Y., 1964

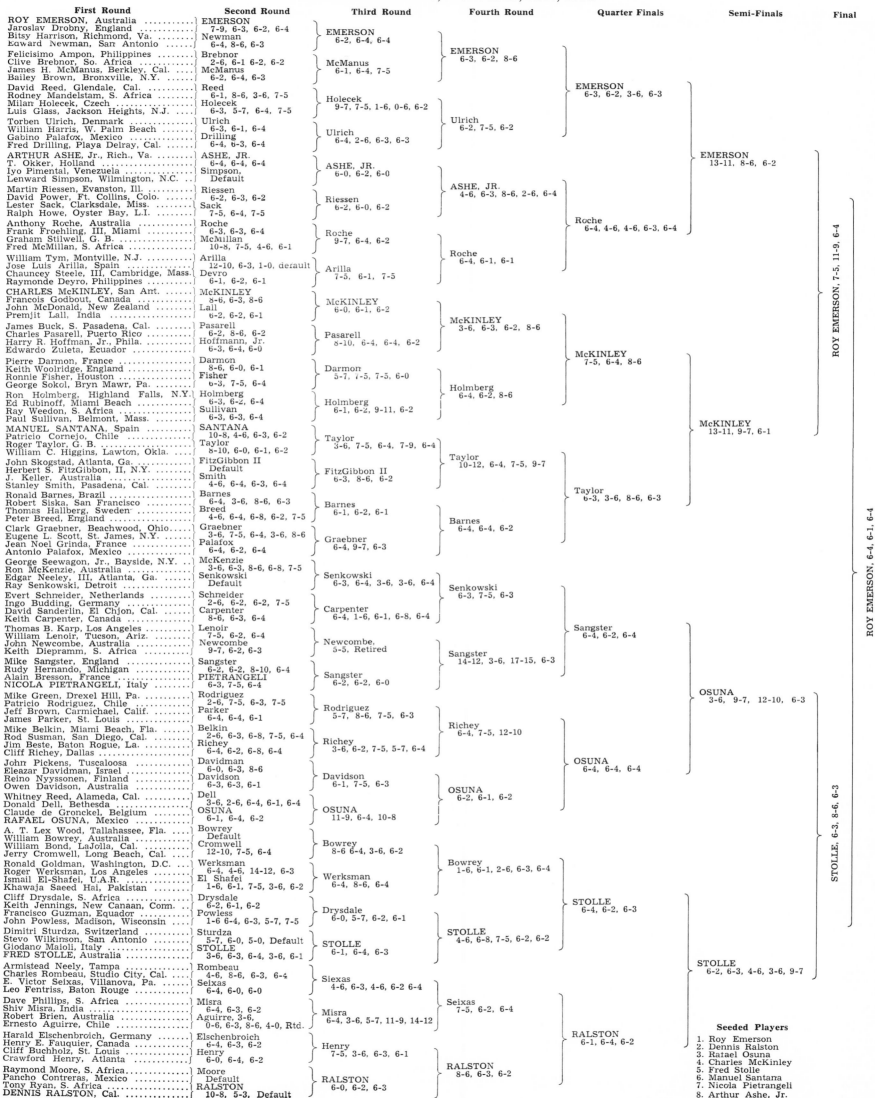

EIGHTY-FOURTH USLTA MEN'S SINGLES CHAMPIONSHIPS
West Side Tennis Club, Forest Hills, N.Y., 1965

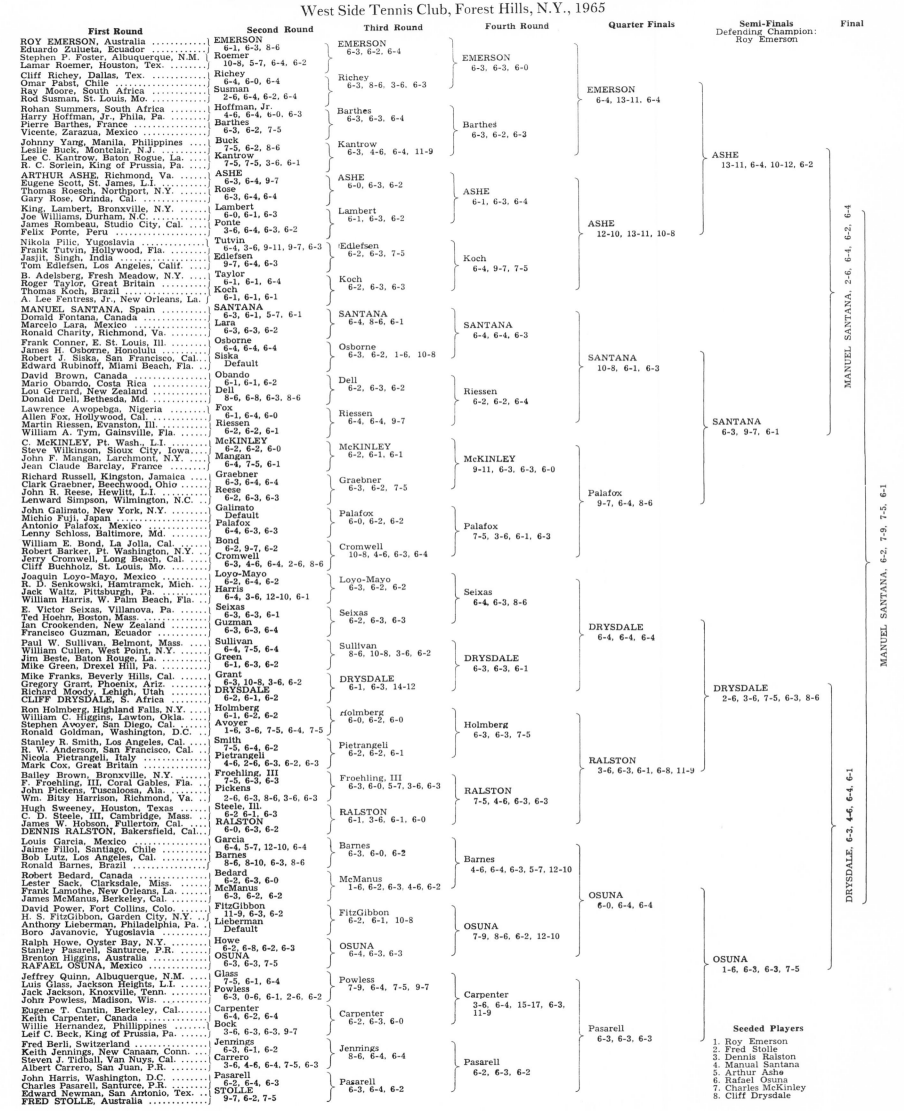

First Round	Second Round	Third Round	Fourth Round	Quarter Finals	Semi-Finals	Final

Defending Champion: Roy Emerson

First Round:
- ROY EMERSON, Australia
- Eduardo Zulueta, Ecuador
- Stephen P. Foster, Albuquerque, N.M.
- Lamar Roemer, Houston, Tex.
- Cliff Richey, Dallas, Tex.
- Omar Pabst, Chile
- Ray Moore, South Africa
- Rod Susman, St. Louis, Mo.
- Rohan Summers, South Africa
- Harry Hoffman, Jr., Phila, Pa.
- Pierre Barthes, France
- Vicente, Zarazua, Mexico
- Johnny Yang, Manila, Philippines
- Leslie Buck, Montclair, N.J.
- Lee C. Kantrow, Baton Rogue, La.
- R. C. Sorlein, King of Prussia, Pa.
- ARTHUR ASHE, Richmond, Va.
- Eugene Scott, St. James, L.I.
- Thomas Roesch, Northport, N.Y.
- Gary Rose, Orinda, Cal.
- King, Lambert, Bronxville, N.Y.
- Joe Williams, Durham, N.C.
- James Rombeau, Studio City, Cal.
- Felix Ponte, Peru
- Nikola Pilic, Yugoslavia
- Frank Tutvin, Hollywood, Fla.
- Jasjit, Singh, India
- Tom Edlefsen, Los Angeles, Calif.
- B. Adelsberg, Fresh Meadow, N.Y.
- Roger Taylor, Great Britain
- Thomas Koch, Brazil
- A. Lee Fentress, Jr., New Orleans, La.
- MANUEL SANTANA, Spain
- Donald Fontana, Canada
- Marcelo Lara, Mexico
- Ronald Charity, Richmond, Va.
- Frank Conner, E. St. Louis, Ill.
- James H. Osborne, Honolulu
- Robert J. Siska, San Francisco, Cal.
- Edward Rubinoff, Miami Beach, Fla.
- David Brown, Canada
- Mario Obando, Costa Rica
- Lou Gerrard, New Zealand
- Donald Dell, Bethesda, Md.
- Lawrence Awopebga, Nigeria
- Allen Fox, Hollywood, Cal.
- Martin Riessen, Evanston, Ill.
- William A. Tym, Gainsville, Fla.
- C. McKINLEY, Pt. Wash., L.I.
- Steve Wilkinson, Sioux City, Iowa
- John F. Mangan, Larchmont, N.Y.
- Jean Claude Barclay, France
- Richard Russell, Kingston, Jamaica
- Clark Graebner, Beechwood, Ohio
- John R. Reese, Hewlitt, L.I.
- Lenward Simpson, Wilmington, N.C.
- John Galinato, New York, N.Y.
- Michio Fuji, Japan
- Antonio Palafox, Mexico
- Lenny Schloss, Baltimore, Md.
- William E. Bond, La Jolla, Cal.
- Robert Barker, Pt. Washington, N.Y.
- Jerry Cromwell, Long Beach, Cal.
- Cliff Buchholz, St. Louis, Mo.
- Joaquin Loyo-Mayo, Mexico
- R. D. Senkowski, Hamtramck, Mich.
- Jack Waltz, Pittsburgh, Pa.
- William Harris, W. Palm Beach, Fla.
- E. Victor Seixas, Villanova, Pa.
- Ted Hoehn, Boston, Mass.
- Ian Crookenden, New Zealand
- Francisco Guzman, Ecuador
- Paul W. Sullivan, Belmont, Mass.
- William Cullen, West Point, N.Y.
- Jim Beste, Baton Rouge, La.
- Mike Green, Drexel Hill, Pa.
- Mike Franks, Beverly Hills, Cal.
- Gregory Grant, Phoenix, Ariz.
- Richard Moody, Lehigh, Utah
- CLIFF DRYSDALE, S. Africa
- Ron Holmberg, Highland Falls, N.Y.
- William C. Higgins, Lawton, Okla.
- Stephen Avoyer, San Diego, Cal.
- Ronald Goldman, Washington, D.C.
- Stanley R. Smith, Los Angeles, Cal.
- R. W. Anderson, San Francisco, Cal.
- Nicola Pietrangeli, Italy
- Mark Cox, Great Britain
- Bailey Brown, Bronxville, N.Y.
- F. Froehling, III, Coral Gables, Fla.
- John Pickens, Tuscaloosa, Ala.
- Wm. Bitsy Harrison, Richmond, Va.
- Hugh Sweeney, Houston, Texas
- C. D. Steele, III, Cambridge, Mass.
- James W. Hobson, Fullerton, Cal.
- DENNIS RALSTON, Bakersfield, Cal.
- Louis Garcia, Mexico
- Jaime Fillol, Santiago, Chile
- Bob Lutz, Los Angeles, Cal.
- Ronald Barnes, Brazil
- Robert Bedard, Canada
- Lester Sack, Clarksdale, Miss.
- Frank Lamothe, New Orleans, La.
- James McManus, Berkeley, Cal.
- David Power, Fort Collins, Colo.
- H. S. FitzGibbon, Garden City, N.Y.
- Anthony Lieberman, Philadelphia, Pa.
- Boro Javanovic, Yugoslavia
- Ralph Howe, Oyster Bay, N.Y.
- Stanley Pasarell, Santurce, P.R.
- Brenton Higgins, Australia
- RAFAEL OSUNA, Mexico
- Jeffrey Quinn, Albuquerque, N.M.
- Luis Glass, Jackson Heights, L.I.
- Jack Jackson, Knoxville, Tenn.
- John Powless, Madison, Wis.
- Eugene T. Cantin, Berkeley, Cal.
- Keith Carpenter, Canada
- Willie Hernandez, Phillippines
- Leif C. Beck, King of Prussia, Pa.
- Fred Berli, Switzerland
- Keith Jennings, New Canaan, Conn.
- Steven J. Tidball, Van Nuys, Cal.
- Albert Carrero, San Juan, P.R.
- John Harris, Washington, D.C.
- Charles Pasarell, Santurce, P.R.
- Edward Newman, San Antonio, Tex.
- FRED STOLLE, Australia

Second Round:
- EMERSON 6-1, 6-3, 8-6
- Roemer 10-8, 5-7, 6-4, 6-2
- Richey 6-4, 6-0, 6-4
- Susman 2-6, 6-4, 6-2, 6-4
- Hoffman, Jr. 4-6, 6-4, 6-0, 6-3
- Barthes 6-3, 6-2, 7-5
- Buck 7-5, 6-2, 8-6
- Kantrow 7-5, 7-5, 3-6, 6-1
- ASHE 6-3, 6-4, 9-7
- Rose 6-3, 6-4, 6-4
- Lambert 6-0, 6-1, 6-3
- Ponte 3-6, 6-4, 6-3, 6-2
- Tutvin 6-4, 3-6, 9-11, 9-7, 6-3
- Edlefsen 9-7, 6-4, 6-3
- Taylor 6-1, 6-1, 6-4
- Koch 6-1, 6-1, 6-1
- SANTANA 6-3, 6-1, 5-7, 6-1
- Lara 6-3, 6-3, 6-2
- Osborne 6-4, 6-4, 6-4
- Siska Default
- Obando 6-1, 6-1, 6-2
- Dell 8-6, 6-8, 6-3, 8-6
- Fox 6-1, 6-4, 6-0
- Riessen 6-2, 6-2, 6-1
- McKINLEY 6-2, 6-2, 6-0
- Mangan 6-4, 7-5, 6-1
- Graebner 6-3, 6-4, 6-4
- Reese 6-2, 6-3, 6-3
- Galinato Default
- Palafox 6-4, 6-3, 6-3
- Bond 6-2, 9-7, 6-2
- Cromwell 6-3, 4-6, 6-4, 2-6, 8-6
- Loyo-Mayo 6-2, 6-4, 6-2
- Harris 6-4, 3-6, 12-10, 6-1
- Seixas 6-3, 6-3, 6-1
- Guzman 6-3, 6-3, 6-4
- Sullivan 6-4, 7-5, 6-4
- Green 6-1, 6-3, 6-2
- Grant 6-3, 10-8, 3-6, 6-2
- DRYSDALE 6-2, 6-1, 6-2
- Holmberg 6-1, 6-2, 6-2
- Avoyer 1-6, 3-6, 7-5, 6-4, 7-5
- Smith 7-5, 6-4, 6-2
- Pietrangeli 4-6, 2-6, 6-3, 6-2, 6-3
- Froehling III 7-5, 6-3, 6-3
- Pickens 2-6, 6-3, 8-6, 3-6, 6-3
- Steele, Ill. 6-2 6-1, 6-3
- RALSTON 6-0, 6-3, 6-2
- Garcia 6-4, 5-7, 12-10, 6-4
- Barnes 8-6, 8-10, 6-3, 8-6
- Bedard 6-2, 6-3, 6-0
- McManus 6-3, 6-2, 6-2
- FitzGibbon 11-9, 6-3, 6-2
- Lieberman Default
- Howe 6-2, 6-8, 6-2, 6-3
- OSUNA 6-3, 6-3, 7-5
- Glass 7-5, 6-1, 6-4
- Powless 6-3, 0-6, 6-1, 2-6, 6-2
- Carpenter 6-4, 6-2, 6-4
- Bock 3-6, 6-3, 6-3, 9-7
- Jennings 6-3, 6-1, 6-2
- Carrero 3-6, 4-6, 6-4, 7-5, 6-3
- Pasarell 6-2, 6-4, 6-3
- STOLLE 9-7, 6-2, 7-5

Third Round:
- EMERSON 6-3, 6-2, 6-4
- Richey 6-3, 8-6, 3-6, 6-3
- Barthes 6-3, 6-3, 6-4
- Kantrow 6-3, 4-6, 6-4, 11-9
- ASHE 6-0, 6-3, 6-2
- Lambert 6-1, 6-3, 6-2
- Edlefsen 6-2, 6-3, 7-5
- Koch 6-2, 6-3, 6-3
- SANTANA 6-4, 8-6, 6-1
- Osborne 6-3, 6-2, 1-6, 10-8
- Dell 6-2, 6-3, 6-2
- Riessen 6-4, 6-4, 9-7
- McKINLEY 6-2, 6-1, 6-1
- Graebner 6-3, 6-2, 7-5
- Palafox 6-0, 6-2, 6-2
- Cromwell 10-8, 4-6, 6-3, 6-4
- Loyo-Mayo 6-3, 6-2, 6-2
- Seixas 6-2, 6-3, 6-3
- Sullivan 8-6, 10-8, 3-6, 6-2
- DRYSDALE 6-1, 6-3, 14-12
- Holmberg 6-0, 6-2, 6-0
- Pietrangeli 6-2, 6-2, 6-1
- Froehling, III 6-3, 6-0, 5-7, 3-6, 6-3
- RALSTON 6-1, 3-6, 6-1, 6-0
- Barnes 6-3, 6-0, 6-2
- McManus 1-6, 6-2, 6-3, 4-6, 6-2
- FitzGibbon 6-2, 6-1, 10-8
- OSUNA 6-4, 6-3, 6-3
- Powless 7-9, 6-4, 7-5, 9-7
- Carpenter 6-2, 6-3, 6-0
- Jennings 8-6, 6-4, 6-4
- Pasarell 6-3, 6-4, 6-2

Fourth Round:
- EMERSON 6-3, 6-3, 6-0
- Barthes 6-3, 6-2, 6-3
- ASHE 6-1, 6-3, 6-4
- Koch 6-4, 9-7, 7-5
- SANTANA 6-4, 6-4, 6-3
- Riessen 6-2, 6-2, 6-4
- McKINLEY 9-11, 6-3, 6-3, 6-0
- Palafox 7-5, 3-6, 6-1, 6-3
- Seixas 6-4, 6-3, 8-6
- DRYSDALE 6-3, 6-3, 6-1
- Holmberg 6-3, 6-3, 7-5
- RALSTON 7-5, 4-6, 6-3, 6-3
- Barnes 4-6, 6-4, 6-3, 5-7, 12-10
- OSUNA 7-9, 8-6, 6-2, 12-10
- Carpenter 3-6, 6-4, 15-17, 6-3, 11-9
- Pasarell 6-2, 6-3, 6-2

Quarter Finals:
- EMERSON 6-4, 13-11, 6-4
- ASHE 12-10, 13-11, 10-8
- SANTANA 10-8, 6-1, 6-3
- Palafox 9-7, 6-4, 8-6
- DRYSDALE 6-4, 6-4, 6-4
- RALSTON 3-6, 6-3, 6-1, 6-8, 11-9
- OSUNA 6-0, 6-4, 6-4
- Pasarell 6-3, 6-3, 6-3

Semi-Finals:
- ASHE 13-11, 6-4, 10-12, 6-2
- SANTANA 6-3, 9-7, 6-1
- DRYSDALE 2-6, 3-6, 7-5, 6-3, 8-6
- OSUNA 1-6, 6-3, 6-3, 7-5

Final:
- MANUEL SANTANA, 2-6, 6-4, 6-2, 6-4
- DRYSDALE, 6-3, 4-6, 6-4, 6-1
- MANUEL SANTANA, 6-2, 7-9, 7-5, 6-1

EIGHTY-FIFTH USLTA MEN'S SINGLES CHAMPIONSHIPS
West Side Tennis Club, Forest Hills, New York, 1966

First Round	Second Round	Third Round	Fourth Round	Quarter Finals	Semi-Finals	Final
MANUEL SANTANA, Spain	SANTANA 6-1, 6-1, 6-2	SANTANA 6-1, 6-1, 6-3			Defending Champion MANUEL SANTANA	
Fred Berli, Switzerland						
Frank Tutvin, Hollywood, Fla.	Ttuvin 3-6, 2-6, 6-1, 6-1		SANTANA 3-6, 6-2, 6-3, 8-6			
John Managan, Harrison, N.Y.						
Jack Darrah, Morgan, Cal.	Moore 6-2, 6-4, 6-1	Moore 6-4, 6-2, 6-2		SANTANA 9-7, 9-7, 8-6		
Ray Moore, South Africa						
John Reese, Hewlett, N.Y.	Reese 6-1, 6-4, 7-5					
Pedro Rossello, Puerto Rico						
William Tym, Peoria, Ill.	Tym 1-6, 6-4, 6-2	McKinley 6-2, 6-3, 6-4				
Hugh Sweeney, Houston, Texas						
Christopher Bovett, Australia	McKinley 6-4, 6-1, 6-1		McKinley 6-2, 6-4, 6-0			
Charles R. McKinley, N.Y. City						
Michael Marcin, San Gabriel, Cal.	Marcin 7-5, 9-7, 6-1	Carrero 6-2, 6-4, 3-6, 6-4			SANTANA 6-8, 6-2, 8-6, 5-7, 6-4	
John Yang, Philippines						
Alberto Carrero, Puerto Rico	Carrero 6-3, 7-5, 6-4					
Lester Sack, Clarksdale, Miss.						
CLIFF DRYSDALE, South Africa	DRYSDALE 6-3, 6-3, 6-1	DRYSDALE 6-3, 6-2, 6-3				
Tom Gorman, Seattle						
Fred Kovaleski, New York City	Cantin, 9-7, 1-6 3-6, 6-1, 7-5		Bowrey 6-1, 8-6, 8-6			
Eugene Cantin, Berkeley, Cal.						
John Mudd, South Orange, N.J.	Bowrey 6-1, 6-0, 6-0	Bowery 6-4, 6-3, 6-4		Bowrey 6-3, 6-2, 6-4		
William W. Bowery, Australia						
Eugene L. Scott, New York City	Scott 6-3, 6-3, 6-4					
Paul Sullivan, Belmont, Mass.						
Jaime Subirats, Mexico	Subirats, 6-3, 6-4, 2-6, 3-6, 6-3	Subirats 6-4, 3-6, 9-11, 6-3, 6-0				
George Seewagen, Bayside, N.Y.						
Kingman Lambert, Bronxville, N.Y.	DeGronckel 2-6, 6-4, 6-4, 6-2		Osborne 9-7, 6-8, 6-2, 6-1			
Claude DeGronskel, Belgium						
Cliff Buchholz, St. Louis, Mo.	Osborne, 6-8, 6-3, 6-3, 21-19	Osborne 6-3, 6-4, 7-5				
James Osborne, Hawaii						
Patrice Beust, France	Beust 6-2, 6-3, 6-4					
Peyton Watson, Greenville, S.C.						
TONY ROCHE, Australia	ROCHE 6-4, 6-3, 6-4	ROCHE 6-4, 8-0, 6-3, 8-6				
Marcella Lara, Mexico						
Jose Villarete, Manila	Stewart, 14-12, 7-5, 2-6, 3-6, 6-3		Cox 10-8, 6-4, 7-5			
Sherwood Stewart, Baytown, Tex.						
E. Victor Seixas, Jr., Villanova, Pa.	Seixas, Jr., 6-3, 6-4, 2-6, 2-6, 6-4	Cox 6-3, 8-6, 6-3		Cox 10-8, 6-4, 7-5		
Stanley Smith, Los Angeles						
Mark Cox, England	Cox 6-4, 6-2, 6-2					
Stephen Stockton, Garden City, N.Y.						
Mike Estep, Dallas	Obando 7-5, 6-4, 3-6, 7-5	Jackson 6-0, 6-4, 6-1			Newcombe 3-6, 6-1, 3-6, 6-2, 6-1	
Mario Obando, Costa Rica						
Jack Jackson, Knoxville, Tenn.	Jackson 9-7, 6-1, 3-6, 6-0		Crookenden 6-4, 4-6, 6-2, 6-2			
Chauncey Steele, III, Camb., Mass.						
Steve Avoyer, San Diego, Cal.	Crookenden, 6-2, 6-2, 8-10, 5-7, 6-4	Crookenden, 1-6, 6-3, 5-7, 6-4, 6-4				
Ian Crookenden, New Zealand						
James McManus, Berkeley	McManus 7-5, 6-4, 6-2					
Stanley Pasarell, Puerto Rico						
ARTHUR ASHE, JR., Richmond, Va.	ASHE, JR. 15-3, 6-2, 6-0	ASHE, JR. 8-6, 5-6, 6-3, 6-4				
Lamar Roemer, Houston						
Ronald Holmberg, H'l'd Falls, N.Y.	Holmberg 6-4, 6-2, 6-4		Newcombe 6-2, 6-3, 6-4			
Jerry Cromwell, Long Beach, Cal.						
John Pickens, Tuscaloosa, Ala.	Newcombe 8-6, 3-6, 6-0, 6-4	Newcombe 6-3, 16-14, 6-4		Newcombe, 9-11, 5-7, 6-2, 6-2, 6-2		
John Newcombe, Australia						
James G. Pressley, Jr., Palm Bch, Fla.	Ryan 6-1, 6-1, 6-2					
Terry Ryan, South Africa						
Wilhelm Bungert, West Germany	Bungert 6-1, 6-2, 6-4	Bungert 9-7, 6-3, 8-6				
Mike Sprengelmeyer, Dubuqe, Ia						
Peter Fishbach, Great Neck, N.Y.	Fillol 6-2, 6-4, 4-6, 6-3		Bungert 6-0, 6-0, 6-1			
Jaime Fillol, Chile						
Robert McKinley, St. Louis	McKinley 3-6, 6-4, 2-6, 6-2, 6-4	Tacchini 1-2, Retire				
Cliff Montgomery, Roslyn Hgts, N.Y.						
Lancelot Lumsden, Jamaica	Tacchini 10-12, 6-2, 6-3, 6-2					
Sergio Tacchini, Italy						
Gary Kesel, St. Louis, Mo.	Dell 6-8, 6-1, 6-0, 6-1	Dell 6-4, 6-4, 3-6, 6-0				
Donald Dell, Bethesda, Md.						
Zan Guerry, Lookout Mt., Tenn.	Guerry 6-4, 6-4, 3-6, 7-5		Stilwell 5-7, 6-3, 10-8, 6-4			
Alberto Olmedo, Peru						
Joaquin Loyo-Mayo, Mexico	Loyo-Mayo 4-6, 6-4, 6-2, 6-3	Stilwell 6-3, 6-2, 8-6		GRAEBNER 9-11, 8-6, 6-3, 7-5		
Allan Stone, Australia						
Luis Glass, Jackson Heights, N.Y.	Stilwell 6-0, 6-4, 6-3					
Graham Stilwell, England						
David Power, Ft. Collins, Colo.	Power 16-14, 6-3, 6-4	Power 6-0, 6-4, 6-1				
Brian Cheney, Santa Monica, Cal.						
Wolfgang Spannagel, W. Germany	Schloss 6-4, 6-2, 6-2		GRAEBNER 6-4, 6-2, 3-6, 6-1		Stolle 6-3, 6-4, 6-2	
Leonard Schloss, Baltimore, Md.						
Richard Dell, Bethesda, Md.	Leach 6-3, 3-6, 2-6, 11-9, 8-6	GRAEBNER 6-2, 6-2, 6-3				
Richard Leach, El Monte, Cal.						
Francisco Guzman, Ecuador	GRAEBNER 6-2, 7-5, 6-2					
CLARK GRAEBNER, Beachwood, O.						
Theodore Gorski, Jr., Ft. Worth	Stolle 6-2, 6-4, 6-4	Stolle 6-4, 6-1, 6-4				
Fred Stolle, Australia						
Roy Barth, San Diego, Cal.	Barth 6-3, 6-1, 6-0		Stolle 10-8, 6-2, 8-6			
Nick Kouridas, Forest Hills, L.I.						
Keith Carpenter, Montreal	Carpenter, 6-8, 2-6, 6-0, 6-4, 6-2	Contet 6-4, 8-6, 6-2		Stolle 7-5, 6-3, 9-7		
Bailey Brown, Bronxville, N.Y.						
Samuel P. Bowe, Haverford, Pa.	Contet 6-4, 6-2, 6-3					
Daniel Contet, France						
Arthur Carrington, Elizabeth, N.J.	Beck 6-2, 6-1, 6-1	Osuna 7-5, 6-2, 7-5				
Leif Beck, King of Prussia, Pa.						
Raphael Osuna, Mexico	Osuna, 4-6, 6-4, 4-6, 6-4, 6-4		RALSTON 6-1, 6-4, 6-3			
Ronald Barnes, Brazil						
Thomas B. Karp, Los Angeles	Mulligan 4-6, 6-2, 6-3, 6-2	RALSTON 6-1, 6-4, 6-3				
Martin Mulligan, Australia						
Jasjit Singh, India	RALSTON 6-1, 6-3, 7-5					
R. DENNIS RALSTON, B'field, Cal.						
Armistead Neeley, Tampa, Fla.	Neeley, 10-8, 4-6, 6-4, 4-6, 8-6	Ruffels 6-1, 8-6, 6-3				
Eduardo Zuleta, Ecuador						
Ray Ruffels, Australia	Ruffels 6-1, 6-0, 6-0		Ruffels 3-6, 10-8, 6-4, 6-3			
James Schwitters, Hawaii						
William Tully, White Plains, N.Y.	Froehling, III 6-3, 6-3, 6-3	Froehling, III 6-1, 6-1, 6-2		Davidson 3-6, 6-2, 6-1, 6-1		
Frank A. Froehling, III, N.Y. City						
Peter Van Lingen, South Africa	Van Lingen, 4-6, 7-5, 6-3, 5-7, 6-3		Garcia 6-1, 6-3, 6-4			
Ralph E Howe, Oyster Bay, N.Y.						
John Powless, Hinsdale, Ill.	Powless 6-4, 6-3, 6-4	Garcia 6-1, 6-3, 6-4				
Frank Connor, E. St. Louis						
Luis Garcia, Mexico	Garcia, 6-3, 2-6, 6-4, 3-6, 12-10		Davidson 6-1, 6-4, 6-0		EMERSON 10-12, 6-4, 6-3, 6-2	
Richard Russell, Jamaica						
Owen Davidson, Australia	Davidson 6-0, 6-4, 6-3	Davidson 7-5, 8-6, 6-1				
Turner Howard, III, Kn'xville, Tenn.						
Keith Jennings, New Canaan, Conn.	RICHEY 6-3, 6-2, 6-3					
CLIFF RICHEY, San Angelo, Tex.						
Steven Tidball, Van Nuys, Cal.	Buding 6-1, 6-4, 6-3	Keldie, 8-6, 1-6, 6-8, 6-2, 6-4				
Inbo Buding, West Germany						
Robert Siska, San Francisco	Keldie, 2-6, 2-6, 6-0, 10-8, 6-1		Riessen 6-3, 6-1, 6-4			
Ray Keldie, Australia						
Lt. Walter Oehrlein, Orlando, Fla.	Oehrlein 8-6, 6-4, 6-2	Riessen 6-1, 6-2, 6-4		EMERSON 2-6, 6-3, 7-5, 6-3		
James Rombeau, Studio City, Cal.						
Robert C. Lutz, Los Angeles	Riessen 6-4, 7-5, 7-5		Gerrard 6-4, 6-3, 6-2			
Martin Riessen, Evanston, Ill.						
Tom Leonard, Arcadia, Cal.	Leonard Default	Gerrard 6-4, 6-3, 6-2				
Miguel Olvera, Ecuador						
Ted Hoehn, Winchester, Mass.	Gerrard 1-6, 6-3, 3-6, 6-3, 6-2		EMERSON 6-0, 6-4, 6-1			
Lew Gerrard, New Zealand						
Charles F. Darley, Rochester, Minn.	Harrison, 6-3, 1-6, 8-10, 11-9, 13-11	EMERSON 4-6, 6-1, 8-6, 6-2				
Bitsy Harrison, Richmond, Va.						
Ismail El Shafei, United Arab Rep.	EMERSON 6-3, 9-7, 9-7					
ROY EMERSON, Australia						

Semi-Finals / Final results:
- Newcombe, 6-4, 6-8, 8-6
- Newcombe, 6-3, 6-4, 6-8, 8-6
- Fred Stolle, 4-6, 12-10, 6-3, 6-4
- Stolle, 6-4, 6-1, 6-1

PICTURE CREDITS